Questions & Answers
Evidence

CAROLINA ACADEMIC PRESS
QUESTIONS & ANSWERS SERIES

Questions & Answers: Sales & Leases
Aviva Abramovsky

Questions & Answers: Administrative Law,
Third Edition
Linda D. Jellum, Karen A. Jordan

Questions & Answers: Antitrust
Shubha Ghosh

Questions & Answers: Bankruptcy, Second Edition
Mary Jo Wiggins

Questions & Answers: Business Associations,
Second Edition
Douglas M. Branson

Questions & Answers: Civil Procedure,
Fourth Edition
William V. Dorsaneo, III, Elizabeth Thornburg

Questions & Answers: Constitutional Law,
Third Edition
Paul E. McGreal, Linda S. Eads, Charles W. Rhodes

Questions & Answers: Contracts, Second Edition
Scott J. Burnham

Questions & Answers: Copyright Law
Second Edition
Dave Fagundes, Robert C. Lind

Questions & Answers: Criminal Law,
Third Edition
Emily Levine, Paul Marcus

Questions & Answers: Criminal Procedure—
Police Investigation, Third Edition
Neil P. Cohen, Michael J. Benza, Wayne A. Logan

Questions & Answers: Criminal Procedure—
Prosecution and Adjudication, Third Edition
Neil P. Cohen, Michael J. Benza, Wayne A. Logan

Questions & Answers: Environmental Law
Dru Stevenson

Questions & Answers: Evidence, Fourth Edition
Paul Giannelli

Questions & Answers: Family Law, Second Edition
Mark Strasser

Questions & Answers: Federal Estate & Gift
Taxation, Second Edition
Elaine Gagliardi

Questions & Answers: Federal Income Tax
David L. Cameron

Questions & Answers: Intellectual Property,
Second Edition
Gary Myers, Lee Ann W. Lockridge

Questions & Answers: International Law
Rebecca Bratspies

Questions & Answers: Patent Law
Cynthia Ho

Questions & Answers: Payment Systems,
Second Edition
Timothy R. Zinnecker

Questions & Answers: Professional Responsibility,
Fourth Edition
Patrick Longan

Questions & Answers: Property, Second Edition
John Nagle

Questions & Answers: Remedies
Rachel Janutis, Tracy Thomas

Questions & Answers: Secured Transactions,
Third Edition
Bruce A. Markell, Timothy R. Zinnecker

Questions & Answers: Taxation of Business Entities
Kristofer Neslund, Nancy Neslund

Questions & Answers: The First Amendment,
Third Edition
Russell L. Weaver, William D. Araiza

Questions & Answers: Torts, Fourth Edition
Anita Bernstein

Questions & Answers: Trademark and
Unfair Competition
Vince Chiappetta

Questions & Answers: Wills, Trusts, and Estates,
Third Edition
Thomas Featherston

Questions & Answers
Evidence

FOURTH EDITION

Multiple-Choice and Short-Answer
Questions and Answers

Paul C. Giannelli
DISTINGUISHED UNIVERSITY PROFESSOR EMERITUS
WEATHERHEAD PROFESSOR OF LAW EMERITUS
CASE WESTERN RESERVE UNIVERSITY

CAROLINA ACADEMIC PRESS
Durham, North Carolina

ISBN 978-1-5310-0991-5
e-ISBN 978-1-53100-992-2
LCCN 2018936042

Carolina Academic Press, LLC
700 Kent Street
Durham, North Carolina 27701
Telephone (919) 489-7486
Fax (919) 493-5668
www.cap-press.com

Printed in the United States of America

To David Leonard—
A great teacher, scholar, and person.

Contents

Preface

The law of evidence is complex, but if you work hard at it, you can develop an understanding of the individual rules and of the way the rules interact to form a coherent system. The key to learning evidence law is to ask several questions about each problem:

(1) What is the questioned evidence? (This is a very important step; isolating the exact evidence at issue often provides clues to the rules that must be satisfied for the evidence to be admissible.)

(2) What is the evidence offered to prove?

(3) Is the evidence relevant when offered for that purpose?

(4) If the evidence is relevant, are there any other rules of evidence that might require its exclusion?

These simple steps will always get you off to a good start. You can also develop a series of more specific questions for each area of evidence law. For example, if you suspect that the problem might deal with witness impeachment, here are the questions you should ask after you have answered those listed above:

(1) Is the evidence offered to impeach or support the credibility of a witness?

(2) If the evidence is offered to impeach or support a witness's credibility, what method of impeachment is involved? (Among many possibilities: Is this impeachment by contradiction? Is it impeachment by showing a bad character for truthfulness? Is it impeachment by showing that the witness did not have a good opportunity to observe the event about which she has testified, or by showing that her capacity to observe, remember, or narrate is impaired?)

(3) Are there any specific rules that govern the use of the evidence for that method of impeachment? If so, have those rules been followed? To determine whether the rules have been followed, ask:

(a) Is the evidence admissible only after the opponent has offered evidence to the contrary?

(b) Are there limits on the form the evidence may take?

(4) If there are no rules that specifically govern this method of impeachment, would admission of the evidence violate any other rules, such as FRE 403?

(5) Do any foundational requirements apply, such as giving the witness an opportunity to explain or deny the statement or showing the evidence to the witness, apply? If so, have those rules been followed?

If you work methodically through each problem, and if you *read the rules* with care, you will succeed.

Though the explanations in this book contain a good deal of information you will find useful, the purpose of this book is not to teach you the rules of evidence. The book's main purposes are to test what you have learned from reading your primary course materials and from the classroom, to broaden your understanding of that material, and to help you to see where you might need to devote additional study time. In this book, you will find questions and answers in sixteen main subject areas that correspond to the basic topics you are likely to cover in an evidence course. There is also a practice final exam that tests your knowledge of rules from most of these subject areas. The practice final also contains questions that require you to apply two or more different rules. Though the book is organized in roughly the same way as some of the popular texts, it will work for you even if your class covers the material in a different order.

The problems in this book are based almost entirely on the Federal Rules of Evidence. The Federal Rules have been extremely influential in the development of state evidence codes, and where there are differences between federal practice and the law of particular states, those differences are usually quite easy to learn once you have mastered the Federal Rules. Because the Multistate Bar Examination tests federal evidence law, you need to learn the Federal Rules in any event. Throughout the book, "Federal Rules of Evidence" is abbreviated "FRE."

One final thought: Take the time to answer every question as carefully as possible. If the question calls for a short answer, write out the entire answer. It is easy to look at a problem, think briefly about how you would answer the question, and then read the answer printed in the book. Try to avoid this shortcut. It is a much better test of your understanding, and much more beneficial to the learning process, for you to write out an answer to each short answer question before you look at the response printed in the book.

About the Author

Paul C. Giannelli is a Distinguished University Professor Emeritus and the Weatherhead Professor of Law Emeritus at Case Western Reserve University. He is the author of numerous law review articles and the author or co-author of more than 10 books, including *Understanding Evidence, Scientific Evidence,* and *Courtroom Criminal Evidence.* He has taught evidence for 45 years.

The late David Leonard of Loyola Law School, Los Angeles, was the author of the first two editions of this book. Leonard was the author of numerous law review articles as well as two volumes of *The New Wigmore: A Treatise on Evidence.* Along with Roger C. Park and Steven H. Goldberg, he was co-author of the hornbook *Evidence Law: A Student's Guide to the Law of Evidence as Applied in American Trials.*

Questions

Topic 1: Questions

Preserving Error; Appellate Review

Civil action by P against D. During the direct examination of one of P's witnesses who claims to have seen the crucial event, D's attorney raises a specific objection to a question asking the witness to relate what she saw. After extensive argument on the evidentiary point, the court sustains the objection.

1. Which of the following best reflects what P's lawyer should do next?

   (A) P's lawyer should move on to the next question.

   (B) P's lawyer should ask the court to have the record reflect P's disagreement with the court's ruling, and move on to the next question.

   (C) P's lawyer should cease his examination of the witness because continuing with the examination will create a risk that an appellate court would find that P impliedly waived his right to appeal the court's ruling.

   (D) P's lawyer should place in the trial record a statement of what the witness would have testified if permitted to answer the question.

At the trial of a civil action between P and D following an intersection collision between their cars, P calls W, who was the only other witness to the accident. Just after P's attorney asks W a question, D's attorney says, "I object, your honor. That question is clearly improper." The court overrules the objection. D loses the case and appeals the judgment on the basis of the court's ruling on the objection.

2. Which of the following statements is most accurate?

   (A) Because D objected at the appropriate time, the appellate court will reverse if any error in the court's ruling affected a substantial right of D.

   (B) If the record clearly reflects the nature of the error, the appellate court will reverse because W's testimony was crucial to P's case.

   (C) Unless the record clearly reflects both the nature of the error and that it affected a substantial right of D, the appellate court will not reverse.

   (D) Because D did not state a ground for the objection, the appellate court will not reverse.

A party fails to object to testimony that would be inadmissible if an objection were lodged.

3. Which of the following is correct?

    (A) The court may, on its own motion, prevent the offering party from eliciting that testimony or strike it from the record if the witness has already testified.

    (B) The court must, on its own motion, prevent the offering party from eliciting that testimony, or, of the witness has already testified, must strike it from the record.

    (C) The court must protect the party against whom the testimony is offered by asking the party's attorney if she wishes to interpose an objection.

    (D) The court must not interfere.

Prosecution of D for the murder of V. D's only witness is W1, who testifies that he was with D in another country when the crime was committed. During its rebuttal case, the prosecution calls W2 to testify that V was a "beautiful person who gave generously to charity and never hurt anyone."

4. D moves to strike W2's testimony as "incompetent, irrelevant, and immaterial." Which of the following statements is correct?

    (A) Because D did not object before W2 testified, D has waived any objection.

    (B) Because "incompetent, irrelevant, and immaterial" is not the proper objection, the trial court may not strike W2's testimony.

    (C) Even though "incompetent, irrelevant, and immaterial" is not the proper objection, the court may grant D's motion.

    (D) The court should deny D's motion because W2's testimony is admissible.

Prosecution of D for murder. D denies involvement. During its case-in-chief, the prosecution calls W, who has lived in the same community as D for many years, and asks W to testify about D's community reputation for violence or peacefulness. D's attorney does not object, and W testifies that D has a community reputation for being a very violent person. D is convicted, and appeals, claiming that this evidence should have been excluded under FRE 404(a).

5. Which of the following statements is most accurate?

    (A) Because the record clearly reflects that the court violated FRE 404(a) by admitting the evidence, the appellate court will reverse.

    (B) Because the record clearly reflects that the court violated FRE 404(a) by admitting the evidence, the appellate court will reverse if the error affected a substantial right of D.

    (C) Because the trial court has discretion to admit character evidence that has substantial probative value, the trial court's error, if any, is not plain error. Because D did not make a specific objection, the appellate court will not reverse.

    (D) Because D did not state a ground for the objection, the appellate court will not reverse.

Prosecution of D for the murder of V. At trial, the prosecution offered into evidence a series of gruesome photographs of V's body. D objected on FRE 403 grounds: that the probative value of the photos was substantially outweighed by the danger of unfair prejudice. The court overruled the objection and admitted the photos after stating that the probative value of the evidence was great under the circumstances, and that the danger of unfair prejudice was not too great to warrant exclusion. D was convicted and appeals on the ground that the court erred by admitting the photos.

6. Which of the following statements is most accurate?

(A) Because rulings based on FRE 403 are solely committed to the discretion of the trial court, the appellate court will not review this alleged error.

(B) Because rulings based on FRE 403 involve the exercise of discretion that partly concerns matters that the trial court is in a better position to evaluate than is the appellate court, the appellate court will only find error if it determines that the trial court abused its discretion.

(C) Because the test set forth in FRE 403 is a legal standard that does not involve the exercise of discretion, the appellate court will review the alleged error *de novo*.

(D) Because the trial court applied the wrong standard to its ruling on the FRE 403 objection, the appellate court will reverse and remand for a new trial.

Prosecution of D for assault and battery on V. During its case-in-chief, the prosecution called W, a long-time acquaintance of D, and sought to elicit W's opinion about D's character for violence. D objected on the ground that this question sought inadmissible character evidence pursuant to FRE 404(a). The court overruled D's objection and permitted W to answer the question. W testified that in her opinion, D was a violent person. D was convicted and appeals on the ground that the court should have excluded this testimony.

7. Which of the following statements is most accurate?

(A) Because rulings based on the exclusionary provision of FRE 404(a) are solely committed to the discretion of the trial court, the appellate court will not review this alleged error.

(B) Because rulings based on the exclusionary provision of FRE 404(a) involve the exercise of discretion that partly concerns matters that the trial court is in a better position to evaluate than is the appellate court, the appellate court will only find error if it determines that the trial court abused its discretion.

(C) Because the exclusionary provision of FRE 404(a) is a legal standard that does not involve the exercise of discretion, the appellate court will review the alleged error *de novo*.

(D) Because the trial court applied the wrong standard to its ruling on the FRE 404(a) objection, the appellate court will reverse and remand for a new trial.

Objections to the Form of the Question

Slander action by P against D. P alleges that in a speech at the American Bar Association convention, D called P a "damned liar." D claims he said P was a "kind lawyer." At trial, P calls W, who attended D's speech. W testifies that D called P a "damned liar." On cross-examination, D's attorney asks W, "Isn't it correct that you were sitting near the back of the auditorium?"

8. Which of the following statements is most accurate?

   (A) The question is unobjectionable.

   (B) If P makes a relevance objection, the court will sustain the objection.

   (C) If P objects to the question as leading, the court will sustain the objection.

   (D) If P objects to the question on the ground that the question assumes a fact not in evidence, the court will sustain the objection.

Prosecution of D for assault and battery on V, a law professor. The attack took place at the corner of First and Main Streets. At trial, the prosecutor calls W, who witnessed the attack. After a few preliminary questions, the prosecutor asks W where he was late on the evening the crime occurred. W says he cannot remember. The prosecutor then asks if W was standing on the corner of First and Main Streets.

9. Which of the following statements is most accurate?

   (A) The question is unobjectionable.

   (B) If D's attorney objects to the question as assuming a fact not in evidence, the court will sustain the objection.

   (C) If D's attorney objects to the question as leading, the court will sustain the objection.

   (D) If D's attorney objects on the basis that the question has already been asked and answered, the court will sustain the objection.

Negligence action by P against D arising from a collision between the two in-line skaters. At trial, P testifies that she suffered permanent damage to her knee in the collision. On cross-examination, D asks P if it isn't true that P injured her knee playing basketball about a year before the accident in question. P objects to the question on the ground that it goes beyond the scope of the direct examination.

10. How should the court rule? Why?

ANSWER:

Prosecution of D for burglarizing a rare coin shop. To prove D's involvement, the prosecution calls W, who testifies that she saw D leaving the shop about an hour after it closed on the night the crime took place. On cross-examination, D asks W if it isn't true that W and D were former business partners who had a falling out about a month before the crime was committed. The prosecutor objects to the question on the ground that it goes beyond the scope of the direct examination.

11. How should the court rule? Why?

ANSWER:

Prosecution of D for the murder of V. The prosecution calls W, a close friend of V. W testifies that she spoke with V's husband the day after the killing. The prosecutor then asks, "What did V's husband say?" W answers, "V's husband told me he saw D kill V." Assume the testimony concerning the husband's statement is inadmissible hearsay.

12. What should D do?

   (A) D should object to the question on the ground that it calls for inadmissible hearsay.

   (B) D should move to strike the testimony on hearsay grounds.

   (C) D should move to strike the testimony on hearsay grounds, and ask the court to instruct the jury to ignore W's answer.

   (D) There is nothing D can do because W has already answered the question.

Negligence action by P against D arising from an intersection collision. P calls W, and after some introductory questions establishing that W was near the scene, P's attorney asks, "Where exactly were you at the time of the collision, and what happened?"

13. Discuss two possible objections to this question, and how P's attorney can correct any problems.

ANSWER:

Negligence action by P against D arising from an intersection collision. As her first witness, P's attorney calls W, and after some introductory questions establishing that W was near the scene, P's attorney asks, "Did you see D's car run the red light?"

14. What objection should D make to this question, and how should P's attorney correct any problems?

ANSWER:

Prosecution of D for assault and battery on V. The incident occurred close to an elementary school playground. The prosecution's first witness is W, a 6-year-old child who observed the incident. When the prosecutor asks W to describe what happened, W says she does not remember.

15. The prosecutor then asks, "Did you see D walk up to V?" Which of the following statements is most accurate?

   (A) The question is improperly leading.

   (B) The question is improper because it assumes a fact not in evidence.

   (C) Because W lacks the capacity to remember and relate accurately, the court should not permit W to testify.

   (D) The witness is competent and the question is proper.

A joint criminal trial of two defendants is being conducted.

16. If a particular item of evidence is admissible against one defendant but inadmissible against another defendant, which of the following may the court do?

   (A) The court may only instruct the jury regarding the limited admissibility of the evidence.

   (B) The court may only sever the trials.

   (C) The court may only exclude the evidence entirely.

   (D) All of the above are permissible in appropriate circumstances.

P sues D following a car crash. At trial, P calls W. Before establishing that W was at the scene, P asks W if D's car ran a red light.

17. D objects, claiming P has not established W's personal knowledge. Which of the following statements is correct?

   (A) The court should not allow W to answer because P must convince the court that W had personal knowledge before W may testify about the fact.

   (B) The court should not allow W to answer because P must offer evidence sufficient to support a finding of personal knowledge before W may testify about the fact.

   (C) The court should allow W to answer the question, but strike the testimony later on D's motion if the court finds that there was not evidence sufficient to support a finding that W had personal knowledge.

   (D) The court should allow W to answer the question, but strike the testimony later on D's motion if the court finds that W did not have personal knowledge.

Prosecution of D for a murder that took place in Denver. D claims she was in Los Angeles at the time of the murder. To prove D was in Denver, the prosecution calls PO, a Denver police officer, and asks PO whether she saw D in Denver on that day. PO says she cannot remember.

18. The prosecutor then shows PO a speeding ticket she issued to D in Denver on that day, and asks PO if she now remembers seeing D in Denver that day. If permitted, PO will testify that she now remembers seeing D in Denver that day. Which of the following is correct?

(A) PO's testimony is admissible under the doctrine of recorded recollection.

(B) PO's testimony is admissible, and the prosecutor may offer the ticket into evidence as an exhibit.

(C) PO's testimony is admissible, and although the prosecutor may not offer the ticket into evidence as an exhibit, D may do so.

(D) PO's testimony is inadmissible because police reports and other police records may not be used against a criminal defendant.

Topic 3: Questions

Witness Competency

Prosecution of D for assault and battery. The prosecution calls W, who was present when the altercation took place. W is four years old. D objects on the ground that W is not competent to be a witness.

19. How should the court rule, and why?

ANSWER:

Action by P against the estate of X for non-payment of a promissory note. P filed the action in federal court under its diversity jurisdiction. The estate claims that X paid the note in full before her death. The state in which the federal court sits had enacted a "dead man statute." At trial, P wishes to testify that shortly before her death, X acknowledged that the debt remained unpaid. The estate objects.

20. Which of the following statements is true?

    (A) The court should sustain the objection because of the dead man statute.

    (B) The court should sustain the objection because P's testimony constitutes inadmissible hearsay.

    (C) The court should sustain the objection both because of the dead man statute and because of the hearsay rule.

    (D) The court should overrule the objection because there is no federal dead man statute and FRE 601 removes such a ground of witness incompetence.

During the trial of a case, a prospective witness refuses to take the oath or affirmation in the words prescribed by the court, claiming that "honesty" is superior to "truth" and proposing to affirm, instead, that she will testify with "fully integrated honesty." The opponent objects, and asks the court to refuse to permit the person to testify.

21. How should the court rule, and why?

ANSWER:

In the middle of a trial at which a factual issue about the layout of a particular street corner is hotly contested, the trial judge takes the witness oath, testifies that she is personally familiar with that particular intersection, and then gives a detailed description of its layout. The testimony is consistent with the position taken by P. P prevails at trial.

22. Which of the following statements is most accurate?

   (A) The judge has committed error. D was not required to object. The appellate court will reverse if the error affected a substantial right of D.

   (B) The judge has committed error. D was not required to object. The appellate court will reverse automatically.

   (C) The judge has committed error, and the appellate court will review the error if D objected at trial.

   (D) Because the matter about which the judge testified is subject to easy verification, the judge did not err by testifying. Her action was consistent with the goals of efficiency and accurate fact-finding.

Product liability action by P, a ten-year-old child, against D, the manufacturer of a bicycle that P alleges was defectively designed, causing him to lose control and crash, suffering serious injuries. Specifically, P claims the bike's frame was not strong enough to handle even the weight of a ten-year-old, and that it collapsed under him while he was riding. Although the actual bike was accidentally destroyed before trial, P produces another bike of the same model and exhibits it to the jury during the trial. The judge allows the jury to take the bike to the jury room. After the jury renders a verdict for D, the bailiff tells P's lawyer that when he entered the jury room to deliver some water, he saw the jurors taking apart the bike and examining its suspension system, something that was not done in open court. Based on this information, P moves for a new trial and asks the court to hold a hearing so the bailiff can testify about what he saw.

23. How should the court rule?

   (A) The court should hold the hearing because if true, the jury's conduct amounted to the taking of new testimony without the parties present.

   (B) The court should hold the hearing because the jurors are not allowed to handle exhibits.

   (C) The court should not hold the hearing because the bailiff may not testify to impeach the verdict.

   (D) The court should not hold the hearing because it is improper for a party to inquire about, or receive information about, the factors that motivated the jurors to render their verdict.

Following a murder conviction, a juror approaches defendant's attorney and complains about several things that occurred during deliberations.

24. If defendant makes a motion for a new trial, and asks the court to hold a hearing at which the juror may testify, which of the following would the court permit the juror to describe at the hearing?

   (A) Several of the jurors announced at the beginning of deliberations that they made up their minds right at the end of the prosecution's case-in-chief that the defendant was guilty, and that they paid little attention to the defendant's case.

   (B) During a lunch break while the trial was still going on, several of the jurors drank beer to the point of obvious intoxication.

   (C) One of the jurors told the other jurors that a publisher had approached her about a book deal if the jury voted to convict.

   (D) One of the jurors now believes that the jury misunderstood the jury instructions.

State court prosecution of D for assault and battery. The charge arises from an altercation that left both D and the alleged victim severely injured. D wishes to testify at trial. The prosecution objects on the ground that prior to testifying, D was hypnotized to help her remember the facts better, and that this makes her incompetent under the state's rule forbidding a previously hypnotized witness from testifying.

25. How should the court rule?

   (A) The court should sustain the objection because the rule forbids D from testifying.

   (B) The court should sustain the objection if it finds that there is an equally good alternative to D's testimony.

   (C) The court must overrule the objection unless it finds that under the circumstances, the evidence is so untrustworthy as to overcome D's constitutional right to testify in her own behalf.

   (D) The court must overrule the objection because D has a constitutional right to testify at her own trial.

Prosecution of D for murder. After deliberating for two days, the jury renders a guilty verdict, the judge discharges the jury, and the judge enters a judgment of conviction. Two days later, X, one of the jurors, tells D's attorney that four jurors spent most of the time during deliberations putting together a Super Bowl pool, and that when the other jurors tried to convince them to participate in the discussions, they paid little attention, saying they'd already made up their minds.

26. Based on this information, D moves for a new trial and asks the court to conduct a hearing so Juror X can testify to this information. Which of the following statements is correct?

   (A) Because the court already entered judgment and discharged the jury, it is improper for the court to consider any challenges to the jury's verdict.

(B) Because D has not presented the type of information that can be used to impeach the jury's verdict, the verdict and judgment will stand.

(C) Because D has presented information suggesting that some jurors might have based their verdicts on inaccurate information or not taken the deliberations seriously, the court should grant D's motion.

(D) Because it is unlawful for D's attorney to speak with a juror after trial, the court may sanction the attorney.

Topic 4: Questions

Logical Relevance; Exclusion for Reasons of Prejudice or Other Dangers

Prosecution of D for the murder of V. D admits killing V, but claims she acted in self-defense. To prove V started the fight, D offers evidence that V had committed numerous acts of violence in the months prior to the killing. D was unaware of these acts when the killing occurred. The prosecution objects on relevance grounds.

27. How should the court rule? Why? If you believe the evidence is relevant, set forth the chain of inferences that demonstrates its relevance, and include the generalizations that show how the inferences are linked.

ANSWER:

Prosecution of D for conspiracy to murder a well-known political figure. At trial, the prosecution calls W to testify that a week before the killing, W saw D talking to X, the confessed trigger-person, in a nightclub. D objects on relevance grounds.

28. How should the court rule? Why? If you believe the evidence is relevant, set forth the chain of inferences that demonstrates its relevance, and include the generalizations that show how the inferences are linked.

ANSWER:

Prosecution of D for burglary. D claims she never left home on the day the crime took place. To prove she was home all day, D testifies that she reads her horoscope every morning in order to help her decide what to do that day, and that on the day in question her horoscope said that she should not "undertake any risky endeavors." The prosecution objects on relevance grounds.

29. How should the court rule? Why? If you believe the evidence is relevant, set forth the chain of inferences that demonstrates its relevance, and include the generalizations that show how the inferences are linked.

ANSWER:

Civil rights action by P against D police department for using excessive force in arresting P at P's home. The officers went to P's home to execute an arrest warrant resulting from P's failure to pay fifty parking tickets. It is undisputed that as soon as P opened her front door, the officers grabbed P and beat her with their night sticks until she lost consciousness. D claims its officers acted in the reasonable belief that such force was necessary. To prove this, D wishes to offer evidence that on two occasions not long before this incident, P had acted violently when confronted with police officers. The two officers involved in this incident were not aware of these previous confrontations. P objects on relevance grounds.

30. How should the court rule? Why? If you believe the evidence is relevant, set forth the chain of inferences that demonstrates its relevance, and include the generalizations that show how the inferences are linked.

ANSWER:

Prosecution of D for the murder of V, D's ex-wife. D denies involvement. To prove that D committed the crime, the prosecution wishes to call W, a friend of D's, to testify that a few days after the killing occurred, D told W, "I dreamed last night that I killed V." D objects on relevance grounds.

31. How should the court rule? If you believe the evidence is relevant, set forth the chain of inferences that demonstrates its relevance, and include the generalizations that show how the inferences are linked.

ANSWER:

Prosecution of D for the murder of V in V's home. D claims she was on vacation in another state when the crime took place. To prove that D could have been in V's home at the time of the murder, the prosecution wishes to offer evidence that D was a federal inmate on work-release who worked for V as a housekeeper.

32. Which of the following statements is most accurate?

(A) The evidence is relevant, and because it goes to a central issue in the case, its probative value cannot be substantially outweighed by the danger of unfair prejudice.

(B) The evidence concerning D's job as a housekeeper is relevant but her status as an inmate on work-release is not. Because the probative value of that aspect of the evidence is zero, the court must not allow the jury to hear that D was an inmate on work-release.

(C) The evidence is relevant, but if the court finds that the probative value of any part of the evidence is substantially outweighed by the danger of unfair prejudice, the court may exclude that part.

(D) The evidence is irrelevant.

Prosecution of D for first degree murder of V. D admits shooting V but claims she acted in self-defense when V attacked her. At trial, the prosecution calls W, a forensic pathologist who conducted the autopsy on V. W testifies that she found three entry wounds on the back of V's head. The prosecution then shows W a series of photographs, which W states were taken of V's upper body and head during the autopsy. The photographs clearly show the bullet wounds to the back of V's head that W had testified about. The prosecution offers the photographs into evidence. D objects.

33. Which of the following statements is most likely correct?

(A) Because the photographs are cumulative, they are irrelevant and must be excluded.

(B) Although the photographs are relevant, the fact that they merely corroborate W's testimony deprives them of all but minimal probative value, and they must be excluded.

(C) Although the photographs are relevant, the court may exclude them if it finds that they are less reliable evidence of the condition of V's body than is W's oral testimony.

(D) Although the photographs are relevant, the court may exclude them if it finds that their probative value is substantially outweighed by the danger that the jury will convict D for the wrong reasons.

Wrongful death action by P against D arising from a horrible head-on automobile collision that killed P's deceased. To prove that D was traveling considerably above the speed limit of 25 miles per hour at the time of the crash, P wishes to offer into evidence several photographs taken at the scene. The photographs show P's mangled car, reduced to half its original size. Blood stains can be seen through the windshield. D offers to stipulate that she was traveling at least 60 miles per hour, and asks the court to exclude the photographs. P refuses to accept D's stipulation and insists on offering the photographs.

34. How should the court rule?

(A) Because the photographs would provide the jury with a greater understanding of the accident, the court should deny D's motion and allow P to offer the photographs.

(B) Because D's stipulation would give P everything the photographs would have shown, the court should grant D's motion and exclude the photographs.

(C) Because a party may prove its case with any otherwise admissible evidence, and may never be forced to accept a stipulation, the court should deny D's motion and allow P to offer the photographs into evidence.

(D) Because trial courts generally exclude gory photographs, which tend to invite unfair prejudice by inflaming the jury's passions against the opponent, the court would exclude them even without D's offered stipulation.

Action by P, who was struck in a crosswalk by driver D. P wishes to offer evidence that D is a wealthy person.

35. Which of the following statements is most likely correct?

(A) The evidence might be relevant if P's action is brought on an intentional tort theory and P seeks punitive damages.

(B) Because a wealthy person is not likely to be concerned about the potential financial impact of a tort judgment against her, the evidence is relevant if P's action is brought on a negligence theory.

(C) Regardless of the substantive theory supporting P's action, the evidence is relevant.

(D) Regardless of the substantive theory supporting P's action, the evidence is irrelevant.

Prosecution of D for being a felon in possession of a firearm and for assault with a deadly weapon. Prior to trial, D offers to stipulate that he is in fact a "felon" as defined in the applicable statute. In return, he asks the court to order the prosecution not to offer evidence that D's prior felony conviction was for assault with a deadly weapon. The prosecutor refuses to accept D's offered stipulation on the ground that the prosecution is entitled to offer evidence to prove each element of the crimes.

36. Of the following, which constitutes D's strongest response?

(A) The prosecution is required to accept any factual stipulation offered by a criminal defendant.

(B) Because D's stipulation gives the prosecution everything it can prove legitimately, any additional evidence has no marginal effect on the probability of D's guilt and poses a substantial risk of unfair prejudice.

(C) D's stipulation renders any evidence of his felon status irrelevant.

(D) D has a due process right to limit the amount of prejudicial evidence offered by the prosecution.

Prosecution of D for bank robbery. The bank is next door to a multiplex movie theater. Prosecution witness W has testified that she was standing in line to buy tickets for the movie "Bar Wars: Episode 2" when she saw D emerging from the bank with a gun in one hand and a large sack in the other. On cross-examination D wishes to ask W if it isn't true that W was standing in line to buy tickets to "Bar Wars: Episode 3," not Episode 2. The prosecution objects on relevance grounds.

37. Discuss whether the evidence is relevant.

ANSWER:

Prosecution of D for murder. D denies committing the crime. The prosecution calls an eyewitness who describes the killer as a "white male with blond hair." The prosecution then calls a police officer who testifies that she collected blood samples from the scene. The prosecutor then calls an expert who testifies that she conducted DNA tests on the blood samples, separated the victim's blood from blood assumed to be from the perpetrator, tested a sample of blood from D, found a "match," and calculated that only one in 500,000 white men could have produced the sample found at the scene. D does not dispute the validity of the DNA tests, nor does he call his own DNA expert. During final argument, the prosecutor makes the following statement to the jury: "Based on the expert's testimony, which was uncontradicted, there would only be a one in 500,000 chance that you would be wrong if you convicted D. That is certainly 'beyond a reasonable doubt.'"

38. Discuss the validity of this argument.

ANSWER:

Same case as in the previous question. Assume D offers evidence that over 5 million people live in the metropolitan area in which the crime was committed. During final argument, D's attorney makes the following statement to the jury: "Based on the expert's testimony, there are at least ten people in this metropolitan area who could have produced the sample found at the crime scene. That means there is only a one in ten chance you would be correct if you convicted D of the crime. There is more than reasonable doubt of D's guilt in this case, and so you must acquit."

39. Discuss the validity of this argument.

ANSWER:

Prosecution of D for murder. The prosecution calls the only eyewitness, who describes the perpetrator as a Caucasian male with brown hair. D is a Caucasian male with brown hair. A tissue sample, almost certainly from the perpetrator, was retrieved from under one of the victim's fingernails. A qualified lab extracts the DNA from the sample, compares it to a DNA database containing only Caucasian males, and calculates that the likelihood of a random Caucasian male leaving such a sample is 1 in 500,000.

40. Which of the following best describes the usefulness of Bayes' Theorem in evaluating all of this evidence?

(A) It will help the jury determine whether the eyewitness testimony and the DNA evidence are statistically independent factors.

(B) It will help the court determine whether the lab chose the proper database from which to calculate probabilities.

(C) It will help the jurors calculate the effect of the DNA evidence on the jurors' prior assessment of the likelihood that D was the perpetrator.

(D) Bayes' Theorem is not useful in this situation.

Topic 5: Questions

Preliminary Questions of Admissibility

Negligence action by P against D arising from a skateboard collision. P claims D skated into P's path, causing the collision. D denies doing this, and claims it was just the other way around. To prove D skated into P's path, P calls W, who will testify that immediately after the collision, W heard someone scream, "D just got in P's way!" Assume this statement is hearsay, but that it will be admissible as an "excited utterance" if the declarant (the person who made the statement) was speaking under the "stress of excitement" caused by a "startling event or condition" (FRE 803(2)). D admits that the accident was a "startling event or condition," but claims that it has not been sufficiently established that the declarant was still under the stress of excitement when making the statement.

41. How should the court rule?

   (A) The court should overrule the objection if it finds that there is sufficient evidence to support the jury's conclusion that the declarant was speaking under the stress of excitement caused by the accident.

   (B) The court should overrule the objection if it finds by a preponderance of the evidence that the declarant was speaking under the stress of excitement caused by the accident.

   (C) The court must admit the evidence because whether the declarant was speaking under the stress of excitement caused by the accident is a question of fact, which the jury must decide.

   (D) The court must exclude the evidence because, as a matter of law, it is not possible to conclude that the declarant was speaking under the stress of excitement caused by the accident without identifying the declarant and having him or her testify at trial.

Prosecution of D for murder. The prosecution wishes to offer into evidence a confession D admittedly signed. At trial, D moves to suppress the confession, however, claiming that the police did not read her the Miranda rights before beginning the questioning that led to the confession. A police officer testifies that he did read D her Miranda rights.

42. How should the court rule?

   (A) The court should deny D's motion if it finds by a preponderance of the evidence that the officer read D her Miranda rights.

   (B) The court should deny D's motion if it finds by clear and convincing evidence that the officer read D her Miranda rights.

(C) The court should deny D's motion if it finds beyond a reasonable doubt that the officer read D her Miranda rights.

(D) The court should deny D's motion if it finds that there is evidence sufficient to support a finding that the officer read D her Miranda rights.

43. Assume D's claim is that she confessed only after 24 hours of non-stop torture, including infliction of physical pain, threats against D's family, and sleep deprivation. D claims she would have signed anything to end the torture. The police deny categorically that any torture took place, and claim D confessed quickly and willingly. How should the court rule on D's suppression motion?

(A) The court should grant D's motion if it finds by a preponderance of the evidence that D's story is true.

(B) The court should grant D's motion if it finds that there is evidence sufficient to support a finding that D's story is true.

(C) The court should let the jury decide the question because the voluntariness of a confession is a question of fact that is always for the jury.

(D) The court should decide the question because the admissibility of evidence is always a decision for the court.

Negligence action by P against D arising from a skateboard accident. P claims D, owner of a small skateboard shop, improperly fixed the wheels on P's skateboard, causing P to crash. D denies negligence, and claims P assumed the risk by riding a defective skateboard. To prove assumption of risk, D wishes to testify that when P showed D the skateboard and asked her to fix it, D told P, "all I can do is tighten the wheel trucks, but it won't do any good. If you don't replace the trucks, the wheels will fall off when you're riding." D will testify that after she said this, P gave her an angry look and took back the skateboard. Assume this statement would only be admissible to prove assumption of risk if P "adopted" D's statement as true, making it a party admission under FRE 801(d)(2)(B). P claims D has not proven adoption.

44. How should the court rule?

(A) The court should overrule the objection if it finds that there is sufficient evidence to support the jury's conclusion that P adopted D's statement as true.

(B) The court should overrule the objection if it finds, by a preponderance of the evidence, that P adopted D's statement as true.

(C) The court must admit the evidence because P's purported adoption of D's statement is a question of fact that the jury must decide.

(D) The answer depends on the approach taken by the jurisdiction.

45. Explain why questions of preliminary fact that do not involve "conditional relevancy" should be decided by the court rather than the jury.

ANSWER:

Negligence action by P against D arising from an automobile collision. P calls W, who testifies that she was standing at the intersection waiting to cross the street when D ran a red light and struck P's car broadside. On cross-examination, D establishes that W was toward the back of a large crowd on the sidewalk before the crash and had only a partial view of the street, that W was looking in the direction of the bright sun, that W has poor eyesight and was not wearing her glasses at the time, and that just after the crash, someone told W that D had run the red light. D moves to strike W's testimony due to lack of personal knowledge, and asks the court to instruct the jury to disregard W's testimony.

46. Which of the following statements is correct?

(A) The court should deny the motion if it concludes that W had first-hand knowledge of the accident.

(B) The court should deny the motion if it finds that there is evidence sufficient to support a finding that W had first-hand knowledge of the accident.

(C) The court should deny the motion because whether W had firsthand knowledge is always a question for the jury.

(D) The court should deny the motion regardless of whether W had firsthand knowledge because W has already testified about the crash.

47. Using the facts of this problem, explain why the conditional relevancy doctrine might be illogical.

ANSWER:

Criminal prosecution of D. The prosecution calls E to testify as an expert.

48. Which of the following is correct?

(A) The court may admit E's testimony only if it decides beyond a reasonable doubt that E is a qualified expert.

(B) The court may admit E's testimony only if it decides by a preponderance of the evidence that E is a qualified expert.

(C) The court may admit E's testimony only if it decides that there is evidence sufficient to support a finding that E is a qualified expert.

(D) The court must leave the question of the E's qualifications to the jury in order to preserve the defendant's right to trial by jury.

Classification of Evidence as Hearsay or Not Hearsay

Prosecution of D for the murder of V. To prove she did not commit the crime, D wishes to testify that after the murder was committed, X, a member of the Jets, a violent street gang, told her the Jets had "whacked" V. D is not a member of the Jets.

49. Which of the following statements is most likely correct?

(A) Because D's testimony concerning X's statement would be highly self-serving, the court should exclude it as a waste of time.

(B) Although X's statement is relevant to D's innocence, it is hearsay when offered for that purpose.

(C) X's statement is not hearsay when offered to prove D's innocence, but it must be excluded because its probative value is substantially outweighed by the danger of unfair prejudice.

(D) X's statement is relevant non-hearsay when offered to prove D's innocence.

Prosecution of D for the murder of V. D claims X committed the crime. To prove X killed V, D calls W to testify that just after the killing, which took place in a secluded area, and before V's body was discovered, X told her he had just killed a person, and described in detail the exact manner of killing (which was very unusual) and where the body could be found. All details given by X were accurate.

50. Which of the following statements is most likely correct?

(A) X's statement to W is only relevant to prove that X killed V, and is hearsay when considered for that purpose.

(B) X's statement to W is relevant both to prove that X killed V and to prove that X had knowledge of certain key details, but is hearsay when offered for either purpose.

(C) X's statement to W is relevant both to prove that X killed V and to prove that X had knowledge of certain key details. The statement is hearsay when offered for the first purpose, but not hearsay when offered for the second.

(D) X's statement is relevant both to prove that X killed V and to prove that X had knowledge of certain key details. However, because the testimony concerning X's statement is so self-serving and because D did not call X, the court should exclude it.

Personal injury action by P against D following a slip-and-fall in D's store. P calls W to testify that shortly before the fall, W told D that there was a big puddle of liquid on the floor.

51. Which of the following statements is most accurate?

    (A) W's testimony is hearsay if offered to prove the floor was slippery, but not hearsay if offered to prove that D knew the floor was slippery.

    (B) W's testimony is not hearsay if offered to prove the floor was slippery (because W didn't say the floor was slippery), but is hearsay when offered to prove that D knew the floor was slippery.

    (C) W's testimony is hearsay when offered for either purpose.

    (D) W's testimony is not hearsay when offered for either purpose.

Prosecution of D for burglary of V's home. To prove that D committed the crime, the prosecution wishes to offer evidence that as D was being led through the police station, V, who was at the station giving a statement, saw D and screamed, "You are the scum of the Earth." D objects on hearsay grounds.

52. Which of the following statements is most likely correct?

    (A) The statement is more likely hearsay under an assertion-based definition of hearsay than under a declarant-based definition.

    (B) The statement is more likely hearsay under a declarant-based definition of hearsay than under an assertion-based definition.

    (C) The statement would be hearsay under either definition.

    (D) Without further information, it is not possible to predict whether the statement is more likely to be admitted under one definition than the other.

Prosecution of D for kidnapping V, her 6-year-old niece. The prosecution alleges that D hid V in a very small container for several days. D admits V was with her for several days, but claims she was babysitting V and never hid V in a container. At trial, the prosecution calls V, who testifies that D locked him in a small "box" for "a long time." On cross-examination, D attacks V's credibility on grounds of mental difficulties affecting V's ability to distinguish reality from fantasy. The prosecution now wishes to offer evidence that when the police interviewed V shortly after D's arrest, V gave a detailed description of the container, right down to certain unique markings on its interior walls. Other evidence demonstrates that D possessed a container with that description before the events at issue.

53. D makes a hearsay objection to the testimony concerning V's detailed description. Of the following, which is the prosecution's strongest response?

    (A) Because of V's age, it is natural to expect him to lack credibility as a witness, and given the importance of the matter to D's guilt, the need for the evidence outweighs the hearsay dangers of the evidence.

    (B) The evidence is admissible as non-hearsay prior identification.

    (C) The evidence is not admissible to prove what the container looked like, but to prove that V knew what the container looked like.

    (D) The evidence is admissible as a prior consistent statement.

Prosecution of D for assault and battery on V. D admits striking V but claims self-defense. To prove her self-defense claim, D testifies that the day before the altercation, X told D that V was planning to kill D the next time they saw each other.

54. Discuss the hearsay implications of X's statement to V.

ANSWER:

Libel action by P, a prominent philanthropist, against D, a newspaper, alleging that D published a false story stating that P supported neo-Nazi organizations. D wishes to present evidence that it received the information from X, a reliable source. Assume two defenses are (1) that the story is true; and (2) that even if false, D acted in good faith because it did not know the story was false and did not act in reckless disregard for the truth.

55. Which of the following statements is most accurate?

    (A) The evidence is relevant and not hearsay both to prove the story is true and to prove that D published the story in good faith.

    (B) The evidence is hearsay for either purpose.

    (C) The evidence is hearsay if offered to prove the story was true but not hearsay if offered to prove D's good faith in publishing the story.

    (D) This question cannot be answered without more information.

Prosecution of D for assault and battery on V. To prove she acted in self-defense, D calls W to testify that V had a reputation for being violent. D did not know V's reputation at the time of the altercation.

56. The evidence of V's reputation is

    (A) irrelevant if D's theory is that D acted in reasonable fear of V, and relevant non-hearsay if D's theory is that V attacked first.

    (B) irrelevant if D's theory is that D acted in reasonable fear of V, and relevant but hearsay if D's theory is that V attacked first.

(C) relevant under either theory but hearsay under both.

(D) irrelevant under either theory.

Breach of contract action by P against D. To prove a contract existed, P wishes to call W, her friend, to testify that the night the negotiations ended, P called him and said, "I just accepted D's offer!"

57. Is P's statement hearsay? Why or why not?

ANSWER:

Will contest. To prove the testator lacked testamentary capacity when she signed her will leaving everything to her law school alma mater, P calls W, the testator's former servant, to testify that on the day the testator signed her will, she asked the servant to make her a "Moon sandwich with Jupiter cheese on Martian brain bread" for lunch.

58. The evidence of the testator's statement to W is

(A) more likely hearsay under a declarant-based definition than under an assertion-based definition.

(B) more likely hearsay under an assertion-based definition than under a declarant-based definition.

(C) clearly hearsay under both definitions.

(D) clearly non-hearsay under both definitions.

Libel action by P against D, a well-known entertainer. P alleges that in front of a comedy club audience, D called P a "slimy, scum-sucking bottom-feeder who wouldn't free his own mother if she was tied to a railroad track." D denies saying this. To prove D uttered the words, P wishes to offer in evidence two things: (1) the testimony of a person who was in the audience that night, who will state that D spoke the words; and (2) a newspaper review of D's performance mentioning what D said.

59. Discuss the hearsay implications of each item of evidence.

ANSWER:

For the following questions, indicate whether each utterance or act is hearsay for the purpose for which it is offered, and explain why. Apply the Federal Rules of Evidence. If something would not be hearsay under the Federal Rules, call it non-hearsay. Also, do not assume that a declarant is a party unless the facts indicate such.

60. To prove P has become the owner of a piece of land by adverse possession, P calls W to testify that one day, X approached her and said, "P's going around saying she owns the lot."

ANSWER:

61. Slander action by P against D. To prove he suffered significant harm to his reputation when D called him an "airhead" in front of a large audience, P testifies that prior to this incident, he was known in the community as a brilliant corporate leader.

ANSWER:

62. Civil rights action by P against D, a police officer. P claims that D shot her without reason during a confrontation before a sporting event. D claims she acted in self-defense. To prove she acted reasonably, D testifies that while en route to the sports arena, the dispatcher told D that P was armed.

ANSWER:

63. Negligence action against D, the builders of a suspended pedestrian bridge that collapsed. To prove that the bridge was sturdy, D calls W to testify that she was present when, a day before the accident, a structural engineer walked onto the bridge in front of a large crowd and proceeded to jump up and down. (The bridge did not shake or collapse.)

ANSWER:

64. Personal injury action by P against D arising from a skateboard collision. To prove that D was at fault, P testifies that just after the collision, D said to P, "Sorry I cut you off, dude."

ANSWER:

65. Prosecution of D for the murder of V. At trial, the prosecution calls W, who claims to have witnessed the killing. When asked who killed V, W points to D.

ANSWER:

66. To prove that the weather at the beach on a certain day was very sunny, W testifies that most people at the beach put on sunscreen.

ANSWER:

67. To prove that it was raining at a certain time, W testifies that at that time, a weather reporter on a local news program said, "Dust off those umbrellas!"

ANSWER:

68. To prove that P and D entered into a contract, P calls W, her secretary, to testify that after P and D completed a negotiation session, and while D's back was turned, P whispered to W, "I just sold those leftover Sugar Boys CDs."

ANSWER:

69. To prove that a physician feared contracting AIDS from X, the physician's nurse testifies that before examining X, the physician put on latex gloves.

ANSWER:

70. To prove that D liked X, W testifies that D introduced X to her as "my favorite person in the whole world."

ANSWER:

71. To prove that X was W's mother, W testifies, "X is my mom."

ANSWER:

72. To prove that X was the owner of a certain dog, W testifies that she saw the dog run up to X wagging its big bushy tail.

ANSWER:

73. To prove that a certain event occurred at 5:10 p.m. W testifies that she was sitting in Professor Wigmore's evidence class one day when the professor looked in the direction of the clock and said, "I see our time is up." The class ended at 5:10.

ANSWER:

74. To prove that P, a big-screen TV store owner, was a sales leader in the business, P calls W to testify that she heard P say at the end of a radio advertisement, "I *am* the king."

ANSWER:

75. To prove that Elvis is dead, W testifies that she visited Graceland and saw a tombstone with the name "Elvis Aaron Presley" chiseled on it.

ANSWER:

76. To prove that D's red car hit P's blue car, P testifies that just after the accident, she turned to her companion and said, "that red car just rammed right into us."

ANSWER:

77. Personal injury action by P against D following an automobile collision. D calls W, who testifies that D had the green light. To impeach W's credibility, P calls X to testify that shortly after the accident, W told her that *P* had the green light.

ANSWER:

78. To prove that X was close to Y's car, W testifies that as X walked past Y's car, an automated voice from Y's car stated, "Back off! You are too close to the vehicle."

ANSWER:

79. Negligence action by P against D arising out of an automobile collision. To prove that he suffered emotional distress as a result of the accident, P calls W to testify that at the scene just after the accident, P was sobbing.

ANSWER:

80. Slander action by P, a film director, against D arising out of a speech D gave to an audience of film critics. To prove that the slander was uttered, P testifies that in the speech, D said that P was the illegitimate offspring of the unholy mating of a pig and a wolf and that he possessed the morality of a buzzard hovering over a corpse.

ANSWER:

81. Prosecution of D for the murder of V. To prove D's guilt, the prosecution offers testimony that while being transported to the police station following her arrest, D said, "that creep I just killed deserved to die."

ANSWER:

82. Negligence action by P against D after the two roller skaters collided on a beach sidewalk. To prove that D was responsible, P calls W, who came on the scene shortly after the collision. P wishes to have W testify that as soon as she saw what had happened, she asked a bystander which skater was responsible, and that the bystander pointed to D. D lodges a hearsay objection to W's testimony about the bystander's pointing motion.

ANSWER:

83. Civil action by P against D bank for wrongful discharge. P alleges that D's president fired P for improper reasons. Assume a valid defense is that the employee has been convicted of a crime involving dishonesty, and that D raises such a defense. To prove its defense, D wishes to call its president to testify that before firing P, she heard that before coming to work for the bank, P had been convicted of embezzlement.

ANSWER:

84. Will contest initiated by P, who claims to have been the deceased's best friend but who was granted nothing in the will. To prove that the deceased intentionally left P out of the will, the deceased's executor calls W to testify that on the day she made her will, the deceased called P "a bloody leech who would con a homeless baby out of her spot on a steam grate on a cold winter night."

ANSWER:

85. Negligence action by P against D arising out of an intersection collision between their cars. Both drivers claim they had the green light. To prove she had the green light, D testifies that a few moments before the collision, the driver in front of D, who had been stopped at the intersection, began to move forward.

ANSWER:

86. Breach of contract action by P, a music wholesaler, against D, a record store owner. P alleges that in a telephone conversation, P and D entered an oral contract for the sale of two cartons of "Sneezer" CDs at a specified price, but that D failed to pay for the CDs after they were delivered. D denies that a contract existed. To prove a contract existed, P offers to testify that after D offered to purchase the CDs, P responded, "I accept your offer."

ANSWER:

87. Prosecution of D for willful neglect of his pet fish. To prove that D had not been feeding his fish, the prosecution wishes to offer evidence that when the police came to D's home to arrest him and approached the tank in which the poor fish lived, all the fish immediately swam to the surface and began moving about wildly.

ANSWER:

88. Prosecution of D for the murder of V, her husband. D admits killing V, but claims she was provoked, which may reduce murder to manslaughter. To prove provocation, D wishes to testify that just before the killing, X told her that V had been arrested for engaging in lewd conduct with a prostitute.

ANSWER:

89. Wrongful death action by P against Taikachanz Airlines (D) following a fatal crash that killed P's deceased spouse. P alleges that the plane in which P's deceased spouse was riding was not airworthy. To prove the plane was airworthy, D calls W to testify that D's pilot visually inspected the outside of the plane just before she went aboard.

ANSWER:

90. Civil action by P against D bank for wrongful discharge. P alleges that D's president fired P for improper reasons. Assume a valid defense to the action is that D acted in good faith in firing the employee, and that D raises such a defense. To prove good faith, D calls Y, its president, to testify that before firing P, she heard that P had been convicted of embezzlement a year earlier.

ANSWER:

91. Prosecution of D for the murder of V. In order to establish that the killing took place at noon, the prosecution calls W, who witnessed the killing, to testify that just after the killing occurred, he turned to his friend, asked her what time it was, and that the friend then looked at her watch and said, "12:00 sharp." D objects to the evidence of the friend's statement.

ANSWER:

92. Prosecution of D for a murder that took place in State X on a summer day. D claims she was a thousand miles away in State Y when the killing took place. At trial, D testifies that she remembers the day well because in State Y on that day, the weather was unbearably hot. To corroborate her testimony, D wishes to offer in evidence a newspaper article from State Y dated the following day. The article states, "the heat wave continued unabated yesterday."

ANSWER:

93. Action for civil commitment of a law professor due to insanity. To prove insanity, plaintiff offers evidence that right in the middle of an evidence class, the professor jumped on the podium and shouted, "I am the king of the Federal Rules!"

ANSWER:

94. To prove an accident happened at dawn, a farmer testifies that just before the crash, her husband poked her and said, "rooster's crowing. Time to get up."

ANSWER:

95. To prove that X is dead, a party offers into evidence the original death certificate, obtained from the county recorder's office.

ANSWER:

96. To prove that A and B, two companies, had agreed to merge, a party calls W to testify that X, a corporate officer, told W that she heard A's president said to B's president, "I propose that we merge our companies," and that B's president responded, "I accept your offer."

ANSWER:

97. To prove that X had conveyed a piece of land to Y, a party offers in evidence a deed signed by X conveying X's interest in the property to Y.

ANSWER:

98. To prove that X is a blond, W testifies that at a party, Y pointed to X and said, "Have you ever seen such blond hair in all your life?"

ANSWER:

99. Negligence action by P against D arising from an automobile accident. To prove that P was in pain following the accident, W testifies that she saw P sitting alone on the sidewalk crying.

ANSWER:

100. Prosecution of D for passing counterfeit money. To prove that D was aware that the notes she passed were not genuine, a prosecution witness testifies that before D passed the notes, X told D that they were "bogus."

ANSWER:

101. Prosecution of D for the murder of V. To prove her innocence, D calls W to testify that X confessed to the crime.

ANSWER:

102. Prosecution of D for a murder committed in a supermarket at 8:00 p.m. on a Sunday night. To prove that she did not commit the crime, D calls W to testify that at 7:45 on the night of the murder, D said to W, "'The Shrimptons' is my favorite television program." It is undis-

puted that "The Shrimptons" is televised at 8:00 on Sunday evenings, including the evening in question.

ANSWER:

103. Prosecution of D for burglary. To prove D committed the crime, a prosecution witness testifies that D confessed to the police.

ANSWER:

104. Negligence action by P against D arising from an automobile accident. To prove that P did not suffer a broken arm in the accident, W testifies that a few minutes after the accident, she saw P playing catch using the arm in question.

ANSWER:

105. During a criminal trial, X, sitting in the audience, rises and proclaims that she, rather than D, committed the crime.

ANSWER:

106. To prove that Y, a law student, understood evidence law well, Y testifies that X, Y's evidence teacher, wrote a note on Y's final exam stating, "excellent work."

ANSWER:

107. To prove X hated Y, W testifies that when X saw Y at a party, X said, "Y is a stupid person."

ANSWER:

108. To prove that X is dead, W testifies that she saw officials of the coroner's office placing X's body into their van.

ANSWER:

109. Sexual harassment action by P against D Corp., her employer. To prove the harassment occurred, P testifies that one of D's managers, who served as P's boss, cornered P one evening after everyone else had left and said, "You have the most amazing eyes I've ever seen."

ANSWER:

110. To prove X liked Y, W testifies that X said to Y, "I hope you'll go out with me some time."

ANSWER:

111. To prove that a prototype automobile was working satisfactorily, W testifies that after taking the car for a test drive, the driver looked toward the control booth and raised one thumb.

ANSWER:

112. Prosecution of D for the murder of V. To prove she did not kill V, D calls W, a deputy sheriff, to testify that shortly after the killing, X, another person, confessed to having committed it.

ANSWER:

113. To prove that the pilot of a small plane survived for a time after a crash, P calls an air traffic controller to testify that moments after the impact, the pilot radioed, "Mayday, Mayday! I've been hit!"

ANSWER:

114. Prosecution of D for burglarizing V's home. V testifies for the prosecution that he heard a noise downstairs in the home at 3:00 a.m. On cross-examination, to impeach V's credibility, D's attorney asks V to acknowledge that on the day after the burglary, V told the police that he heard a noise downstairs at 11:00 p.m.

ANSWER:

115. To prove that X is able to swim, W testifies that after she asked X if she could swim, X dove into the deep end of a pool and swam to the other end.

ANSWER:

116. Prosecution of D for the murder of V. D claims she killed V in self-defense because she believed V was about to attack her. To prove she had reason to fear V, D testifies that a week before the killing, X, a friend of hers, told her that Y, another friend, had told X that V was very angry at D.

ANSWER:

117. Personal injury action arising out of an automobile accident. To prove the accident happened at 5:00, P testifies that a moment after the crash, the radio announcer said, "It's 5:00 and time for the news."

ANSWER:

118. Breach of contract action by P's estate against D, P's daughter, arising out of D's failure to pay for a car P allegedly sold to D. D claims the car was a gift. To prove the transfer of the car to D was not a gift, P's administrator offers in evidence P's will, in which P wrote, "I intentionally leave nothing by this will to my daughter D, who is nothing but a leach."

ANSWER:

119. To prove that X is a lawyer, a witness testifies that she attended the new attorney swearing-in ceremony, and that X raised her hand and took the attorney's oath.

ANSWER:

120. Prosecution of D for the murder of V. To prove D committed the crime, the prosecution calls W to testify that a bloodhound was brought to the place where V was found, and that the dog ran straight to D's home (its nose to the ground), stopped there, and began barking loudly.

ANSWER:

121. Prosecution of D for the murder of V, her husband. The prosecution calls W, who shared a jail cell with D on the night of D's arrest. W testifies that after she asked D what she was in for, D said, "I killed my husband."

ANSWER:

122. Prosecution of D for the murder of V. D claims she killed V in self-defense because she believed V was about to attack her. To prove she had reason to fear V, D calls W to testify that a week before the killing, X, a friend of D, told W that he had told D that V was angry at D.

ANSWER:

123. Prosecution of D for assault on V. V testifies that after the assault, while he was being treated by a paramedic, he saw D standing nearby and that he told the paramedic that D was the one who attacked him.

ANSWER:

124. Prosecution of D for the murder of V. D claims she killed V in self-defense because she believed V was about to attack her. To prove she had reason to fear V, D calls W to testify that a week before the killing, D told W that V was angry at D.

ANSWER:

125. To prove that Brand X laundry detergent works better than all others, an expert witness testifies that more shoppers choose Brand X than all other brands.

ANSWER:

126. To prove that a certain law professor is insane, W, a student in the professor's class, testifies that one day, the professor started teaching linear algebra instead of evidence.

ANSWER:

127. Breach of contract action by P, a door-to-door encyclopedia sales company, against D, who agreed to purchase the set of books. The contract gave D a three-day period in which to cancel the deal by notifying P in writing. To prove the contract was canceled, D offers his letter to P, dated the day after the contract was signed, stating that he was canceling the agreement.

ANSWER:

128. P sues D for personal injuries following an auto accident. D denies negligence. To prove that D exercised reasonable care, W testifies that just before leaving the house on the fateful day, D told him that he planned to drive very carefully on this trip.

ANSWER:

129. Prosecution of D for the attempted murder of V during a bar brawl. W, a physician, treated D for multiple cuts after the brawl. The prosecution calls W to testify that while treating D, he said to D, "You tried to kill V, didn't you," and that D looked back at W and smiled broadly.

ANSWER:

130. Prosecution of D for burglarizing V's home. V testifies for the prosecution that he heard a noise downstairs in the home at 3:00 a.m. On cross-examination, to prove that the burglary occurred at a different time, D's attorney asks V to admit that the day after the burglary, V told the police he heard a noise downstairs at 11:00 p.m.

ANSWER:

131. Product liability action by P, administrator of X's estate, against Purple Giant, a canned food maker, for selling tainted canned pork and beans. To prove X ate Purple Giant's pork and beans, P calls W to testify that a week before X became ill, she said, "I just love Purple Giant pork and beans!"

ANSWER:

132. Prosecution of D for arson following the destruction of a small food market. D claims X committed the crime. To prove that X committed the crime, D authenticates and offers into ev-

idence a surveillance videotape showing a person strongly resembling X running away from the market moments before the building burst into flames.

ANSWER:

133. To establish the landowner's ownership of a particular portion of a corn crop, the tenant farmer testifies that on a particular day, she stood with the landowner on the farm, pointed to a particular stack of corn, and said, "that corn over there is yours, in payment of the rent."

ANSWER:

Exceptions to (and Exemptions from) the Hearsay Rule

<u>Note</u>: To answer many of the following questions, you must have covered the material on preliminary questions (FRE 104), the exceptions to the hearsay rule (FRE 803, 804, and 807), and exemptions from the hearsay rule (FRE 801(d)).

Prosecution of D for the murder of V. To prove that D committed the murder, the prosecution calls W, who was with V when he died. The prosecution wishes to have W testify that just before V died, W said to him, "Where did this happen?", and that V pointed to D, who was standing in a corner of the room, and said, "his house." D lodges a hearsay objection to W's proposed testimony.

134. Which of the following statements is most accurate?

    (A) Because W's out of court statement is hearsay for which no exception applies, it is inadmissible.

    (B) Because neither W nor V have made statements as defined in the hearsay rule, W will be permitted to testify both to what he said to V and to V's nodding conduct.

    (C) If V is found to have adopted W's assertion as his own, both W's statement and V's response will be admissible.

    (D) If V heard W's statement and if V believed he was about to die, W's question and V's pointing will be admissible.

Prosecution of D for the murder of V in a city plaza. It is undisputed that at the time of the killing, D was standing in a grassy area on the east side of the plaza, about 50 feet from V. D claims, however, that she had nothing to do with the killing. At trial, a critical issue is the direction from which the shots were fired. The prosecution claims the shots came from the grassy area, while D claims they came from a six-story building on the west side of the plaza. To prove that the shots issued from the grassy area, the prosecution calls W, and wishes to have her testify that she was in the plaza at the time of the killing, that she heard the sound of gunfire, and that moments later, she saw X, a bystander who she'd noticed had been in the plaza for several minutes, raise her arm and point toward the grassy area. D lodges a hearsay objection to W's testimony about X's actions.

135. Which of the following statements is most accurate?

(A) The judge must decide whether X was asserting the direction from which the shots were fired. If the judge decides that she was, the evidence will be hearsay but admissible as a present sense impression.

(B) The judge must decide whether there is sufficient evidence to support the conclusion that X was asserting the direction from which the shots were fired. If the judge makes that finding, she will allow the jury to hear the evidence of X's conduct.

(C) Because the foundational elements for the excited utterance exception are clearly satisfied, the court must admit the evidence.

(D) Because X's conduct is irrelevant if he was not asserting the place from which the shots were fired, and inadmissible hearsay if X was in fact asserting the place from which the shots were fired, the judge must exclude the evidence.

Breach of contract action by the P Opinion Survey Co. (P) against D, an unsuccessful presidential candidate. P claims that D failed to pay a large bill for political polling P had performed. D claims that she never hired P to do any work for her. At trial, P calls W, a news reporter, and wishes to have W testify that during the campaign, he attended a press conference conducted by X, D's husband, and that at that press conference, X said, "according to figures put together for us by the P Opinion Survey Co., we have a 19 percentage point lead over our closest rival."

136. Which of the following constitutes P's strongest argument that the evidence of X's statement is admissible?

(A) Because the making of X's statement constitutes the very fact in issue, it is an act of independent legal significance, and is thus admissible as non-hearsay.

(B) Because X's statement does not assert that D hired P, it is admissible non-hearsay.

(C) Because X was probably authorized to speak for D, X's statement is admissible as an authorized admission under FRE 801(d)(2)(C).

(D) Because X was speaking about a matter within the scope of his employment, X's statement is admissible as an agency admission under FRE 801(d)(2)(D).

Prosecution of D for conspiracy to sell illicit drugs. D denies that he was involved in any conspiracy. The prosecution calls one witness who testifies that she was a part of the conspiracy but backed out before the drug sales took place. To prove D's involvement in the conspiracy, the prosecution wishes to call PO, an undercover officer, to testify that she infiltrated the organization which allegedly planned the crime, and that on the day before the "big deal" was going to "go down," X, a member of the organization, said to PO, "D and I need a driver for tomorrow's big buy. Can you help out?" D lodges a hearsay objection to PO's testimony concerning X's statement.

137. Which of the following statements is most accurate?

  (A) The existence of a conspiracy is a preliminary fact which must be found in order for X's statement to be admissible. It is also a fact which the jury must ultimately decide in order to convict D. As a result, the jury should decide the preliminary fact.

  (B) The existence of a conspiracy is a preliminary fact which must be found in order for X's statement to be admissible. It is also a fact which the jury must ultimately decide in order to convict D. Therefore, although the existence of the preliminary fact will be for the court to decide, the court must apply the reasonable doubt standard in making that determination.

  (C) Because the statement asserts that a conspiracy existed, which is the very thing the court must decide in order to determine the admissibility of the statement, it would be improper "bootstrapping" to allow the court to consider the statement as evidence of the existence of the conspiracy.

  (D) Even though the statement asserts that a conspiracy existed, which is the very thing the court must decide in order to admit the statement, the court may consider the statement as it determines the preliminary fact question.

138. Assume X's statement was the only evidence the prosecution offers to prove that a conspiracy existed. Will the trial court be acting properly if it decides as a preliminary fact that a conspiracy existed and allows the case to go to the jury? (Assume that the other preliminary facts necessary to the admissibility of the statement have been found to exist.) Explain.

ANSWER:

  Prosecution of D for burglary of V's home. V died before trial. To prove D did not commit the burglary, D calls W to testify that just before V died, V said, "The end is near. I don't know if I picked the right guy out of the lineup." At the lineup, V picked D as the perpetrator.

139. The prosecution makes a hearsay objection to W's testimony about V's statement to W. Of the following, which is D's strongest argument for admitting W's testimony concerning V's statement?

  (A) The statement is not hearsay.

  (B) The statement is hearsay but admissible as a declaration against interest.

  (C) The statement is hearsay but admissible as a dying declaration.

  (D) Although the statement is hearsay and does not fall within an exception, the court must admit it to protect D's constitutional right to due process and to present a defense.

Prosecution of D for assault and battery on V, a hitchhiker who was driven by his attacker to a remote location and brutally assaulted before being dumped in an alley. D denies that he was the attacker. At trial, the prosecution calls V to testify about the incident, and then calls PO, a police officer, to testify that while V was recuperating in the hospital the day after the attack, V told her that he expected to die and then described the inside of the van in which he was attacked, saying that the interior was upholstered with red and white striped leather, and that the walls of the van were covered with "gang-style" graffiti and photographs of a well-known political figure. It is undisputed that D owns a van meeting the description given by V. D lodges a hearsay objection to PO's testimony concerning V's out of court statement.

140. Which of the following constitutes the prosecution's strongest argument in favor of admissibility?

(A) Although the statement is hearsay because it is offered to prove the appearance of the interior of the attacker's van, there are sufficient indications of trustworthiness to warrant admission.

(B) Although the statement is hearsay because it is offered to prove the appearance of the interior of the attacker's van, the statement is admissible as a present sense impression.

(C) Although the statement is hearsay because it is offered to prove the appearance of the interior of the attacker's van, the statement is admissible as a dying declaration.

(D) The statement is not offered to prove the appearance of the interior of the attacker's van, but to demonstrate V's knowledge of its quite unique interior under circumstances indicating that V must have been inside the van.

Prosecution of D, a woman, for assault and battery following a fight with V, a man, in a bar. The primary issue is whether it was D or V who started the fight. At trial, to prove that D started the fight, the prosecution calls W to testify that moments after the fight began, X screamed, "that woman just ran up and slugged that guy!" D lodges an objection to the testimony concerning X's statement on both hearsay and personal knowledge bases. The prosecution responds that the statement is admissible as an excited utterance and that X did in fact have personal knowledge of the facts.

141. Which of the following best describes the procedure the court should follow?

(A) The court should decide by a preponderance of the evidence whether X had personal knowledge of the fight and whether the foundational requirements for the excited utterance exception have been satisfied.

(B) The court should decide beyond a reasonable doubt whether X had personal knowledge of the fight and whether the foundational requirements for the excited utterance exception have been satisfied.

(C) The court should decide whether there is sufficient evidence to support a jury finding that X had personal knowledge of the fight, and should then decide by a preponderance of the evidence whether the foundational requirements for the excited utterance exception have been satisfied.

(D) The court should decide whether there is sufficient evidence to support a jury finding that X had personal knowledge of the fight, and whether there is sufficient evidence to support a jury finding that the foundational requirements for the excited utterance exception have been satisfied.

Breach of contract action by P against D. P claims that D promised to hire P to work for her law firm, that P turned down another job offer in reliance on this promise, and that D then failed to hire P. Assume it is given that D's firm planned to hire only one new person. At trial, D calls W, her secretary, and wishes to have him testify that just after P completed his interview with the law firm, D said to W, "I think I'll go downstairs to start the paperwork to hire Q for the job." P lodges a hearsay objection to W's testimony concerning D's statement.

142. Which of the following arguments has the greatest chance of succeeding?

   (A) Because D's statement tends to make it more likely that D did not promise to hire P, it is relevant. Because the statement only circumstantially indicates his state of mind, it is not hearsay. It is therefore admissible.

   (B) Because D's statement tends to make it more likely that D did not promise to hire P, it is relevant. Though the statement asserts D's state of mind, and is therefore hearsay, it fits within the exception for statements of then existing state of mind. It is therefore admissible.

   (C) Because D's statement tends to make it more likely that D did not promise to hire P, it is relevant. However, because the statement asserts D's state of mind, it is hearsay, and it does not fit within the state of mind exception because it refers to the future status of a third person.

   (D) Because D's statement does not make it more likely that D did not promise to hire P, it is irrelevant and therefore inadmissible.

Prosecution of D, a law student, for vandalizing the offices of Bigue Biggere & Biggeste, a law firm which denied her a summer clerkship. At trial, the prosecution wishes to call W to testify that the day before the crime was committed, she overheard X, who had also been denied an offer, mumbling the following to himself: "I think I'll go with D tomorrow night to the offices of Bigue Biggere and leave those idiots a message even they will understand." X has already been convicted of this crime and now resides in the state penitentiary. D lodges a hearsay objection to W's testimony concerning X's statement.

143. Which of the following constitutes the prosecution's strongest response?

   (A) The statement is not hearsay because it is not offered to prove the truth of what it asserts.

   (B) The statement is admissible as a coconspirator statement.

   (C) The statement is hearsay but admissible as a declaration against interest.

   (D) The statement is hearsay but admissible under the state of mind exception.

144. Which of the following constitutes D's strongest policy argument <u>against</u> admitting W's testimony concerning X's statement?

(A) Admission of the statement would violate D's 6th Amendment confrontation right.

(B) Because the main purpose for admitting the statement was to establish the intent (and by implication the future conduct) of a person other than the declarant, the foundation that makes state of mind statements reliable drops away, and we are left with an arguably unreliable statement the credibility of which cannot be tested contemporaneously with its making.

(C) The probative value of the evidence in establishing D's intentions and future conduct was substantially outweighed by the danger of unfair prejudice arising from the jury's inability or unwillingness to abide by an instruction that the evidence is to be considered only for that purpose.

(D) Because the statement did not directly assert the declarant's state of mind, the state of mind doctrine does not apply at all to the case, and the evidence should have been excluded.

Prosecution of D, a popular actor, for the murder of V in Chicago. To prove D was in Chicago on the day of the murder, the prosecution calls PO, a police officer, to testify that she attended a press conference held by A, D's agent, on the day before the murder, and that A said, "D is looking forward to traveling to Chicago tomorrow for the start of shooting on her new blockbuster film."

145. D objects to this testimony on hearsay grounds. Of the following, which is the prosecution's strongest argument for admissibility of A's statement to PO?

(A) The statement is admissible non-hearsay.

(B) The statement is hearsay but admissible as a party admission.

(C) The statement is hearsay but admissible as a declaration against interest.

(D) The statement is hearsay but admissible under the residual exception.

Prosecution of D1 and D2 for the murder of V. The prosecution calls W, D1's cellmate in county jail, to testify that just before the trial, D1 told her that she and D2 killed V.

146. If D1 and D2 object on hearsay grounds, how should the court rule?

ANSWER:

Negligence action by P against D, an auto dealer, following an accident in which the car in which P was riding crashed into a tree. The car was driven by X, one of D's employee-salespeople, and occurred as X demonstrated the car's sporty handling. At trial, P wishes to testify that after the accident, X told P, "I took that turn too fast. My boss will pay your medical bills."

147. D objects to the testimony concerning X's statement. How should the court rule?

ANSWER:

Prosecution of D for bank robbery. The prosecution calls X, a teller, who testifies about the robbery. The prosecution then calls PO, a police officer who arranged a line-up for X. PO will testify that when X saw D in the lineup, X said, "That's her," and pointed to D.

148. D objects to admission of X's statement. Which of the following is correct?

(A) The court should admit X's statement as a statement of prior identification.

(B) The court should exclude X's statement because X, rather than PO, must testify about the identification of D at the lineup.

(C) The court should admit X's statement if the prosecution recalls X to verify that she in fact identified D.

(D) The court should exclude X's statement if a better record of the line-up, such as a videotape, exists.

Prosecution of D, a blond man, for bank robbery. The prosecution alleges that D participated with X in committing the crime. At trial, the prosecution calls PO, a police officer, and wishes to have PO testify that two days after the crime, she arrested X, and that on the way to be booked, X said, "Yeah, me and some blond guy did it. So what?" Two days later, X died of food poisoning while he was being held in the county jail. D lodges a hearsay objection to PO's testimony concerning X's statement.

149. Which of the following rulings would be most supportable?

(A) The court should admit the evidence as an admission.

(B) The court should admit the evidence as a declaration against interest.

(C) The court should admit the evidence as a dying declaration.

(D) The court should exclude the evidence as irrelevant.

Prosecution of D for assault and battery on V. V was attacked in a dimly lit alley late one night, with the perpetrator jumping V from behind. A struggle ensued, during which V got a glimpse of the perpetrator. The day after the assault, while V was recuperating in the hospital from serious head injuries, he described his attacker to PO, a police officer, as a white male between 25 and 35, medium height, with long brown hair. PO then showed V some photographs of men generally meeting the description V gave. V picked D's photograph out of this group. At trial, V testifies generally about the crime, but is unable to provide much detail because, he claims, he remembers little. V remembers looking through some photographs, but does not remember who, if anybody, he selected. The prosecutor then calls PO and wishes to have PO testify that V chose D's photograph. D lodges a hearsay objection to PO's testimony insofar as it relates that V selected D's photograph.

150. Which of the followings statements is most accurate?

(A) PO's testimony concerning V's selection of D's photograph is admissible under the prior identification rule.

(B) Because V remembers so little about both the attack and identification procedure, admitting PO's testimony would violate D's right to confront the witnesses against him.

(C) Because PO did not know whether V chose the correct person when he selected D's photograph from the book, PO's testimony is inadmissible.

(D) Because V could not have gotten a good look at the attacker, V did not have personal knowledge. Thus, V would not have been allowed to testify about who attacked him. If V could not have testified to this fact, neither can PO.

Prosecution of D for attempted murder of V by poison. To prove V took the poison voluntarily in a suicide attempt, D calls W, V's oldest friend and confidante, to testify that on the day V was released from the hospital, V had lunch with W and told her, in reference to the day she became ill from the poison, "I was so depressed that day."

151. V died before trial in an unrelated auto accident. The prosecution objects to W's testimony concerning V's statement. How should the court rule?

ANSWER:

Prosecution of D for the murder of V. D denies involvement. To prove the murder took place at D's apartment at 8:00 p.m. on a certain date, the prosecution calls W to testify that earlier that day, V told W that she was planning to drop something off at D's apartment that night.

152. Which of the following is most likely correct?

(A) W's testimony is admissible as it stands.

(B) W's testimony is admissible only to prove V's plans, and the court should redact any reference to D.

(C) W's testimony is inadmissible for any purpose because it is impossible to remove any reference to D from V's statement.

(D) W's testimony is inadmissible because the probative value of the evidence is substantially outweighed by the danger of unfair prejudice.

Wrongful discharge action by P, a law professor, against D University, his employer. P claims he was fired without cause. D claims it fired P because rather than teaching Evidence, P taught quantum mechanics. P denies this. To prove that P was teaching quantum mechanics, D calls W, a student in P's class, to testify about the contents of a certain class session. Despite efforts to refresh W's recollection, she cannot recall what took place on that day. D then asks W if she took notes during the class on that day and whether the notes accurately reflected what took place in the classroom. W answers "yes" to both questions. D then asks W to read aloud a page of her notes. The notes state that D discussed Schroedinger's cat, a quantum mechanics thought experiment. P makes a hearsay objection.

153. Which of the following statements is most accurate?

(A) W's notes are not hearsay because they are not offered to prove the truth of P's statements about quantum mechanics. The notes may be read into the record.

(B) W's notes are hearsay and because W had no legal duty to record P's words accurately, no hearsay exception applies.

(C) W's notes are hearsay but admissible under the recorded recollection exception.

(D) W's notes are not hearsay because D is merely using them to refresh the witness's recollection. They may therefore be read into the record.

Negligence action by P against D arising out of a collision between the two skateboarders. At trial, to prove damages, P calls W to testify that she saw the collision, and ran over to P (who was lying on the ground) immediately after it. P then wishes to have W testify that when he saw W, P said, in an anguished tone, "My leg is all twisted the wrong way and I don't have any feeling in it at all." D lodges a hearsay objection to the evidence concerning P's response.

154. Which of the following statements is most accurate?

(A) The statement is not hearsay because it is an admission.

(B) The statement is hearsay, and it is admissible only under the exceptions for excited utterances and present sense impressions.

(C) The statement is hearsay, and it is admissible only under the exceptions for statements of then existing physical condition.

(D) The statement is hearsay, and it is probably admissible under the exceptions for excited utterances, present sense impressions, statements of then existing physical condition, and statements made for purposes of medical diagnosis or treatment.

Prosecution of D for the murder of V in a barroom brawl. D claims she was attending a World Series game when the murder took place. The prosecutor calls W, who testifies that he was in the bar when the killing occurred and clearly saw the killer's face. The prosecutor then wishes to have W testify that the day after the killing, W was shopping with his girlfriend at a supermarket when W saw D coming down the same aisle; that W walked up to D and said, "You're the woman who killed that old man"; and that D continued walking down the aisle. D lodges a hearsay objection to the testimony about W's statement to D, and a relevancy objection to the evidence concerning D's failure to respond.

155. Which of the following constitutes the prosecution's best response?

(A) W's statement to D is hearsay but admissible as an excited utterance. The court should then admit the evidence of D's silence if it finds that by her conduct, D admitted the truth of W's accusation.

(B) W's statement to D is not hearsay because it constitutes a prior identification. The court should then admit the evidence of D's silence if it finds that by her conduct, D admitted the truth of W's accusation.

(C) W's statement to D is not hearsay because it constitutes a prior identification. The court should then permit the jury to decide whether by her conduct, D admitted the truth of W's accusation.

(D) The court should allow the jury to decide whether W's statement to D constitutes a prior identification. The court should then permit the jury to decide whether by her conduct, D admitted the truth of W's accusation.

Breach of contract action by P against D, a music retailer. P alleges D breached by failing to deliver an order by the specified date, and that by the time the CDs arrived, there was no market for them. To prove she delivered the cartons to P's store personally and on time, D testifies that as she was driving back to her office after making the delivery, she wrote herself a note about the CDs and that she dated the note. D wishes to read the note into the record. The note reads "CDs delivered to P today."

156. P objects on hearsay grounds. How should the court rule?

ANSWER:

Prosecution of D for arson arising out of a fire that destroyed D's insured building. Earlier, D had sued her fire insurer after it refused to pay. At the trial of that action, the insurer called W, D's friend, who testified that he saw D place an incendiary device in the shop just before the fire. D cross-examined W at that time, trying to shake his story. W is now dead, killed in a fire in another store. In D's criminal trial, the prosecution offers the transcript of W's testimony under the former testimony exception.

157. Which of the following statements is most accurate?

(A) The transcript is inadmissible because in the criminal action, D has much to lose and thus a strong motive to more vigorously cross-examine W.

(B) The transcript is inadmissible because the civil trial came first.

(C) The transcript is inadmissible because its admission would violate D's constitutional right to confront the witnesses against him.

(D) The transcript is admissible.

158. Assume that in this criminal trial, the state has also named X as a defendant. X is the person from whom D had bought the store a few months before the fire. X was not a party in D's civil action against the insurance company. X bases his defense on the same theory as D—that the fire was accidental. At trial, the prosecution wishes to offer against X the transcript of W's testimony from the previous civil action. Which of the following statements is most accurate?

(A) The transcript is inadmissible because in the first action, D had a different motive in cross-examining W than X has in this criminal trial.

(B) The transcript is inadmissible because X was not a party to the civil action.

(C) The transcript is admissible because X is D's predecessor in interest and is bound by D's actions.

(D) The transcript is admissible against X because it is admissible against D.

P sues D following a surfing collision. P calls W1, who saw the accident. W1 testifies that D was "not watching out for other surfers." To prove D was surfing carefully, D calls W2 to testify that on the day after the accident, X told her, "W1 says D was surfing carefully." D later called W1 to give her a chance to explain or deny the statement.

159. Assume W2's testimony is offered to prove D was surfing carefully. Which of the following is correct?

(A) The testimony relates inadmissible hearsay.

(B) The testimony relates non-hearsay but it is inadmissible because W1 was not given a chance to explain or deny the statement *before* D proved the statement with extrinsic evidence.

(C) The testimony relates hearsay but it is admissible as a declaration against interest.

(D) The testimony relates admissible non-hearsay.

Prosecution of D for bank robbery. To prove that W, not D, committed the crime, D calls W and asks if W committed the crime. W denies this. D then asks W if she admitted during grand jury testimony that she had robbed the bank. W denies making such a statement.

160. To prove W's guilt, D wishes to offer W's grand jury testimony admitting responsibility. Which of the following is correct?

(A) The evidence is inadmissible hearsay.

(B) The evidence is admissible as a party admission of W.

(C) The evidence is admissible only if D did not know that W would deny making the statement to the grand jury.

(D) The evidence is admissible non-hearsay to prove that W committed the crime.

Civil action by P against D arising out of a hit-and-run accident. D claims that though she drives the same kind of car that was involved in the accident, she had nothing to do with the accident. D claims that X was the responsible party, and she subpoenas X to appear at trial. However, X refuses to testify (even when ordered to do so by the court), raising an invalid claim of privilege. Consequently, D wishes to call W to testify that a week after the accident, he was introduced to X for the first time, and that X told W that he had just been involved in an accident and "took off before the cops arrived."

161. Which of the following statements is most accurate?

(A) The evidence concerning X's statement to W is hearsay but admissible as a declaration against interest.

(B) The evidence concerning X's statement is admissible as an admission.

(C) The evidence concerning X's statement is admissible as an excited utterance.

(D) The evidence concerning X's statement is inadmissible because X is not unavailable.

Prosecution of D for possession of cocaine. D claims he did not know that the substance found in his apartment was cocaine. To prove D knew it was cocaine, the prosecution calls W to testify that he saw X hand the substance to D while saying, "here is the coke you ordered."

162. Which of the following statements is correct?

(A) X's statement is inadmissible hearsay.

(B) X's statement is hearsay but admissible as a present sense impression.

(C) X's statement is admissible as an admission of D.

(D) X's statement is not hearsay.

Products liability action by P against D, a new car dealer from whom she bought a car, alleging that a construction defect in the steering mechanism caused the accident that led to P's injury. At trial, to prove the defect, P testifies that after the accident, she showed her car to X, D's service manager. P states that X told her that the car's steering mechanism was not assembled correctly.

163. Which of the following statements is correct?

(A) If the judge finds that X was speaking about a matter within the scope of her employment, X's statement is admissible as an admission of D.

(B) If the judge finds that there is evidence sufficient to support a finding that X was speaking about a matter within the scope of her employment, X's statement is admissible as an admission of D.

(C) Even if the statement appears to qualify as an adoptive admission, it is inadmissible for lack of personal knowledge.

(D) The statement is inadmissible hearsay.

Prosecution of D for a double murder. To prove her innocence, D calls W to testify that shortly after D's arrest, W attended a press conference given by X, D's friend who was also her lawyer, and that at the press conference, X stated, "I was with D in another state on the day these horrible crimes took place, and D would not, could not, and did not commit these crimes."

164. Which of the following objections to this testimony is most appropriate?

   (A) Irrelevant.

   (B) Lack of personal knowledge.

   (C) Hearsay.

   (D) Unfair prejudice substantially outweighs probative value.

   Prosecution of D for importing and selling bootleg copies of the software program "Mirrors XP," and with conspiracy to commit that act. To prove D's guilt, the prosecution calls W, who testifies that a few weeks before the police arrested D, X, and Y for the crime, she overheard a conversation between X and Y in which X stated, "D's bringing in a shipment of MXP on TAL flight 612, and we'll be meeting him at O'Hare."

165. Which of the following statements is correct?

   (A) If the judge finds that there is evidence sufficient to support a finding both that there was a conspiracy and that X was involved in it, the evidence is admissible under the co-conspirator rule.

   (B) If the judge finds that there was a conspiracy and that X was involved in it, the evidence is admissible under the coconspirator rule.

   (C) Because the existence of a conspiracy is a fact the jury must ultimately decide, the judge need not make any preliminary determination of that fact. However, the evidence will not be admissible unless the judge finds that X was involved in any conspiracy the jury might decide existed.

   (D) X's statement is admissible as a simple party admission under FRE 801(d)(2)(A).

   Prosecution of D for murder. D calls W, D's closest friend, to testify that D was not at the scene at the time the murder was committed. The prosecution objects to this testimony on grounds of lack of personal knowledge, claiming that W was not at the scene and had no other basis of knowledge about the facts.

166. Which of the following statements is correct?

   (A) The court should sustain the objection if it finds that W lacked personal knowledge.

   (B) The court should sustain the objection if it finds that there is not evidence sufficient to support a finding that W had personal knowledge.

   (C) The court should sustain the objection because even if W had personal knowledge, her testimony is manifestly self-serving and thus unreliable.

   (D) The court should overrule the objection.

   Prosecution of D for the murder of V. D calls W to testify that just before he died, V said, "X did this to me." D claims the statement is admissible as a dying declaration.

167. In determining whether V's statement was made while believing his death was imminent, the trial court may consider

(A) the circumstances surrounding the statement.

(B) the statement itself.

(C) other evidence, including inadmissible evidence, unless that evidence has been found to be privileged.

(D) all of the above.

Prosecution of D for burglary of a mansion on Hilltop Drive. The stolen goods were recovered from a self-storage facility in River City. Shortly after the crime was committed, X told a friend, "I did that big house up on Hilltop last night, if you know what I mean. I stashed the stuff out in River City." At trial, D calls X to testify about this statement, but X refuses to answer on grounds of self-incrimination, even though he has already been granted immunity from prosecution for reasons unrelated to this problem. The court orders X to answer, but X still refuses to do so. D then calls the friend of X to testify about X's involvement in the crime.

168. Which of the following statements is most likely correct?

(A) X's statement is admissible as an admission.

(B) X's statement is against his interest but does not fall within the exception for declarations against interest.

(C) X's statement is admissible as a declaration against interest.

(D) X's statement is inadmissible unless it comes in through the friend's testimony rather than X's.

Breach of contract action by P against D. P claims that D failed to deliver CDs that P ordered. To prove D did not deliver the CDs, P wishes to testify that after a telephone conversation with D, P told her secretary, "D is not planning to deliver those CDs on time."

169. Which of the following statements is correct?

(A) P's testimony is hearsay but admissible as an admission.

(B) P's testimony is hearsay but admissible under the state of mind exception.

(C) P's testimony is not hearsay because it constitutes words of independent legal significance (D's repudiation of the contract).

(D) P's testimony is inadmissible hearsay.

Civil action by P against D Corp. following a collision between P's car and a D Corp. delivery truck driven by X. P has also named X as a defendant. P claims X drove negligently, and that D Corp. should be held liable under the doctrine of respondeat superior. Prior to the trial in this case, X was prosecuted for reckless driving for the same collision. At the trial of that case, the prosecution called W, a hitchhiker X picked up a few minutes before the accident. On direct examination, W testified that X was not paying much attention to the road and was swerving from one side of the road to the other. W died before the trial of P's civil action against D Corp. At the civil trial, X and D Corp. deny that X was driving recklessly at the time of the accident. P offers in evidence the transcript of W's testimony from the criminal trial.

170. Which of the following statements is most likely correct?

(A) The transcript of W's testimony is not hearsay because it was not offered to prove the truth of the matter asserted.

(B) The transcript of W's testimony is not hearsay because it was not made out of court.

(C) The transcript of W's testimony is hearsay but admissible under the former testimony exception.

(D) The transcript of W's testimony is inadmissible hearsay.

Prosecution of D for bank robbery. To prove D participated in the crime, the prosecution calls PO, a police officer, to testify that she obtained judicial permission to conduct a wiretap of the telephone of X, an alleged accomplice of D, and that while listening to a conversation between X and Y, she heard X tell Y, "D is gonna be the lookout."

171. Which of the following statements is correct?

(A) The court should exclude PO's testimony about the conversation under the best evidence rule if an audiotape of the conversation is available.

(B) If the court finds that the preliminary facts for a coconspirator statement are present, the court should admit PO's testimony.

(C) Because X's statement concerns the intentions of another person to do something in the future, PO's testimony concerning the conversation is inadmissible.

(D) Because D has not been charged with conspiracy, PO's testimony concerning the conversation is inadmissible.

Prosecution of D for possession of cocaine. At trial, the prosecution calls a number of witnesses, including D's roommate X. D admits that the cocaine was found in her apartment, but claims it belonged to X. To prove that fact, D calls W, who arrived at the scene a few minutes after D was placed under arrest. If permitted, W will testify that when D was being led to the police car, D turned to X, said "Those drugs were yours," and that X just smiled back.

172. Which of the following statements is correct?

(A) D's allegation and X's response are admissible as an admission of X.

(B) D's allegation is hearsay but admissible as an excited utterance, and X's smiling response is admissible non-hearsay.

(C) D's allegation is inadmissible hearsay. X's smiling response is then irrelevant.

(D) D's allegation and X's smiling response are admissible as a declaration against interest by X.

P sues D for medical malpractice after D allegedly botched P's surgery, requiring another surgeon to repair the damage. To prove the amount he had to pay the second surgeon, P offers a document which he claims is a bill he received by mail from the second surgeon.

173. What objections to the purported bill could D reasonably make?

ANSWER:

Wrongful death action by P, administrator of V's estate, against Smith and Jones arising from the killing of V. Smith was tried criminally. At Smith's criminal trial, the prosecution called W, who testified that she saw Jones hand Smith a gun, and that Smith used it to shoot V. Smith cross-examined W, and also called an alibi witness to show that she was in another city when the crime occurred. Smith was acquitted. At the wrongful death trial, Smith still denies killing V. Jones testifies that she had nothing to do with the killing.

174. P calls W, but W claims a bogus privilege and refuses to testify even when ordered to do so. P calls the court reporter from the criminal trial to authenticate and read the transcript of W's testimony. Smith and Jones both raise hearsay objections. How should the court rule?

ANSWER:

Breach of contract action by P, a construction contractor, against D, a lumber wholesaler. P claims that D failed to make a timely delivery of a load of lumber, causing P to suffer significant anticipated consequential damages. D claims it delivered the lumber on time. P calls W, its custodian of records. P's attorney shows W a document, which W identifies as a record of the kind prepared by its job foreperson any time building materials are delivered to a construction site. W testifies that P kept the document in the company files, as was customary. The document appears to concern the questioned shipment, and bears a delivery date two weeks after the shipment was due. Evidence shows that the person who dated the document was unaware of any potential dispute between P and D. P offers the document into evidence.

175. Which of the following statements is correct?

(A) The document is hearsay and admissible as a business record.

(B) The document is hearsay and admissible under the exception for recorded recollection.

(C) The document is hearsay and does not satisfy the business records exception because W did not have personal knowledge of the accuracy of its contents.

(D) The document is not hearsay. It was used solely to refresh the recollection of the witness.

Prosecution of D and X, business partners, for participating in a fraudulent real estate scheme. Earlier, X had been sued by P, an investor who lost a great deal of money. At that civil trial, P testified about the scheme and identified X as the one who enticed her into investing her life savings. P died before the criminal trial. At the criminal trial, the prosecution wishes to call W, a newspaper reporter who was in the courtroom during P's testimony at the civil trial, to testify about P's trial testimony.

176. W's testimony concerning P's civil trial testimony is

   (A) hearsay, and inadmissible against both D and X because it does not satisfy the former testimony exception because of the "similar motive" requirement of the former testimony exception.

   (B) hearsay, and inadmissible against both D and X because it is not offered in the form of the trial transcript.

   (C) hearsay, and admissible against X, but not against D.

   (D) hearsay, and admissible against both D and X.

Prosecution of D for arson. D denies committing the crime. At trial, D calls PO, a police officer who interviewed V, the owner of the burned building. D shows PO a document, which PO identifies as the report she prepared after the interview. The report describes the physical condition of the building and states that PO showed V a group of photographs, and that V identified an individual as the one she saw running from the building just before the fire broke out. That individual was not D. D represents that she will call V to testify later in the trial. D now offers PO's report into evidence.

177. Which of the following statements is most likely correct?

   (A) The report is hearsay and inadmissible under the public records exception because it contains matters observed pursuant to duty imposed by law as well as factual findings resulting from an investigation. V's statement is thus also inadmissible.

   (B) The report is hearsay and admissible under the public records exception. V's statement is admissible non-hearsay if V testifies and is subject to cross-examination concerning the statement.

   (C) The report is hearsay and the description of the building is admissible under the public records exception. The part of the report describing V's identification of the perpetrator is inadmissible, however, because PO lacks personal knowledge of who committed the crime.

   (D) The report is non-hearsay because it is not offered to prove the truth of the matter asserted.

Prosecution of D for murder. At trial, the prosecution offers against D a written statement prepared by X, a witness to the crime, at the request of the investigating police officer. X is now dead. Her statement includes a description of the perpetrator, and the characteristics match those of D. The court holds that the written statement is hearsay that does not fit within the regular exceptions to the hearsay rule, but that it satisfies the residual exception (FRE 807). D claims that the evidence should not be admitted because it would violate her confrontation rights under the Sixth Amendment.

178. Which of the following statements is most likely correct?

(A) Because the evidence satisfies the requirements of the residual hearsay exception, which include considerations of reliability, X's statement is admissible despite the Confrontation Clause.

(B) Because X's statement is testimonial in nature, because D never had a chance to cross-examine X, and because X is unavailable, the court must exclude the statement.

(C) Because X's statement is not testimonial, the court may admit it despite the Confrontation Clause.

(D) Because the residual exception is not "firmly rooted," the court may not admit X's statement unless it finds the statement trustworthy after an independent inquiry.

Prosecution of D for a murder that took place in Boston. D claims she was in Denver on the day of the murder. To prove D was in Boston that day, the prosecution calls PO, a Boston police officer, and asks PO whether she saw D in Boston on that day. PO states that she cannot remember. The prosecutor shows PO a speeding ticket she issued to D that day, and asks PO if she now recalls seeing D in Boston on that day. PO states that she still cannot recall. PO then testifies that she gave one speeding ticket on the day in question, that she wrote the ticket as she was talking to the person to whom she issued it, that she issued it to the name that appeared on the driver's license the person showed her, and that she recorded the information correctly. D's name appears on the ticket.

179. The prosecutor asks PO to read aloud the name on the ticket. Which of the following arguments most strongly supports D's argument for exclusion of the evidence?

(A) The ticket is inadmissible hearsay within hearsay.

(B) The ticket is inadmissible because it does not satisfy the requirements of any hearsay exception.

(C) The ticket is inadmissible because its probative value is substantially outweighed by the danger of unfair prejudice.

(D) Even though the ticket satisfies the hearsay exception for recorded recollection, it should be excluded to effectuate the policy of the rule excluding certain public records when offered against criminal defendants.

Personal injury action by P against D arising from a collision between P's blue car and D's red car. P calls W, who testifies that she saw the accident and that D's red car ran a red light and struck P's blue car. On cross-examination, D asks W if it isn't true that a few moments after the collision, X came upon the scene and screamed, "Oh, no! That blue car just ran the light and struck the red car!"

180. Which of the following statements is correct?

(A) If P objects to D's question as impermissibly leading, the court will sustain the objection.

(B) X's statement is admissible as a prior inconsistent statement to impeach W's credibility.

(C) X's statement is admissible as an excited utterance.

(D) X's statement might be admissible as an excited utterance only if the court finds that there is evidence sufficient to support a finding that X had personal knowledge of the accident.

Breach of contract action by P against D. P claims that D failed to deliver the CDs that P ordered. To prove that D did in fact deliver the CDs, D calls W, her secretary, to testify that just before delivery was due, D said, "I'm planning to meet all orders."

181. Which of the following statements is correct?

(A) D's statement is admissible as an admission.

(B) D's statement is hearsay but admissible under the state of mind exception.

(C) D's statement is hearsay and fits within the state of mind exception, but because it is not clear that D was referring to this particular order from P, the court should exclude it as potentially irrelevant.

(D) D's statement is hearsay but admissible because its probative value substantially outweighs any danger of unfair prejudice.

Negligence action by third-grader P against classmate D arising from a playground collision. To prove that she suffered an arm injury, P calls her father to testify that when he took P to the hospital, he told the admitting nurse, "my daughter's arm really hurts and she can't move it."

182. Which of the following statements is correct?

(A) P's father's statement to the nurse is hearsay but admissible as a statement made for purposes of medical diagnosis or treatment.

(B) P's father's statement to the nurse is hearsay but admissible as an excited utterance.

(C) P's father's statement is not hearsay because it is not offered to prove the truth of the matter asserted.

(D) P's father's statement is inadmissible hearsay.

183. As additional evidence that she suffered an arm injury from the collision, P calls W, the hospital's records clerk. W authenticates P's hospital record and testifies that the record was prepared by hospital personnel based on information they knew firsthand or which was provided by people with knowledge, that it was kept in the ordinary course of business, and that hospital procedure requires such records to be kept. P offers into evidence a portion of the record in which the attending physician wrote, "P says felt significant arm pain after having a collision with another person." Which of the following statements is most likely correct?

(A) P's statement to the doctor is hearsay but admissible as a statement made for purposes of medical diagnosis or treatment. However, the statement is inadmissible because the document that contains it is hearsay for which no exception likely applies.

(B) P's statement to the doctor is hearsay but admissible as a statement made for purposes of medical diagnosis or treatment. The hospital record containing the statement is likely admissible under the business records exception.

(C) P's statement to the doctor is hearsay but admissible as a statement made for purposes of medical diagnosis or treatment. Because the doctor's statement about what P said is not offered to prove the truth of the matter asserted, it is not hearsay. Thus, this portion of the hospital record is admissible.

(D) P's statement to the doctor is inadmissible hearsay and must be excluded because it is self-serving.

Personal injury action by P against D arising from an automobile collision. P claims the accident caused a permanent leg injury and that he is not able to continue to work at his job. To prove the permanent impairment, P calls W, the custodian of records of the office of Dr. X, an orthopedic specialist who examined P to determine eligibility for state disability benefits. W states that the office keeps charts on all persons examined by Dr. X. W identifies P's chart. The chart contains Dr. X's notation, "Prognosis: Significant permanent impairment of motion in left leg."

184. Which of the following is correct?

(A) The notation is hearsay but admissible as an expert opinion.

(B) The notation is hearsay but admissible as a business record.

(C) The notation is inadmissible because of physician-patient privilege.

(D) The notation is inadmissible hearsay.

Prosecution of D for assault and battery on V. The prosecution calls W, who testifies that she was present in the bar where the altercation took place, and that just after the fight started, she heard X, another patron who was sitting close to V, scream, "Oh, my Lord, D just attacked that poor person from behind!" D claims the evidence constitutes inadmissible hearsay and that even if it satisfies the hearsay rule, its admission would violate her confrontation rights.

185. Which of the following statements is most likely correct?

(A) X's statement is hearsay but admissible as an excited utterance. The court may admit it despite the Confrontation Clause without further inquiry.

(B) X's statement is hearsay but admissible as an excited utterance. The court may admit it despite the Confrontation Clause only if it finds that the statement bears sufficient independent indicia of reliability.

(C) X's statement is not hearsay and its admission does not violate the Confrontation Clause.

(D) X's statement is hearsay but admissible as an excited utterance. The Confrontation Clause will only be satisfied if X is produced or is found to be unavailable.

Breach of contract action by P, an ad agency, against D, a corporation that hired the agency. P alleges that D approved P's proposed print ad at a board meeting and was thus required to pay P's fee, but that D never paid. To prove that D did not approve P's ad, D calls W, the board secretary, who identifies a copy of the board minutes from the meeting in question. W testifies that he wrote these minutes, that he keeps all board minutes in a special file at the corporate office, and that the minutes were approved at a subsequent meeting. D offers in evidence a portion of the minutes containing the following statement: "After looking at the ad, Chairperson P said, 'What a piece of junk!'"

186. This portion of the minutes is most likely

   (A) inadmissible hearsay.

   (B) inadmissible because it is irrelevant.

   (C) inadmissible because it is too unreliable.

   (D) admissible.

Product liability action by P against D, a drug manufacturer. P claims he took D's drug for many years and suffered liver damage as a result. To prove the extent of his harm, P calls W, his physician. W identifies a document as a report she prepared in connection with an application P had made for health insurance. W testifies that the report was prepared in the ordinary course of her medical practice, that it was her usual practice to prepare such reports regarding her patients, and that she kept the report in her office. The report states that P has suffered "significant decline in liver function over the past several years." The report was prepared before P learned that D's drug might have caused her liver ailment. P offers the document into evidence.

187. Which of the following statements is most likely correct?

   (A) The report is hearsay but admissible as an authorized admission.

   (B) The report is hearsay but admissible as a business record.

   (C) The report is hearsay but admissible as a statement made for purposes of medical diagnosis or treatment.

   (D) The report is inadmissible hearsay.

Prosecution of D for burglary. The prosecution calls W, a police officer who investigated the crime. After testifying to certain facts, W states that she cannot remember anything else. The prosecutor shows W a document, which W identifies as the report she wrote in connection with her investigation. W testifies that she wrote the report in the ordinary course of her work, and that it was the normal procedure to prepare such a report. The report contains the statement, "Officer X states that D waived her Miranda rights and admitted that at the relevant time, she was in the neighborhood where the burglary was committed." The prosecution offers this statement into evidence.

188. Which of the following statements is most likely correct?

   (A) D's statement is admissible as an admission, and the rest of the statement is admissible as a business record.

   (B) D's statement is admissible as an admission, and the rest of the statement may be read to the jury under the recorded recollection exception.

   (C) D's statement is admissible as an admission, and the rest of the statement is admissible as a declaration against interest.

   (D) The entire statement is inadmissible hearsay.

Personal injury action by P against D after an automobile accident between P's red car and D's blue car. P claims D ran the red light. D denies this. To prove D ran the red light, P calls W, a claims adjuster for P's insurance company who was assigned to handle the case. P asks W if she remembers what she learned in her investigation, and W is only able to give a few details. P then asks W if she interviewed any witnesses, and W testifies that she did, but that she cannot remember anything about the interviews. P shows W a document which W identifies as a note she wrote to herself at home one evening during her investigation. She states that she wrote it as a reminder of a talk she had with a witness to the accident, and that when she wrote the note, the conversation was fresh in her memory. She found the note at home recently. The note states that a witness said D ran the red light.

189. Which of the following statements is correct?

   (A) The note is hearsay but satisfies the recorded recollection exception. It may be read to the jury but not received as an exhibit.

   (B) The note is hearsay but satisfies the recorded recollection exception. It may be admitted as an exhibit.

   (C) The note is hearsay but admissible as a business record.

   (D) The note is inadmissible hearsay.

Prosecution of D for murder. Eyewitnesses state that they saw two men commit the crime. To prove she had nothing to do with the crime, D calls W to testify that just after the murder, she overheard X, a friend of D, tell a police officer, "Two of us killed that guy. But D wasn't the other one involved. We dumped the body in the lake just outside of River City." At the time X made the statement, the body had not yet been found. After talking to X, the police located the body where X said it would be. X died in an auto accident before the trial. The prosecution lodges a hearsay objection to this statement.

190. Analyze whether the court should admit the statement.

ANSWER:

Negligence action by P against D Corporation arising from the collision of P's green car and D's delivery truck. D denies negligence. To prove the accident was caused by P's negligence rather than any fault on the part of the truck driver, D calls its custodian of records who identifies an "accident report" which appears to have been written by the employee who drove the delivery truck. The custodian states that within 24 hours of any accident, employees with knowledge of the facts are required to make a report on this form and give it to their supervisors for inclusion in the company's files. D offers the report into evidence. The report states, "I was driving in my lane just below the speed limit when a green car veered into my lane, just ahead of me. I tried to avoid colliding with it, but was unable to do so." P objects on hearsay grounds.

191. How should the court rule, and why?

ANSWER:

Breach of contract action by P against D, an electronic parts wholesaler. P claims she placed an order with D and included a check with the order, but that D neither shipped the ordered parts nor returned the check. D denies ever receiving an order from P on or around the date P claims to have sent it. To prove that it did not receive an order from P, D calls its custodian of records, who identifies an "order log" kept by its order department. The log shows all orders received from one week before until one week after P claims to have placed the order. P's name appears nowhere on the report. P objects on hearsay grounds.

192. How should the court rule, and why?

ANSWER:

After a car driven by X struck and killed V while V was crossing the street in a crosswalk, P, the administrator of V's estate, sued X for wrongful death. At trial, P called W, who testified that he saw X run a red light and strike V in the crosswalk. The jury returned a verdict for P. Within the limitations period, the state decided to prosecute X and D, the owner of the car, for criminal negligence. The state's theory against D is that D knew X to be a reckless driver and that D should not have loaned X the car. Before this trial could take place, W died. The prosecution therefore wishes to offer in evidence the transcript of the testimony W gave in the earlier trial. X and D object.

193. How should the court rule, and why?

ANSWER:

Prosecution of D for the murder of V. V was a business rival of D. D denies involvement. At trial, the prosecution wishes to call W, a friend of V, to testify that a week before V was killed, V told a friend that D was planning to kill him (V).

194. D objects to W's testimony. How should the court rule?

(A) The court should overrule the objection because the testimony is admissible under the state of mind exception.

(B) The court should overrule the objection because the testimony is admissible under the "forfeiture by wrongdoing" exception.

(C) The court should sustain the objection because the testimony would violate D's right to confrontation.

(D) The court should sustain the objection because the testimony relates hearsay to which no exception applies.

Negligence action by P against D arising from an auto collision. To prove D caused the accident by driving recklessly, P calls W to testify that she was at home speaking to X, who was using her cell phone while driving to an appointment, and that at one point, W heard the sound of a horn, and X immediately said, "a blue Exterminator is weaving in and out of lanes like it's a sports car." Other evidence establishes that D was driving a blue Exterminator, that the accident happened on the same road X was traveling at the time, and that the collision occurred less than a minute after X made this statement.

195. Which of the following statements is correct?

(A) X's statement is hearsay but admissible as a present sense impression.

(B) X's statement is inadmissible hearsay because there was nobody present to verify the accuracy of X's statement.

(C) X's statement is inadmissible because it constitutes an improper lay opinion.

(D) X's statement is admissible as an excited utterance.

P sues D after an automobile collision. D admits negligence but denies P was injured. P calls W1, a hitchhiker P picked up a few minutes before the accident. W1 testifies that P was "bleeding badly." D then offers evidence that a month after the collision, P offered W1 a job.

196. To prove that P did in fact suffer an injury, P calls and seeks to elicit W2's testimony that before W1 learned of the job offer, W1 told W2 that P was bleeding badly in the car. D objects on hearsay grounds. How should the court rule?

ANSWER:

Action by P, a hospital, against D, after D refused to pay a bill. D claims she was never treated at the hospital. To prove D was treated at the hospital, P calls W, its custodian of records, who authenticates a computerized "admissions-discharge log" from the dates of D's alleged hospital stay. W testifies that the log is updated daily, and that the names and identification codes of all patients admitted and discharged are entered at the times of admission and discharge. The log contains entries showing D's admission and discharge.

197. D objects to admission of the log. Which of the following is correct?

 (A) The court most likely will admit the log.

 (B) The court most likely will exclude the log because it is self-serving and therefore unreliable.

 (C) The court most likely will exclude the log because it is easy to tamper with computerized records such as these.

 (D) The court most likely will exclude the log unless P calls an expert to testify that the software used to create the log produces accurate results.

Prosecution of D for assault and battery on V, D's wife. The incident occurred on the driveway of the home D and V shared. D admits that an altercation occurred, but claims he struck V in self-defense. At trial, the prosecution calls W, a 911 operator, who will testify that at the time of the incident, she received a call from X, who claimed to be a neighbor of D and V. X died before the trial. The prosecutor then asks W to relate the substance of the conversation with X.

198. If permitted, W will testify that X sounded "hysterical" and said, "several minutes ago, D punched V over and over again" and that D had run into the house. D objects to this testimony on hearsay and confrontation grounds. Which of the following is correct?

 (A) The testimony is hearsay but qualifies as an excited utterance, and does not violate D's confrontation right.

 (B) The testimony is hearsay but qualifies as a present sense impression, and does not violate D's confrontation right.

 (C) The testimony is otherwise admissible hearsay but violates D's confrontation right.

 (D) The testimony is hearsay and does not satisfy any exception, so the court does not need to reach the confrontation issue.

Prosecution of D for bank robbery. At trial, the prosecution calls PO, one of the police officers who investigated the crime and who arrested X, an alleged coconspirator. PO questioned X about the crime. Before D's trial, X pleaded guilty pursuant to a plea bargain. X died shortly after entering prison. The prosecutor asks PO to testify about what X told PO concerning the crime.

199. If permitted, PO will testify that X admitted entering the bank with D and stated that he served as lookout while D approached the teller and pulled a weapon. D objects to this testimony on hearsay and confrontation grounds. How should the court rule?

ANSWER:

Prosecution of D for murder. At trial, the prosecution wishes to offer evidence that in testimony before the grand jury, X, who died before trial, stated that both she and D planned and carried out the murder.

200. D objects to admission of X's statement. Which of the following is correct?

(A) The evidence is hearsay, and though it might satisfy the exception for declarations against interest, it is inadmissible under the Confrontation Clause.

(B) The evidence is hearsay and satisfies the exception for former testimony, but is inadmissible under the Confrontation Clause.

(C) The evidence is hearsay and satisfies the exception for declarations against interest, but is not admissible unless the prosecution presents evidence showing that the statement is trustworthy.

(D) The evidence is hearsay, satisfies the exception for declarations against interest, and is admissible under the Confrontation Clause without any additional showing.

Prosecution of D for the murder of V. D denies committing the crime. The prosecution calls W to testify that immediately after the murder, W saw X pointing in D's direction and screaming, "Stop him! Stop him!"

201. D makes a hearsay objection to W's testimony concerning X's statement. Which of the following statements is correct?

(A) W's testimony is inadmissible because unless X testifies, it is not possible to lay the foundation for the excited utterance or present sense impression exceptions.

(B) W's testimony is inadmissible because X might be available.

(C) W's testimony is inadmissible because it is unreliable.

(D) W's testimony is admissible.

Personal injury action by P against D following a hit-and-run bicycle accident. To prove P suffered a serious injury, P calls W to testify that she approached P moments after the collision, and that P cried out, "that guy just ran over my head with a bike and I'm going to die!"

202. Which of the following is correct?

(A) W's testimony concerning P's statement is most likely admissible as a party admission.

(B) W's testimony concerning P's statement is most likely admissible as a dying declaration.

(C) W's testimony concerning P's statement is most likely admissible as an excited utterance.

(D) W's testimony concerning P's statement is most likely inadmissible.

Evidence of Character, "Other Crimes, Wrongs, or Acts," Habit, and Similar Events

Assume that in a certain trial, a party wishes to present evidence that the opponent claims constitutes inadmissible character evidence. The proponent's response is that the evidence is not of a character "trait," so is not character evidence.

203. Assuming it concerns the evidence at issue, which of the following is a court *least likely* to treat as testimony that relates to a "trait" of character?

    (A) X is a careless driver.

    (B) X has epilepsy.

    (C) X is frugal.

    (D) X is an alcoholic.

Prosecution of D for assault and battery. D claims self-defense. During its case-in-chief, to prove D was the aggressor in the fight, the prosecution calls W, who testifies that she has lived in the same community as D for many years, that she is familiar with D's community reputation for violence or peacefulness, and that D's reputation is that she is a very violent person. D objects.

204. Which of the following statements is correct?

    (A) The court should sustain D's objection because the evidence is hearsay for which no exception applies.

    (B) The court should sustain the objection because this is impermissible character evidence.

    (C) The court should overrule the objection because D's character is in issue.

    (D) The court should overrule the objection if the probative value of the evidence substantially outweighs the danger of unfair prejudice.

Prosecution of D for fraud arising from D's management of several people's finances. D testifies that her clients' losses were caused by market decline and that she did not divert any of the clients' money to her own use. D calls W to testify that D has a reputation in the community as a peaceful person.

205. The prosecutor objects on the ground that the question seeks to elicit inadmissible character evidence. How should the court rule?

ANSWER:

Prosecution of D for molestation of V, a child. D claims she was not the one who committed the crime. To prove that D molested V, the prosecution offers evidence that several years earlier, D molested another child. D objects.

206. Which of the following statements is correct?

(A) The evidence is inadmissible character evidence.

(B) The evidence is admissible unless the court finds that the probative value of the evidence is substantially outweighed by the danger of unfair prejudice.

(C) The evidence is admissible to prove *modus operandi* to molest children, and thus prove D's identity as the perpetrator.

(D) The evidence is admissible regardless of the balance of probative value and unfair prejudice.

Civil action by P against D for battery during a professional basketball game. D had been cheering for the visiting team when P asked her to "cut it out." P claims D then punched P. D claims she never touched P. To prove her defense, D calls W to testify that she was with D at another game when D cheered for the visiting team, that a home team fan asked D to stop, and that D just shrugged it off. P objects.

207. Which of the following statements is correct?

(A) The evidence is admissible character evidence.

(B) The evidence is admissible habit evidence.

(C) The evidence is inadmissible because it is offered in the form of specific instances of conduct rather than reputation or opinion.

(D) The evidence is inadmissible because D may not use character evidence to support her defense in this situation.

Libel action by P against D after D, the owner of a newspaper, published an article accusing P of committing a string of burglaries in the city. D claims the story was true. To prove P committed the burglaries, D offers evidence that P had been convicted of several burglaries in another city within the past few years. P objects.

208. Which of the following statements is correct?

(A) The evidence is admissible because character is in issue.

(B) The evidence is admissible because it tends to show D's good faith.

(C) The evidence is inadmissible because it is offered in the form of specific instances of conduct rather than reputation or opinion.

(D) The evidence is inadmissible because D may not use character evidence to support her defense in this situation.

Negligence action by P against D. P claims that D failed to yield the right of way at an intersection and smashed into P. To prove that D failed to yield, P calls W to testify that a number of D's friends told her that D frequently drives through that intersection and almost always fails to yield. D objects.

209. Which of the following statements is correct?

(A) W's testimony is inadmissible because character is not admissible in this situation.

(B) W's testimony is inadmissible because behavior will only constitute a habit if it is repeated invariably.

(C) W's testimony is inadmissible hearsay.

(D) W's testimony is admissible habit evidence.

Prosecution of D for the murder of V. To prove she acted in self-defense, D calls W, who has known D for many years, to testify that in her opinion, D is a peaceful person. The prosecution objects.

210. Which of the following statements is correct?

(A) The court should sustain the objection because D may not offer character evidence to prove action in accordance with that character on a specific occasion.

(B) The court should sustain the objection because, although character evidence is admissible in this situation, D may only prove character by offering evidence of her community reputation.

(C) The court should sustain the objection because the witness is biased.

(D) The court should overrule the objection.

Prosecution of D for the murder of V while both were watching their sons compete in a high school football game. To prove self-defense, D offers the testimony of W that D is a peaceful person. The prosecution does not object. On cross-examination, the prosecutor asks W, "Did you know that D was involved in a barroom brawl just last year?" D objects.

211. How should the court rule?

(A) The court should overrule the objection.

(B) The court should sustain the objection because specific instances of conduct may not be used in this situation.

(C) The court should sustain the objection because the question is impermissibly leading.

(D) The court should sustain the objection because the circumstances of the barroom brawl were different than the brawl that led to V's death.

Prosecution of D for assault and battery on V. D calls W, who testifies that she has lived in the same community as D for more than twenty years, and that D has a reputation as a peaceful person. The prosecution wishes to ask W whether she heard that D had once started a fight in a yogurt store. The prosecutor admits that although stories about D's involvement in the fight were all over town, it was actually someone else who was involved. D objects.

212. How should the court rule?

(A) The court should sustain the objection because D was not involved.

(B) The court should sustain the objection because the question should have been framed as "did you know?" rather than "have you heard?"

(C) The court should sustain the objection because the question concerns a specific instance of conduct.

(D) The court should overrule the objection unless the court determines that the probative value of the evidence is substantially outweighed by the danger of unfair prejudice.

Prosecution of D for the murder of V. To prove self-defense, D calls W to testify that V had a reputation in the community as a very violent person. The prosecution objects.

213. How should the court rule, and why?

ANSWER:

Prosecution of D for the murder of V. D claims V attacked her, and that D acted in self-defense. To prove self-defense, D calls W1 to testify that she saw V attack D. To rebut D's self-defense claim, the prosecution calls W2 to testify that she knew V for many years and that in her opinion, V was a non-violent person. D objects.

214. How should the court rule, and why?

ANSWER:

Prosecution of D for the murder of V in a pet shop. D admits killing V with a sharp stick, but claims she did so accidentally when she was trying to part two fighting puppies. During its case-in-chief, the prosecution calls W to testify that shortly before V's killing, D and V had been partners in a criminal fraud that had netted the pair more than $2 million.

215. Which of the following statements is correct?

    (A) W's testimony is inadmissible character evidence.

    (B) W's testimony is inadmissible because of lack of similarity between the charged and the uncharged act.

    (C) W's testimony is inadmissible because of the nature of D's defense.

    (D) W's testimony is admissible.

Prosecution of D for robbing a pet shop of cash, hamsters, and kittens. The robbery was committed by a masked bandit who threatened to fling a bag of monkey excrement at a clerk if the clerk did not turn over all the cash, hamsters, and kittens. D denies involvement.

216. To prove D's involvement, the prosecution wishes to present evidence that a year earlier, D committed a pet shop holdup in a very similar way, except that she demanded only hamsters and money, not kittens. D was never charged in connection with the earlier holdup. Which of the following is correct?

    (A) This evidence is inadmissible because D was never charged in the prior incident.

    (B) This evidence is inadmissible to prove identity because the incidents are not sufficiently similar.

    (C) This evidence is admissible to prove identity if the court finds by a preponderance of the evidence that D committed the earlier robbery.

    (D) This evidence is admissible to prove identity if the court finds that there is evidence sufficient to support a finding that D committed the earlier robbery.

Prosecution of D, a trustee, for embezzling funds from the trust. D admits that the trust was depleted, but claims someone else was stealing the funds. To rebut D's defense, the prosecution wishes to present evidence that after the charged act, D embezzled more funds from the same trust. D objects.

217. How should the court rule?

    (A) The court should overrule the objection because the evidence is admissible to prove a plan, and thus D's identity as the perpetrator.

    (B) The court should overrule the objection because the evidence is admissible to impeach D by contradiction.

(C) The court should sustain the objection because the uncharged act took place after the charged event.

(D) The court should sustain the objection because this is inadmissible character evidence.

Prosecution of D for embezzling money from her employer. D declines to testify in her own behalf. To prove she did not embezzle, D calls W1 and W2, each of whom testify that they have known D for many years, and that in their opinion, D is an honest person. To rebut the testimony of W1 and W2, the prosecution calls W3 to testify that she has also known D for many years, and that in her opinion, D is dishonest. D objects.

218. How should the court rule, and why?

ANSWER:

Prosecution of D for assault and battery on V. To prove V was the first aggressor, D calls W1 to testify that V has a reputation in the community as a violent person. In rebuttal, the prosecution wishes to call W2 to testify that D has a community reputation as a violent person. D objects.

219. How should the court rule?

(A) The court should sustain the objection because the prosecution may not offer evidence of D's bad character unless and until D offers evidence of her good character.

(B) The court should sustain the objection because D's community reputation is inadmissible hearsay.

(C) The court should sustain the objection because the prosecution may not call its own character witness to rebut D's witness, but must rely on cross-examination.

(D) The court should overrule the objection.

Prosecution of D for robbing a store. The robber entered before closing, put on a salesperson's uniform, and pretended to work there. After the store closed and everyone else left, the robber shed the uniform and stole all the DVD players. D denies involvement. To prove D's guilt, the prosecution offers evidence that a month earlier, D stole all the DVD players from a different store using the same method. D denies committing the prior robbery, and objects.

220. How should the court rule?

(A) The court should sustain the objection unless D was charged criminally for that robbery.

(B) The court should sustain the objection unless the prosecution convinces the court by a preponderance of the evidence that D committed the prior robbery.

(C) The court should sustain the objection unless the prosecution offers evidence sufficient to support a finding that D committed the prior robbery.

(D) The court should sustain the objection even if D admits committing the prior robbery.

Prosecution of D, a home care nurse, for the murder of V by poison. D testifies, denying involvement. D also calls two character witnesses to vouch for her non-violent character. The prosecution establishes that D makes a living caring for patients placed in his home, and that D cares for only one or two patients at a time. The prosecution calls several witnesses to testify that on three prior occasions, home care patients in D's care died of poisoning. D objects.

221. How should the court rule?

   (A) The court should overrule D's objection because this evidence is admissible to rebut the evidence offered by D's character witnesses.

   (B) The court should overrule D's objection because this evidence is admissible to prove D's guilt by means of the "doctrine of chances."

   (C) The court should overrule D's objection because this evidence is admissible to impeach D.

   (D) The court should sustain D's objection unless the prosecution proves D's guilt of each of the three prior offenses.

Prosecution of D for the rape of V. D and V met at a gym. D claims V consented to the sexual conduct.

222. To prove consent, D calls W to testify that on several occasions in the past year, V went to the same gym, met a stranger, and had sex at the stranger's house. Which of the following statements concerning W's testimony about V's encounters with these several different men is most likely correct?

   (A) The testimony is admissible to prove a pattern, and thus consent.

   (B) The testimony is admissible to prove a habit, and thus consent.

   (C) The testimony is admissible to prove V's character with respect to sexual relationships with strangers, and thus consent.

   (D) The testimony is inadmissible.

Civil action by P against D for assault and battery. P claims D sexually assaulted her after the two began to converse in a private booth in a restaurant/bar. D claims P consented to the sexual contact.

223. At trial, D wishes to present evidence that on three prior occasions in the two months preceding the incident in the bar, P conversed with several other men in the same restaurant/bar and consented to the same kind of sexual contact with each of those men. P objects. How should the court rule?

ANSWER:

Prosecution of D for knowingly passing a counterfeit $100 bill. D admits passing the bill, but testifies that she did not know it was counterfeit. In rebuttal, the prosecution calls W, a convenience store clerk, to testify that the day before the charged act, D tried to buy a six pack of beer using the same $100 bill, and that W told D she could not accept the bill because it was "phony." D objects.

224. How should the court rule, and why?

ANSWER:

Personal injury action by P against D arising from an automobile collision. P alleges that D wasn't paying attention and allowed the car to drift across the center line, striking P's car. D denies losing attention, and claims it was P's car that drifted across the center line. To prove she was paying attention, D calls W, a long-time friend who often rides with D to work, to testify that in her opinion, D is a careful driver who always pays attention. P objects.

225. How should the court rule?

(A) The court should overrule the objection because this is admissible habit evidence.

(B) The court should overrule the objection because by testifying that she did not lose attention, D has placed her character in issue.

(C) The court should overrule the objection because this is admissible evidence of D's good character for careful driving.

(D) The court should sustain the objection.

Prosecution of D1 and D2 for the murder of four restaurant patrons. D1 and D2 deny involvement in the crime. The prosecution wishes to call W to testify that she knows D1 and D2 as well as the victims, that all were illegal drug dealers, and that not long before the killings, the victims had tried to "muscle in" on territory controlled by D1 and D2. D objects.

226. How should the court rule?

(A) The court should overrule the objection because the evidence is admissible to show a tendency toward violent behavior.

(B) The court should overrule the objection because the evidence is admissible to show a motive to kill the victims.

(C) The court should sustain the objection because the evidence constitutes inadmissible hearsay.

(D) The court should sustain the objection because the probative value of the evidence is substantially outweighed by the danger of unfair prejudice.

Prosecution of D for murder. D claims she did not commit the crime, and calls W to testify that a long-time friend of D told her that D was as "gentle as a lamb." The prosecution objects.

227. How should the court rule?

    (A) The court should overrule the objection because the evidence is hearsay but admissible to prove that D did not commit the crime.

    (B) The court should overrule the objection because the evidence is admissible to show lack of a pattern of violent conduct.

    (C) The court should sustain the objection because the evidence constitutes inadmissible hearsay.

    (D) The court should sustain the objection because the evidence is inherently unreliable.

Prosecution of D for the murder of V. The prosecution alleges that D and V, two strangers, had a quarrel in a bar, that D left the bar momentarily, retrieved a shotgun from her car, returned to the bar, and shot V to death. D admits having an argument with V, but claims she never returned to the bar after she left. The prosecution calls W to testify that twice in the past five years, D has physically attacked strangers with whom she has had serious arguments. D does not deny that these prior events occurred, but objects to admission of the evidence.

228. How should the court rule?

    (A) The court should overrule the objection because this is admissible habit evidence.

    (B) The court should overrule the objection because this evidence is admissible to show a pattern of conduct or a common scheme or plan, and from that, D's intent.

    (C) The court should overrule the objection because this evidence is admissible to show a pattern of conduct, or a common scheme or plan, and from that, to prove D shot V.

    (D) The court should sustain the objection.

Fraud action by P against D, a car dealership. P claims that the car D sold to her only got 11 miles per gallon, even though D's salesperson told P that it would get "in the mid-twenties." D denies its salesperson made any such representation. To prove the representation was made, P wishes to offer the testimony of five other customers that the salesperson made the same representation to them about the same model of car. D does not deny that the other representations were made, but objects to admission of the evidence.

229. How should the court rule?

    (A) The court should overrule the objection because the evidence is admissible pattern evidence to show that the representation was made.

    (B) The court should overrule the objection because the evidence is admissible habit evidence.

    (C) The court should sustain the objection because the evidence is inadmissible character evidence.

    (D) The court should sustain the objection because the evidence, though relevant non-character evidence, is inadmissible because this is a civil action.

Negligence action by P against D, owner of a department store, after P was injured in a fall from an escalator. P claims D improperly maintained the escalator, causing it to jerk and throw P down. D admits that P was injured, but denies that the escalator jerked while P was riding it. At trial, P wishes to offer the testimony of several people that they were thrown down by the same escalator in the year prior to P's fall. D objects.

230. What information would you need in order to determine how the court should rule, and why? If the court admits the evidence, is D entitled to a limiting instruction?

ANSWER:

Negligence action by P against D, the owner of a football stadium, for injuries P suffered after a slip-and-fall accident on the steep stairs leading to her assigned seat. P claims the stairs are too steep and that the absence of handrails compounds the danger. To prove that the condition was safe, D wishes to offer the testimony of its stadium manager that in the two years prior to P's fall, it received no reports of other injuries in that location. P objects.

231. What information would you need in order to determine how the court should rule, and why?

ANSWER:

Civil action against D for sexually molesting V, a child. In her case-in-chief, P wishes to call W to testify that D has molested other children.

232. Which of the following is most likely correct?

(A) W's testimony is inadmissible hearsay.

(B) W's testimony is inadmissible unless W testifies to the factual basis for her testimony.

(C) W's testimony is admissible character evidence.

(D) W's testimony is admissible because exclusion would violate P's due process rights.

Evidence of Subsequent Remedial Measures, Compromise, Humanitarian Assistance, Criminal Pleas, and Liability Insurance

Personal injury action by P against D arising from P's fall on the floor in D's supermarket. P fell on a liquid spill that was not visible to her as she walked down the aisle, and claims D was negligent for not cleaning it up before the accident. D denies negligence. To prove D did not act reasonably, P wishes to offer evidence that a week after the accident, D's employees began patrolling for spills twice as often as before the accident. D objects.

233. Which of the following statements is correct?

    (A) The evidence is inadmissible hearsay.

    (B) The evidence is inadmissible because it is irrelevant.

    (C) The evidence is relevant but inadmissible.

    (D) The evidence is relevant and admissible.

Personal injury action by P against D arising from P's fall on the floor in D's supermarket. P fell on a liquid spill that was not visible to her as she walked down the aisle, and claims D was negligent for not cleaning it up before the accident. W, D's manager, testifies that she had her employees patrol the aisles frequently, and that "we've had no reason to change the way we do things around the store." In rebuttal, P wishes to offer evidence that a week after the accident, W ordered store employees to patrol for spills twice as often as before the accident. D objects.

234. Which of the following statements is correct?

    (A) The evidence is inadmissible hearsay.

    (B) The evidence is inadmissible because it is irrelevant.

    (C) The evidence is relevant but inadmissible.

    (D) The evidence is admissible to impeach W.

Negligence action by P against D, a supermarket owner, following P's slip and fall in the produce section. P claims D allowed slippery matter to collect on the floor, leading to his fall. P fell nearly an hour after D's employees last cleaned the floor. W, D's manager, testifies that she was not aware of anything slippery on the produce section floor at the time of P's fall. In rebuttal, P wishes to offer evidence that shortly after P's accident, D started requiring its employees to clean the produce section floor every thirty minutes instead of once an hour. D objects.

235. Which of the following statements is correct?

(A) The evidence is admissible to prove that until D changed the policy, D did not have the floor cleaned often enough.

(B) The evidence is admissible to prove that the floor was slippery at the time of the accident.

(C) The evidence is admissible to impeach W by contradiction and to prove the feasibility of more frequent cleaning.

(D) The evidence is inadmissible.

Product liability action by P against D, a window manufacturer, after one of P's windows shattered in a strong wind, causing P's injuries. P claims D made the window with a type of glass that was not appropriate to the expected or foreseeable conditions to which it would be subjected. At trial, an expert witness testifies for D that the window glass used was "the strongest, most wind-resistant type available for windows of this kind." In rebuttal, P wishes to offer evidence that shortly after P's accident, D began using a stronger, more wind-resistant type of glass. D objects.

236. Which of the following statements is correct?

(A) The evidence is admissible because the subsequent remedial measures rule does not apply to this kind of case.

(B) The evidence is admissible to prove D's awareness of the weakness of the glass used.

(C) The evidence is admissible to impeach the expert and prove that it was feasible to use a more wind-resistant glass.

(D) The evidence is inadmissible.

237. Assume that instead of testifying that the glass used was the strongest available, the expert had testified that the glass used was the most "cost-effective" glass for this particular project. Describe D's best argument for excluding the evidence if P claims it is being offered to prove feasibility of precautionary measures.

ANSWER:

Negligence action by P against D City following an accident in which P's car was badly damaged when it hit a huge pothole in the middle of the small street on which P was driving. D City claims that the street on which the accident took place was a small private lane over which it had no authority. At trial, P wishes to call W to testify that a day after the accident, a D City road crew repaired the street, covering the pothole.

238. Which of the following statements is most accurate?

    (A) The evidence is relevant but inadmissible for reasons of policy.

    (B) The evidence is irrelevant and therefore inadmissible.

    (C) The evidence is relevant and admissible as an act of independent legal significance.

    (D) The evidence is relevant and admissible to demonstrate that D City had control over the street.

Product liability action by P against D Corp., the manufacturer of the bicycle P was riding at the time of the accident that caused P's injuries. P claims the bike was defective because the metal used for the frame was too weak to support the weight of a normal person. D denies that the metal was too weak, and calls an expert witness who testifies that the metal was the same strength as that used by other manufacturers.

239. During his rebuttal case, P calls W to testify that after the accident, D started using a stronger alloy on the frame of that model, and that if this alloy had been used on P's bike, the accident would not have occurred. D objects to W's testimony. How should the court rule?

ANSWER:

Personal injury action by P against D following an automobile collision. P claims she suffered $25,000 in damages. D wishes to testify that a week before trial, P approached her and said, "You were negligent, but I was distracted by something on the side of the road and was looking away at the time of the crash. I'll dismiss the action if you'll pay $5000."

240. Which of the following statements is most accurate?

    (A) P's statement about being distracted is admissible as a party admission. The rest is inadmissible.

    (B) P's entire statement is admissible as a party admission.

    (C) P's entire statement is admissible as a declaration against interest.

    (D) P's entire statement is inadmissible.

Negligence action by P against D arising from a car crash. P alleges that D suddenly swerved into P's lane. D claims it was P who swerved. At trial, P wishes to testify that after P wrote D demanding $20,000, D wrote back offering to pay P $100, "which is all I've got."

241. P authenticates and offers D's letter into evidence. D objects on the basis of the compromise rule. Of the following, which is P's strongest response?

    (A) D's letter is not a compromise offer.

    (B) Even if D's letter is a compromise offer, it is admissible as a party admission.

(C) Even if D's letter is a compromise offer, it is admissible as a declaration against interest.

(D) Even if D's letter is a compromise offer, its probative value substantially outweighs any unfair prejudice its admission might cause.

Breach of contract action by P against D. To prove D breached by failing to deliver a load of child's trading cards, P testifies that a week after P threatened to sue, D called P and said, "I simply blew it and forgot to ship the cards. Now, unfortunately, I'm sold out. Will you settle for a load of baseball cards instead?"

242. What if any part of D's statement is admissible?

(A) The entire statement is admissible as an admission of D.

(B) Only the part of the statement in which D admitted failing to deliver the cards is admissible.

(C) Only the part of the statement in which D offered to ship P the baseball cards is admissible.

(D) The entire statement is inadmissible.

Negligence action by P against D arising from an automobile accident. P was the sole occupant of her car, and D was the driver of a car in which W was riding. Both P and W were injured in the accident, and sued D for their injuries. Prior to trial, D and W settled, and at trial, W testifies for D that P's car crossed the center line and crashed into D's car. On cross-examination of W, P wishes to inquire about the settlement between D and W. D objects.

243. How should the court rule?

(A) The court should exclude the evidence.

(B) The court should admit the evidence only to prove D's negligence.

(C) The court should admit the evidence only to impeach W by showing bias.

(D) The court should admit the evidence both to prove D's negligence and to impeach W by showing bias.

Negligence action by P against D after the car D was driving struck P in a crosswalk. P seeks $1,000,000 compensation for personal injuries, pain and suffering, and lost earnings. Before trial, D's attorney approaches P's attorney and states, "My client does not deny negligence, but believes your client did not suffer the damages she alleges. We offer to pay $125,000 if you will dismiss the case." P's attorney turns down the offer after consulting with her client. At trial, P wishes to offer into evidence the part of D's attorney's statement that admitted negligence. D objects.

244. How should the court rule?

(A) The court should sustain the objection because the statement is inadmissible hearsay.

(B) The court should sustain the objection because of the compromise rule.

(C) The court should overrule the objection because liability was not contested.

(D) The court should overrule the objection because the probative value of the evidence substantially outweighs any unfair prejudice that might result from its admission.

Prosecution of D for murder. Initially, D pleaded guilty, but she changed her mind about the plea, and the court allowed her to withdraw the plea and enter a plea of not guilty.

245. The prosecution wishes to offer evidence of D's original guilty plea. D objects. How should the court rule?

ANSWER:

Civil action by P against D for battery. P wishes to offer evidence that D was criminally charged with assault and battery arising from the same incident, and that D had pleaded guilty and paid a small fine. D objects.

246. Which of the following statements is correct?

(A) The evidence is inadmissible because its probative value is substantially outweighed by the danger of unfair prejudice.

(B) The evidence is inadmissible character evidence.

(C) The evidence is inadmissible because there are many reasons other than guilt why P might have pleaded guilty.

(D) The evidence is admissible.

P sues D claiming D's car struck P in a crosswalk. D claims P was crossing illegally in the middle of the block. P received a jaywalking ticket for the incident and paid the fine by mail.

247. If D wishes to present evidence of P's payment of the jaywalking fine, which of the following is correct?

(A) The court should exclude the evidence if it finds that most people who receive jaywalking citations pay the fine even if they believe themselves innocent.

(B) The court should exclude the evidence if it finds that allowing it to be used would make people unwilling to pay fines for minor violations because they would fear admissibility in subsequent litigation, which would clog the courts.

(C) The court should exclude the evidence because it is irrelevant.

(D) The court should admit the evidence.

Prosecution of D for murder. Previously, D had pleaded guilty, but the court permitted her to withdraw her plea and enter a plea of not guilty. At trial, the prosecution wishes to offer evidence of D's earlier guilty plea. D objects.

248. How should the court rule?

(A) The court should sustain the objection.

(B) The court should overrule the objection but allow the evidence only to impeach D's credibility if she testifies that she did not commit the crime.

(C) The court should overrule the objection but allow the evidence only to prove D's guilt.

(D) The court should overrule the objection and allow the evidence for any relevant purpose.

Prosecution of D for robbery. The prosecution claims D and W committed the crime. W plea bargained and received a light sentence. At D's trial, W testifies for the prosecution that she and D committed the crime.

249. The prosecution then seeks to prove that shortly after her arrest, while talking with police officers in hopes of making a plea bargain, W said the same thing—that she and D committed the crime together. Which of the following statements concerning the evidence concerning W's earlier statement is most likely correct?

(A) The evidence is hearsay but admissible as a declaration against interest.

(B) The evidence is admissible non-hearsay.

(C) The evidence is both inadmissible hearsay and inadmissible because of the rule excluding evidence of plea bargaining statements.

(D) The evidence is inadmissible hearsay.

Prosecution of D for murder. D agrees to plead guilty, and a hearing is held at which the plea is to be entered. During the hearing, the court asks D whether the charges are accurate, and D answers, "Yes, Your Honor. I am guilty of killing the victim." The court accepts D's guilty plea and sets a date for sentencing. Before the sentencing hearing, D has a change of heart and the court allows her to withdraw her guilty plea and enter a plea of not guilty. At trial, the prosecution wishes to offer into evidence D's statement at the earlier hearing. D objects both on hearsay grounds and on the basis of FRE 410.

250. How should the court rule, and why?

ANSWER:

Prosecution of D for importation of a large shipment of illegal drugs. D was arrested a few days after the crime was committed. On the way to the police station, after having been given his *Miranda* warnings, D said to one of the officers, "If you try to get me probation, I'll tell you who else was involved." At trial, the prosecution wishes to offer D's statement. D objects both on hearsay grounds and on the basis of FRE 410.

251. How should the court rule, and why?

ANSWER:

Negligence action by P against D arising from the collision of their cars on a busy highway. P alleges that D merged into P's lane without looking, colliding with P's car. D denies improperly merging. At trial, P wishes to offer evidence that the police issued D a traffic citation for illegal lane change, and that D pleaded guilty and paid the $75 fine by mail. D objects on the ground that the evidence is irrelevant because many people plead guilty to traffic violations to avoid the inconvenience of going to trial, not because they are guilty.

252. How should the court rule, and why?

ANSWER:

Civil action for battery by P against D. P was attacked from behind as he was leaving a football game. D denies being the attacker. At trial, P wishes to testify that immediately after P was knocked to the ground, D offered to take P to the hospital. D objects.

253. Which of the following statements is correct?

    (A) D's statement is admissible as a party admission.

    (B) D's statement is inadmissible because of the compromise rule (FRE 408).

    (C) D's statement is a party admission but is inadmissible.

    (D) D's statement is inadmissible because it is irrelevant.

Negligence action by P against D after P was struck by a car while she was crossing the street. D denies driving the car that struck P. To prove D's involvement, P wishes to testify that immediately after P was struck by the car, D walked up to P, said, "I didn't see you in the street," and offered to pay P's medical bills. D objects.

254. Which of the following statements is correct?

    (A) D's entire statement is admissible as a party admission.

    (B) D's entire statement is inadmissible because it constitutes an effort to compromise.

    (C) D's entire statement is inadmissible under the rule barring evidence of payment and offers to pay medical and similar expenses.

    (D) Only the statement, "I didn't see you in the street" is admissible.

Negligence action by P against D after the two surfers collided while trying to catch the same wave. P was injured and his board was broken in half. D denies negligence. To prove D's fault, P wishes to testify that a week after the collision, D gave P a new surfboard. D objects.

255. Which of the following statements is correct?

(A) Evidence of D's conduct is inadmissible because it is irrelevant.

(B) Evidence of D's conduct is inadmissible because of the compromise rule.

(C) Evidence of D's conduct is inadmissible under FRE 409.

(D) Evidence of D's conduct is admissible.

Negligence action by P against D arising from an automobile collision. D denies negligence. To prove D's negligence, P wishes to present evidence that D has liability insurance. D objects on grounds of relevance and FRE 411.

256. How should the court rule, and why?

ANSWER:

Medical malpractice action by P against D, a surgeon. P alleges that D botched a surgical procedure, leaving P with a permanent physical impairment. D denies negligence. At trial, D calls an expert witness, who testifies that D performed the surgery in the appropriate way, and made no errors of medical judgment. To impeach D's expert, P wishes to present evidence that D and the expert both carry malpractice liability insurance with the same company. D objects.

257. How should the court rule, and why?

ANSWER:

Negligence action by P against D arising from a boating accident that left P injured. D was piloting the boat when it capsized, causing P's injury. D denies negligence. P's lawyer learns that D carries liability insurance with a particular carrier. During jury selection, P's lawyer wishes to ask jurors whether any of them are employed by that company. D objects on the ground that this would violate FRE 411.

258. How should the court rule, and why?

ANSWER:

Impeachment and Cross-Examination of Witnesses

Defamation action by P against D. To prove the defamatory utterance was made, P calls W1, who testifies that she was in a group of P's business associates when D told the group that P was a "famous liar." During his case-in-chief, D calls W2, W1's husband, to testify that W1 suffers from moderate hearing loss and often forgets to wear her hearing aids.

259. Which of the following statements is correct?

(A) W2's testimony is admissible only if W1 is given an opportunity to explain or deny the substance of W2's testimony.

(B) W2's testimony is admissible to impeach W1's character for truthfulness.

(C) W2's testimony is admissible to impeach the accuracy of W1's testimony.

(D) W2's testimony is inadmissible because extrinsic evidence may not be used in this situation.

Prosecution of D for perjury. D testifies that she did not lie under oath. D calls W, a long-time friend, to testify that in her opinion, D is a peaceful, non-violent person.

260. This evidence is

(A) admissible only to prove D did not commit the crime.

(B) admissible only to support D's credibility.

(C) admissible both to prove D did not commit the crime and to support D's credibility.

(D) inadmissible.

Civil fraud action by P against D arising from a failed real estate deal. P calls W1, who testifies favorably to P's cause.

261. Later, D calls W2 to testify that W1 has a poor community reputation for veracity. Which of the following is correct?

(A) W2's testimony is admissible to impeach W1's character for truthfulness.

(B) W2's testimony is inadmissible because this evidence may only be elicited during cross-examination.

(C) W2's testimony is inadmissible because this is a civil action.

(D) W2's testimony is inadmissible because only specific instances of conduct may be used under these circumstances.

Negligence action by P against D arising from an intersection collision. P calls W1, who testifies that D ran the red light and hit P's car.

262. D calls W2 to testify that W1 told W2 that a bus partially blocked her line of sight. Which of the following is correct?

(A) W2's testimony is admissible to impeach W1 by prior inconsistent statement.

(B) W2's testimony is admissible to impeach W2 by contradiction.

(C) W2's testimony is admissible to impeach W1 by showing lack of opportunity to observe accurately.

(D) W2's testimony is inadmissible.

Prosecution of D for robbery of a liquor store. D testifies that she was not involved. On cross-examination, the prosecutor wishes to ask D if it isn't true that she is a drug addict with a $500 a day habit.

263. This question is

(A) proper to impeach D's character for truthfulness.

(B) proper to impeach D's recollection of the events.

(C) proper to show a motive to commit the crime.

(D) improper because it goes beyond the scope of the direct examination.

Civil action by P against D arising from a roller skating collision. P claims D ran into her on the sidewalk. D calls W, an eyewitness, who testifies that D was skating on her driveway, not the sidewalk, and that it was P who caused the collision when she lost control and headed up the driveway.

264. P wishes to ask W if it isn't true that shortly after the accident, W told X, a bystander, that D "was just learning to skate and should have stayed off the sidewalk." This question is

(A) permissible both to impeach W and to show that D was on the sidewalk.

(B) permissible only to impeach W.

(C) permissible only to show that D was on the sidewalk.

(D) impermissible.

265. Assume P is permitted to ask W about the statement she made to X shortly after the accident, and that W denies making it. P then wishes to call X to testify to W's statement. X's testimony is

(A) admissible only to impeach W.

(B) inadmissible for any purpose because W was not notified of the time and place of the alleged statement, nor of the persons present when it was made.

(C) inadmissible for any purpose because it constitutes extrinsic evidence of the alleged statement.

(D) admissible both to impeach W and to show that D was on the sidewalk.

266. Assume, again, that W denies making the statement to X. P then wishes to call Z to testify that X told her (Z) that W told X that D was just learning to skate and should not have been on the sidewalk. Z's testimony is

(A) admissible both to impeach W and to show that D was on the sidewalk, as long as W is given an opportunity to explain or deny making the statement.

(B) admissible only to impeach W, and only if W is given an opportunity to explain or deny making the statement.

(C) admissible to impeach W regardless of whether W is given an opportunity to explain or deny making the statement.

(D) inadmissible.

267. P wishes to ask W if it isn't true that in a deposition taken several months after the accident, W testified that D "was just learning to skate and should not have been on the sidewalk." This question is

(A) permissible both to impeach W and to show that D was on the sidewalk.

(B) permissible only to impeach W.

(C) permissible only to show that D was on the sidewalk.

(D) impermissible.

Prosecution of D for setting a forest fire. D testifies that she had nothing to do with the fire. During its rebuttal case, the prosecution calls W to testify that D has a community reputation for being an untruthful person.

268. Which of the following is correct?

(A) W's testimony is admissible only to prove that D set the fire.

(B) W's testimony is admissible only to impeach D's credibility as a witness.

(C) W's testimony is admissible for both purposes.

(D) W's testimony is inadmissible.

Prosecution of D for murder. The prosecution calls W, who testifies that she was jogging past the corner of X and Y Streets in her blue jogging outfit when she saw D pull a knife and stab the victim. On cross-examination, D wishes to ask W if it isn't true that W was wearing her green outfit, not her blue outfit.

269. This question is

   (A) a permissible attempt to impeach W by contradiction.

   (B) a permissible attempt to impeach W by showing her inability to perceive accurately.

   (C) an impermissible attempt to impeach W by contradiction.

   (D) an impermissible attempt to impeach W's character for truthfulness.

Prosecution of D for murder. D calls W, who testifies that she and D were in another country together when the crime was committed. On cross-examination, the prosecutor asks W if it isn't true that a year earlier, she tried to get into a gambling establishment with a false identification showing her to be over 21 years of age when she was in fact only 20.

270. This question is

   (A) an impermissible attempt to impeach W's character for truthfulness.

   (B) an impermissible attempt to impeach by contradiction on a collateral issue.

   (C) impermissible because it is beyond the scope of the direct examination.

   (D) permissible.

A witness testifies at a trial. The witness has been convicted of a crime.

271. In which of the following circumstances is the prior conviction *most* likely to be admissible to impeach?

   (A) The witness is a civil plaintiff and the conviction is a five-year-old conviction for felony robbery.

   (B) The witness is a criminal defendant and the conviction is a five-year-old conviction for felony robbery.

   (C) The witness is a criminal defendant and the conviction is a fifteen-year-old conviction for perjury.

   (D) The witness is a prosecution witness and the conviction is a five-year-old conviction for misdemeanor robbery.

Prosecution of D for burglary. If D testifies, she will deny involvement. Before trial, D moves to preclude the prosecution from offering a previous murder conviction of D for the purpose of impeaching D.

272. Which of the following facts would make it more likely the court would *grant* D's motion?

   (A) The prior conviction occurred nine years ago.

   (B) D is unlikely to testify if the court rules that it will allow the prosecution to impeach her with the prior conviction.

(C) Both facts would make granting of the motion more likely.

(D) Neither fact would make granting of the motion more likely.

Negligence action by P against D. P calls W1, who testifies that she saw D's car swerving all over the road just moments before it struck P's car. D wishes to call W2 to testify that she has lived in the same community as W1 for many years, and that W1 has a reputation as an untruthful person.

273. W2's testimony is

(A) admissible to impeach W1.

(B) inadmissible because W1's reputation for truthfulness has not first been supported.

(C) inadmissible because this is a civil action.

(D) inadmissible because it injects irrelevant issues into the case.

Prosecution of D for murder. D testifies that she and her friend were home all night the evening the murder took place across town. On cross-examination, the prosecutor asks D if it isn't true that she was convicted of murder five years earlier. D objects.

274. Which of the following statements is most accurate?

(A) The court must sustain the objection.

(B) The court must overrule the objection.

(C) The court must sustain the objection unless it finds that the probative value of the evidence on the issue of D's credibility outweighs the danger of unfair prejudice.

(D) The court must overrule the objection unless it finds that the probative value of the evidence on the issue of D's credibility is substantially outweighed by the danger of unfair prejudice.

Prosecution of D for burglary. The prosecution calls W1, who testifies that D admitted committing the crime. D calls W2, W1's former boyfriend, to testify that W1 has been under the care of a psychiatrist for many years because she often loses touch with reality, "remembering" events that never occurred.

275. Discuss D's strongest argument for admission of this testimony to impeach W1.

ANSWER:

Prosecution of D for a murder that took place at 7:00 p.m. in a pool hall. The prosecution calls W1, who testifies that she was walking along the sidewalk in front of the pool hall at 7:00 that evening wearing her blue raincoat when D ran out of the building. D calls W2, W1's spouse, to testify that W1 does not own a blue raincoat.

276. W2's testimony is

    (A) admissible to impeach W1 by contradiction.

    (B) admissible to impeach W1's character for truthfulness.

    (C) inadmissible because it is irrelevant.

    (D) inadmissible because it constitutes extrinsic evidence.

Prosecution of D for murder. D calls W, who claims she and D were home all night the evening the murder took place across town. On cross-examination, the prosecutor asks W if it isn't true that she (W) was convicted of murder five years earlier. D objects.

277. Which of the following statements is most accurate?

    (A) The court must sustain the objection.

    (B) The court must overrule the objection.

    (C) The court must sustain the objection unless it finds that the probative value of the evidence on the issue of W's credibility outweighs the danger of unfair prejudice.

    (D) The court must overrule the objection unless it finds that the probative value of the evidence on the issue of W's credibility is substantially outweighed by the dangers enumerated in FRE 403.

Prosecution of D for robbery. The prosecution calls W1, an alleged accomplice of D, who testifies that D committed the crime. D wishes to call W2, a police officer, to testify that W1 agreed to testify against D in order to avoid prosecution for the crime.

278. Which of the following statements is correct?

    (A) The evidence is admissible.

    (B) This is an impermissible attempt to impeach W1 by extrinsic evidence.

    (C) This is an impermissible attempt to impeach W1's character for truthfulness.

    (D) This is an impermissible attempt to introduce compromise evidence.

Personal injury action by P against D arising out of a slip-and-fall in D's supermarket. P calls W, who testifies that P was walking her cart slowly around the store when she suddenly fell on a clear liquid that was difficult to see. On cross-examination, D wishes to ask W about a two-year-old misdemeanor Medicare fraud conviction. P objects.

279. The court

    (A) should sustain the objection if the probative value of the evidence is substantially outweighed by the danger of unfair prejudice.

(B) should overrule the objection unless the probative value of the evidence is greater than the danger of unfair prejudice.

(C) must overrule the objection regardless of the danger of prejudice.

(D) must sustain the objection.

Prosecution of D for a murder that took place in Los Angeles. At trial, D calls W, who testifies that she had lunch with D in Bologna, Italy on the day the crime was committed.

280. On cross-examination, the prosecutor asks W, "Isn't it true that a week after the murder occurred, you told a police officer that you were in Los Angeles on the day of the murder?" Which of the following is correct?

(A) This statement is admissible only to prove W and D's whereabouts on the day of the crime.

(B) This statement is admissible only to impeach W.

(C) This statement is admissible both to impeach W and to prove W's whereabouts on the day of the crime.

(D) This statement is inadmissible for any purpose because admission of the statement violates D's constitutional right to confrontation.

Personal injury action by P against D following an automobile collision. P testifies that she had the green light. D claims that it was P who ran the red light. In rebuttal, P wishes to call W to testify that at a recent party, P said she, not D, had the green light.

281. W's testimony is

(A) inadmissible hearsay.

(B) inadmissible because a party may not support the credibility of a witness unless the witness has been impeached.

(C) inadmissible because P, not W, must testify about the statement.

(D) admissible.

Prosecution of D for auto theft. The prosecution alleges that on the evening of February 6 at 11:00, D broke into the show room of a luxury car dealer in River City and stole a $75,000 luxury sports sedan. D's defense is an alibi. He claims that on the evening the crime was committed, he was in Cleveland attending a poodle show. As part of its case-in-chief, the prosecution calls W, the security guard for the car dealer. W testifies that at 10:45 on the night of February 6, he was taking a short break at Mel's Diner, across the street from the car lot, and that he saw D sitting in a booth sipping a Diet Coke. On cross-examination, D's attorney asks W if he recalls telling his brother X on February 7 that he had spent the entire previous evening at the movie theater, and that he'd gone home right after the show.

282. Which of the following statements is correct?

    (A) The question is a proper attempt to impeach W with a prior inconsistent statement.

    (B) The question is a proper attempt to establish the whereabouts of W on the evening of February 6.

    (C) Both (A) and (B) are correct.

    (D) Neither (A) nor (B) is correct.

283. Assume W denies making the prior statement. To impeach W's credibility, D calls X (W's brother), to testify that on February 7, W told him that he'd had the previous evening off, that he'd spent the entire evening at the movies, and that he'd gone home right after the show. Which of the following statements is most accurate?

    (A) This is an impermissible attempt to impeach W because once W denies having said such a thing, D is stuck with his answer.

    (B) This is an impermissible attempt to impeach W because the question of his whereabouts is collateral, and D is therefore stuck with the answer which W gave on cross-examination.

    (C) This is a permissible attempt to impeach W with a prior inconsistent statement.

    (D) This is a permissible attempt to impeach W by demonstrating his bad character for truthfulness.

284. Assume that during his cross-examination of W, D seeks to show that W made up his story about being in Mel's Diner on a break because he wanted to hide the fact that he went to the movies instead of going to work that evening. Allegedly, W made up the story on February 13, when his boss confronted him about where he'd been on the night of February 6. After the defense rests, the prosecution recalls W and seeks to elicit from W his testimony that very late on the evening of February 6, he told his children that he'd just seen an interesting man sipping a Diet Coke in a booth at Mel's Diner. Which of the following statements is correct?

    (A) The question is a permissible attempt to establish W's credibility.

    (B) The question is a permissible attempt to establish the whereabouts of W on the evening of February 6.

    (C) Both (A) and (B) are correct.

    (D) Neither (A) nor (B) is correct.

Personal injury action by P against D arising from a brawl at a heavy metal rock concert. To prove D attacked P with a baseball bat, P calls W, who testifies that just after P fell to the ground, X, who was sitting close by, screamed, "D just clubbed that guy!"

285. On cross-examination, D asks W if it isn't true that a few minutes later, X told W that somebody else clubbed P. P objects on hearsay and impermissible impeachment grounds. How should the court rule?

ANSWER:

286. D takes the stand, and on direct examination testifies that he was at the poodle show in Cleveland on February 6. On cross-examination, the prosecution asks D if it isn't true that he hates poodles. Which of the following statements is most accurate?

(A) The question is improper because it calls for irrelevant evidence.

(B) The question constitutes an improper attempt to impeach D by showing his bad character.

(C) The question is a proper attempt to impeach D by showing the implausibility of his alibi.

(D) The question is a proper attempt to impeach D by showing his bias.

Prosecution of D for battery on V. D testifies that V attacked D, forcing D to defend herself. To impeach D, the prosecution wishes to offer evidence that D was convicted of felony battery two years earlier.

287. The conviction evidence is

(A) inadmissible because the crime was the same as that for which D is currently on trial.

(B) admissible unless its probative value for impeachment purposes is substantially outweighed by the danger of unfair prejudice to D.

(C) admissible if its probative value for impeachment purposes outweighs the danger of unfair prejudice to D.

(D) admissible regardless of the balance of probative value and unfair prejudice.

Prosecution of D for attempted murder of V, her husband. D claims she acted in self-defense when V attacked her. D calls W, who testifies that V was the first aggressor. On cross-examination, the prosecution asks W if it isn't true that W and D were then, and are still now, having an affair.

288. This question is

(A) proper to impeach W by showing a motive to testify for D.

(B) proper to prove that D was the first aggressor.

(C) proper both to impeach W by showing a motive to testify for D and to prove that D was the first aggressor.

(D) improper.

Negligence action by P against D arising from a car crash. The only dispute is over who had the green light. P calls W1, who testifies that she was coming out of a movie theater after watching "Bar Wars" when she saw D's car run the red light and strike P's car. D calls W2 to testify that she was with W1 that night, and that the two had been attending a showing of "Beetleman," not "Bar Wars," when they saw the accident. "Beetleman" was playing at the same multiplex theater.

289. W2's testimony is

   (A) an improper attempt to impeach by contradiction.

   (B) improper because D did not give W1 an attempt to explain her testimony before calling W2.

   (C) a permissible attempt to impeach W1's memory.

   (D) permissible impeachment by contradiction.

Prosecution of D for the murder of V. D claims he acted in self-defense when V attacked him. D calls W, who testifies that she was at the scene of the killing when X screamed, "Watch out, D, V is coming at you with a knife!" The prosecution wishes to offer evidence that X was convicted of misdemeanor forgery five years earlier.

290. The conviction evidence is

   (A) inadmissible because X did not testify at the trial.

   (B) admissible unless its probative value for impeachment purposes is substantially outweighed by the danger of unfair prejudice to D.

   (C) admissible if its probative value for impeachment purposes outweighs the danger of unfair prejudice to D.

   (D) admissible regardless of the balance of probative value and prejudice.

Prosecution of D for stealing a child's trading cards while the child was playing with them. D testifies that she paid the child for the cards. The prosecutor declines to conduct any cross-examination of D. D then calls W to testify that she has known D for years, and that in her opinion, D is an untruthful person.

291. W's testimony is

   (A) admissible.

   (B) inadmissible character evidence.

   (C) inadmissible because honesty is not a pertinent trait of character.

   (D) inadmissible hearsay.

Prosecution of D for burglary. D testifies that she was in another state when the crime was committed. To impeach D, the prosecution gives appropriate notice that it wishes to offer evidence of D's fifteen-year-old conviction for misdemeanor perjury, and supplies evidence about the circumstances supporting the probative value of the conviction.

292. The evidence is

(A) admissible.

(B) admissible if the court finds that the probative value of the conviction outweighs the danger of unfair prejudice.

(C) admissible if the court finds that the probative value of the conviction, supported by specific facts and circumstances, substantially outweighs the danger of unfair prejudice.

(D) inadmissible.

A grand jury investigating the murder of V hears the testimony of W, who denies any involvement and claims to have been with D in another state when the crime was committed. Based on the testimony of other witnesses, the grand jury indicts D for murder. W is D's girlfriend. Prior to the trial, the prosecutor learns that after giving her grand jury testimony, W admitted to a friend that she and D were in town at their apartment on the day the murder was committed, and that D left the apartment around the time the killing occurred nearby. Even though the prosecutor is aware that W will continue to support her boyfriend by supplying the same alibi she gave before the grand jury, the prosecutor calls W at trial. W testifies that she and D were in another state on the relevant day. The prosecutor then seeks to introduce, for purposes of impeachment, W's statement to the friend. D objects.

293. How should the court rule?

(A) The court should overrule the objection because a party may impeach her own witness.

(B) The court should overrule the objection because the jury is entitled to observe W's demeanor when she supplies the alibi.

(C) The court should sustain the objection because a party who calls a witness vouches for the witness's story, and may not impeach her.

(D) The court should sustain the objection because a party may not call a witness for the sole purpose of impeaching her.

Wrongful death action by P, the administrator of the estate of X, against D, arising from an automobile accident that resulted in the death of X about a week later. X was driving a red car, and D was driving a blue car. D denies negligence. At trial, P calls W1, who testifies that immediately after the crash, Z, a bystander, screamed, "That blue car just rammed that red car!" D now calls W2 to testify that just a few minutes later, Z said that it was the red car that rammed the blue car. The estate objects, and D responds that the evidence is being offered to impeach Z with an inconsistent statement.

294. How should the court rule, and why?

ANSWER:

Action to quiet title to a disputed piece of land that borders the property of both P and D. To prove it owns the disputed property, P calls W, a professional surveyor, who testifies to a location of the boundary that would give P all of the disputed land. On cross-examination, D asks, "isn't it true that your religion teaches that people with blue eyes are evil?" P objects to this question.

295. How should the court rule, and why?

ANSWER:

296. In the prior question, assume P is a church, and that W, the surveyor, is a member of the congregation. On cross-examination, D asks W, "is it not true that you are a member of the P church?" D objects. How should the court rule, and why?

ANSWER:

Negligence action by P against D arising from an automobile accident. At trial, P calls W1, who testifies that she saw the accident occur, ran up to P's car, and noticed that P was crying and kept repeating, "why did that car hit me?" Unfortunately, P does not remember the accident, and does not testify at trial. D denies striking P's car, and in fact testifies that P's car backed into his car. D now calls W2, who, if permitted, will testify that she knows P's community reputation for truthfulness, and that P is generally known as a "liar extraordinaire." P objects to W2's testimony.

297. How should the court rule, and why?

ANSWER:

Prosecution of D for bank robbery. D claims he wasn't involved. At trial, the prosecution calls W1, who testifies that she was in the bank when D entered carrying a shotgun and ordered everyone to lie down on the floor. W1 testifies that D demanded that all the tellers empty their cash drawers and place the money in sacks which D gave them. On cross-examination, D's attorney asks W1 what the weather was like on the day of the robbery. W1 answers that it was a rainy day. D's attorney asks W1 if it isn't a fact that it was warm and sunny on the day of the robbery. W1 insists that it was raining. D now wishes to call W2, a meteorologist, to testify that the day of the robbery was warm and sunny. The prosecutor objects.

298. If the court applies common law rules, how should the court rule, and why?

ANSWER:

Prosecution of D for assault and battery on V. D testifies that she did not commit the crime. On cross-examination, the prosecutor asks D if it isn't true that shortly after the crime occurred, D told X that she (D) "taught V a lesson he'll never forget."

299. D objects to admission of her statement to X. Which of the following is correct?

   (A) The evidence is admissible only to impeach D's credibility.

   (B) The evidence is admissible only to prove D committed the crime.

   (C) The evidence is admissible for both purposes.

   (D) The evidence is inadmissible for either purpose.

Breach of contract action by P against D. P claims D failed to deliver ten cases of a certain Beethoven CD on a certain date as promised. To prove she delivered the goods, D calls W1, who testifies that on the day in question, she was in P's store buying a Mozart CD when she saw D's truck unloading cases of the Beethoven CDs in question. P then wishes to call W2 to testify that on the same day, X, who is W1's sister, told W2 that W1 had just bought a Mahler CD (not a Mozart CD).

300. If D objects to W2's testimony on the ground that this is an improper attempt to impeach W1, how should the court rule?

ANSWER:

Topic 11: Questions

Authentication

Negligence action by P against D's Heating and Cooling for injuries suffered when D allegedly failed to fix P's heater during a sub-zero cold snap. P, who is elderly and housebound, alleges that she phoned D as soon as the heater failed, that D promised to respond "within two hours," that P waited in vain for an entire night, and that D never appeared. While waiting for D, P alleges that she suffered cold-related injuries to her fingers and toes. P testifies that she placed her call to the number for D listed in the phone book, and that a voice answered, "heating service." D denies ever receiving the call and moves to strike P's testimony from the record.

301. How should the court rule?

   (A) The court should deny D's motion because there is sufficient evidence to support a finding that the call was actually placed to D.

   (B) The court should deny the motion if it finds that the call was not placed to D.

   (C) The court should grant the motion because the party answering the phone did not identify itself as D's Heating and Cooling.

   (D) The court should deny the motion because P has already testified, and it is too late to keep the evidence from the jury.

Prosecution of D for assault with a deadly weapon, a baseball bat. At trial, the prosecution wishes to authenticate a particular baseball bat as the one used by D. Assume the bat has no marks that would distinguish it from other bats of its type.

302. What is the best way for the prosecution to authenticate the bat?

ANSWER:

Negligence action by P against D arising from an intersection collision controlled by traffic signals. P was driving east on one street, and D was driving north on the cross-street. Both parties claim the other ran the light at the intersection, leading to the collision. At trial, P wishes to use a photograph to show the positions of the cars about fifteen minutes after the collision. The photograph was taken by a passerby, who gave it to P. The passerby is not called to testify. P seeks to authenticate the photograph by testifying that it accurately depicts the scene as it appeared immediately after the collision. D objects, claiming lack of authentication.

303. How should the court rule?

   (A) The court should sustain the objection because P has not called the photographer to testify.

   (B) The court should sustain the objection because the cars might have been moved between the time of the collision and the time the photograph was taken (fifteen minutes later).

   (C) The court should sustain the objection because the photograph is not the best evidence of what happened at the time of the accident.

   (D) The court should overrule the objection.

Prosecution of D for burglarizing V's store and stealing a box of CDs of the New York Philharmonic's performance of Beethoven's 9th Symphony. A carton of CDs of the same title was found in D's home. The prosecutor calls V, shows V a carton of CDs, and asks if she recognizes it. V identifies it as the carton of CDs that was stolen from her store. When asked why she was able to say so, V answered that she recognizes a crushed corner of the carton.

304. D objects. Which of the following is correct?

   (A) V's testimony is admissible if the court finds the box presented at trial is in fact the box that was stolen from V's store.

   (B) V's testimony is admissible if the court finds that there is evidence sufficient to support a finding that this is the same box that was stolen from V's store.

   (C) V's testimony is inadmissible because it is impossible to tell one box of CDs from another.

   (D) V's testimony is inadmissible because only D is qualified to identify the box.

Negligence action by P against D arising from an automobile accident. P claims that a week after the accident, she received a handwritten letter from D accepting responsibility. D claims the letter is a forgery.

305. Discuss two ways P may authenticate the letter.

ANSWER:

Breach of contract action by P against D. P claims D failed to deliver the goods called for in the contract. D asserts the doctrine of impossibility, based on the claim that severe storms caused flooding which destroyed all the goods in D's warehouse. To prove impossibility, P offers in evidence what appears to be a newspaper published in the town in which D's business is located, and which is dated a few days before D was supposed to ship P's order. An article in the paper reports the loss of all the goods in D's warehouse due to storm-related flooding. D objects on grounds of lack of authentication.

306. How should the court rule?

(A) The court should sustain the objection if it finds that P has failed to show by a preponderance of the evidence that this is the newspaper P claims it to be.

(B) The court should sustain the objection because the newspaper is not the best evidence of whether flooding caused the destruction of the goods in D's warehouse.

(C) The court should sustain the objection if it finds that there is insufficient evidence to support a finding that this is the newspaper P claims it to be.

(D) The court should overrule the objection.

The Best Evidence Rule

Medical malpractice action by P against D, a surgeon. P claims D failed to treat a leg injury properly, and that as a result of improper treatment, her leg had to be amputated. At trial, P wishes to testify that her leg required amputation due to complications that occurred during D's treatment. D objects on best evidence rule grounds, asserting that P's medical records must be used to prove the cause of the condition leading to amputation.

307. How should the court rule?

   (A) The court should sustain the objection because the medical records are the best evidence of P's medical condition.

   (B) The court should sustain the objection unless P offers to produce the records to support her testimony.

   (C) The court should sustain the objection unless P demonstrates that her medical records are not available for reasons beyond P's control.

   (D) The court should overrule the objection.

Second trial of a murder case after the first trial ended with a hung jury. At the first trial, X testified for the prosecution. X died before the second trial. The prosecution wishes to call W, a family member of the victim who was in the courtroom during X's testimony, to recount X's testimony in the first trial. Defendant makes a best evidence rule objection to W's testimony.

308. How should the court rule?

   (A) The court should sustain the objection because the reporter's transcript is the best evidence of X's testimony.

   (B) The court should sustain the objection unless the prosecution offers to produce the transcript to support W's testimony.

   (C) The court should sustain the objection unless the prosecution demonstrates that the transcript of the first trial was destroyed through no fault of the prosecution.

   (D) The court should overrule the objection.

Personal injury action by P against D arising from an inline skating collision. To prove P broke her leg in the collision, P calls Dr. W, who testifies that she concluded that P broke her leg by reviewing an X-ray of P's leg taken an hour after the accident. D objects on best evidence rule grounds.

309. How should the court rule?

(A) The court should sustain the objection.

(B) The court should overrule the objection because an X-ray is not covered by the best evidence rule.

(C) The court should overrule the objection because the jury is not capable of interpreting an X-ray, making it a waste of time to produce it.

(D) The court should overrule the objection because Dr. W is testifying about her own impressions of the X-ray, not the contents of the X-ray itself.

Breach of contract action by P against D. P claims that D breached the written contract by failing to deliver 200 crates of apples by the specified date. At trial, D wishes to testify that the contract only called for delivery of 100 crates. P makes a best evidence rule objection.

310. How should the court rule?

(A) The court should sustain the objection.

(B) The court should overrule the objection because a contract is an agreement brought about by the meeting of two minds, not a writing. The writing is only a memorandum of the agreement, not the contract itself.

(C) The court should overrule the objection because D is not testifying about the contents of the writing, but about her understanding of the agreement. Thus, the best evidence rule does not apply.

(D) The court should overrule the objection because the central issue in the case concerns the terms of the agreement, and the jury is entitled to hear D's interpretation of the terms.

During the trial of a case, it is important for a party to prove that a certain parked automobile had a parking ticket on its windshield at a certain time. To prove this fact, a witness is called to testify that she saw a parking ticket on the car's windshield at that time.

311. Discuss the best evidence rule implications of this testimony.

ANSWER:

To prove that Elvis Presley is dead, a party calls a witness to testify that she visited Graceland in Memphis, Tennessee, and that she saw a tombstone on which were etched the lines "Elvis Aaron Presley," "January 8, 1935," and "August 16, 1977."

312. Discuss the best evidence rule implications of this testimony. If you have studied the hearsay rule, discuss the hearsay implications of this testimony as well.

ANSWER:

P sues D following a freeway pile-up. P claims D was going 85 mph, lost control, and caused the accident. D claims she was going only 50.

313. To prove she was not speeding, D testifies that the impact of the crash "froze" the speedometer, and that the instrument on the wrecked car registers 50 mph. P objects to D's testimony about the odometer reading on both hearsay and best evidence rule grounds. How should the court rule?

ANSWER:

Negligence action by P against D arising from a unicycle collision. To prove D's negligence, P wishes to offer in evidence a photocopy of a letter from D accepting responsibility for the accident. D admits writing the letter but claims P altered it to appear as though D accepted responsibility when in fact she did not. Thus, D claims the photocopy violates the best evidence rule.

314. How should the court rule?

    (A) The court should overrule the objection because the photocopy is a duplicate and a duplicate is admissible to the same extent as an original.

    (B) The court should sustain the objection because a photocopy is not a duplicate.

    (C) The court should sustain the objection because even though the photocopy qualifies as a duplicate, it would be unfair to allow P to offer the duplicate.

    (D) The court should overrule the objection because the jury should be permitted to view the photocopy and make its own decision about whether it was tampered with.

Negligence action by P against D after the elevator in D's building stalled while P was riding in it. P was injured during the rescue. P alleges that D failed to maintain the elevator properly. To prove this allegation, P wishes to testify that while she was waiting to be rescued, she noticed that the elevator permit posted on the wall had expired five years earlier. P asked D to produce the permit at the trial, but D failed to do so even though D has the permit.

315. D objects to P's proposed testimony about the permit on hearsay and best evidence rule grounds. How should the court rule?

ANSWER:

Judicial Notice

Assume each of the following facts is relevant to the determination of a factual dispute at issue in a case.

316. Which would probably <u>not</u> be a proper subject of judicial notice?

    (A) That palm trees grow better in warm climates than in cold climates.

    (B) That deuterium is an isotope of hydrogen in which the nucleus of the atom contains both a proton and a neutron.

    (C) That a certain road was not plowed for twenty-four hours after a particular snow storm.

    (D) That stores in the state in which the case is being tried are not allowed to sell packaged liquor on Sundays.

Negligence action by P against D after the Expunger SUV D was driving struck P in a crosswalk, injuring P. D admits striking P, but denies negligence, claiming that he was momentarily blinded by an extremely bright sun shining directly into his eyes just before the accident. P asks the court to take judicial notice that the sun was obscured by heavy clouds for the entire day. To support judicial notice, P presents the court with an official National Weather Service log showing that on the day in question, the entire area was shrouded by heavy clouds. After hearing argument, the court agrees to take judicial notice.

317. Which of the following statements is correct?

    (A) After the court takes judicial notice, D may offer a witness to testify that the day was sunny.

    (B) During closing argument, D may encourage the jury to find that she was momentarily blinded by bright sunshine at the time of the accident.

    (C) The court may instruct the jury to accept as conclusive that the sun was obscured by heavy clouds for the entire day.

    (D) The court must instruct the jury to accept as conclusive that the sun was obscured by heavy clouds for the entire day.

Civil rights action by P, a prison inmate, against D, the warden, for requiring him to subject himself to a test for AIDS. D argues that the intrusion on P is justified because of the danger posed by the disease. At trial, however, D presents no evidence of the danger caused by the disease. Instead, she asks the court to take judicial notice of the danger.

318. Which of the following statements is most likely true?

   (A) It would be proper for the court to take judicial notice.

   (B) Because these facts are central to D's defense, it would be improper for the court to take judicial notice. D should be required to offer evidence.

   (C) Because D waited until the trial had begun before requesting the court to take judicial notice, it would be improper for the court to take notice.

   (D) Because proof of these facts would require the consideration of inadmissible hearsay, it would be improper for the court to take judicial notice.

Prosecution of D for child molestation. One element of the crime is that the victim be under the age of 18. V, the alleged victim, is a prosecution witness, but the prosecutor neglects to ask V his age or to submit other evidence of V's age at the time of the alleged crime. At the close of all evidence, D moves for an acquittal on the ground that the prosecution has not offered any evidence that V was under 18 years of age at the time of the alleged crime. The prosecutor responds by showing the court a certified copy of V's birth certificate, and asks the court to take judicial notice of V's age. The birth certificate contains a birth date that would have made V seven years old at the time of the alleged crime, which was only six months prior to trial.

319. Which of the following statements is correct?

   (A) Because this is a criminal case, the court may not take judicial notice of any fact that would operate against the defendant.

   (B) Because this is a criminal case, the court may not take judicial notice of any fact that constitutes an element of the crime.

   (C) The court may take judicial notice of the fact but must instruct the jury that it is not required to accept the fact as conclusively established.

   (D) The court may take judicial notice of the fact and may instruct the jury that it must consider the fact to be conclusively established.

Negligence and strict liability action by P against D, a pharmaceutical company, for serious injury allegedly caused by a drug D manufactured and which was prescribed to P. D moves to dismiss the strict liability count on the ground P must prove negligence to prevail. The state has not previously decided the precise question raised by D's motion: whether a pharmaceutical company may be held strictly liable for a design defect in its drug that causes personal injury. During argument on the motion, D asks the court to take "judicial notice" of the fact that strict liability would discourage the development of new and useful drugs.

320. May the court take notice of this fact? Why or why not?

ANSWER:

Topic 14: Questions

Burdens of Proof and Presumptions

Negligence action by P against D arising from an automobile accident. P has the burden of production as to the essential elements of the cause of action, which include duty, breach, causation, proximate cause, and damages. Assume that on the question of D's negligence, P calls a witness who testifies that she saw D's car cross the center line and strike P's car head-on.

321. Which of the following statements best indicates what should happen if D fails to present any evidence contesting this item of evidence?

    (A) The court should allow the jury to decide whether P has presented sufficient evidence to persuade the jury by a preponderance of the evidence that D acted negligently.

    (B) The court should instruct the jury that D was negligent.

    (C) The court should instruct the jury that D now has the burden of persuasion on the negligence question, and allow the jury to decide whether P has convinced the jury by a preponderance of the evidence that D was not negligent.

    (D) The court should direct a verdict for P and award judgment.

322. Assume P fails to offer any evidence as to D's negligence, and only calls witnesses to testify that P suffered serious injuries in the collision. If D moves for a directed verdict at the close of P's case, what should the court do?

    (A) The court should deny the motion because the jury is entitled to decide whether to render a verdict for P.

    (B) The court should deny the motion and order D to present her case.

    (C) The court should withhold a ruling on the motion until D has presented her case.

    (D) The court should grant the motion.

323. Assume P produces no evidence of D's negligence. In opposition to D's motion for directed verdict, P admits that she can produce no witnesses who have first-hand knowledge of the accident. P argues, however, that if given an opportunity, she can, through cross-examination of D's witnesses, either get them to admit that D was negligent or demonstrate to the jury that the demeanor of D's witnesses shows that they are lying. Should the court grant or deny D's motion for directed verdict under these circumstances?

ANSWER:

Paternity action by P against D. D claims that he was not the father of the child. Assume that the following rebuttable presumption applies: *A child born within ten months of the last date on which a male and female were cohabiting is rebuttably presumed to have been fathered by the male.* This is the only presumption that applies in the case. The action is being tried in a jurisdiction that adheres to the majority ("bursting bubble") theory of presumptions. At trial, P testifies that she and D cohabited continuously for five years and only stopped living together one month before the baby was born. D, in turn, calls an expert witness who testifies that she performed blood tests on D and on the child, and determined that there is only a tiny probability that D could have fathered the child. At the close of all evidence, P's attorney asks the court to instruct the jury that if it finds that the child was born within ten months of the last date on which P and D were cohabiting, it must find that D was the father.

324. The court should

    (A) find that P has produced sufficient evidence to meet her burden of production on the foundational facts, and give P's requested instruction.

    (B) find that all of the foundational facts are true, and instruct the jury that D is the father.

    (C) find that D's expert has produced sufficient evidence to support the conclusion that D could not have been the father of the child, and not give P's requested instruction.

    (D) find that the expert is correct that D could not have been the father of the child, and not give P's requested instruction.

Action by P against D to quiet title to a piece of land. Both P and D claim ownership. Assume that the following rebuttable presumption applies to the case: *A deed purporting to create an interest in real property is presumed to be authentic if it is at least 30 years old, is in such condition as to create no suspicion as to its authenticity, was kept in a place where such a writing would likely be found, and has been acted upon as authentic by persons having an interest in the matter.* At trial, P offers the deed in evidence after testifying that it is 40 years old, was never altered, was kept in her safe deposit box, and that it has always been treated as authentic. The deed purports to convey to P a fee simple interest in the property. D then calls W, P's sister, who testifies that for many years, P has kept the purported deed in the glove compartment of his car, and has never kept the document in a safe deposit box. At the close of all evidence, P's attorney asks the court to instruct the jury that it must find that the deed is authentic if it finds that it is at least 30 years old, is in such condition as to create no suspicion as to its authenticity, was kept in a place where such a writing would likely be found, and has been acted upon as authentic by persons having an interest in the matter.

325. The court should

    (A) find that P has produced sufficient evidence to meet her burden of production on all of the foundational facts, and give P's requested instruction.

    (B) find that all of the foundational facts are true, and give P's requested instruction.

(C) find that D has produced sufficient evidence to support the conclusion that the deed was not kept in the safe deposit box, and not give P's requested instruction.

(D) find that the deed was not kept in the safe deposit box, and not give P's requested instruction.

Prosecution of D for possession of a firearm in violation of a statute forbidding convicted felons from possessing firearms. At trial, the prosecution presents evidence that D is a convicted felon, and that D was arrested when a firearm was found under the front seat of a car in which she was riding as a passenger. D stipulates that she is a convicted felon, but declines to take the stand in her own defense or call any witnesses. The jurisdiction in which the case is being tried maintains the following rebuttable presumption: *All occupants of a vehicle are presumed to be in possession of any firearm contained in the vehicle.*

326. Which of the following jury instructions would it be appropriate for the court to issue?

(A) If you find that D was an occupant of the vehicle at the time the firearm was found in the vehicle, you must find that D was in possession of the firearm.

(B) If you find that D was an occupant of the vehicle at the time the firearm was found in the vehicle, you may, but need not, find that D was in possession of the firearm.

(C) If you find that D was an occupant of the vehicle at the time the firearm was found in the vehicle, you must find that D was in possession of the firearm unless D has persuaded you otherwise.

(D) No jury instruction would be appropriate in this situation.

Paternity action by P, the mother of a child, against D, whom P alleges to be the child's father. The jurisdiction in which the case is being tried has the following statute: *The child of a wife cohabiting with her husband, who is not impotent or sterile, is conclusively presumed to be a child of the marriage.* P presents evidence that P and D are married, that they were cohabiting, and that D is not impotent. In his defense, D wishes to present evidence of a blood test that establishes that he could not have fathered the child.

327. Which of the following statements is correct?

(A) The court should allow D to present the blood test evidence but should instruct the jury that it should weigh the value of the presumption against D's evidence.

(B) The court should allow D to present the evidence but should instruct the jury that D has the burden of persuading the jury that he is not the father.

(C) The court should not allow D to present the evidence, and should instruct the jury that D is the father.

(D) The court should not allow D to present the evidence, and should instruct the jury that if it finds that P and D were married and cohabiting, and that D is not sterile, it must find that D is the father of the child.

P sues D to collect a debt. To prove the debt was not paid, P offers into evidence a note signed by D for the amount of the debt. The jurisdiction maintains a rebuttable presumption that "an obligation possessed by the creditor is presumed not to have been paid." Assume a note qualifies as an "obligation."

328. D testifies that she (D) possessed the note prior to trial, and that she only let P borrow it during the trial to make a photocopy. The jurisdiction has adopted the "bursting bubble" theory of presumptions. D rests without offering any evidence that she paid the note. Which of the following statements is correct?

(A) The court should instruct the jury that if it finds by clear and convincing evidence that P possessed the note other than to make a photocopy, it must find that the note was not paid.

(B) The court should instruct the jury that if it finds by a preponderance of the evidence that P possessed the note other than to make a photocopy, it must find that the note was not paid.

(C) The court should instruct the jury that the note was not paid, and that the jury's responsibility is only to assess damages.

(D) The court should not instruct the jury at all concerning the presumption.

Evidentiary Privileges

Prosecution of D for the murder of V. At trial, the prosecution calls D's attorney as a witness, and asks the attorney if it isn't true that during an interview in the attorney's office, D admitted to her that she killed V and asked for help to "beat this charge." Assume D did make this statement to the attorney. The attorney objects on grounds of the attorney-client privilege.

329. How should the court rule?

   (A) The court should overrule the objection because, if the prosecutor knows about D's statement to her attorney, D must have waived the privilege.

   (B) The court should overrule the objection because D sought her attorney's help to cover up the crime.

   (C) The court should overrule the objection as to D's asking for help to "beat this charge," but sustain the objection as to D's statement that she killed V.

   (D) The court should sustain the objection.

330. Assume D's husband and the attorney's secretary were present in the attorney's office when D made the statement to the attorney. How should the court rule on D's attorney's objection?

   (A) The court should overrule the objection because the husband's presence waives the attorney-client privilege.

   (B) The court should overrule the objection because the secretary's presence waives the attorney-client privilege.

   (C) The court should overrule the objection unless D can show that her husband's assistance is needed for her defense.

   (D) The court should sustain the objection.

Negligence action by P against D, a grocery store owner, following a slip-and-fall in the produce section of D's store. P claims she slipped on a puddle of liquid, and that D either should have prevented the liquid from spilling on the floor or cleaned it up sooner. Before trial, the former secretary for D's attorney, angry at being fired, contacted P's attorney and told her that she sat in on a conversation in which D and the attorney discussed paying off store employees who saw the accident to get them to deny that there was any liquid on the floor and to state that P tripped because she was running through the produce section. The secretary told P's attorney that the meeting was taped, and gave P's attorney her notes of this meeting, which summarize the conversation, but without detail. P subpoenas the tape of the meeting. D objects on grounds of privilege. P responds that the conversation was not privileged due to the crime-fraud exception, and asks the court to conduct an *in camera* inspection of the tape.

331. Discuss the procedure the court should follow in deciding on the admissibility of the secretary's testimony.

ANSWER:

Negligence action by P against D in federal court under the court's diversity jurisdiction. D admits negligently running into P, but claims P's injuries were minor. To prove this fact, D calls W, the doctor who treated P after the accident, to testify about the extent of the injuries. P objects on grounds of privilege. Assume the state in which the federal court sits has adopted a general physician-patient privilege but that the federal courts in that circuit have held that there is no such privilege.

332. Which of the following statements is correct?

(A) Because the federal courts have not adopted a general physician-patient privilege, there is no privilege and the court should allow W to testify.

(B) Even though the privilege applies here, the court should allow W to testify if it finds W's testimony is the best available evidence of P's injuries.

(C) If the state recognizes the patient-litigant exception to the privilege, the privilege does not apply and the court should allow W to testify.

(D) Even if no privilege applies, the court should exclude W's testimony if W relied in part on P's own statements to diagnose P's condition.

Prosecution of D for masterminding a fraudulent investment scheme. X, D's former secretary, contacts the prosecution and provides damaging information about a meeting attended by X, D, and A, D's attorney. X prepares an affidavit claiming that at that meeting, which X attended to take notes and which was tape recorded, D sought A's assistance in avoiding police detection of the scheme. The prosecution presents X's affidavit to the court and moves to compel D to produce the tape of the meeting so the court may conduct *in camera* inspection and, ultimately, play the tape for the jury.

333. D objects to *in camera* review on grounds of attorney-client privilege. Which of the following is correct?

(A) The judge should conduct the *in camera* review of the tape recording if she finds, based on X's affidavit, that there are reasonable grounds to believe that such review may yield evidence that establishes the applicability of the crime-fraud exception to attorney-client privilege, and that it would otherwise be appropriate to conduct the review.

(B) The judge should conduct the *in camera* review of the tape recording regardless of the strength of X's affidavit, because the court is not bound by rules of evidence when making admissibility rulings.

(C) The judge should refuse to conduct *in camera* review because the court is bound by rules of privilege when determining the admissibility of evidence, and the tape might be subject to the attorney-client privilege.

(D) The judge should hold, even without *in camera* review, that the attorney-client privilege does not apply because X's presence at the meeting waived the privilege.

Negligence action by P against D arising from a scooter collision. P claims she suffered severe back injuries in the accident. Prior to trial, P's attorney referred P to Dr. X to obtain an opinion about the prospects for P's long-term recovery. X examined P and sent a report directly to P's attorney. D wishes to take Dr. X's deposition in order to ask about her examination and report. P objects on grounds of privilege.

334. How should the court rule?

(A) The court should sustain P's objection because the examination and report are subject to the attorney-client privilege.

(B) The court should sustain P's objection because the examination and report are subject to the physician-patient privilege.

(C) The court should sustain P's objection because the examination and report are subject to both the attorney-client privilege and the physician-patient privilege.

(D) The court should overrule P's objection.

Federal prosecution of D for the murder of V. V's killer lay in wait outside V's house one rainy night, and shot V when V returned. That same night, D went out alone. When D returned an hour later, W and a friend, who had been watching television together, noticed that D's clothes were wet and his shoes muddy. W is D's wife. At the time of the trial, W's friend is in another country. The prosecutor wishes to have W testify to what she saw that night. W is willing to testify, but D objects.

335. How should the court rule?

(A) The court should sustain the objection based on the privilege for confidential communications between spouses.

(B) The court should sustain the objection based on the privilege against adverse spousal testimony.

(C) The court should sustain the objection based on both privileges.

(D) The court should overrule the objection.

336. Assume W was alone in the house when D returned home, and that in addition to the other facts, D whispered to W, "I don't think V is going to bother you anymore." After V's murder but before the trial, D and W obtained a divorce. The prosecution wishes to have W testify to what she saw when D came home as well as to what D told her. D objects on grounds of the privilege for confidential communications between spouses and the adverse spousal testimony privilege. How should the court rule?

(A) The court should sustain the objection as to what D told W, but should allow W to testify to what she saw.

(B) The court should sustain the objection as to what W saw, but allow her to testify to what D told her.

(C) The court should sustain the objection as to both aspects of W's proposed testimony.

(D) The court should overrule the objection in its entirety.

P and D were involved in an auto accident. P's estate has brought a negligence action against D's estate. Plaintiff alleges that D struck and killed P while P was in a crosswalk. D was also severely injured in the accident, and died of her wounds a few days later.

337. At trial, plaintiff calls A, D's attorney, and asks A whether just before she died, D told A, in confidence, that she knew she was dying and that she probably should have been paying closer attention. Which of the following statements is correct?

(A) D's statement to A is inadmissible because of the attorney-client privilege.

(B) D's statement to A is inadmissible hearsay.

(C) D's statement to A is admissible if plaintiff demonstrates that the statement is the only available evidence that D was not paying attention.

(D) D's statement to A is admissible even if the statement is not the only available evidence that D was not paying attention.

Prosecution of D for battery on his wife, W. W testifies that D struck her repeatedly late one night when the children were sleeping and nobody else was home. The prosecution then asks W to relate anything D said to her during the beating.

338. D objects to W's testimony concerning his statement on both hearsay and privilege grounds. Assume the court has held that both spouses hold the privilege for confidential communications. How should the court rule?

ANSWER:

Federal diversity action by P against D following an auto accident. At trial, P calls W, D's minor child, to testify about a confidential conversation she had with D concerning the accident.

339. W refuses to testify, claiming a parent-child confidential communication privilege. The federal circuit in which the district court sits does not recognize such a privilege, but the state in which the court sits does. Which of the following is correct?

(A) The court should order W to testify because the federal courts do not recognize the privilege W claims.

(B) The court should ask the United States Supreme Court for a definitive ruling on whether there is a federal privilege, and rule accordingly after the Supreme Court issues its opinion.

(C) The court should refuse to order W to testify because state privilege law applies.

(D) The court should order W to testify because, even though state privilege law applies, there is no privilege regarding conversations relevant to a party's fault in the event giving rise to the action.

Negligence action by P against D arising from an automobile accident. D learns that at trial, P plans to call W, who will state that she was at the scene at the time of the accident and that she saw D's car run a red light and strike P's car. D also learns that W has been under the care of PSW, a psychiatric social worker, for several years. Hoping to develop evidence that W is an unreliable witness, D takes the deposition of PSW and asks about the nature of the treatment. At W's request, PSW objects to any questions concerning her treatment of W. D makes a motion to compel PSW to answer the questions.

340. Which of the following statements is correct?

(A) The court should overrule the objection because this is only discovery and not trial, and the rules of evidence do not apply. The court should order PSW to answer the questions.

(B) The court should overrule the objection because neither W nor PSW is a party to the action, and they may not assert any privilege. The court should order PSW to answer the questions.

(C) The court should overrule the objection because there is no privilege in federal court between a patient and her psychiatric social worker. The court should order PSW to answer the questions.

(D) The court should sustain the objection.

Imagine you are a state legislator. You are trying to decide how to vote on a bill that would create a privilege for confidential communications between a parent and a minor child.

341. Explain why few states recognize a privilege for confidential communications between parent and child.

ANSWER:

Action in federal court by P, a clothing manufacturer, against D Corp., a competitor. P alleges that D Corp. unlawfully interfered with P's contractual relationship with Store, a large department store chain, leading the chain to drop P's clothing line and start selling D Corp.'s line. D Corp. denies any wrongdoing. Prior to trial, P takes the deposition of W, a sales representative for D Corp. who is now in charge of the Store account. P asks W to relate any communications she had with D Corp.'s attorney concerning the contract with Store. D objects on grounds of attorney-client privilege. Assume W's boss told W that any communications she had with the attorney were to be treated as confidential.

342. Which of the following statements is correct?

(A) If W is not in a high enough position within D Corp. to act on any legal advice given by the attorney, communications between W and the attorney are not privileged.

(B) If W's communications with the attorney took place in order to secure legal advice for D Corp., upper echelon management did not possess all the information needed to obtain proper legal advice, and the communications concerned matters within the scope of W's job, they are subject to the attorney-client privilege.

(C) Because a corporation does not enjoy any attorney-client privilege, W's communications with the attorney are not privileged.

(D) Because W worked for D Corp., W's communications with the attorney are subject to the attorney-client privilege.

Legal malpractice action by P against Attorney. Attorney formerly represented P in a breach of contract case. P lost that case, and now claims it was because of incompetent representation by Attorney. Attorney claims she represented P competently, and that early in the litigation process, she advised P to take certain action to maximize her chances of prevailing, but that P refused to follow her advice. At trial, Attorney wishes to testify about the advice she gave P and P's responses. P objects on grounds of attorney-client privilege.

343. How should the court rule?

(A) The court should sustain the objection because P is the holder of the privilege, and P has manifested her intention to maintain the privilege.

(B) The court should sustain the objection because the attorney-client privilege continues as long as there is a client in existence.

(C) The court should overrule the objection because there is no privilege for communications relevant to an alleged breach of duty by the attorney or client arising from their relationship.

(D) The court should sustain the objection as to statements made by P to Attorney, but overrule the objection as to the advice Attorney gave to P.

Lay and Expert Opinion; Scientific Evidence

Assume each of the opinions listed below is relevant to a case.

344. Which of the following opinions is a court *least likely* to allow a lay witness to give?

(A) The house smelled of gas just before the explosion.

(B) The car that passed us as we were trying to cross in the crosswalk was going at least 50 miles per hour.

(C) The damage to the basement was caused by the water that seeped into the basement.

(D) The driver appeared to be intoxicated when he stepped out of the car moments after the crash.

Prosecution of D for burglary. To prove innocence, D calls W, a six-year-old child, who will testify that D was home watching television at the time the crime was committed. To establish W's basis for knowing D's whereabouts, D's lawyer asks W to state her relationship to D. If permitted, W will testify that D is her mother.

345. Of the following objections to W's testimony, which is the most appropriate (even if it might not succeed)?

(A) Improper opinion.

(B) Lack of personal knowledge.

(C) Hearsay.

(D) The child is incompetent to testify.

Negligence action by P against D arising from an automobile accident. P claims the accident was caused by D's careless driving.

346. Of the following, which statement by an eyewitness is the court *most likely* to permit?

(A) D was driving carelessly.

(B) D was driving negligently.

(C) D was driving erratically.

(D) D was driving recklessly.

Negligence action by P against D arising from an automobile accident. D alleges she suffered permanent injuries to her legs as a result of the way her car crumpled.

347. Which of the following statements would a court be *least likely* to permit P's expert, an orthopedic surgeon, to make?

(A) P's legs were fractured by the sudden, extreme, inward movement of the steering column and instrument panel.

(B) A force slightly less than that exerted by the crash would not have fractured P's legs.

(C) A more strongly designed passenger cage would not have collapsed from the force exerted in the accident, and thus would not have fractured P's legs.

(D) Even after the fractures in P's legs have healed, P is likely to suffer permanent impairment of motion.

Prosecution of D for arson. To prove the fire was set intentionally, the prosecution calls W, a police arson investigator who has served in that capacity for ten years after spending several years as a beat officer. W never attended college and had no special schooling in arson investigation, but learned investigative techniques from a senior investigator with whom she worked for two years. From techniques learned through this experience, W spoke with eyewitnesses who saw the fire at various stages, and concluded from that information as well as her own investigation of the fire scene that the fire was set intentionally.

348. Which of the following objections to W's testimony is the court likely to sustain, if either?

(A) W is not a qualified expert.

(B) W's testimony about the cause of the fire should be excluded as inadmissible hearsay.

(C) The court is likely to sustain both of these objections.

(D) The court is likely to overrule both of these objections.

349. The prosecution wishes to have W testify not just to her conclusion that the fire was caused by arson, but also to the basis for that conclusion. Such testimony would include repeating what the eyewitnesses told her about the fire. If D requests the court to issue a limiting instruction concerning the testimony about the bystander statements, which of the following would be most appropriate?

(A) You may consider the bystander statements only for the purpose of showing that the fire proceeded as described by the witnesses, and not to explain the basis of W's testimony.

(B) You may consider the bystander statements only for the purpose of explaining the basis for W's testimony, and not as proof that the fire proceeded as described by W.

(C) You may consider the bystander statements only for the purpose of demonstrating the bystanders' belief about how the fire proceeded, and not as proof of how the fire actually proceeded.

(D) No limiting instruction is appropriate in this situation.

Class action by a group of homeowners against D, owner of a chemical plant, alleging that seepage from the plant's underground chemical storage tanks caused severe illnesses. After offering evidence that the seepage occurred and that the chemicals contaminated plaintiffs' drinking water wells, plaintiffs call W, a Ph.D. toxicologist, as an expert witness. If allowed, W will testify that using a new scientific technique, she has determined that there is a causal connection between the contamination of plaintiffs' drinking water and the illnesses.

350. If D objects to W's testimony, which of the following factors may the court consider in making its ruling?

(A) The court may consider only whether W's technique has achieved general acceptance in the relevant scientific community.

(B) The court may consider only whether W has published her technique in a peer-reviewed journal.

(C) The court may consider only whether it is possible to determine the error rate of W's technique.

(D) The court may consider all of the above.

Prosecution of D for murder. D claims insanity. To support the insanity defense, D wishes to call W, a psychiatrist who examined D.

351. Which of the following opinions would the court be *least likely* to permit the expert to state?

(A) At the time of the killing, D suffered from paranoid schizophrenia.

(B) At the time of the killing, D suffered from a severe mental disease that made it impossible for her to appreciate the nature and quality or the wrongfulness of her acts.

(C) At the time of the killing, D was mentally ill.

(D) At the time of the killing, D suffered from psychosis.

Prosecution of D for sexual molestation of V, a child. D denies committing the crime. At trial, V testifies about the molestation.

352. D calls Dr. W, a psychiatrist, to testify that based on her observations of V for several hours under various circumstances, she has concluded that V suffers from a psychiatric disorder that causes V to fantasize a great deal. On the basis of Dr. W's testimony, D moves to strike V's testimony. Which of the following is correct?

(A) The court should strike V's testimony because the testimony concerns the existence or non-existence of a mental state.

(B) The court should allow the jury to determine whether V is competent to testify, and instruct the jury to ignore V's testimony if it finds him incompetent.

(C) The court should not strike V's testimony but should allow Dr. W's testimony to impeach V's credibility if the court finds that Dr. W is a qualified expert and that the testimony is based on information of a type on which experts in the field rely.

(D) The court should not permit Dr. W to testify because this is not a situation in which expert testimony is permitted.

Negligence action by P against D arising from a motorcycle collision. P claims serious emotional injuries as a result of the accident. D denies that P suffered any such injuries. To prove her injuries, P wishes to call W, a psychiatrist.

353. From which of the following sources may W learn the facts or data that form the basis of her opinion?

(A) Personal observations and testing of P.

(B) Tests performed by a clinical psychologist.

(C) A hypothetical question posed to W before or during W's testimony.

(D) All of the above are permissible sources of information.

Product liability action by P action against D, manufacturer of an implantable medical device designed to regulate pancreas function. A surgeon implanted the device in P, and P later developed pancreatic cancer. P claims the device was the cause of the cancer. To prove causation, P calls W, a Ph.D. in biochemistry who works for a major university. If permitted, W will testify that based on certain animal studies she conducted on D's device, she has concluded that the device can cause pancreatic cancer. D objects to W's proposed testimony on the ground that it is not valid science.

354. If the action is tried in a state court that follows the *Frye* test, which of the following best states the principle the court should use in ruling on the admissibility of W's testimony?

(A) W's testimony will only be admissible if the court finds that it is based on a theory or method that is generally accepted in the relevant scientific community.

(B) W's testimony will only be admissible if the court finds that there is evidence sufficient to support a conclusion that it is based on a reliable scientific theory or method and that the application of the theory or method is relevant to the case.

(C) W's testimony will only be admissible if the court finds that it is based on a reliable scientific theory or method and that the application of the theory or method is relevant to the case.

(D) W's testimony will only be admissible if it is based on a theory or method that has been subjected to publication and peer review.

355. If the action is tried in federal court, which of the following best states the principle the court should use in ruling on the admissibility of W's testimony?

(A) W's testimony will only be admissible if the court finds that it is based on a theory or method that is generally accepted in the relevant scientific community.

(B) W's testimony will only be admissible if the court finds that there is evidence sufficient to support a conclusion that it is based on a reliable scientific theory or method and that the application of the theory or method is relevant to the case.

(C) W's testimony will only be admissible if the court finds that it is based on a reliable scientific theory or method and that the application of the theory or method is relevant to the case.

(D) W's testimony will only be admissible if it is based on a theory or method that has been subjected to publication and peer review.

356. Assume the trial court applies the *Daubert* standard and holds that the testimony of W is inadmissible. D prevails, and P appeals. Based on the standard of review applicable to this situation, discuss the likelihood of P obtaining a reversal.

ANSWER:

Questions

Practice Final Exam

This exam has two parts. The first part consists of multiple choice questions. The second part is a series of short answer questions. Try to answer all questions in no more than two hours.

Part I:
Multiple Choice Questions

Prosecution of D for robbing a yogurt shop. D claims that the police arrested the wrong person. To prove that he was not at the shop at the time of the robbery, D calls W, a police officer, and shows W a document that W identifies as a report she made of an interview conducted at D's home on an unrelated matter, and notes that it records a date and time of the interview that correspond to the time of the yogurt shop robbery. W further testifies that she is required to make and file reports of all citizen interviews.

357. Which of the following statements is most accurate?

(A) The document may be read into the record under the doctrine of refreshing recollection.

(B) The document is hearsay but is admissible under the recorded recollection exception.

(C) The document is hearsay but is admissible as a public record.

(D) The document is inadmissible.

Libel action by P against D, the publisher of a newspaper. P claims that D published an article calling P a "notorious gangster," which P claims is completely false. At trial, P wishes to testify about the allegedly libelous statements in the article.

358. Which of the following statements is most accurate?

(A) Though P's testimony is not hearsay, it is inadmissible because it violates the best evidence rule.

(B) P's testimony violates the best evidence rule and constitutes inadmissible hearsay.

(C) P's testimony does not violate the best evidence rule but constitutes inadmissible hearsay.

(D) P's testimony is admissible.

Prosecution of D for armed robbery of a bank. The prosecution alleges that D and several colleagues, all wearing red, white, and blue berets, entered the bank carrying shotguns, forced the tellers to perform a specific dance, then took all the $5, $10, and $20 bills from the cash drawers. D denies participating in the robbery. The prosecution wishes to offer evidence that three years before this event, D robbed another bank in the same way. D denies involvement in the earlier robbery as well.

359. Which of the following statements is most accurate?

    (A) The trial judge must determine whether there is sufficient evidence from which the jury could conclude that D took part in the first robbery. If the court believes sufficient evidence exists, the judge must allow the jury to hear about that event.

    (B) The trial judge must determine whether there is sufficient evidence from which the jury could conclude that D took part in the first robbery. Even if such evidence exists, the judge must still determine its relevance to the crime for which D is charged and whether the probative value of the evidence is substantially outweighed by the danger of unfair prejudice.

    (C) The trial judge must determine whether D took part in the first robbery, but even if it makes that finding, the judge must still determine its relevance to the crime for which D is charged and whether the probative value of the evidence is substantially outweighed by the danger of unfair prejudice.

    (D) Because the first robbery is not sufficiently similar to the act for which D has been charged, the evidence is inadmissible.

Prosecution of D for bank robbery. At trial, the prosecution calls W, who testifies that an hour after the robbery, she was riding on a bus and saw D, whom she knew. If permitted, W will then testify that she walked up to D, said "That was quite a bank job you pulled off today," and that D laughed. D makes a hearsay objection to W's testimony concerning her out-of-court statement to D and D's response.

360. Which of the following constitutes the prosecution's strongest argument in favor of admissibility?

    (A) W's statement is hearsay but admissible as an excited utterance.

    (B) W's statement is hearsay but admissible as a present sense impression.

    (C) Standing alone, W's statement is inadmissible hearsay. However, D's response makes both statements admissible as a declaration against interest.

    (D) Standing alone, W's statement is inadmissible hearsay. However, by his response, D adopted W's statement, making it admissible as an adoptive admission.

Prosecution of D1 and D2 for stealing V's wallet as V was waiting to cross a busy street. The prosecution alleges that defendants accomplished their crime by having D1 stand in front of V at a busy downtown intersection, while D2 stood behind V. When the "Walk" signal went on, D1 allegedly started to cross, and then stopped suddenly, causing V to bump into D1. While V was distracted by this event, D2 allegedly reached into V's back pocket and removed his wallet. This is a common scheme used by pickpockets. D1 and D2 were found in possession of V's wallet, but claim they picked it up on the street and were planning to return it. At trial, the prosecution wishes to offer evidence that when they were arrested, D1 and D2 were found to possess two other wallets that had been reported stolen by their owners several weeks earlier. D1 and D2 claim they were planning to return these wallets also, and object to admission of this evidence.

361. Which of the following statements is most likely correct?

(A) The evidence is admissible to show intent.

(B) The evidence is admissible to establish the identity of the pickpockets by means of showing *modus operandi*.

(C) The evidence is admissible to establish a habit of stealing wallets which was likely repeated in this instance.

(D) The evidence is inadmissible.

Personal injury action by P against D arising out of a skateboard accident. P alleges that the accident caused him permanent, painful impairment of his right leg. At trial, D calls Dr. W, the physician who treated P for the injuries she sustained in the accident. Dr. W proves to be antagonistic to D's questions, so the court permits D to proceed with leading questions. D asks Dr. W whether it isn't true that when P first consulted her, P said his right leg "isn't hurting too badly." P objects.

362. Which of the following statements is most likely true?

(A) P's statement is not hearsay and is not subject to any privilege.

(B) P's statement is inadmissible hearsay and is subject to the physician-patient privilege.

(C) P's statement is not hearsay but is subject to the physician-patient privilege.

(D) P's statement is admissible hearsay and is not subject to any privilege.

Prosecution of D for assault with a deadly weapon on V. At trial, the prosecution calls several witnesses who testify that D and V were standing next to each other at a bar when suddenly and without provocation, D punched V in the stomach. D then testifies that he only punched V after seeing that V was about to bash him with a large moose head which V had dislodged from the wall. D then wishes to call W to testify that in the lobby of the courthouse during jury selection, D told W that V had attacked D with a moose head.

363. Which of the following constitutes the court's most likely ruling?

(A) W's testimony is only admissible to establish that D acted in self-defense.

(B) W's testimony is only admissible to establish D's credibility by virtue of prior conduct evidencing a character for truthfulness.

    (C) W's testimony is admissible both to establish that D acted in self-defense and to establish D's credibility.

    (D) W's testimony is inadmissible.

Prosecution of D for murder. D claims she was in another country when the crime was committed. At trial, the prosecution wishes to offer into evidence a transcript of a meeting between D and her lawyer. D objects that the transcript is subject to the attorney-client privilege. The prosecution responds that the privilege does not apply because of the crime-fraud exception. Assume the transcript of the conversation was obtained legally.

364. Which of the following statements is most accurate?

    (A) Without any showing by the prosecution, the court may conduct an *in camera* hearing to determine the admissibility of the transcript. At the hearing, the court will not be bound by the rules of evidence.

    (B) Without any showing by the prosecution, the court may conduct an *in camera* hearing to determine the admissibility of the transcript. At the hearing, the court may consider any evidence, admissible or not, except evidence which has been claimed to be privileged.

    (C) If the prosecution produces evidence sufficient to support a reasonable belief that an *in camera* review may yield evidence showing that the crime or fraud exception applies, the court may conduct an *in camera* hearing to determine the admissibility of the transcript. At that hearing, the court may consider any evidence it wishes.

    (D) If the prosecution produces evidence sufficient to support a reasonable belief that an *in camera* review may yield evidence showing that the crime or fraud exception applies, the court may conduct an *in camera* hearing to determine the admissibility of the transcript. At that hearing, the court may consider any evidence except material that has been found privileged.

Prosecution of D for setting a brushfire that destroyed hundreds of canyon homes. D claims it was X, rather than he, who set the fires. At trial, D calls W to testify that a week before the fires started, X, a close friend of W, told W to take all her valuables out of her canyon home.

365. Which of the following statements is most accurate?

    (A) X's statement would be admissible as an admission under the Federal Rules.

    (B) X's statement would be admissible non-hearsay under the Federal Rules.

    (C) X's statement would be admissible non-hearsay under a declarant-based definition of hearsay.

    (D) X's statement would be admissible non-hearsay under both the Federal Rules and a declarant-based definition of hearsay.

Prosecution of D for theft of a series of valuable bicycles that were chained together in a parking lot. D claims she had nothing to do with the theft. At trial, the prosecution wishes to call W, D's husband, to ask W whether D told him on the night of the crime that she had participated in it.

366. Which of the following statements is most accurate?

    (A) If D objects to W's testimony on privilege grounds, W may not testify even if she is willing to do so.

    (B) Even if D does not object on privilege grounds, D can raise a successful hearsay objection to W's testimony.

    (C) If W does not claim his privilege, D cannot prevent W from testifying.

    (D) Because no privilege is applicable to these facts, W must answer the question even if he does not wish to do so, and even if D objects.

Prosecution of D for the murder of V. D admits killing V, but claims that she acted in self-defense when V attacked her. To prove that V attacked D, D wishes to offer evidence that V had a community reputation as a violent person. D was unaware of this fact at the time she killed V.

367. Which of the following statements is most accurate?

    (A) Because D was unaware of the story about V at the time she killed V, the evidence is irrelevant.

    (B) Even though D was unaware of the story about V at the time she killed V, the evidence is relevant and admissible to show that V was the first aggressor in the fight.

    (C) The evidence is relevant but is an improper attempt to impeach V.

    (D) The evidence is relevant but is an improper attempt to use character evidence to prove V's out of court conduct.

Wrongful death action by P against D Corp. arising out of a collision between a D Corp. truck and P's car. Several people including P's deceased were killed in the crash. P alleges that the driver of the D Corp. truck was drunk at the time of the accident. At trial, P calls W to testify that the day after the collision, X, an officer of D Corp., called the spouse of P's deceased and said, "I speak for the company when I tell you how sorry we are about this accident. We plan to review our procedures for enforcing our policy against alcohol consumption by truck drivers." D Corp. makes a hearsay objection to this testimony.

368. Which of the following statements is most accurate?

    (A) If the trial court finds that X was authorized to speak for the company, the statement is admissible as an authorized admission.

    (B) Because X is not a party and no hearsay exception applies, X's statement is inadmissible hearsay.

(C) When deciding whether to admit the statement, the court may not take the statement itself into account in determining if X had authority to speak for D Corp.

(D) If the court finds that a reasonable jury could decide that X had authority to speak for D Corp., the court should admit the statement.

Prosecution of D for the murder of V. At trial, the prosecution calls W, and wishes to have her testify that she was with V just before he died, and that V winced in pain, pulled W close to his face, and whispered, "I know this is the end. D did this to me." D objects to this statement on grounds its admission would violate her 6th Amendment right to confront the witnesses against her.

369. Which of the following statements is most accurate?

(A) If the court determines that the statement satisfies the dying declaration exception and that the circumstances of its making demonstrate its reliability, the court should admit the statement.

(B) If the court determines that the statement satisfies the dying declaration exception and that D's guilt is corroborated by other evidence, the court should admit the statement.

(C) If the court determines that the statement satisfies the dying declaration exception, the court should admit the statement.

(D) Because the defendant never had an opportunity to confront V, the court should not admit the statement.

Negligence action by P against D arising from a car accident. At trial, P calls W, a police officer, who testifies that she arrived at the scene moments after the accident and saw X, a bystander, sitting on the curb sobbing uncontrollably. When she walked up to X, X immediately screamed, "That red car just ran right through the light and cut that blue car in half!" D makes a hearsay objection, and P responds that the evidence is admissible under the excited utterance exception. D then offers to prove by W2, another witness to the accident, that just before X made the statement to the police officer (but still after the accident), X was chatting with W2 about the weather.

370. Which of the following statements is most accurate?

(A) The court must sustain D's objection because X's statement concerning the accident does not satisfy the excited utterance exception.

(B) The court will admit both of X's statements and instruct the jury that if it finds that X's statement concerning the accident was made under the stress of excitement caused by the accident, it should consider the statement, but if it finds that X's statement was not made under such stress, it must disregard the statement.

(C) The court will determine whether X's statement concerning the accident was made under the stress of excitement caused by the accident. If it finds that it was, the court will admit that statement and exclude the earlier statement concerning the weather, which is irrelevant.

(D) The court will determine whether X's statement concerning the accident was made under the stress of excitement caused by the accident. If it finds that it was, the court will admit the statement as an excited utterance, but will also admit the earlier statement concerning the weather.

Prosecution of D for running a house of prostitution. At trial, the prosecution calls W, a police officer who took part in the raid on D's establishment. The prosecution wishes to have W testify that moments after the raid began, the phone rang three times, and on each occasion, the caller asked to make an appointment with a particular woman at a particular time that evening.

371. Which of the following statements is most accurate?

(A) The callers' statements are more likely to be classified as hearsay under the assertion-based definition of hearsay than under the declarant-based definition.

(B) The callers' statements are more likely to be classified as hearsay under the declarant-based definition of hearsay than under the assertion-based definition.

(C) The callers' statements are hearsay under either definition.

(D) Because the police officer is on the stand and subject to cross-examination, the callers' statements are not hearsay under either definition.

Negligence action by P against D arising out of an automobile collision. As part of her case-in-chief, P calls D to the stand. During the direct examination of D, P's attorney asks, "Isn't it true that at the time of the accident, you were going 65 miles per hour?"

372. Which of the following statements about this question is accurate?

(A) The question is leading but proper.

(B) The question is an improper leading question.

(C) The question is not leading and is proper.

(D) The question is not leading but assumes a fact not in evidence.

Prosecution of D for the murder of V. D claims he killed V in self-defense after V viciously attacked D with a knife. At trial, D calls W to testify that she is well-acquainted with V's community reputation, and that V had a reputation as a very violent person.

373. Which of the following statements is most accurate?

(A) The evidence is inadmissible because it is irrelevant.

(B) The evidence constitutes inadmissible hearsay.

(C) The evidence is inadmissible because D is not permitted to offer character evidence in this situation.

(D) The evidence is admissible.

Prosecution of D for burglary. D fears that if he chooses to testify at trial, the prosecution will seek to impeach his credibility by cross-examining him about a prior burglary conviction. Before trial, D makes a motion *in limine* to prevent the prosecution's use of the prior conviction. The court denies the motion. D does not take the stand at trial and is convicted. D has now appealed on the basis that the court should have granted his motion *in limine*.

374. Which of the following constitutes the prosecution's strongest response to D's claim?

(A) The trial court was correct to deny D's motion because it had no discretion to exclude this relevant evidence.

(B) The determination of whether to admit this evidence rests solely with the sound discretion of the trial court, and that court's decision may not be overturned on review.

(C) Because D did not take the stand at trial, D may not raise this issue on appeal.

(D) Because it would be a denial of due process to refuse to allow the prosecution to offer this impeaching evidence, the trial court's ruling was clearly correct and should not be overturned on appeal.

Prosecution of D for embezzlement from V, D's employer. At trial, D testifies that she never took any money from V. On cross-examination, the prosecutor wishes to ask D to acknowledge that three years ago, D was convicted of misdemeanor perjury.

375. Which of the following statements is most accurate?

(A) This evidence is admissible only to impeach D's credibility.

(B) This evidence is admissible both to impeach D's credibility and to establish that D is the kind of person who would embezzle.

(C) This evidence is admissible only to impeach D and only if the probative value of the evidence outweighs the danger of unfair prejudice to D.

(D) This evidence is inadmissible.

Fraud action by P against D, a used car seller, arising from the sale of a car. P claims D advertised the car as new when in fact its odometer had been set back to zero from 5,000 miles. Prior to trial, P took the deposition of W, D's sales manager. During the deposition, which was taken under oath, W admitted that the seller sometimes set back odometers on cars before they were sold. At trial, *D* calls W, who testifies that he "preps" all cars for D and that no odometers were ever set back while W worked for D. On cross-examination, P asks W whether he remembers having his deposition taken and stating that odometers sometimes were set back. W admits to having had his deposition taken but denies making the statement. P wishes to read into evidence that portion of W's deposition transcript containing W's statement that odometers sometimes were set back.

376. Which of the following statements is most accurate?

(A) The portion of the transcript is admissible only to impeach W's credibility.

(B) The portion of the transcript is admissible both to impeach W's credibility and to prove that the odometer was set back.

(C) The portion of the transcript is inadmissible for either purpose because W is not unavailable.

(D) The portion of the transcript is inadmissible for either purpose unless D's lawyer cross-examined W at the deposition.

Prosecution of D for car theft. At trial, the prosecution calls W, the custodian of records for D's employer. W is shown a document which W identifies as D's personnel record. That record contains the statement, "Following investigation, it has been determined that D has been stealing office supplies from our storeroom. Personnel has notified D of this finding and informed D that any further infractions will result in immediate termination." W testifies that written personnel records are kept of each employee, and that items in each record are written by individuals with personal knowledge of the matters recorded.

377. Which of the following statements is most accurate?

(A) The document is admissible as a business record.

(B) The document is inadmissible because it is irrelevant.

(C) The document is hearsay and fails to satisfy the business records exception.

(D) The document satisfies the business records exception and is relevant, but is inadmissible.

Prosecution of D for burglarizing V's home. At trial, the prosecution calls V to testify about the items he found missing after the break-in. V can remember some of the items, but not all. The prosecutor then shows V a document listing all missing items, asks V to read it to himself, takes it back, and asks V if he now remembers what else what missing. V says he does. The prosecutor then wants V to list the other missing items.

378. Which of the following statements is most accurate?

(A) Because V has not laid the proper foundation for the recorded recollection exception, V should not be permitted to list the other missing items.

(B) Because the document is offered against a defendant in a criminal case, it is inadmissible.

(C) Because the document has not been shown to have been prepared in the ordinary course of business, it is inadmissible.

(D) V will be allowed to list the other missing items.

D drove a car that struck and killed V as V was crossing a street. P, the administrator of V's estate, sued D for wrongful death. At trial, P called W, who testified that he was standing on a street corner near where the accident took place and saw D run a red light and strike V in a crosswalk. The jury returned a verdict for P. Within the limitations period, the state decides to prosecute D for involuntary manslaughter. At trial, W raises a wholly improper "privacy" claim and refuses to testify even when ordered by the trial court. The prosecution therefore wishes to offer in evidence the transcript of W's testimony in the earlier trial.

379. Which of the following statements is most likely correct?

(A) Because the prosecution cannot succeed without W's testimony, the transcript is admissible.

(B) Because the transcript is admissible hearsay and its use does not violate the Confrontation Clause, the transcript is admissible.

(C) Because W is available to testify, the transcript is inadmissible.

(D) Because the civil trial came first, D's confrontation rights would be violated if the transcript were used. Therefore, the transcript is inadmissible.

Proceeding for injunctive relief brought by the state of Muckaska against Messon Oil Co. to compel Messon to complete the cleanup of Muckaska beaches which were badly soiled when a Messon Oil tanker ran aground and spilled millions of gallons of crude into a pristine bay. To prove that Messon does not intend to resume cleanup operations after the winter season, Muckaska offers evidence that at the end of the warm season, Messon's public relations officer held a press conference in which she stated, "Mission Accomplished! We think the entire bay is prettier and cleaner than ever!"

380. Which of the following constitutes Muckaska's strongest argument for admissibility of this statement?

(A) The statement is hearsay but admissible as a declaration against interest.

(B) The statement is hearsay but admissible as an excited utterance.

(C) The statement is not hearsay because it is not offered to prove the truth of the matter asserted.

(D) The statement is admissible as an authorized admission.

Prosecution of D for murder. At trial, D testifies that she was in another country when the crime took place. D also calls W1 to testify that she was with D at that time. On rebuttal, the prosecution wishes to call W2 to testify that W1 has been D's lover for five years.

381. Which of the following statements is most accurate?

(A) W2's testimony is admissible to impeach W1 by showing that she has a bad character for truthfulness.

(B) W2's testimony is admissible to impeach W1 by showing that W1 has a reason to testify in D's favor.

(C) W2's testimony is admissible to impeach W1 by contradiction.

(D) W2's testimony is inadmissible.

Slander action by P, the owner of an art gallery, against D. P alleges D gave a public speech in which she asserted that P was a "well-known art forger." At trial, D testifies that she was not the person who made the speech. Also during the trial, P calls W, who testifies that he was in the audience during the speech but because he was not wearing his glasses, he could not see the speaker clearly. However, W testifies that he made a tape recording of the speech on a very high-quality machine and brought it to court with him. P wishes to play for the jury that portion of the tape recording in which the speaker calls P a "well-known art forger."

382. Which of the following statements is most accurate?

(A) If the court finds that the jury, comparing the voice on the tape with D's, could conclude that the voice is D's, the court should allow the jury to hear the tape.

(B) If the court finds that the voice on the tape is D's, the court should allow the jury to hear the tape.

(C) Even if the tape has been authenticated, the court must not allow the jury to hear the tape because it constitutes inadmissible hearsay.

(D) Because P did not call an expert to identify the voice on the tape as D's, the court must not allow the jury to hear the tape.

Prosecution of four police officers for using excessive force when arresting V. A witness recorded the incident on videotape. The tape, played for the jury, clearly shows the officers inflicting more than forty blows on V with night sticks, and kicking V as well. At trial, the officers each take the stand in their own defense, and none deny that the blows were inflicted on V. Despite what appears to be overwhelming evidence of guilt, the jury acquits the officers of the criminal charges.

383. Which of the following statements is accurate?

(A) The prosecution may ask the court to set aside the verdicts of acquittal and order a new trial on the basis that the verdicts are against the overwhelming weight of the evidence.

(B) The prosecution is entitled to a hearing at which it will present affidavits of jurors that demonstrate that the jury ignored crucial evidence.

(C) The prosecution is entitled to a hearing at which it will present affidavits of jurors that demonstrate that the jury ignored the court's jury instructions.

(D) The prosecution has no recourse.

Negligence action by P against D after P's bicycle and D's bicycle collided. At trial, P testifies that D was riding with "no hands" and lost control of his bike when he hit some sand on the road. D testifies that both of his hands were on the handlebars. P wishes to call W to testify that he has gone on bicycle rides with D at least 20 times, and that on each occasion D rode for at least part of the time with "no hands."

384. Which of the following constitutes P's strongest argument in favor of the admissibility of W's testimony?

(A) The evidence is admissible to show that D is a careless bicycle rider.

(B) The evidence is admissible to show that D habitually rides with "no hands."

(C) The evidence is admissible impeachment by contradiction.

(D) The evidence is admissible to establish D's intent to ride with "no hands."

Prosecution of D for child molestation. At trial, the prosecution calls W, the 10-year-old alleged victim. After establishing W's competency to testify, the prosecution asks W about the alleged assault. W states that he cannot remember what happened. The prosecution then asks W, "Now, you went to an apartment with D, didn't you?"

385. Which of the following statements concerning this question is most accurate?

(A) The question is leading but proper.

(B) The question is not leading and is proper.

(C) The question is leading and improper.

(D) The question is argumentative, compound, and improper.

Prosecution of D for bank robbery committed by use of a sophisticated and little-known safe-cracking technique. The prosecution wishes to offer evidence that twice before, D robbed other banks using the same technique. D claims that he was in another state when the charged crime took place.

386. Which of the following statements is most accurate?

(A) The evidence is irrelevant and therefore inadmissible.

(B) The evidence is irrelevant because its probative value is substantially outweighed by the danger of unfair prejudice to D.

(C) The evidence is relevant because the fact that D committed bank robberies on other occasions using this unusual technique makes it somewhat more likely that he was the one who committed the robbery for which he is being tried. Therefore, the evidence is admissible.

(D) The evidence is relevant for the reasons explained in answer (C), but the court may exclude the evidence if it finds that the probative value is substantially outweighed by the danger of unfair prejudice.

Negligence action by P against D Construction Co. arising out of a collision between P's car and a truck driven by W, an employee of D. At trial, the jury found for P, and the court entered judgment accordingly. However, D appealed and the appellate court reversed because of errors unrelated to evidence issues and remanded for a new trial. Unfortunately for P, W died before the second trial could be held. At the first trial, P had called W as an adverse witness, and W admitted that she ran a red light, causing the collision. At the second trial, P calls X, a friend who was in the courtroom during the entire first trial. If permitted, X will testify that W gave this testimony at the first trial.

387. Which of the following statements is most accurate?

(A) Because the transcript, and not X's testimony, is the best evidence of W's testimony at the first trial, X's testimony is inadmissible.

(B) Because W was called as an adverse witness and D would have no motive to conduct a searching cross-examination, the transcript is inadmissible.

(C) Because W's testimony is so central to the case that it would be unfair to D to allow it to be entered into evidence, the transcript is inadmissible.

(D) X's testimony is admissible.

Paternity action by P against D. D claims that he was not the father of the child. Assume that the following rebuttable presumption applies: *A child born within ten months of the last date on which a male and female were cohabiting is rebuttably presumed to have been fathered by the male.* Assume that this is the only presumption that applies in the case. Assume further that this action is being tried in a jurisdiction that adheres to the minority (Morgan/McCormick) theory of presumptions. At trial, P testifies that she and D cohabited continuously for five years and only stopped living together one month before the baby was born. D, in turn, calls an expert witness who testifies that she performed blood tests on D and on the child, and determined that D could not have fathered the child. At the close of all evidence, P's attorney asks the court to instruct the jury that if it finds that the child was born within ten months of the last date on which P and D were cohabiting, it must find that D was the father unless D persuades the jury that he was not.

388. Which of the following statements is most accurate?

(A) If the court finds that P has produced sufficient evidence to meet her burden of production on the foundational facts, the court should issue the instruction.

(B) If the court finds that all of the foundational facts are true, the court should issue the instruction.

(C) If the court finds that D's expert has produced sufficient evidence on which the jury could find that D could not have been the father of the child, the court should not issue the instruction.

(D) If the court decides that the expert is correct that D could not have been the father of the child, the court should not issue the instruction.

Prosecution of D for murder. D admits killing the victim but claims she was insane at the time she did so.

389. Which of the following may serve as the basis of an expert psychiatrist's testimony concerning the psychiatric condition of a criminal defendant?

(A) The witness's pre-testimony psychiatric treatment of defendant.

(B) The defendant's "raw scores" on a battery of psychological tests performed by another expert who testified about those tests prior to this witness's testimony.

(C) A hypothetical question posed by counsel to the psychiatrist on the stand, which is based on facts supported by testimony in the case.

(D) All of the above are permissible bases of the psychiatrist's testimony.

Prosecution of D for child molestation. At trial, the prosecution calls W, the 5-year-old alleged victim. Prior to taking testimony about the event, the judge takes W into her chambers, along with the attorneys, D, and the court reporter. The judge then asks W whether he understands what it means to tell the "truth." W says he does. After probing this issue in more detail, the judge asks W whether he understands that he must tell the truth when they go back into the courtroom. W says he does. The group then returns to the courtroom, where the prosecution questions W concerning the facts of the case.

390. Which of the following statements concerning the proceedings in the judge's chambers is most accurate?

(A) Because FRE 602 does away with all tests of witness competency, the judge acted improperly in questioning W before taking his testimony.

(B) Because the child's competency to testify has not been determined beyond a reasonable doubt, the court has committed error by permitting him to testify to the facts of the case.

(C) Because a 5-year-old is unable to truly understand the concept of "truth" and the obligation to tell the truth when under oath, the court has committed error by permitting W to testify to the facts of the case.

(D) The court acted properly.

Negligence action by P against D, the owner of the amusement park Sidneyland. P claims that the "Bar Tours" ride was not properly maintained, causing her to be injured when it lurched forward suddenly, pitching her out of the vehicle. D claims that there was nothing wrong with the ride, and that P must have stood up while the vehicle was moving. P denies doing so. At trial, P wishes to call W to testify that he went on the ride a week before the accident, that he was sitting in his seat in the proper manner, and that the vehicle lurched forward suddenly, nearly throwing him out. The ride is indoors, and had not been altered between the two events.

391. Which of the following statements concerning W's testimony is most accurate?

(A) The evidence is admissible to show a similar event under similar circumstances, making it more likely that the accident happened as P claims.

(B) The evidence is admissible to show that D tends to be careless in maintaining the "Bar Tours" ride, making it more likely that the accident happened as P claims.

(C) The evidence is admissible to show that D habitually fails to maintain the "Bar Tours" ride.

(D) The evidence is inadmissible.

Medical malpractice action by P against D after D performed unsuccessful brain surgery on P. At trial, P calls Dr. W to prove that D failed to use proper surgical techniques. P's attorney establishes Dr. W's experience, but D's attorney objects to Dr. W's testifying as an expert, claiming that she has not been shown to be an expert on the matters involved in this case. The court hears arguments concerning D's objection and then sustains the objection, refusing to allow Dr. W to testify on P's behalf. P has no other experts waiting in the wings to testify.

392. Which of the following represents P's best course of action?

(A) P's attorney should ask to have the jury excused and then should make a record of what Dr. W would have said if she had been permitted to testify.

(B) P's attorney has already placed on the record his response to D's objection. This preserves the point for appeal.

(C) P's attorney should ask that the court allow Dr. W to testify after reminding the jury that it must disregard his testimony if it finds him unqualified as an expert in the matters involved in this case.

(D) P's attorney should threaten to gather up her marbles and go home unless the court changes its mind.

Libel action by P against D. P alleges that D wrote a letter to a newspaper stating that P was a "major drug kingpin." D denies writing any such letter. At trial, P offers the letter in evidence. The letter bears D's name on the signature line. In addition, P offers a letter containing a signature which D admits to be his.

393. Which of the following statements is most accurate?

(A) Because P has not called a handwriting expert to compare the signatures and offer an opinion, no reasonable jury could find that the signature was D's, and the court should exclude the letter.

(B) Because P has not called a handwriting expert to compare the signatures and offer an opinion, P has not offered enough evidence for the court to find that the signature on the letter is genuine, and the court should exclude the letter.

(C) Even without expert testimony, the court may determine that there is sufficient evidence from which the jury can decide that the letter is genuine, and the court can therefore admit the letter.

(D) Even without expert testimony, the court may decide that the signature is genuine and admit the letter.

P sues D, a private elementary school, for negligence following an accident in which P was struck by a car while trying to cross a street in front of the school. P does not base her claim on the theory of respondeat superior, but rather on the theory that D was itself negligent for retaining an unreliable employee. D admits that its crossing guard was absent on that occasion, but denies any negligence in hiring or retaining the guard. At trial, P wishes to offer evidence that the guard had been absent twice in the previous month.

394. Which of the following statements is most likely correct?

   (A) If offered to prove the guard was absent on the day of the accident, the evidence is relevant and admissible.

   (B) If offered to prove D had notice that the guard was unreliable, the evidence is irrelevant because the number of past absences is insufficient to establish a pattern. Therefore, the evidence is inadmissible.

   (C) If offered to prove that the guard was unreliable, and that D had notice of this fact, the evidence is relevant and admissible.

   (D) If offered to prove D had notice that the guard was unreliable, the evidence is relevant, but the court must exclude it because its low probative value is substantially outweighed by the danger of unfair prejudice.

Civil action by P against D arising out of a business dispute. At trial, P calls W, whose testimony helps to establish P's version of the facts. On cross-examination, D wishes to ask W if it isn't true that W has sued D's spouse in an unrelated matter. W denies that this is true. D now wishes to call X, the court clerk, to testify that W has indeed filed such an action.

395. Which of the following statements is most accurate?

   (A) X's testimony should not be permitted because the existence of a lawsuit between W and D's spouse is irrelevant to the present case.

   (B) X's testimony should not be permitted because it would constitute impermissible use of extrinsic evidence to impeach.

   (C) X's testimony should not be permitted because it would constitute improper use of specific instances of the conduct of a witness to impeach the witness's credibility.

   (D) X's testimony is admissible.

Wrongful death action by P, administrator of V's estate, against D. P alleges that V was walking on a sidewalk adjacent to a construction site when he was crushed by a steel crane which fell onto the sidewalk. D admits that V was struck by the crane, but claims that at the time, V was trespassing on the construction site. (The position of V's body following the accident leaves doubt as to where he had been walking.) To prove that V was on the sidewalk outside of the construction site, P calls W to testify that as he was lying on the ground just before he died, V told W, "I've had it! You aren't safe anymore on the sidewalks of the city." D makes a hearsay objection to this evidence.

396. Which of the following statements is most accurate?

(A) Because the statement is relevant and is not offered to prove the truth of the matter asserted, it is admissible non-hearsay.

(B) The statement is hearsay and does not satisfy the dying declarations exception because it does not concern the causes or circumstances of V's impending death.

(C) The statement is hearsay, but if the court finds that V believed he was about to die when he made the statement and that the statement concerns the cause or circumstances of what V believed to be his impending death, it will be admissible under the dying declarations exception.

(D) The statement is hearsay, but if the court finds that there is evidence sufficient to support a finding that V believed he was about to die when he made the statement, it will be admissible under the dying declarations exception.

Prosecution of D for the murder of V. D admits shooting V but claims she acted in self-defense when V advanced on her with a knife.

397. To disprove self-defense, the prosecution offers in evidence a series of photographs showing the blood-covered body of V along with several easily perceptible bullet entry wounds in the back of the head. Which of the following is correct?

(A) The court will most likely exclude the photographs because D's admission to killing V renders them irrelevant.

(B) The court will most likely exclude the photographs because, even if relevant, their probative value is substantially outweighed by the danger of unfair prejudice.

(C) The court will most likely exclude the photographs because the prosecutor's purpose in offering the photographs is to inflame the passions of the jury.

(D) The court will most likely admit the photographs.

Prosecution of D for knowingly passing a counterfeit $50 bill at a department store. D denies knowing the bill was fake.

398. The prosecution calls W to testify that a month before the charged event, D tried to spend the same bill at W's liquor store and that W told D he wouldn't take it because it was phony. Which of the following is correct?

(A) W's testimony about the liquor store incident is admissible only if D knew the bill was fake when she gave it to W.

(B) W's testimony about the liquor store incident is inadmissible because the circumstances of the charged and uncharged events were not similar enough.

(C) W's testimony about the liquor store incident is admissible unless the probative value of the evidence is substantially outweighed by the danger of unfair prejudice.

(D) W's testimony about the liquor store incident is inadmissible hearsay.

Action by P, a mail order video retailer, against D for refusing to pay for 20 videos. D admits ordering the videos but claims she canceled the order within the time allotted and did not receive them. To prove she followed proper procedures, D testifies that she phoned P's published number, that a person answered, "Videos," and that the person stated that the order would be cancelled.

399. Which of the following statements concerning D's testimony about the phone conversation is correct?

(A) The testimony relates inadmissible hearsay.

(B) The testimony is inadmissible unless D testifies that she recognized the voice.

(C) The testimony is inadmissible because the best evidence of D's cancellation is P's record of the call, not D's recollection of the phone conversation.

(D) The testimony is admissible.

Negligence action by P against D following a freeway pile-up. P claims D was going 85 mph at the time of impact. D claims she was traveling no faster than 50. To prove she was not speeding, D testifies that just before impact, she looked at her speedometer, and that it registered 50 mph.

400. Which of the following statements is correct?

(A) D's testimony is inadmissible hearsay.

(B) D's testimony is inadmissible because of lack of authentication.

(C) D's testimony is inadmissible because of the best evidence rule.

(D) D's testimony is admissible.

Prosecution of D for assault and battery on V. D claims V started the fight and that D struck back in self-defense.

401. To prove V started the fight, D calls W to testify that she is familiar with V's community reputation for violence, which is that she is short-tempered and belligerent. Which of the following statements is correct?

(A) W's testimony concerning V's reputation is both inadmissible hearsay and inadmissible character evidence.

(B) W's testimony concerning V's reputation is not hearsay but inadmissible character evidence.

(C) W's testimony concerning V's reputation is admissible.

(D) W's testimony concerning V's reputation is admissible only if the prosecution has placed V's character in issue.

Negligence action by P, a concert-goer, against D, a rock guitarist, after P was injured by sparks flying from D's Stratocaster guitar. P testifies without objection that a few days after the concert, she received a letter signed by D stating, "Those sparks really hurt you. I hope you're feeling better."

402. During his case-in-chief, D wishes to read to the jury another part of the same letter in which D wrote, "If you hadn't run onto the stage while I was playing, you wouldn't have been hurt." Which of the following statements about D's proposed testimony is most accurate?

    (A) The court should exclude the testimony because it constitutes inadmissible hearsay.

    (B) Even though the testimony is hearsay for which no exception applies, the court should admit it because its probative value substantially outweighs any danger of unfair prejudice.

    (C) The court should admit D's proposed testimony as a party admission.

    (D) The court should admit the testimony under the completeness doctrine.

P sues D after a freeway collision. Each claims the other caused the accident. At trial, P authenticates and offers into evidence a letter from D. In it, D states, "I know this was my fault but your car was barely scratched. I'll give you $10,000 if you'll drop the matter."

403. Which of the following is correct?

    (A) D's letter is inadmissible hearsay.

    (B) D's letter is non-hearsay but probably inadmissible because made during the course of an effort to compromise.

    (C) D's letter is non-hearsay and probably admissible because D's admission of responsibility is not part of an offer to compromise.

    (D) D's letter is non-hearsay and admissible because D failed to state that the statement about running into P's car was made "arguendo" or "without prejudice."

In a trial, a party calls an expert witness to give opinion testimony within the area of her expertise.

404. Which of the following expert opinions would most likely *not* be proper even if the witness is an expert in the area?

    (A) In a homicide prosecution, the prosecution calls an expert on gangs to testify that in her opinion, the killing was "consistent with gang behavior."

    (B) In a prosecution for possession of narcotics with intent to distribute, the prosecution calls an expert to testify that the amount of drugs possessed by the defendant was "common among those who sell drugs."

    (C) In a prosecution for transporting contraband across state lines with intent to distribute, the prosecution calls an expert to testify that based on the evidence adduced at trial, the defendant was "crossing state lines with intent to distribute contraband."

    (D) None of the above opinions would likely be improper.

Toxic tort case. P alleges that pollutants from D's chemical plant several miles from P's home seeped into the soil and made their way into P's drinking water, causing P's cancer. To prove the pollutants were in P's drinking water, P calls an expert forensic chemist to testify that she used a new scientific technique for tracking pollutants and concluded that the pollutant in question did in fact reach P's drinking water. The expert's technique was recently published in a peer reviewed journal and has been praised for its theoretical soundness and its low error rate, but P's expert is the only forensic chemist who accepts the validity of the technique as of the date of the trial.

405. D objects on the ground that the testimony is "junk science." Which of the following statements is correct?

  (A) The testimony is probably admissible both under the common law and in a federal court.

  (B) The testimony is probably admissible under the common law but inadmissible in a federal court.

  (C) The testimony is probably admissible in a federal court but inadmissible under the common law.

  (D) The testimony is probably inadmissible in both federal and under the common law.

Prosecution of D for murder. The prosecution offers hearsay evidence that satisfies the requirements of the residual exception and is "non-testimonial" in nature.

406. D objects on confrontation grounds. Which of the following is correct?

  (A) The court should exclude the evidence unless the prosecution offers other evidence corroborating it.

  (B) The court should exclude the evidence unless the prosecution demonstrates by a preponderance of the evidence that there are particularized guarantees of trustworthiness, a standard which may not be met with corroborating evidence.

  (C) The court should exclude the evidence unless the prosecution demonstrates by clear and convincing evidence that there are particularized guarantees of trustworthiness, a standard which may not be met with corroborating evidence.

  (D) The court should admit the evidence.

Prosecution of D for the murder of V. D denies involvement. The prosecution calls W to testify that immediately after the killing, W saw X pointing in D's direction and screaming, "Stop him! Stop him!"

407. D objects on Confrontation Clause grounds to admission of W's testimony concerning X's statement. Which of the following is correct?

  (A) The court should sustain the objection because D never had the opportunity to cross-examine X.

  (B) The court should sustain the objection because the prosecution has not demonstrated X's unavailability.

(C) The court should sustain the objection because the prosecution has not offered testimony independently indicating the reliability of X's statement.

(D) The court should overrule the objection.

Five years after V was killed, D1 and D2 are charged with the murder. Earlier, P, V's legal representative, had sued D1 for wrongful death and prevailed. At the wrongful death trial, P called W, who testified that she saw D1 kill V. W is unavailable.

408. In the criminal trial of D1 and D2, which of the following is correct?

(A) The transcript of W's testimony is admissible against both D1 and D2.

(B) The transcript of W's testimony is inadmissible against D1 but admissible against D2.

(C) The transcript of W's testimony is inadmissible against both D1 and D2.

(D) The transcript of W's testimony is admissible against D1 but inadmissible against D2.

P sues D for negligence following a sidewalk collision. During her case-in-chief, P calls W, who testifies that he saw D run into P from behind.

409. P also offers into evidence a portion of the transcript of W's deposition, at which W made a similar statement about the accident. On the facts stated, which of the following is most likely correct?

(A) The transcript is admissible as a prior consistent statement.

(B) The transcript is hearsay but admissible under the former testimony exception.

(C) The transcript is admissible only to prove W's opinion about what happened, not to prove what actually happened.

(D) The transcript is inadmissible.

Prosecution of D for a burglary that took place in Big City. D claims she was in Smalltown when the crime was committed. To prove D was in Big City at the time of the crime, the prosecution calls W to testify that the day before the crime, she was with D in Smalltown and that D said, "I'm heading back to Big City tonight."

410. Which of the following is correct?

(A) D's statement is hearsay but admissible as a party admission.

(B) D's statement is admissible as a party admission, which is non-hearsay.

(C) D's statement is hearsay and inadmissible as a party admission because the statement was not against D's interest when it was made.

(D) D's statement is hearsay but admissible as a declaration against interest.

P sues D for negligence after P fell on the floor of D's market. To prove negligence, P wishes to testify that after the fall, X, D's assistant store manager, told P that the store would pay P's medical bills and compensate her for pain and suffering.

411. Which of the following is correct?

    (A) P's testimony is inadmissible.

    (B) P's testimony is only admissible if the court decides that X was authorized to speak for D.

    (C) P's testimony is only admissible if the court decides that there is evidence sufficient to support a finding that X was authorized to speak for D.

    (D) P's testimony is only admissible if the court finds that X had personal knowledge of the circumstances of the accident.

In a trial, a party wishes to ask the court to take judicial notice of a fact.

412. Which of the following is *least likely* to be a proper subject of judicial notice, even if the party asking the court to take notice supplies supporting information?

    (A) The standard height of a rear bumper on a certain model of vehicle.

    (B) The mailing address of the County Recorder's office.

    (C) The names of all direct descendants of a particular person.

    (D) The existence of a stop sign at a certain intersection.

In an action, a party calls a lay witness to give opinion testimony.

413. Which of the following opinions would a court be *least* likely to allow the witness to give?

    (A) D maliciously killed the victim.

    (B) D appeared to be intoxicated.

    (C) D was choking the victim.

    (D) The car was swerving all over the road.

P sues D for negligence after the two kids collided on a playground. At trial, P calls W to testify that moments after P and D collided, X, another child, screamed, "D just ran into P!"

414. Before W answers the question that would elicit this testimony from W, D objects on hearsay grounds. After argument, the court sustains the objection. Which of the following is correct?

    (A) P should place into the record the testimony W would have given.

    (B) P should repeat the question to W and hope D does not object again.

    (C) P should move to the next question so as not to anger the judge.

    (D) P should stop questioning W completely so there will be a record of the harm caused to the case by disallowing the evidence about X's statement.

Prosecution of D for the murder of V. D calls W1, who testifies that he was with D in another city on the day of the murder. During its rebuttal case, the prosecution calls W2, who had been a long-time friend of V, to testify that V was a "great person who gave generously to charity."

415. D moves to strike W2's testimony but does not give a specific reason. The trial court denies D's motion. D is convicted. On appeal, D claims this ruling was error. Which of the following statements is correct?

(A) Because D did not specify the ground for the objection, the appellate court may not review this matter.

(B) Because W2 already answered the question, there is no ground for appeal.

(C) Because the record clearly reveals that the evidence was inadmissible, the appellate court will reverse D's conviction.

(D) Because the record clearly reveals that the evidence was inadmissible, the appellate court may review the matter and decide whether to reverse D's conviction.

Action by P against D to collect a debt. To prove the debt was not paid, P offers a note signed by D for the amount of the debt. The jurisdiction maintains a rebuttable presumption that "an obligation possessed by the creditor is presumed not to have been paid." Assume a note qualifies as an "obligation." D does not dispute that the note was in P's possession prior to trial, but testifies that she paid the obligation.

416. If the jurisdiction has adopted the "bursting bubble" theory of presumptions, which of the following statements is correct?

(A) The court should instruct the jury that if it finds by a preponderance of the evidence that P possessed the note, it must find that the note was not paid.

(B) The court should instruct the jury that if it finds by clear and convincing evidence that P possessed the note, it must find that the note was not paid.

(C) The court should instruct the jury that the note was not paid, and that the jury's only responsibility is to assess damages.

(D) The court should not instruct the jury at all concerning the presumption.

Prosecution of D in federal court for the murder of V at Moe's Bar. The prosecution calls W, D's spouse, and asks whether an hour after the murder, D announced to a group including W that she had just come from Moe's.

417. D objects to W's testimony on grounds of privilege. Which of the following statements is correct?

(A) Because D's statement was not made in confidence to W, no privilege applies, and W must testify.

(B) Even though D's statement was not made in confidence to W, the court may not compel W to testify if W does not wish to do so.

(C) Even though D's statement was not made in confidence to W, the court may not allow W to testify if D objects.

(D) Regardless of the applicability of any privilege, the court should refuse to allow W to testify concerning D's statement because the statement is inadmissible hearsay.

Prosecution of D for murder. The prosecution calls an expert in DNA analysis to testify that a DNA test of a blood sample from D "matched" that of blood found at the scene of the crime, and that the crime-scene blood could have been produced by only 1 in 1,000,000 of the people inhabiting the large urban area in which the crime took place. In all, there are 10,000,000 people in the urban area.

418. Which of the following statements best represents the meaning of this evidence?

(A) If the crime was committed by a person inhabiting this urban area, the odds are 1 in 1,000,000 that D did not commit the crime.

(B) If the crime was committed by a person inhabiting this urban area, D is one of approximately 10 people who could have been the source of the blood left at the crime scene.

(C) If the crime was committed by a person inhabiting this urban area, there is only a 1 in 10 chance that D was the one who committed it.

(D) If the crime was committed by a person inhabiting this urban area, D is probably the person who committed it.

Prosecution of D for possession of cocaine. D testifies that she did not possess the drugs found hidden in her apartment or even know the drugs were present. During its rebuttal case, the prosecution calls W, D's friend, to testify that D is a cocaine user.

419. D objects. Of the following, which is the prosecution's strongest argument supported by the law?

(A) The court should admit W's testimony only to impeach D's character for truthfulness.

(B) The court should admit W's testimony only to prove D's guilt.

(C) The court should admit W's testimony both to impeach D and to prove D's guilt.

(D) The court should admit W's testimony unless D shows that W has a reason to lie.

Prosecution of D for setting a forest fire. D testifies that she had nothing to do with the fire.

420. D then calls W to testify that she has known D for many years, and that in her opinion, D is an honest person. Which of the following statements is correct?

(A) W's testimony is inadmissible.

(B) W's testimony is admissible only to prove that D did not set the fire.

(C) W's testimony is admissible only to support D's credibility as a witness.

(D) W's testimony is admissible both to prove D did not set the fire and to support D's credibility.

Prosecution of D for the murder of V by use of a bomb. W1 testifies for the prosecution that a few minutes after the bombing and just before he died, V told W1 that he knew he was dying and wanted W1 to know that he saw D set off the bomb. V died at the scene a few minutes later.

421. D calls W2 to testify that she knew V for many years, and that in her opinion, V was a "liar." Which of the following is correct?

(A) W2's testimony is inadmissible because it is irrelevant.

(B) W2's testimony is inadmissible because V never testified at the trial.

(C) W2's testimony is inadmissible extrinsic evidence offered to impeach V.

(D) W2's testimony is admissible.

Prosecution of D for murder. D testifies that she did not commit the crime. During its rebuttal case, the prosecutor authenticates and offers into evidence a "judgment of conviction" of D for misdemeanor assault in an unrelated matter, dated two years earlier.

422. Which of the following is correct?

(A) The judgment of conviction is inadmissible to impeach D.

(B) The judgment of conviction is admissible to impeach D.

(C) The judgment of conviction is inadmissible to impeach D unless D was given an opportunity to explain or deny the conviction.

(D) The judgment of conviction is inadmissible to impeach D unless the court finds that the probative value of the conviction substantially outweighs its prejudicial effect.

Part II:
Short Answer Questions

Prosecution of D for robbing V on a street corner. D claims that the police arrested the wrong person. At trial, the prosecution calls W, a police officer, who testifies that after the robbery, she interviewed X, a bystander, and that during the interview, X pointed to D (who was standing on the corner), and said, "He's the one who robbed V." The prosecution does not call X to testify at trial. D moves to strike the officer's testimony.

423. How should the court rule, and why?

ANSWER:

Medical malpractice action by P against D Utility Co. following the death of X, P's father, from cancer. P's theory is that D caused X's cancer by placing high voltage electrical lines too close to X's residence. D denies that the high voltage lines could have caused X's cancer. At trial, P wishes to call W, an M.D. engaged in cancer research who holds a faculty position at a major research hospital. If permitted, W will testify that the electromagnetic fields produced by high voltage lines are capable of causing cancer.

424. Assume W's view is held by only a small minority of cancer experts. D objects to P's testimony. How should the court analyze this problem?

ANSWER:

Prosecution of D for the crime defined in the statute as "aiding and abetting in the possession of narcotics with intent to sell." D admits that the narcotics were in his car when he was arrested, but claims the drugs belonged to a passenger and that he did not intend to participate in any illegal transactions, including distribution of the drugs. At trial, the prosecution calls W, a 30-year veteran of the police force with extensive experience in investigation of narcotics offenses. Prior to trial, the prosecutor informed W of each of the facts on which she intended to offer evidence to establish D's guilt. When W takes the stand, the prosecutor first establishes W's experience in investigating narcotics offenses, and then asks W whether he has an opinion concerning D's conduct in relation to the drugs. If permitted, W will answer that in his opinion, D "aided and abetted in the passenger's possession of narcotics with the intent to sell." D objects to W's proposed testimony.

425. How should the court rule, and why?

ANSWER:

Personal injury action by P against D following an incident in which D's car struck P as P crossed the street. P claims he was in a crosswalk when D struck him. D claims P ran out from between two parked cars in the middle of the block. At trial, P calls W, who testifies that she had just emerged from a movie theater on the corner after watching "Cohasset Park" when she saw D's car strike P as he crossed the street in a crosswalk. On cross-examination, D asks W if it isn't true that she could not possibly have been emerging from a showing of "Cohasset Park" because that movie did not open until a year later. P objects to the question on the ground that it constitutes improper impeachment.

426. How should the court rule, and why?

ANSWER:

Prosecution of D for burglary of a home. The prosecution alleges that D climbed down the chimney of the home and made off with only the owners' expensive cowboy boots. D claims she was in another state when the crime took place. At trial, the prosecution calls W to testify that the city police chief told him that on two prior occasions, D entered homes through the chimney and stole only the owners' expensive cowboy boots. D objects to this testimony as offered.

427. How should the court rule, and why? If the court should sustain the objection, is there a way the prosecution could present the evidence of D's other burglaries without violating the rules of evidence? Explain.

ANSWER:

Negligence action by P against D arising from an intersection collision between their automobiles. P claims D ran a red light, causing the accident. At trial, P wishes to testify that a police report of the accident records a bystander's statement, taken an hour after the accident, that D ran the red light. D objects based on both the hearsay rule and the best evidence rule.

428. How should the court rule, and why?

ANSWER:

Prosecution of D for the burglary of several homes during a serious brush fire. At trial, D calls W, who testifies that she was with D in another state at the time the fire and burglaries took place. On cross-examination, the prosecution wishes to ask W if it isn't true that seven years prior to this trial, she was convicted of filing a false federal income tax return. D objects.

429. How should the court rule, and why?

ANSWER:

Prosecution of D for killing the neighbor's cat. At trial, the prosecution calls W, D's spouse, and wishes to have W testify that on the night of the killing, D had cat hair all over him and that when they went to bed, D told W that he'd "just taken care of that howling animal." W is willing to testify about these matters. D objects to W's testimony both about the cat hair and about what D said.

430. How should the court rule, and why?

ANSWER:

Prosecution of D for bank robbery. D denies involvement. A few days before trial, X, an eyewitness who would have identified D as the perpetrator, suddenly left the country for a foreign destination. X refuses to return and is beyond the court's subpoena power. The prosecution calls PO, a police officer, to testify that shortly after the robbery, X told PO that she saw D rob the bank. D objects on hearsay grounds. The prosecution responds that D threatened to kill X unless X left the country.

431. How should the court rule on D's hearsay objection, and why?

ANSWER:

Prosecution of D for fraud. The prosecution alleges that D fraudulently induced V to invest in an illegal pyramid scheme. D claims she was the victim of V's inducement, and not the other way around. To prove this, D calls W1, who testifies that V has a community reputation for dishonesty in business dealings. The prosecution wishes to call W2 to testify that D has a community reputation for business dishonesty. D objects on the ground that the prosecution's evidence constitutes an impermissible use of character evidence.

432. How should the court rule on D's character evidence objection, and why?

ANSWER:

Prosecution of D for bank robbery. D denies involvement.

433. The prosecution wishes to present evidence that the day before the robbery, D stole the car that was used as the getaway vehicle in the robbery. D objects on the ground that the question seeks to elicit inadmissible character evidence. How should the court rule?

ANSWER:

Prosecution of D for sexual assault on V, whom D met in a bar. D denies involvement. To prove D is guilty, the prosecution calls W and seeks to elicit W's testimony that a year earlier, D sexually assaulted her after she met him in a bar.

434. D objects on the ground the question seeks to elicit inadmissible character evidence. How should the court rule?

ANSWER:

P sues D, a rock star, after P was injured by sparks flying off D's guitar at a concert. At trial, P identifies a letter she received after the concert, purportedly signed by D, stating, "Those sparks hurt you. I hope you're feeling better." P is not familiar with D's signature.

435. D objects to admission of the letter on the ground that because P is not familiar with D's signature, P has not authenticated the letter as coming from D. How should the court rule?

ANSWER:

Prosecution of D for assault and battery on V. D calls W, who testifies that she observed the fight and that V, not D, started it.

436. To prove V did not start the fight, the prosecutor asks W, "isn't it true that V has a community reputation as a peaceful person?" D objects. How should the court rule?

ANSWER:

Negligence action by P against D after P fell in the produce section of D's market. D testifies that the floor was swept every half hour. To prove the floor was not swept for over an hour before he fell, P calls W, D's custodian of records, and shows W a "sweep log." W testifies that the log is posted near the produce section, and that each time an employee sweeps the floor, the employee records on the log the time she did so. The log contains no marks between an hour before and an hour after P's fall.

437. P offers the log into evidence. D objects. How should the court rule?

ANSWER:

Bank robbery prosecution of D. The prosecution claims D committed the robbery with X and Y, presents evidence of the plan and X's participation, and also calls W to testify that the day before the robbery, she overheard X say to Y, "D needs a getaway car." X is available, but the prosecution does not call her as a witness. Eyewitnesses to the robbery said several people including X committed it.

438. If D objects on hearsay and confrontation grounds, how should the court rule?

ANSWER:

P sues Smith and Jones for wrongful death after V, P's spouse, was killed in River City. Defendants claim they were together in Bigtown at the time. Earlier, Smith was prosecuted for the murder of V but was acquitted. Jones was not charged. At Smith's criminal trial, the prosecution called W, who testified that she saw Smith and Jones in River City on the day of the killing. W is now unavailable. At the civil trial, Smith and Jones both claim they were in Bigtown when the crime occurred.

439. P wishes to introduce the transcript of W's criminal trial testimony. Assume P is able to authenticate the transcript. Smith and Jones both object on hearsay grounds. How should the court rule?

ANSWER:

Negligence action by P against D after D's car allegedly hit P in a crosswalk. To prove P was injured in the collision, P calls W to testify that moments after the collision, W ran over to P, and that P said, "Call 911! My leg is killing me!"

440. D objects on hearsay grounds. How should the court rule?

ANSWER:

Product liability action by P against D. P claims that a defective design in D's product caused P's injury. At trial, D calls W, D's director of product design, who testifies that the product involved in the accident was "sound."

441. On cross-examination, P wishes to ask W if it isn't true that after P's accident, D redesigned the product. Assume that if the redesign had been in effect when P purchased the product, P would not have been injured. D objects on the ground the evidence is excluded by the subsequent remedial measures rule. How should the court rule?

ANSWER:

Product liability action by P against D Corp. for injuries suffered in a bicycle accident. D Corp. manufactured P's bicycle. P claims the bike was defective because the metal used for the frame was too weak to support the weight of a normal person. D denies the metal was too weak, and calls an expert witness who testifies that the metal was the strongest available.

442. During his rebuttal case, P calls W and seeks to elicit W's testimony that after the accident, D started using a stronger alloy for the frame of that model of bike, and that had this alloy been used on P's bike, the accident would not have occurred. The alloy was available all along. P objects. How should the court rule?

ANSWER:

Prosecution of D for possession of illegal drugs. D testifies that she did not possess the drugs found in her apartment or even know the drugs were present.

443. On cross-examination, the prosecution asks D if it isn't true that on a recent job application, D stated that she had never been convicted of a crime, when in fact she had been convicted of misdemeanor theft. D objects on the ground the evidence is not admissible to prove D's guilt or to impeach D's credibility. How should the court rule?

ANSWER:

Prosecution of D for burglary. D calls W, who testifies that she and D were in another city when the burglary took place. On cross-examination, the prosecutor asks W to acknowledge that W was convicted of misdemeanor perjury seven years earlier.

444. D objects on the ground that this is improper impeachment evidence. How should the court rule?

ANSWER:

Prosecution of D for possession of cocaine. The drugs were found hidden in D's apartment. D testifies that she did not know there were drugs in the apartment.

445. During its rebuttal case, the prosecution calls W to testify that D recently applied for a job in W's store and stated on the application that she had never been convicted of a crime. In fact, she had been convicted of petty theft, a misdemeanor carrying a maximum 60-day jail sentence. D objects. How should the court rule?

ANSWER:

Negligence action by P against D following an automobile collision. At trial, P calls W, who testifies that he observed the accident and that D ran a red light.

446. On cross-examination, D asks W, "Isn't it true that you cheated on a college American History exam?" P objects on grounds the question is leading and that it is an impermissible attempt to impeach W. How should the court rule?

ANSWER:

P sues D after they collided while rushing to get to Evidence class on time. P calls W1, who testifies that she saw D run into P. On cross-examination, W1 denies ever having said that it was the other way around (that P ran into D).

447. D calls W2 to testify that an hour after the accident, she heard W1 tell X, "P ran right into D." P objects on hearsay and improper impeachment grounds. How should the court rule?

ANSWER:

P sues D for negligent entrustment after a car owned by D and loaned to X struck P in a crosswalk. P suffered serious injuries. To prove X was a reckless driver, P wishes to present testimony that X had been involved in five auto accidents in the past year.

448. D objects to this testimony on grounds it violates the character evidence rule. How should the court rule?

ANSWER:

Prosecution of D for bank robbery. During the course of the bank robbery, the mask worn by X, one of the bank robbers, slipped off his face. When X noticed that a teller was looking right at his face, X warned the teller to "pack up and leave the state and never come back or I'll track you down and kill you." The teller did just that after calling her friend W and telling her what she'd seen take place in the bank. All efforts to locate the teller so she could testify at the trial failed.

449. At trial, the prosecution calls W for the purpose of having W relate what the teller said before leaving the state. D objects on hearsay grounds. How should the court rule?

ANSWER:

P sues D for battery after D allegedly attacked P for no reason. D alleges that she was an innocent bystander who had nothing to do with the attack.

450. At trial, to prove D attacked P, P wishes to testify that just before an ambulance took P away, D offered to pay P's hospital bill and said, "I don't know what came over me." D objects to this testimony. How should the court rule?

ANSWER:

Prosecution of D for murder. Following D's conviction, a juror approached defendant's attorney and complained about another juror's conduct. That juror made a disparaging remark about the defendant's racial background, and stated that people of that race "just commit these crimes like it was nothing." The defense attorney submits a motion for a new trial on grounds of juror misconduct. The prosecutor objects.

451. How should the court rule, and why?

ANSWER:

Personal injury action by P against D arising from an automobile accident in which D's car hit P's car at an intersection. P claims D drove through a red light. At the scene W, an eyewitness, told a police officer (PO) that P had a green light. At trial, P calls W, who testifies that P had a green light at the time of the accident. On cross-examination, D's attorney asks W: "Isn't it true that you recently suffered a stroke and that your memory has since been deficient?" W responds that the stroke has caused some memory issues. P wishes to call PO to testify about the statement W gave PO at the time of the accident. The defense attorney objects.

452. How should the court rule, and why?

ANSWER:

Prosecution of D for the murder of V. D denies involvement. At trial, the prosecutor calls W, a friend of V's, who testifies that a week before V's death, V told W that she "was afraid of D." D moves to strike W's testimony and asks the court to instruct the jury to disregard it.

453. How should the court rule, and why?

ANSWER:

Prosecution of D for rape of V. D claims consent. At trial, the prosecutor calls W, a friend of V's, who testifies that a day before the rape, V told W that she "was afraid of D." D moves to strike W's testimony and asks the court to instruct the jury to disregard it.

454. How should the court rule, and why?

ANSWER:

Prosecution of D for child abuse of V, his 4-year-old son. V's preschool teacher, W, noticed bruising on V's cheek. When W asked about the bruising, V was reluctant but eventually reported that D had beaten him again. When the prosecutor calls W to testify about V's statement, D objects on confrontation grounds.

455. How should the court rule, and why?

ANSWER:

Answers

Topic 1: Answers

Preserving Error; Appellate Review

1. **Answer (D) is correct.** When the court sustains an objection to evidence a party wishes to offer, the party must place on the record an indication of what the evidence would have been, i.e., an offer of proof. Sometimes a reviewing court will need to know what the evidence would have been in order to determine whether the trial court erred. And almost always, a court will have to know what the evidence would have been in order to determine whether any error "affects a substantial right of the party" (FRE 103(a)) ("harmless error" rule). In this case, the evidence would have consisted of a witness's oral testimony, so the lawyer should make sure the record reflects the answer the witness would have given.

   Answer (A) is incorrect because moving on to the next question would not leave any record of what the evidence would have been. This would place a reviewing court in the position of guessing, something it is unlikely to do.

   Answer (B) is incorrect because it is not necessary to make a formal "exception" to the ruling. Also, this would not indicate what the evidence would have been.

   Answer (C) is incorrect because simply by continuing with the witness's examination, the party does not waive the right to appeal. Such a rule would make no sense because it would prevent the party from offering other admissible testimony from that witness.

2. **Answer (C) is correct.** FRE 103(a)(1) requires that objections to evidence be "timely" and that they state "the specific ground, unless it was apparent from the context." The facts do not indicate that the context makes clear what the ground of the objection was. Assuming that is correct, FRE 103(e) offers D the only refuge. That rule (the "plain error" rule) allows an appellate court to take notice of "a plain error affecting a substantial right, even if the claim of error was not properly preserved." Even so, the record will have to show clearly what the court's error was. In addition, reversal is not appropriate unless that error "affects a substantial right of the party" (FRE 103(a)).

   Answer (A) is incorrect because an objection at the appropriate time is not sufficient to preserve error. As noted above, the objecting party should also state the ground of the objection.

   Answer (B) is incorrect because, as explained above, it is not enough that the trial court erred. The error must also have been prejudicial (affected a substantial right of the party).

   Answer (D) is incorrect because it does not take account of the "plain error" rule.

3. **Answer (A) is correct.** Normally, the trial court will not interfere with evidentiary matters if the parties do not raise them. This is consistent with the feature of the adversary system that gives the parties control over how the trial will be conducted (within the rules, of course). The court has authority to act, however. This is called "acting on its own motion." Thus, the judge, on her own motion, may order a party not to elicit certain testimony or may strike the testimony if it has already been given.

    Answer (B) is incorrect because the court is not required to exclude inadmissible evidence in the absence of an objection, nor is it required to strike inadmissible evidence in the absence of a motion to strike.

    Answer (C) is incorrect because the court need not ask a party if it wishes to object.

    Answer (D) is incorrect because the court has the authority to act.

4. **Answer (C) is correct.** A court may grant a motion to strike even if the stated ground for the objection is incorrect. Here, the correct objection would be that the testimony violates FRE 404(a)(2)(B), which forbids the prosecution from using evidence of the character of the victim unless certain facts are shown, none of which are present here.

    Answer (A) is incorrect because the proper thing for the opponent to do if the witness has already answered a question is to move to strike the witness's testimony.

    Answer (B) is incorrect for the reasons stated above. The court may grant the motion. It does not have to do so.

    Answer (D) is incorrect because evidence of the good character of the crime victim is not admissible under these circumstances. (For example, D has not testified that V had a bad character for some trait "pertinent" to the defense being used. In that situation, the prosecution would have been permitted to offer evidence of V's good character for that trait. Or, if D's defense was that V was the first aggressor, the prosecution would be allowed to offer evidence of V's peaceful character.)

5. **Answer (B) is correct.** FRE 103(e) sets forth the "plain error" doctrine, which permits the appellate court to take notice of "a plain error affecting a substantial right, even if the claim of error was not properly preserved." FRE 404(a) categorically forbids the prosecution from offering character evidence during its case-in-chief to prove circumstantially that the defendant acted in a particular way on a specific occasion. The record clearly reflects the error. If the error affected a substantial right of D, the appellate court will reverse.

    Answer (A) is incorrect because it assumes automatic reversal once error is found. Unless the error affected a substantial right of a party, the appellate court will not reverse.

    Answer (C) is incorrect because FRE 404(a) is categorical; there is no rule allowing the trial court to admit prosecution character evidence in this situation, even if the evidence has substantial probative value. Thus, the error is plain.

    Answer (D) is incorrect because it fails to take account of the plain error doctrine.

6. **Answer (B) is correct.** Rulings based on FRE 403 involve the exercise of discretion. Though the appellate court might be in as good a position as the trial court to determine the probative value of the evidence if it is accurate, the trial court is in a much better position than the appellate court to assess the likely prejudicial effect of the evidence. The likely effect on this particular jury, for example, is something that the appellate court cannot determine as well as the trial court. Thus, because the standard of FRE 403 requires the exercise of discretion, the appellate court will apply an "abuse of discretion" standard of review to the alleged error.

Answer (A) is incorrect because the existence of trial court discretion does not mean the appellate court has no review authority. To say that review is deferential in this type of situation is not to say the appellate court lacks authority to review.

Answer (C) is incorrect because, as explained above, the proper standard of review in this situation is "abuse of discretion."

Answer (D) is incorrect because there is no indication that the trial court applied an incorrect standard. On the contrary, the court's ruling suggests that it understood and applied the applicable standard.

7. **Answer (C) is correct.** FRE 404(a) sets up a categorical rule that does not involve the exercise of discretion. It is clear from the rule that in a murder prosecution, the prosecution may not offer evidence of the character of a person in order to prove how that person behaved on a particular occasion. The facts also demonstrate categorically that none of the exceptions stated in the rule apply. Thus, the appellate court should review the trial court's action as an error of law, sometimes referred to as "*de novo*" review.

It should be noted that not all appellate courts recognize that some evidence rules are not discretionary. It is common, for example, to see statements in appellate opinions such as, "We review alleged errors in the admission and exclusion of evidence on an abuse of discretion standard."

Answer (A) is incorrect because, as explained above, this rule does not grant the trial court discretion. Even if it did, the appellate court would still possess the authority to review.

Answer (B) is incorrect because, as explained above, "abuse of discretion" is not the proper standard of review.

Answer (D) is incorrect because the trial court's application of the wrong standard does not automatically result in reversal. The appellate court must also determine whether the error affected a substantial right of D. If the ruling did not have that effect, the error will be deemed harmless.

Topic 2: Answers

Objections to the Form of the Question

8. **Answer (A) is correct.** The question is unobjectionable.

   Answer (B) is incorrect because the evidence sought by the question is relevant to whether W correctly heard D's statement.

   Answer (C) is incorrect because, although the question is leading, it is permissible (and in fact desirable) to lead a witness on cross-examination.

   Answer (D) is incorrect because the question does not assume any facts not in evidence.

9. **Answer (A) is correct.** The question is unobjectionable.

   Answer (B) is incorrect because the question does not assume W was standing on the corner of First and Main; it seeks that information.

   Answer (C) is incorrect because it is permissible to lead a witness on direct examination if the witness is having difficulty remembering the facts.

   Answer (D) is incorrect because even though the question was asked, W did not answer it. In addition, the questioning party has a right to ask a question in a different way if the purpose is to help develop the witness's testimony.

10. The court should overrule the objection. A question is within the scope of the direct examination if it concerns a subject that was explicitly raised on direct examination or if the matter is implied by something that was the subject of the direct examination. P's testimony on direct examination left the impression that any impairment to P's knee resulted from the skating accident. Under the circumstances, the court should allow D to raise doubt about that matter. It would not be fair to force D to wait until it is time to present her own case, when she might recall P as a witness or otherwise present evidence correcting the impression left by P's testimony.

11. The court should overrule the objection. In addition to questions that inquire about matters explicitly or impliedly raised during direct examination, a question is considered within the scope of the direct examination if it relates to the credibility of the witness. Here, the question goes to W's credibility. If W and D were former business partners who had a falling out shortly before the crime was committed, it is possible that W would be biased against D and would therefore testify against D. D's question seeks to reveal this possible source of bias or motive.

12. **Answer (C) is correct.** If a question calls for inadmissible testimony, the opponent should always try to object before the witness has an opportunity to answer. This will prevent the jury from hearing the inadmissible evidence, which it might find difficult to ignore even if instructed to do so. Sometimes, however, the opponent is unable to object in time. In such a case, the opponent should move to strike the witness's testimony, state the ground of the motion, and also ask the court to instruct the jury to ignore the testimony.

    Answer (A) is incorrect because an objection is not timely.

    Answer (B) is incorrect because it fails to mention the request for a jury instruction to ignore the testimony.

    Answer (D) is incorrect because, as explained above, there is something the opponent can do. In fact, if the opponent does not make a motion to strike, there is a real possibility that the record will not be preserved for appeal.

13. D should object on the ground that this is a *compound question*. A witness is supposed to be given only one question at a time, whether on direct examination or cross-examination.

    D should also object that the second part of the question *calls for a narrative*. Particularly on direct examination it is appropriate to ask the witness to relate some information, but questions are supposed to be reasonably confined. A witness should not be asked to tell a full, unstructured story. "What happened?" is very open-ended, and the problem usually can be solved by asking questions such as "What happened next?" or "What was the first thing you saw?"

    Many common trial objections—such as compound questions, questions calling for a narrative, and misleading questions—are not specifically mentioned in the Federal Rules. However, FRE 611(a) gives the trial judge broad authority to "exercise reasonable control over the mode and order of examining witnesses and presenting evidence."

14. D should object on the ground that the answer assumes a fact not in evidence: that D's car ran the red light. W was P's first witness, and there is no suggestion that D has stipulated that she ran the red light. Thus, the question assumes, without any testimony in the record to support it, that D ran the red light. The way to cure the problem is to ask what W saw, without suggesting that W might have seen a particular thing. It might take several questions to get to the testimony that W saw D run the red light, but this is the appropriate way to elicit that testimony.

15. **Answer (D) is correct.** This question raises issues of witness competence and the proper use of leading questions. Under FRE 601, every person is competent to be a witness. The exception for diversity cases does not apply to criminal prosecutions. Thus, W is competent. Under FRE 611(c), leading questions are proper when they are "necessary to develop the witness's testimony." One common example is with a witness who is having memory problems or who is reluctant, which is often true of child witnesses.

    Answer (A) is incorrect for the reason given above.

    Answer (B) is incorrect because the question doesn't assume any fact.

    Answer (C) is incorrect for the reason given above.

16. **Answer (D) is correct.** This question raises the problem of limited admissibility. Under FRE 105, when evidence is admissible for one purpose but not another, or against one party but not another, the court must take appropriate steps to protect the opponent if the opponent makes a request (the court may act even if a request is not made). Usually, the remedy is a jury instruction about the limited admissibility of the evidence. In joint criminal trials where evidence is admissible only against one defendant, severance is a remedy, especially when the evidence is the statement of another person that names both defendants. Sometimes, the court will exclude the evidence entirely. The rule gives the court room to fashion the best remedy in the particular circumstances.

    Answers (A), (B), and (C) are each possible remedies, but, as stated above, the rule gives the court the authority to choose the most effective remedy.

17. **Answer (C) is correct.** FRE 602 requires that a lay witness may testify to a fact only if "evidence is introduced sufficient to support a finding" that the witness has personal knowledge of the fact. The rule does not require that personal knowledge be established *before* the witness testifies to the fact (though usually, the proponent chooses to do so). If the witness testifies but it is later shown that the "sufficient to support a finding" requirement has not been met, the court, on motion, should strike the testimony.

    Answer (A) is incorrect for the reasons given. The court need not find that the witness had personal knowledge, but only that there is evidence "sufficient to support" that finding.

    Answer (B) is incorrect for the reason given. The witness may testify before the evidence of personal knowledge is offered.

    Answer (D) is incorrect because, as noted above, the court need not believe the witness had personal knowledge, but need only find that there is evidence "sufficient to support" that finding.

18. **Answer (C) is correct.** This is a simple example of refreshing a witness's recollection. Except as noted below, there are no evidentiary rules that limit the use of a document (or anything else, for that matter) to refresh a witness's recollection. All that needs to happen is for the witness to testify that her recollection has been refreshed, if indeed it has been. FRE 612 states that when a writing is used to refresh a witness's recollection for the purposes of testifying, the opponent must be shown the writing, and the opponent (not the party using it) may offer the writing into evidence.

    Answer (A) is incorrect because the ticket is not being used as evidence. The witness's memory is the source of the testimony. Thus, no hearsay issue arises.

    Answer (B) is incorrect because, as noted above, the party using the writing to refresh a witness's recollection may not introduce it into evidence. Here, the prosecutor used the writing to refresh PO's memory.

    Answer (D) is incorrect because the ticket is not being used as evidence.

Topic 3: Answers

Witness Competency

19. The court should overrule D's objection. FRE 601 removes all common law grounds of incompetence by providing that "[e]very person is competent to be a witness unless these rules provide otherwise." There is no provision regarding the age of the prospective witness. At common law, a party was usually required to prove that the prospective witness was capable of accurate observation, recollection, and narration, and that the person understood the obligation to tell the truth while testifying. That rule is not preserved by FRE 601, which generally leaves such matters to the fact-finder as questions of weight. If a prospective witness is so clearly useless that it would be a waste of time to take the person's testimony, the court has authority under FRE 403 to refuse to permit the person to testify.

20. **Answer (A) is correct.** FRE 601 provides that "in a civil case, state law governs the witness's competency regarding a claim or defense for which state law supplies the rule of decision." Because the claim in this case is governed by state law, that state's rules of witness competency apply, and the state's dead man statute would forbid P from testifying to statements made by the deceased prior to his death.

    Answer (B) is incorrect because X's statement would almost certainly constitute a declaration against interest under FRE 804(b)(3). X is unavailable and the statement is so far contrary to X's pecuniary interest that a reasonable person in X's position would not have made the statement unless believing it to be true. Thus, hearsay is not a proper ground of objection.

    Answers (C) and (D) are incorrect for the reasons just given.

21. The court should overrule the objection. FRE 603 provides that "[b]efore testifying, a witness must give an oath or affirmation to testify truthfully. It must be in a form designed to impress that duty on the witness's conscience." This rule does not prescribe a particular form of oath or affirmation, and stresses only that the statement be of the kind that calls upon the person's conscience to be truthful. While the word "truthfully" is contained in the rule, there is no requirement that that word be included in the oath or affirmation. This question is based on *United States v. Ward*, 989 F.2d 1015 (9th Cir. 1992), in which the court held that it was error for the trial court to refuse to allow the criminal defendant to testify when she wished to substitute the words "fully integrated Honesty" for the word "truth."

22. **Answer (A) is correct.** Under FRE 605, a judge may not testify in the trial over which she is presiding, and no objection has to be made to preserve the error for appellate review. The appellate court need not reverse, however. The aggrieved party must show that the judge's error affected a substantial right.

Answers (B), (C), and (D) are incorrect for the reasons given. Note that it does not matter that the judge's actions might have been consistent with the goals of efficiency and accuracy; the rule categorically forbids the judge from testifying in a trial over which she is presiding.

23. **Answer (A) is correct.** It is a basic principle that all evidence should be taken in the presence of the parties, and that it is improper for the jurors to investigate the facts during deliberations. At the same time, the jurors are entitled to examine the exhibits and to treat the exhibits consistently with the way they were treated at trial. In this case, neither P nor any other witness took the bike apart in open court, and when the jurors did so, they broke new ground. It would be unfair to allow them to do this without giving the parties an opportunity to meet this new evidence.

    The jury's conduct in this situation therefore probably amounted to the introduction of extraneous prejudicial information. In such a case, FRE 606(b) does not forbid juror testimony (or evidence of juror statements) about what happened in the jury room.

    Even if FRE 606(b) would forbid juror testimony or evidence of juror statements to impeach the verdict, that is not the source of the information in the present case. Here, the bailiff observed the jurors engaging in the experiment. FRE 606(b) does not forbid the bailiff's testimony about her own observations.

    Answer (B) is incorrect because jurors may handle exhibits. They may not do truly new things with the exhibits, as explained above, but they certainly may handle them.

    Answer (C) is incorrect because, as noted above, FRE 606(b) probably does not apply here. Even if it does, the rule only restricts jurors from testifying or providing affidavits (and restricts the use of juror statements for that purpose).

    Answer (D) is incorrect because there is no rule forbidding the parties from interviewing jurors about their verdict. The jurors may decline to discuss the matter, but there is no rule forbidding the inquiry.

24. **Answer (C) is correct.** FRE 606(b)(1) forbids juror testimony about "any statement made or incident that occurred during the jury's deliberations; the effect of anything on that juror's or another juror's vote; or any juror's mental processes concerning the verdict or indictment," except that a juror may testify about "whether *extraneous prejudicial information was improperly brought to the jury's attention.*" (emphasis added) (FRE 606(b)(2)(A)). In *Tanner v. United States*, 483 U.S. 107 (1987), the Supreme Court gave the italicized language a very narrow interpretation, holding that evidence of drunkenness, drug use and drug dealing, and jurors falling asleep were not proper subjects of juror testimony to impeach the verdict. The Court left open juror testimony that would show such activities made the jurors truly *incompetent*, but the facts given were insufficient.

    For the reasons given above, **answers (A), (B), and (D) are incorrect.**

    Answer (C) is correct because a possible book deal clearly amounts to an outside influence brought to bear on the jurors. Jurors are being asked to render their verdict not based on the evidence, but based on a motivation to make money. Defendant may call the juror to testify about this matter.

25. **Answer (C) is correct.** In *Rock v. Arkansas*, 483 U.S. 44 (1987), the Supreme Court held that a state may not apply against a criminal defendant a per se rule that prohibits from testifying any individuals who have been hypnotized to enhance their recollection of the events. The Court did not hold that a criminal defendant always must be permitted to testify, but only that the trial court must make a case-by-case determination of whether the person's testimony would be so unreliable as to overcome the defendant's right to testify at her own trial.

    Answers (A), (B), and (D) are incorrect for the reasons just stated.

26. **Answer (B) is correct.** After the Supreme Court's decision in *Tanner v. United States*, 483 U.S. 107 (1987), conduct such as partying, not paying attention, and other similar things do not qualify as an "outside influence" that can open the jury verdict to impeachment under FRE 606(b).

    Answer (A) is incorrect because it is not improper to consider challenges to the verdict after the court has entered judgment and discharged the jury.

    Answer (C) is incorrect for the reasons noted above.

    Answer (D) is incorrect because the law does not forbid an attorney from speaking to jurors after the trial.

Logical Relevance; Exclusion for Reasons of Prejudice or Other Dangers

27. The evidence is relevant. The evidence is offered to show V's action. A possible chain of reasoning:

EVIDENCE: V committed numerous acts of violence in months before killing.

→ INFERENCE: V was a violent person.

GENERALIZATION: One who commits several acts of violence is more likely a violent person than is a person chosen at random.

→ INFERENCE: V started the fight with D.

GENERALIZATION: One who has a violent character is more likely to start a fight than is a person chosen at random.

→ INFERENCE: D acted in self-defense.

GENERALIZATION: A person who kills another who has attacked her is more likely to have killed in self-defense than is one who kills a person who has not attacked her.

It does not matter that D was unaware of V's prior violent acts because D does not claim she attacked V out of fear that V was about to attack her. Instead, she claims that V started the fight. The evidence tends to show V's possible violent character, which tends to support the claim that V attacked D.

(Note that the fact that the evidence is relevant in this case does not mean it is admissible. In fact, this evidence probably violates FRE 405, which restricts the *types* of character evidence that may be used on direct examination even when character evidence is admissible.)

28. The evidence is relevant. Relevant evidence is evidence having *any* tendency to make more or less likely the truth of any proposition of consequence to the action (FRE 401). This evidence is relevant because it shows D's possible involvement in the crime. A possible chain of reasoning:

EVIDENCE: D spoke with the killer.

→ INFERENCE: D knew the killer.

GENERALIZATION: A person who speaks with another person is more likely to know that other person than is a person chosen at random.

→ INFERENCE: D knew what the killer was about to do.

GENERALIZATION: One who knows another person is more likely to know about that person's impending acts than is one chosen at random.

→ CONCLUSION: D was involved in the killing.

GENERALIZATION: One who knows about another's future acts is more likely to be involved in those acts than is a person chosen at random.

29. The evidence is relevant. It shows D's actions, even if D's beliefs are silly. A possible chain of reasoning:

EVIDENCE: D believed in astrology, and D's horoscope for the day of the crime warned D not to do anything risky.

→ INFERENCE: D read her horoscope that day.

GENERALIZATION: One who believes in astrology is more likely to read her horoscope daily than is one chosen at random.

→ INFERENCE: D believed her horoscope.

GENERALIZATION: One who believes in astrology is more likely to believe in the truth of a horoscope's prediction than is one chosen at random.

→ CONCLUSION: D stayed home that day.

GENERALIZATION: One who believes in astrology is more likely to act consistently with her horoscope than is one chosen at random.

The horoscope need not be a valid predictor of what would happen to D if she undertakes a "risky endeavor." All that matters is that D believed the horoscope was accurate, making it somewhat more likely than it would be without the evidence that D stayed home that day and thus did not commit the crime).

(Note that the evidence here probably violates the best evidence rule (FRE 1002) because it constitutes testimony about the contents of a writing. The best evidence rule requires that the writing itself be produced to prove its contents. None of the exceptions to that rule appear to apply here.)

30. The evidence is not relevant. D claims that the officers reasonably believed that D would act violently. The only basis for such a conclusion revealed by the facts is that P had acted violently when confronted with the police on two prior occasions. If the officers were unaware of these acts of violence, the acts could not have formed the basis of a belief that force was necessary.

31. The answer is unclear. Whether the evidence is relevant depends on the validity of the generalization that one's unconscious thoughts bear some relation to one's actual behavior. If relevant, the reasoning would be as follows:

EVIDENCE: A few days after the murder, D told a friend that he had just dreamed that he killed V.

→ INFERENCE: D believed that he killed V.

GENERALIZATION: One who dreams of having done something is more likely actually to have believed he acted in that way than is a person who has not had such a dream.

→ CONCLUSION: D killed V.

GENERALIZATION: One who believes he acted in a certain way is more likely actually to have acted in that way than is one who does not harbor that belief.

(Note: If faced with a relevance challenge in this case, an interesting question is whether the court should rely on its own knowledge about the nature of dreams, or should instead insist that the party offering the evidence (here, the prosecution) call an expert witness to testify that there is a relationship between unconscious thoughts and waking action. Some judges might not feel qualified to make that judgment without the assistance of expert opinion.)

32. **Answer (C) is correct.** The evidence is relevant because if D was a housekeeper for V, D had some connection with V that might have placed D in V's home. (In more technical language, this evidence gives rise to the inference that D had *opportunity* to commit the crime.) FRE 403, however, allows the court to exclude "relevant evidence *if its probative value is substantially outweighed by a danger of . . . unfair prejudice. . . .*" Prejudice here comes from the reason D had opportunity: her status as an inmate on work release. Hearing that D was an inmate might lead the jury to punish D for her prior crimes rather than for what she might have done on this occasion. Alternatively, the jury might consider the evidence of D's inmate status for the wrong reason: that one who has committed a crime is more likely to have committed the charged crime. As we will learn, this inference is forbidden by the rules of evidence. The issue is whether, in this instance, the danger of unfair prejudice is so great as to substantially outweigh the probative value of the evidence. That is a close question. A court might find that all the jury really needs to know is that D was a housekeeper, not that she held that job as part of a prison work-release program. Answer (C) states the issue that way.

Answer (A) is incorrect because the centrality of a factual issue to a case does not *per se* mean that no evidence offered to prove that fact can be too prejudicial. The balancing must be done on a case-by-case basis.

Answer (B) is incorrect because D's status as an inmate on work-release is relevant to rebut D's defense that she was on vacation in another state at the time of the crime. It is highly unlikely that an inmate on work-release would be allowed to take such distant vacations.

Answer (D) is incorrect because the evidence is relevant.

33. **Answer (D) is correct.** The photographs are relevant because they make it somewhat more likely than it would be without the evidence that V was retreating when shot. The court may exclude the photographs if it finds that their probative value is substantially outweighed by the danger of unfair prejudice or other dangers mentioned in FRE 403. Among those is "needlessly presenting cumulative evidence." The evidence here is cumulative in the sense that it corroborates oral testimony. But the court is unlikely to find them "needlessly cumulative" be-

cause they add something to the oral story: they *show* the jury what the witness was talking about, making it easier to understand the oral testimony. The jurors might also be able to judge whether the witness accurately described the condition of the head. There is also the risk of unfair prejudice if the jury might react emotionally rather than logically to the evidence, and the court should weigh this danger as well. On balance, the court is likely to admit the evidence.

Answer (A) is incorrect because cumulative evidence is relevant.

Answer (B) is incorrect because, as explained above, the probative value of the photographs might be great depending on the circumstances. On the facts given, we cannot judge them to have minimal probative value.

Answer (C) is incorrect because the judge should not be determining the reliability of the evidence. Reliability is a matter to be determined by the trier of fact. The judge should be deciding the probative value of the evidence *if the jury decides it is reliable.*

34. **Answer (A) is correct.** In *Old Chief v. United States*, 519 U.S. 172 (1997), the Supreme Court adopted a very narrow exception to the general principle that a party may prove her case with any otherwise admissible evidence, and may not be forced to accept a stipulation. The exception applied where the issue on which the disputed evidence would have been offered—defendant's status as a felon within the meaning of a statute—was an issue that could not benefit from any "evidentiary richness." D either was or was not a felon within the meaning of that statute, and D essentially offered to stipulate that he was. In this situation, D's offer to stipulate to his speed prior to the crash does tend to establish that he was going considerably in excess of the speed limit, but it does not demonstrate the catastrophic effect of his actions as well as the photographs.

Answer (B) is incorrect because, as explained above, the stipulation would not give P everything that the photographs would have shown.

Answer (C) is incorrect because, as explained above, there are very limited situations in which the general principle does not apply.

Answer (D) is incorrect because the opposite is true: Courts usually admit gory photographs because they generally hold that their probative value is not substantially outweighed by the danger of unfair prejudice.

35. **Answer (A) is correct.** A person's wealth is relevant to the amount of punitive damages that should be awarded because the amount of money it takes to "punish" a person depends in part on the person's wealth. A punitive damage award of $1000 might be significant to a poor defendant, but would likely mean little to a wealthy person.

Answer (B) is incorrect because it relies on a faulty generalization: that a wealthy person is likely to be careless because she will not be concerned about the financial impact of a tort judgment. That generalization is almost certainly wrong.

Answer (C) is incorrect because wealth will not be relevant to all substantive theories of recovery. For example, punitive damages are not awardable in negligence cases, and because all persons are judged according to the same standard (reasonable care under the circumstances), the wealth of a person is irrelevant to the question of reasonable care.

Answer (D) is incorrect because, as explained above, wealth is relevant to the possible award of punitive damages in an intentional tort case.

36. **Answer (B) is correct.** The facts of this hypothetical closely track those of *Old Chief v. United States*, 519 U.S. 172 (1997). The only value of D's status is to show that D qualifies as a "felon" under the statute. There is no "story-telling" value to more information (such as the nature of the prior conviction) because that information does not help the jury understand what happened in the present case. Under these very limited circumstances, the general rule that a party may use any otherwise admissible evidence to prove its case does not apply. Thus, the court may require the prosecution to accept the stipulation D has offered.

Answer (A) is incorrect because, though it is normally true that a party need not accept an opponent's offered stipulation, that is not the case in the rare instance where the stipulation truly gives the party everything it would be entitled to get by the evidence it wishes to offer.

Answer (C) is incorrect because, under FRE 401, evidence offered to prove an undisputed fact is relevant as long as it meets the basic definition in the rule. (In that sense, the rule differs from that of a few states including California, which provide that evidence offered to prove undisputed facts is not relevant. *See* Cal. Evid. Code § 210.)

Answer (D) is incorrect because a due process argument cannot be made in such a generalized way. The court must examine each piece of evidence and determine whether its probative value is substantially outweighed by the danger of unfair prejudice. It is true, however, that the probative value of an item of evidence should be measured in light of other evidence in the case. *See Old Chief.*

37. Under FRE 401, evidence is relevant if it advances or impedes to *any* degree the likelihood of a fact of consequence to the case being true. This is an extremely lenient standard. Here, D wishes to show that W, perhaps because of a faulty memory, was wrong about the movie for which she was buying tickets. D wants to raise the possibility that if W was wrong about this fact, she might also have a faulty memory as to the identity of the person she saw emerging from the bank. Of course, that her memory is faulty concerning a trivial detail (the name of the movie) does not say much about whether she might have a faulty memory about something more striking, but the relevance rule is extremely easy to satisfy. If the evidence is to be excluded, it will have to be based on another rule. (As it happens, this evidence is probably admissible.)

38. The "prosecutor's fallacy" as applied here incorrectly asserts that the probability of error is only one in 500,000, which is not what the statistical evidence suggests. The statistics, if accurate, only show that one in 500,000 white men could have produced this sample. They do not distinguish who, among the small number who could have produced the sample, did in fact produce it. The prosecutor has incorrectly correlated the fact that few people could produce the sample with the probability that it was D who produced it. Finally, the prosecutor's argument encourages the jury to ignore the other evidence in the case that might shed light on D's guilt or innocence, such as an alibi, or the existence of a motive in another person.

39. The "defense counsel's fallacy" as applied here incorrectly characterizes the nature of the statistical evidence. That evidence does not imply that there is only a one in ten chance D committed the crime. At most, it suggests that only one in ten white males who live in the metropolitan area could have left the blood sample found at the scene; it says nothing about who, among those people, was responsible. For example, some of those who could have produced the sample might have been away from the city at the time the crime was committed. As to those people, there is a zero percent chance of guilt. As with the prosecutor's argument, D's argument to the jury over-emphasizes the value of the statistical evidence and encourages the jury to ignore other evidence that might shed light on whether D committed the crime.

40. **Answer (C) is correct.** Bayes' Theorem is a statistical formula for determining the effect that a new piece of evidence has on a fact-finder's prior assessment of probability. That theorem is well-suited to a situation in which statistical evidence such as DNA evidence is added to the jury's assessment of identity based on other evidence in the case. That is what is happening in the hypothetical.

Answers (A), (B), and (D) are incorrect for the reasons stated above.

Topic 5: Answers

Preliminary Questions of Admissibility

41. **Answer (B) is correct.** The preliminary question here is whether the declarant was speaking under the stress of excitement caused by the startling event or condition (the accident). The statement will not be admissible unless the declarant was in that condition. But the statement is relevant even if the declarant wasn't speaking under stress caused by the condition. (The statement is relevant because it says something about how the accident happened.) That means that this is not a situation of "conditional relevancy" governed by FRE 104(b). Instead, FRE 104(a) applies, meaning that the judge must decide whether the fact is true. The standard the judge will use is "preponderance of the evidence."

    Answer (A) is incorrect because it assumes that this is a "conditional relevancy" problem. As explained above, it is not.

    Answer (C) is incorrect because there are some facts the court must decide under FRE 104(a). Indeed, most preliminary facts are for the judge under FRE 104(a); this is the default rule that applies unless the situation involves conditional relevancy. This one does not.

    Answer (D) is incorrect because it is not necessary to identify the declarant to know whether he or she was speaking under the stress of excitement caused by the accident. That fact may be inferred from circumstantial evidence (tone of voice, facial expression, and so forth).

42. **Answer (A) is correct.** This is a question for the court under FRE 104(a) because the confession is relevant whether the police read D her *Miranda* rights or did not do so. Thus, it is not a situation of "conditional relevancy." The Supreme Court has generally declined to impose any higher standard for the determination of preliminary facts relevant to a constitutional question than for other situations. Thus, the proper standard is preponderance of the evidence.

    Answers (B) and (C) are incorrect because they assume a higher standard of proof applies. It does not.

    Answer (D) is incorrect because it assumes this is a situation of "conditional relevancy," which it is not. The confession is relevant even if the police did not read D her *Miranda* rights. In addition, FRE 104(c)(1) provides that "[t]he court must conduct any hearing on a preliminary question so that the jury cannot hear it if … the hearing involves the admissibility of a confession." This suggests that under the Federal Rules, admissibility of confessions is always a question for the court under FRE 104(a).

43. **Answer (A) is correct**, but only because of a specific rule (FRE 104(c)) that provides that hearings on the admissibility of confessions must always be conducted out of the presence of the jury. That means the court must make the finding, and from the previous question, we know that the standard of proof is preponderance of the evidence. (In some states, evidentiary questions that implicate constitutional matters are always decided by the court. **Answer (A) would be correct in those states as well.**)

Answer **(B) is incorrect** for the reasons stated above. This is true even though it seems correct based on the logic of FRE 104(b).

Answer **(C) is incorrect** because no questions of preliminary fact are *always* for the jury. Even if a situation involves conditional relevancy, the jury will only be empowered to decide the question of preliminary fact if the court finds that there is evidence sufficient to support a finding that the preliminary fact is true.

Answer **(D) is incorrect** because, while *admissibility* of evidence is always for the court, some preliminary facts necessary to the *consideration* of evidence are left to the jury. Those situations are ones that fall within FRE 104(b).

44. **Answer (D) is correct.** The answer depends on the jurisdiction. The issue here is whether this is a case of "conditional relevancy" governed by FRE 104(b). The preliminary fact at issue is whether, by his action, P adopted D's statement as true. If, by giving D an angry look and taking back the skateboard, P was adopting D's statement as true, it would tend to show that D knowingly rode a defective skateboard. But who should decide that question, ultimately? There are two approaches. It is not clear which is the "majority" approach.

Some jurisdictions hold that because the evidence (here, D's statement about the skateboard's trucks) is relevant whether or not P adopted it as true, the court must decide adoption pursuant to FRE 104(a). If the matter were left to the jury, these courts reason, the jury might find that P did not adopt the statement but consider it anyway because it tends to show that the wheel trucks were defective. Because it is not admissible for that purpose if P did not adopt the statement as true, the jury would be considering evidence it should ignore. **In these courts the correct answer would be (B).** (Arguably, this is the better approach.)

Other jurisdictions point out that P's response to D's statement (the angry expression and taking back the skateboard) would not be relevant if D was not adopting the truth of D's statement. (It wouldn't advance or impede the finding of any other proposition of consequence to the action.) For that reason, these courts would hold that this is a case of conditional relevancy. **In these courts the correct answer would be (A).**

Answer **(C) is incorrect** because it fails to recognize that some questions of fact are for the court under FRE 104(a).

45. The underlying problem has to do with the roles of judge and jury and the importance of maintaining the rules of evidence. Jurors properly view their primary job to be determining

the truth—figuring out what happened on the relevant occasion. When a person has such a role, she is likely to consider any evidence that is relevant. She is not likely to care much whether a rule of evidence would forbid consideration of certain relevant evidence; she will not understand the reasons for the rule. Courts, on the other hand, understand the importance of evidence rules.

Based on these roles, the judge is the only party who can be trusted to maintain the rules of evidence (e.g., hearsay rule). If a piece of evidence will be relevant even if some preliminary question of fact is not true, letting the jury decide that preliminary question of fact is risky because the jury is likely to consider the underlying evidence even if the fact is not true.

When the underlying evidence will not be relevant unless the preliminary fact is true, there is no real danger that the jury will consider the evidence unless that fact is true. The definition of relevant evidence under FRE 401 is not a technical one. It relies on everyday logic, and does not require legal expertise. If evidence is not relevant, a jury is as likely as a judge to know that fact.

46. **Answer (B) is correct.** FRE 602 provides that a witness may testify to a matter "only if evidence is introduced sufficient to support a finding that the witness has personal knowledge of the matter." This standard is the same as the standard found in FRE 104(b). That is, personal knowledge is treated as a question of conditional relevance. The court need not conclude that the witness had personal knowledge; it need only find that a rational jury could conclude that the witness had personal knowledge.

   Answer (A) is incorrect because it assumes the court must make the finding of personal knowledge.

   Answer (C) is incorrect because if the court concludes that there is *not* sufficient evidence to support a finding that W had personal knowledge, the court should not allow the jury to consider the testimony.

   Answer (D) is incorrect because a motion to strike and a request that the court issue an instruction to the jury to ignore the testimony is the proper vehicle for dealing with a situation in which the witness has already testified to the facts.

47. The conditional relevancy doctrine makes a certain type of assumption about how people think. It assumes that the existence of fact in a person's mind is an on/off question. On the facts of this problem, for example, the theory assumes that the jury will decide conclusively whether W had personal knowledge or not, and that if it decides W lacked personal knowledge, the jury will simply ignore W's testimony. That is not how people think, however. People consider unknowns along a scale from true to false, including every point between. Realistically, that is, jurors are likely to be at least somewhat uncertain about the personal knowledge question. This means they will give W's testimony *some weight* even if they believe it's more likely than not that W lacked personal knowledge of the accident.

48. **Answer (B) is correct.** According to FRE 104(a), the court has the responsibility to determine the qualifications of a person to testify as a witness. When the court has the responsibility to determine the existence of a preliminary question (such as the qualification of a person to be a witness), the "preponderance" standard applies.

Answer (A) is incorrect because it assumes the wrong standard.

Answer (C) is incorrect for the same reason.

Answer (D) is incorrect because, even in criminal trials, the court may make findings concerning preliminary questions; this does not violate the defendant's right to trial by jury.

Topic 6: Answers

Classification of Evidence as Hearsay or Not Hearsay

49. **Answer (B) is correct.** We will assume that "whacked" means killed. The statement, "The Jets whacked V" is relevant because it makes it more likely than it would be without the evidence that the Jets whacked V. This, in turn, makes it less likely that D, who is not a member of the Jets, was involved. The statement is hearsay, however. The declarant (X) made the statement other than while testifying at the trial, it asserts that the Jets killed V, and it is offered to prove that the Jets killed V. Thus, it is relevant but hearsay.

Note: A type of statement that tends to confuse students learning the hearsay rule is one which asserts one thing but *appears* to be "offered to prove" another thing. Here, the statement presumably says the Jets killed V, and the problem states that the evidence is offered to prove D did not commit the crime. This confusion can be cleared up in one of two ways, and they amount to the same thing. (1) For purposes of the hearsay rule, assume that "offered to prove" refers only to the *first inference* from the evidence. In this case, the first inference from the evidence is that the Jets killed V. Because this is the same thing as the assertion contained in the statement (the thing X, the declarant, was trying to say), the evidence is hearsay. (2) Another way to look at it is to ask whether the statement at issue *must be true* in order for it to be relevant for the stated purpose. Here, ask whether it must be true that the Jets killed V in order to be relevant to whether D killed V. The answer, of course, is yes. Thus, X's statement is hearsay.

Answer (A) is incorrect because the purpose of offering evidence is to prove facts favorable to the party offering the evidence. Being self-serving is not, therefore, a proper objection. The evidence is not a waste of time because it bears on a crucial issue and might carry high probative value.

Answer (C) is incorrect because it assumes the evidence is not hearsay when offered to prove D's innocence. Also, there is no meaningful danger of unfair prejudice. It's not *unfairly* prejudicial to the prosecution's case.

Answer (D) is incorrect because the statement is hearsay.

50. **Answer (C) is correct.** This is a very difficult question. First, the statement, "I killed V this way and the body can be found in this place" is relevant because it makes it somewhat more likely than it would be without the evidence that X is the killer. This, in turn, increases the probably that D was not the killer. The problem is that if offered to prove that X was the killer, the statement is hearsay. It was made by X other than while testifying at the trial or hearing,

it asserts that X was the killer (and that the crime was committed in a particular way and that the body could be found in a certain place), and it is offered to prove that X was the killer. Thus, if D offers the statement on this basis, it will be relevant but hearsay.

There is another basis on which the evidence might be used, however. Note that X gave great detail about the crime just after it took place, and thus most likely before it was publicized. The crime was committed in a distinctive way—a way nobody would be likely to guess. Under these circumstances, X's very *knowledge* of the facts might be relevant in itself. The evidence, then, would be used not to prove the facts X stated are true, but to show X's knowledge of those facts. (Other evidence will be offered to prove the facts.) For this purpose, the evidence is not hearsay. The reasoning would be approximately as follows:

EVIDENCE: X described the killing in detail, indicated where the body could be found, and took responsibility for the killing.

→ INFERENCE: X knew these facts.

→ INFERENCE: X was at the scene of V's killing at the time of the killing and disposal of the body.

→ CONCLUSION: X was involved in the killing and disposal of the body.

Some courts have approved this theory. *See, e.g.,* Bridges v. State, 19 N.W.2d 862 (Wis. 1945); United States v. Muscato, 534 F. Supp. 969 (E.D.N.Y. 1982). Students should be cautious about the theory, however. Every statement of fact is also implicitly a statement that the declarant knows the fact or believes the fact to be true. The statement, "The red car hit the blue car" is both an assertion that this happened and circumstantial evidence that the declarant knew or believed that this is what happened. If an attorney were able to assert that the statement, "The red car hit the blue car" is being offered not to prove that this is what happened, but to prove that the declarant knew or believed it to be true, the hearsay rule would be eviscerated because this argument always could be made. It is only when there is something unique about the facts, when the declarant has no other likely source of the information other than to have been present at the relevant time, and when the declarant gives a detailed description, that the theory might be used appropriately.

Answers (A), (B), and (D) are incorrect for reasons that should be clear from the preceding discussion.

51. **Answer (A) is correct.** The statement, "There is a puddle of liquid on the floor" is hearsay if offered to prove the floor was slippery. It was made by W other than while testifying at the trial. It asserts that there was a puddle of liquid on the floor. The first inference in a chain of inference leading to the floor being slippery is that there was, in fact, a puddle of liquid on the floor. Thus, the statement is "offered to prove the truth of the matter asserted." Note that it doesn't matter that W is the declarant as well as the witness testifying about the out-of-court statement. A statement is hearsay even if the person testifying about it is the person who made the statement.

The statement is not hearsay, however, if offered to prove that D had been notified about the puddle. Notice is relevant in itself because a defendant in a negligence case is more likely to be classified as being negligent if she failed to act even when notified of the danger. In other words, notice helps to prove breach of duty. The statement is not hearsay for this purpose because it is not offered to prove that there was a puddle on the floor. The mere fact that the statement was made to D is relevant, as just explained. (Of course, to prevail, P will have to prove that the floor was slippery, which means proving there was a puddle of liquid on the floor. But W's statement will not be proof of that fact because it is hearsay when offered for that purpose.)

Answer (B) is incorrect because, as explained above, the statement is hearsay when offered to prove the floor was slippery even though W didn't say that it was. The first inference is that there was a puddle of liquid, and that inference must be true for the evidence to prove that the floor was slippery. In addition, as explained above, the statement is not hearsay if offered to prove D knew the floor was slippery.

Answers (C) and (D) are incorrect for the reasons explained above.

52. **Answer (B) is correct.** The assertion-based definition of hearsay, which is embodied in FRE 801(c), classifies as hearsay only those statements that assert the matter they are offered to prove. The statement, "You are the scum of the Earth" is not offered to prove that D is the "scum of the Earth." Instead, it is circumstantial evidence that V believed D was the burglar. Because it does not assert that D was the burglar (that is, one must infer that V believed this to be true), it is not hearsay. We would classify the statement as circumstantial evidence of V's state of mind, and not hearsay.

Under a declarant-based definition of hearsay, a statement is hearsay if its value depends on the credibility of the declarant. "Credibility" in this context, means the declarant's perceptions, sincerity, memory, and ambiguity (whether we correctly understand what the declarant was trying to say). In this situation, it is difficult to judge V's sincerity at the time she made the statement. Was V trying to frame D for the crime, for example? Because the declarant-based definition does not require that a statement assert the matter it is offered to prove in order to be classified as hearsay, any situation that leaves meaningful doubt about the declarant's credibility at the time the statement was made might be classified as hearsay.

Thus, the statement is more likely to be classified as hearsay under a declarant-based definition of hearsay than under an assertion-based definition of hearsay. Though we cannot be certain of the outcome, a hearsay objection would have a greater chance of being sustained under a declarant-based definition.

Note that the Federal Rules and virtually every state code use the language of an assertion-based definition of hearsay.

Answers (A) and (C) are incorrect for the reasons given. **Answer (D) is incorrect** because the problem provides sufficient information to answer the hearsay question.

53. **Answer (C) is correct.** V's statement describing the container (especially its unique markings) is hearsay if offered to prove what it asserts: that V was held in a container with that appearance. But some courts have held that in situations of this kind, the evidence may be offered for a different purpose: to show the declarant's *knowledge* of a container of that exact appearance. (Other evidence in the case will establish that D had such a container.) Courts tend to allow this theory when the description is unique, when there is little chance that the declarant obtained the knowledge other than from the circumstances alleged in the case, and where the declarant testifies. All of those factors are present here.

    Answer (A) is incorrect because there is no "reverse-403" rule that allows the court to admit otherwise inadmissible evidence if it has great probative value.

    Answer (B) is incorrect because the statement was not one of identification of a person made after perceiving the person. In addition, it cannot be offered to show that D was the one who locked V in the container.

    Answer (D) is incorrect because the prior statement, though consistent with V's trial testimony, contains key facts that were not present in V's trial testimony. In addition, the requirements of FRE 801(d)(1)(B) are not satisfied because D has not made an express or implied charge of recent fabrication or improper influence of motive, nor is there a showing that the statement was made before such charge or motive arose, nor is the statement offered to rehabilitate the declarant's credibility.

54. The statement, "V is planning to kill you the next time she sees you" is hearsay if offered to prove that V attacked D. That is because the statement was made by V other than while testifying at the trial, it asserts that she was going to kill (attack) D, and it is offered to prove that she did so. The statement is also relevant to show D's fear, however. A valid self-defense claim can exist when one acts out of reasonable fear of imminent attack by the other person. If D heard X's statement, D might reasonably have feared V, and this would justify D's striking V. For that purpose (to prove D believed V was going to attack her), the statement is not hearsay.

55. **Answer (C) is correct.** Assume X's statement to D was, "P supports neo-Nazi organizations." That statement is relevant both to prove that P in fact supported such organizations and to show that D had a good-faith belief that P did so. If offered to prove that P really does support such organizations, the statement is hearsay because it was made by X other than while testifying at the trial and it would be offered to prove the truth of the matter asserted. If offered to prove D's good faith basis for publishing the story, however, the statement is not hearsay. That is because the statement need not be true for it to serve as the basis for good faith. D need only have believed it to be true.

    Answers (A) and (B) are incorrect for the reasons just given.

    Answer (D) is incorrect because the problem provides sufficient information to answer the hearsay question.

56. **Answer (B) is correct.** Though it might not appear so at first glance, reputation can be hearsay. Consider what "reputation" means: it is what people are saying about another person or group. It is, therefore, a sort of group statement. Because it is being made out of court, it is hearsay if

offered to prove the truth of what it asserts. Thus, in this case, the community's statement would be, "V is violent." (Note that the statement is an assertion that V is violent. The statement is *not* that V has a reputation for violence.) That statement is relevant to prove that V attacked first because a person who is violent is more likely to be the first aggressor in a fight than is one who is not violent. However, if the statement is offered to prove that V attacked first, it is hearsay.

Suppose, however, that D claims she attacked V because she reasonably feared that V would attack her imminently. This is also a self-defense claim, albeit based on a different element of a self-defense claim. If this is D's defense, however, the evidence of V's reputation for violence would be irrelevant because D did not know V's reputation at the time of the altercation. Thus, V's reputation could not have served as the basis of a reasonable fear of V.

The result is that the evidence is irrelevant if offered to prove D acted out of a reasonable fear of V, and relevant, but hearsay, if offered to prove that D was the first aggressor.

Answers (A), (C), and (D) are incorrect for the reasons given.

57. P's statement is hearsay. P's statement was made other than while testifying at the trial, it is an assertion that she accepted D's offer, and it is offered to prove that P did so. P's statement does not constitute words of independent legal significance because it is a *statement about* the acceptance of D's offer. It is not the acceptance itself. That occurred prior to the time P made the statement to W, and P is only reporting to W about that event.

58. **Answer (A) is correct.** As discussed in connection with a previous question, a declarant-based definition of hearsay would be likely to classify as hearsay a statement the value of which depends on the credibility of the declarant. Here, if the testator was being insincere, she might have wanted to create the impression that she was insane. One way to do that might be to say something that made no sense. (Other testimonial infirmities, such as problems with the declarant's perceptions, might also be present.) Under the declarant-based definition, therefore, the testator's statement might be classified as hearsay.

The statement would not be hearsay under the assertion-based definition, however. The testator has given an order or made a request here; she has not made an assertion of fact. The statement is relevant not because of what it says, but because of what it *implies* about the testator's sanity. We would call this "circumstantial evidence of the declarant's state of mind" and classify it as non-hearsay.

Answers (B), (C), and (D) are incorrect for the reasons given.

59. The testimony of a witness that D spoke the words would not be hearsay. Even though the witness will be repeating D's out-of-court utterance, the utterance would constitute words of independent legal significance (what some would call a "verbal act"). The utterance, in other words, is not offered as proof of some fact; the utterance is the fact itself that is being proved.

The newspaper review would be hearsay, however. It is an assertion (by the writer of the article) that D uttered the words. This assertion is not being made while the writer of the article is testifying at the trial. It is being made in an out-of-court context (the newspaper review).

For the following questions, indicate whether each item is hearsay for the purpose for which it is offered, and explain your answer. Apply the Federal Rules of Evidence. If something would not be hearsay under the Federal Rules, call it non-hearsay. Also, do not assume that a declarant is a party unless the facts indicate such.

60. **Hearsay.** There are two statements here. P is saying, "I own the lot." That statement is not hearsay because it constitutes words of independent legal significance ("verbal act"). (It is the *act* of open and notorious possession, an element of adverse possession.) X's statement is, "P is saying she owns the lot." That statement is hearsay because it is an out-of-court assertion that P is making the statement, offered to prove that P is making the statement.

61. **Not hearsay.** The community statement (reputation) is, "P is a brilliant corporate leader." That statement is not being offered to prove the truth, but just to show that P enjoyed a great reputation before D's alleged slander.

62. **Not hearsay.** The dispatcher's statement, "P is armed" is not being offered to prove that P was armed, but to show that D had reason to think P was armed. This would help form the basis of a claim that D acted reasonably in shooting P.

63. **Not hearsay.** The circumstances suggest that the structural engineer was trying to assert something about the safety of the bridge, but that does not matter. It makes no difference what was going through the engineer's mind when he jumped up and down on the bridge. All that matters is that W, who observed the event, is subject to cross-examination when she testifies about that event. To test this point, imagine that the engineer believed the bridge was poorly designed or constructed and wanted to show that it would collapse when he jumped up and down on it. That does not matter. Again, this is a situation in which there is an event and a person who observes the event testifies about it.

64. **Not hearsay.** D's statement, offered by P, is an admission under FRE 801(d)(2)(A). All statements that fit into FRE 801(d) are classified as non-hearsay even if offered to prove the truth of the matter asserted. It really is that simple; a statement of a party offered against the party is not hearsay. In this example, the statement is against the party's interest, but it need not be. If D had said, "You cut me off, dude," and P for some reason wanted to offer that statement into evidence to prove the truth of the matter asserted, it would still qualify as an admission. (Keep this in mind; the term "admission" in the law of evidence does *not* mean that the declarant is admitting any sort of fault. Indeed, the title of the subdivision was amended to "opposing party's statements" to reflect this point.)

65. **Not hearsay.** W's statement was the assertive conduct of pointing to D in response to the prosecutor's question. Thus, it is equivalent to the statement, "D killed V." However, W made the statement while testifying at the trial. Therefore, it is not hearsay.

66. **Not hearsay.** The people at the beach were not trying to *assert* that it was sunny. They were simply acting on the belief that it was sunny. (That is what makes their conduct relevant.) Because there is no assertion, the statement is not hearsay. This example fits into the category of non-assertive conduct ("implied assertion").

67. **Hearsay.** The forecaster's statement, understood in context, was an assertion that it was raining. Generally, orders or requests are not hearsay because they do not contain an intended assertion of fact. This one does. If offered to prove that it was raining, the statement is hearsay.

68. **Hearsay.** P's statement is not part of the contract, but is an assertion that there was a contract. The statement is hearsay to prove there was a contract. Note that this is not an admission because P is offering her own statement, not her opponent's statement.

69. **Not hearsay.** The physician's conduct is non-assertive ("implied assertion"). She was not trying to *say* she was afraid of contracting AIDS from X; she was merely acting consistently with such a belief. Thus, the conduct is relevant, but not hearsay.

70. **Hearsay.** D's statement that X is "my favorite person in the whole world" is an assertion that D likes X. The statement is offered to prove that fact, so it is hearsay.

71. **Not hearsay.** Though it is true that the only way W would know that X is her mother is that someone told her, W's testimony does not repeat the out-of-court statement. If W had testified, "Someone told me X is my mom," that would have been hearsay. (If there is any objection to W's testimony here, it might be that W lacks personal knowledge. But even that objection is fairly weak; in virtually any circumstance, the opponent would feel silly objecting.)

72. **Not hearsay.** To be a "statement" within the definition of that term in FRE 801(a), the conduct must be that of a person. FRE 801(b) defines "declarant" as a "*person* who made the statement." (emphasis added). The issue here is one of relevance and probative value, not hearsay.

73. **Hearsay.** Professor Wigmore was asserting that the time was 5:10. The statement is offered to prove that it was 5:10.

74. **Hearsay.** The owner's statement is relevant because, by claiming to be the "king," the declarant meant that he was a sales leader. This is the assertion in the declarant's utterance. Thus, the utterance is hearsay.

75. **Hearsay.** Whoever commissioned the tombstone wished to assert that Elvis is dead. Therefore, the writing on the tombstone is an out-of-court statement. When offered to prove Elvis is dead, it is hearsay.

76. **Hearsay.** P's out-of-court statement was an assertion that the car that, as other evidence will show, was driven by D, hit P's car. It is hearsay when offered to prove that fact. Note that it doesn't matter that P is testifying about her own statement; it is still hearsay.

77. **Not hearsay.** W's prior statement impeaches W's credibility by showing that W spoke inconsistently about the same event. This makes W a less reliable witness than she would be without the inconsistency. Used in this way, the statement is not offered to prove the truth of the matter asserted; it is not offered to prove that P had the green light. Thus, it is not hearsay. (No doubt D will seek a limiting instruction under FRE 105, informing the jury that it may consider the evidence only to impeach W, and not to prove that P had the green light.)

78. **Not hearsay.** The automated message is not treated as a "statement" for purposes of the hearsay rule because no person was present and making an assertion at the time. FRE 801(b) defines "declarant" as a "*person* who made the statement." (emphasis added). As with the conduct of animals, admissibility of things done by mechanical devices is analyzed as a question of relevance and probative value, not one of hearsay.

79. **Not hearsay.** As the facts are stated, P does not appear to have been *asserting* her emotional distress; she was merely reacting to it—i.e., non-assertive conduct ("implied assertion"). Without an assertion, there can be no hearsay.

80. **Not hearsay.** This utterance is the slander itself. It is not evidence of the slander. Thus, it constitutes words of independent legal significance ("verbal act"). (Consider what would happen if the hearsay rule barred this evidence. How would plaintiff in a slander case ever prove that defendant uttered the slander? The law of evidence would be "trumping" the tort law that establishes a cause of action for slander.)

81. **Not hearsay.** This is D's statement, offered by the prosecution. It is therefore an admission, classified as non-hearsay under FRE 801(d)(2)(A) (opposing party's statement).

82. **Hearsay.** The bystander's act of pointing in response to W's question appears to have been an assertion that D was the responsible party. It was made other than while testifying at the trial, and it is offered to prove the truth of the matter asserted. It is therefore hearsay. Note that the bystander's pointing action apparently amounted to the identification of a person made after perceiving the person. Had the bystander testified at the trial, her conduct therefore might have qualified under FRE 801(d)(1)(C). But because the bystander was not a witness at trial, the rule's requirements are not satisfied and the conduct is hearsay.

83. **Hearsay.** The out-of-court statement was, essentially, "P was once convicted of embezzlement." D's defense is that it fired P because P had been convicted of a crime involving dishonesty, and embezzlement is such a crime. Therefore, the statement at issue is being offered to prove the truth of the matter asserted.

84. **Not hearsay.** The deceased's statement is relevant because it *suggests, circumstantially*, that she did not like P. If that is true, it is more likely that she left the deceased out of her will intentionally. Because she did not directly assert that she disliked P, the statement is not hearsay. (Note that if the deceased had said, "I don't like P," the statement would be hearsay. One might reasonably ask at this point whether the law of evidence makes any sense at all. Does admissibility here really depend on the exact words the decedent just happened to utter? Actually, and happily, the answer is no. As worded in the problem, the statement is not hearsay because it is circumstantial evidence of the declarant's state of mind. Thus, it is admissible. If the decedent had said, "I don't like P," the statement would be hearsay, but it would be admissible under FRE 803(3), an exception for statements of the declarant's then-existing state of mind. In both cases, then, the statement is admissible.)

85. **Not hearsay.** The other driver's act of moving forward is relevant because it makes it more likely that the driver was reacting to a green light. But the act is not hearsay because there is no indication that the driver was moving forward to *assert* that the light was green. There is

a difference between acting to assert a fact, and acting *because* of that fact. The former is hearsay. Under modern evidence law, the latter, which we call non-assertive conduct ("implied assertion," is not hearsay. (Note that at common law, non-assertive conduct was more likely to be excluded as hearsay because its value depends on the credibility of the actor.)

86. **Not hearsay.** P's statement to D was not an assertion that a contract existed, but constituted the acceptance of an offer, which is part of the act of making the contract. Thus, it constituted words of independent legal significance ("verbal act"), and is not hearsay.

87. **Not hearsay.** A fish cannot be a declarant. FRE 801(b) defines "declarant" as a "*person* who made the statement." (emphasis added). The conduct of the fish is either relevant or not relevant, but it is not hearsay.

88. **Not hearsay.** This statement is being offered to show its effect on the listener (D). What matters is not whether the statement is true, but whether D believed it to be true. If D held that belief, there is a possible basis for her claim of provocation. Because the statement is relevant even if not true, it is not hearsay.

89. **Not hearsay.** The pilot's behavior is relevant because it suggests that she believed the plane to be airworthy. (If she did not believe the plane was safe, it is unlikely she would have gone aboard and flown off.) Because the pilot did not inspect and board the plane in order to *assert* that it was airworthy, her conduct is not hearsay. It falls into the category of non-assertive conduct ("implied assertion"). (Note that at common law, this conduct probably would have been classified as hearsay because its relevance and probative value depend in part on the credibility of the pilot. Perception might be a particularly important issue. If, for example, the pilot did not do a good job of inspecting the plane, her act of boarding would carry little weight as to the plane's safety.)

90. **Not hearsay.** This is an example of a statement offered to show the effect on the listener, and not to prove the truth of the matter asserted. If D's president believed the story about P was true, it is far more likely she acted in good faith in firing P than if she did not believe the story.

91. **Hearsay.** The declarant in this example is the friend. The friend asserted that it was "12:00 sharp." The statement is being offered to prove that it was in fact 12:00 at that time. Thus, the statement is hearsay. (Note that if the friend had been the witness, and had testified that the killing occurred at 12:00, her testimony that she knew it was 12:00 because she looked at her watch would not be hearsay. In that situation, there would be no declarant because the watch would not be a declarant. FRE 801(b) defines "declarant" as a "*person* who made the statement." (emphasis added).)

92. **Hearsay.** The declarant in this case is the writer of the newspaper article. The writer asserted that the heat wave continued on the previous day. That statement is hearsay because its value depends on its being true.

93. **Not hearsay.** The statement is being offered as circumstantial evidence of the professor's state of mind. The statement suggests that the declarant is insane because a sane person is less likely to make such a claim than an insane person. Thus, the statement is not being offered to prove that the professor is in fact the "king of the Federal Rules."

94. **Hearsay.** The declarant is the husband. His assertion was that the rooster was crowing and that it was time to get up. For this statement to be relevant to whether it was about dawn, the statement must be true. Note that the rooster is not a declarant. FRE 801(b) defines "declarant" as a "*person* who made the statement." (emphasis added).

95. **Hearsay.** The death certificate is an assertion that a person is dead. The declarant is the person who filled out the certificate. Because it is offered to prove that X is dead, the death certificate is hearsay. (The death certificate does not constitute words of independent legal significance. It is true that there are legal consequences to the death certificate. But that document did not kill X; X would be dead whether or not a death certificate existed. The death certificate is only evidence that X is dead. Of course, in some circumstances, the law treats a death certificate as particularly persuasive, or even conclusive, evidence of the person's death. But even in those situations, the death certificate is evidence of the fact.)

96. **Hearsay.** It is important to identify the declarant in this situation. It is not A's president or B's president (though they uttered words). It is X. X has made an out-of-court statement that A's president and B's president uttered these words. For testimony concerning X's statement to be relevant, it must be true. Therefore, it is hearsay. (This is not a hearsay within hearsay case. The words spoken by A's president and B's president are words of independent legal significance, and thus not hearsay.)

97. **Not hearsay.** The execution of the deed is part of the act of conveying the property. The deed therefore constitutes words of independent legal significance ("verbal act"). (It is like a written contract in that sense.) Therefore, it is not hearsay.

98. **Hearsay.** Usually, a question is not an assertion and is therefore not hearsay. In this case, however, the question does contain an assertion, which is that X has blond hair. Because it was made out of court, and is offered to prove that X is a blond, the statement is hearsay.

99. **Not hearsay.** Absent evidence to the contrary, it appears that P was not asserting that she was in pain; she was merely reacting to the pain. The conduct is therefore non-assertive conduct ("implied assertion"), which we classify as non-hearsay. (If P had said, "My leg hurts," there would be an assertion, and it would be hearsay if offered to prove P was in pain.)

100. **Not hearsay.** X's statement to D is not offered to prove that the notes were bogus, but to prove D's knowledge of that fact. This is therefore an example of a statement offered to prove its effect on the listener. (D will almost certainly ask for a limiting instruction under FRE 105 instructing the jury to consider the evidence only to show D's knowledge, and not to prove the notes were counterfeit.) The prosecutor will need to introduce other evidence to prove the money was counterfeit.

101. **Hearsay.** X's confession is an out-of-court statement offered to prove the truth of the matter asserted (that X is guilty). This statement, in turn, is relevant because it makes D's guilt less probable. The statement is therefore hearsay on the question of D's innocence even though X did not assert D's innocence.

102. **Hearsay.** D is the declarant. Her assertion that "The Shrimptons is my favorite television program" is relevant only if true. The reasoning is that if the show is D's favorite, it is more likely D was home at 8:00 that night than if the show was not D's favorite.

103. **Not hearsay.** D's statement is a party admission under FRE 801(d)(2)(A). Even though it is an out-of-court statement offered in evidence to prove the truth of the matter asserted, it is classified as non-hearsay under the Federal Rules.

104. **Not hearsay.** This is non-assertive conduct ("implied assertion"). P was not playing catch using that arm to assert that the arm was uninjured. The evidence is relevant, however, because it tends to make it more likely that P did not suffer an injury than if P was not engaging in this activity.

105. **Not hearsay.** X was not testifying as a witness when she made the statement. As a result, the statement is not being "offered" by any party. *See* FRE 801(c)(2). It is merely an unfortunate event that the people in the courtroom, including the jurors, have witnessed. The court should instruct the jury to ignore the event, or, if the danger of unfair prejudice is too great, declare a mistrial.

106. **Hearsay.** The teacher's assertion that Y did "excellent work" is only relevant to Y's knowledge if it is true. It is therefore hearsay.

107. **Not hearsay.** This statement would be classified as circumstantial evidence of the declarant's state of mind. A person who calls another person "stupid" is less likely to like the other person than is one who makes a more flattering statement about that individual. Because the statement that Y is stupid is not an assertion that X does not like Y, it is not hearsay.

108. **Not hearsay.** The officials were not placing X's body into the van to assert that X was dead. They were doing so *because* X was dead (or perhaps because they believed X was dead). This is therefore an example of nonassertive ("implied assertion") conduct, which we classify as non-hearsay.

109. **Not hearsay.** The manager's utterance constitutes words of independent legal significance ("verbal act"). Making that statement to P is one of the acts of sexual harassment. (This is a better answer than classifying the utterance as non-hearsay because it is not offered to prove the truth of the matter asserted. The utterance is not a statement for purposes of the hearsay rule, so we never reach the question of whether it is offered to prove the truth of the matter asserted.)

110. **Hearsay.** This is a direct statement of X's state of mind. It must be true to be relevant on the question of whether X likes Y. The first inference from the statement is that X does hope Y will go out with her, and the next inference is that X likes Y.

111. **Hearsay.** Under the circumstances, the act of raising one thumb is an assertion that the prototype automobile was working well. If it was not, the act is probably irrelevant. Because this was assertive conduct, and because the assertive conduct is offered to prove the matter asserted, it is hearsay.

112. **Hearsay.** D is offering X's out-of-court statement to prove X committed the crime. If X did it, then D did not. Thus, the evidence is offered to prove the truth of the matter asserted.

113. **Not hearsay.** The evidence is offered only to prove that the pilot was alive at that moment. It does not matter what the pilot said. The evidence is treated as an event, not a statement.

114. **Not hearsay.** This is a prior inconsistent statement offered only to impeach the declarant's (V's) credibility. Thus, it is not offered to prove the truth of the matter asserted. If the prosecutor asks the court to issue a limiting instruction telling the jury not to consider the evidence to prove that the noise actually occurred at 11:00, the court must issue it. *See* FRE 105.

115. **Not hearsay.** This is an event, not a statement for purposes of the hearsay rule. Here is a way to test the concept: Suppose that X, for some irrational reason, wanted to demonstrate that she could *not* swim, and did the same act for that purpose. Wouldn't the evidence be equally probative of her ability to swim (contrary to her own beliefs)? The answer is yes. Thus, there is no reason to treat X as a declarant. It is her act that is important, not what she was trying to say by doing the act. The person the opponent would want to cross-examine is W, to test whether W really saw X perform the act.

116. **Not hearsay.** There are two declarants in this example: X and Y. Y told X, "V is very angry at D." X told D, "Y says V is very angry at you." Neither statement is hearsay. The combined statements are being offered to show the effect on D. If D believed what X told her, then D's self-defense claim is stronger. Test this conclusion: Suppose Y never really told X that V was very angry with D. The evidence that X told D that Y did make the statement still would have value in supporting D's self-defense claim.

    Keep in mind the necessity of distinguishing between the *witness's* statement and the *declarant's* statement. A student might ask, "What if X never told D about what Y said?" That doesn't change the hearsay problem. D made the statement about what X told her *while D was a witness testifying in the case.* Thus, D may be cross-examined concerning the accuracy of D's testimony.

117. **Hearsay.** The declarant is the radio announcer. The statement asserts that it is 5:00. It is offered to prove that fact. This is a simple case of hearsay.

118. **Not hearsay.** The declarant is P, the statement asserts that P is intentionally leaving nothing to D in the will and that D is (essentially) a bad person. The statement is relevant because it strongly implies that P does not like D. If that inference is correct, it is less likely that P would have given D an expensive gift such as a car. Because it doesn't state directly that P doesn't like D, however, the statement is not hearsay.

119. **Not hearsay.** Taking the oath is part of the *act* of becoming an attorney. It is not a statement *about* being an attorney. Thus, the oath fits into the category of words of independent legal significance, the verbal part of an act.

120. **Not hearsay.** There is no statement here because no person is making an assertion out of court. FRE 801(b) defines "declarant" as a "*person* who made the statement." (emphasis added). And what good would it do to cross-examine the bloodhound? The real question is the relevance and probative value of the bloodhound's conduct. How good was the dog at

tracking a scent? Were proper procedures followed in this case? These are matters that should be inquired of W or other witnesses.

121. **Not hearsay.** The statement of D, when offered by the prosecution, is a party admission under FRE 801(d)(2)(A) (opposing party's statement).

122. **Hearsay.** The declarant is X, who said to W, "I told D that V was angry at D." The statement is relevant because it helps to support D's claim that she believed V was going to attack her. The statement is hearsay because it is a out-of-court assertion that the declarant told D that V was angry at her. (Note that the statement is not being offered to prove that V *in fact* was angry at D. All that matters is that X told D that was so. And the assertion that X told D was not made on the witness stand.)

123. **Not hearsay.** V's statement qualifies as a statement of prior identification under FRE 801(d)(1)(C). The declarant (V) testifies at the trial. There is no reason to believe that V is not "subject to cross-examination about a prior statement." The statement is one of identification of a person made after perceiving the person.

124. **Not hearsay.** The declarant is D. D's statement to W is "V is angry at me." The statement is not offered to prove that V actually was angry at D, but only to prove that D *believed* that to be the case. If that inference is correct, D's self-defense claim is supported. Thus, this statement is circumstantial evidence of the declarant's then-existing state of mind.

125. **Not hearsay.** The evidence actually consists of many acts of purchasing Brand X. Those acts are not assertive; the purchasers bought Brand X so they could have detergent, not because they wanted to say anything about Brand X. Thus, there is no statement.

126. **Not hearsay.** The professor's act is relevant because it constitutes circumstantial evidence of his insanity.

127. **Not hearsay.** The letter is part of the *act* of canceling the contract. It is not a statement about cancellation. This is therefore an act that has independent legal significance ("verbal act").

128. **Hearsay.** D is the declarant. His statement is, "I plan to drive very carefully on this trip." From that evidence, one might infer that D did drive carefully. The statement is hearsay because it is a direct statement of D's then-existing state of mind—an intention to drive carefully—and it is offered to prove that fact. This is an example of a *Hillmon*-type statement and falls with the presently existing mental condition exception. *See* FRE 803(3).

129. **Not hearsay.** By his conduct, D appears to have "adopted" W's accusation that D tried to kill V. If that is true, W's statement is an adoptive admission under FRE 801(d)(2)(B) and is therefore not hearsay.

130. **Hearsay.** V's prior statement to the police claiming that he heard a noise at 11:00 p.m. is inconsistent with V's trial testimony that the event occurred at 3:00 a.m. If only offered to impeach V by showing that V was inconsistent, the statement would not be hearsay. However, the problem states that D's purpose was to establish the truth of V's prior statement: that the event took place at 11:00 p.m. It is therefore hearsay.

Note that V's statement does not qualify as non-hearsay under FRE 801(d)(1)(A) because it was not made under oath, subject to the penalty for perjury. It was simply a statement to the police.

131. **Hearsay.** X's statement asserts that she loves Purple Giant pork and beans. The statement is relevant because, if X really loved that product, it is more likely she consumed it than if she did not love the product. The statement is hearsay because it is a direct statement of X's then-existing state of mind, and it is offered to prove her state of mind.

132. **Not hearsay.** The video is relevant because it makes it somewhat more likely that X was the guilty party. There is no statement, however. X was not running away from the market to *assert* that she was the arsonist — i.e., non-assertive conduct ("implied assertion"). Absent some very bizarre circumstances not revealed in the problem, the most reasonable inference is that X was running away to get away.

133. **Not hearsay.** This is a classic example of words of independent legal significance, or a "verbal act." The tenant farmer's pointing and words are part of the *act* of paying the rent.

Topic 7: Answers

Exceptions to (and Exemptions from) the Hearsay Rule

134. **Answer (D) is correct.** W's question to V is not an assertion, so is not hearsay. But V's pointing action probably amounts to a statement that the crime was committed at D's house. It is hearsay because it is being offered to prove that the crime happened at D's house, which, in turn, makes it more likely that D committed the crime. (There is no other relevant purpose for the evidence.) This is a homicide prosecution, V is unavailable, and the statement concerns the cause or circumstances of death. If the judge finds that V believed he was about to die, V's statement will be admissible as a dying declaration. *See* FRE 804(b)(2).

   Answer (A) is incorrect because it assumes no exception applies. **Answer (B) is incorrect** because it assumes V's pointing is not a statement. **Answer (C) is incorrect** because the concept of "adoption" deals with admissions, and V is not a party.

135. **Answer (B) is correct.** Either X was asserting the direction from which the shots were fired, or X's pointing is irrelevant. If X was asserting the direction from which the shots were fired, X would be making a hearsay statement because the only relevant purpose would be to prove the truth of the matter asserted. However, it would likely be admissible as a present sense impression under the circumstances. *See* FRE 803(1). Because it would be irrelevant if not an assertion of the direction from which the shots came, and would be admissible if it was such an assertion, there is no danger in allowing the jury to decide whether it was an assertion (as long as there is evidence sufficient to support that conclusion). *See* FRE 104(b).

   Answer (A) is incorrect because it assumes the judge should make all preliminary factual findings here. **Answer (C) is incorrect** because it assumes the statement could only be admissible as an excited utterance. That's possible if more facts could be shown, but the present sense impression exception seems more applicable here. **Answer (D) is incorrect** because it assumes no hearsay exception would apply.

136. **Answer (C) is correct.** X's statement is analytically hearsay because it asserts that P did the work, and P is offering it to prove that it did. But the statement would be an admission if X was authorized to speak for D, which is most likely the case.

   Answer (A) is incorrect because the making of the statement is not part of the contract itself, but just circumstantial evidence that a contract had been entered into. **Answer (B) is incorrect** because it assumes the statement isn't hearsay, but the first inference is that P did the work, from which one can infer that D hired P to do so. The first inference is one of the things asserted in the statement. **Answer (D) is incorrect** because there is little indication in the facts that D employed X to work with polling information.

137. **Answer (D) is correct.** The judge makes preliminary findings under FRE 801(d)(2)(E) because the statement is still relevant even if the preliminary facts are not present. The statement which is at issue can be used as part of the foundation for its own admissibility. (This is what the Supreme Court held in *Bourjaily v. United States*, 483 U.S. 171 (1987).)

   Answer (A) is incorrect because it assumes the preliminary facts are for the jury. **Answer (B) is incorrect** because preliminary fact questions decided by the court are decided on a preponderance standard. **Answer (C) is incorrect** because the Supreme Court held in *Bourjaily* that the "bootstrapping" rule did not survive the adoption of the Federal Rules.

138. In *Bourjaily*, the Supreme Court explicitly reserved this question. However, Congress amended FRE 801(d)(2)(E) in 1997 to add the following sentence: "The statement must be considered but does not by itself establish the declarant's authority under (C); the existence or scope of the relationship under (D); or the existence of the conspiracy or participation in it under (E)." The effect of that amendment is to render the statement alone insufficient to establish the existence of the conspiracy. The court would not be acting properly if it allows the case to go to the jury.

139. **Answer (D) is correct.** V's statement is hearsay because it constitutes an assertion that V might have been wrong and it is offered to prove that fact and thus D's innocence. The dying declaration exception (FRE 804(b)(2)) does not apply for two reasons: this is not a civil case or a homicide prosecution, and the statement does not concern the cause or circumstances of what V believed to be her impending death. The statement also is not a declaration against interest because the worst a reasonable person in V's position would have believed at the time V made the statement is that the statement might subject V to social criticism for pointing out the wrong person. That is not an "interest" mentioned in FRE 804(b)(3). D's only reasonable argument is that her right to present a defense under the Sixth Amendment and the Due Process Clause would be violated if she is not allowed to testify about V's statement to W.

   Answers (A), (B), and (C) are incorrect for the reasons stated above.

140. **Answer (D) is correct.** The prosecution's strongest argument would be to employ the theory used in cases such as *Bridges v. State*, 19 N.W.2d 529 (Wis. 1945) and *United States v. Muscato*, 534 F. Supp 969 (E.D.N.Y. 1982) that the statements are admissible as non-hearsay to show knowledge of a fact that will be proven with other evidence. V is unlikely to have been shown the van at any time other than when he was assaulted. The description is quite detailed and the interior of the van rather unusual. V testifies, so V can be cross-examined about the statement.

   Answer (A) is incorrect because mere trustworthiness does not render a hearsay statement admissible. **Answer (B) is incorrect** because the statement was not made while observing the van or immediately thereafter. **Answer (C) is incorrect** because V is not unavailable.

141. **Answer (C) is correct.** FRE 602 makes the existence of personal knowledge a fact to be determined under the same standard set forth in FRE 104(b). Preliminary facts for admissibility of excited utterances are decided by the court under FRE 104(a) because the statement would be relevant whether or not the preliminary facts are true.

   Answers (A) and (B) are incorrect because they assume the wrong allocation of responsibility between judge and jury on personal knowledge. In addition, answer (B) assumes the incorrect standard to be applied to the finding. **Answer (D) is incorrect** because it assumes the wrong allocation of responsibility for excited utterances.

142. **Answer (B) is correct.** This appears to be a direct statement of D's then-existing state of mind, which would be relevant to show that he acted in accordance with the statement. Thus, it is an application of the *Hillmon* doctrine (derived from *Mutual Life Ins. Co. of New York v. Hillmon*, 145 U.S. 285 (1892)). FRE 803(3) adopted the *Hillmon* concept.

   Answer (A) is probably incorrect because the statement appears to state directly his feelings or intentions ("I think I'll go."). **Answer (C) is incorrect** because the statement only relates to the declarant's future intentions. **Answer (D) is incorrect** because it assumes the statement is not relevant. Note: The statement is not admissible as an admission because D was offering his own statement; it was not being offered against D.

143. **Answer (D) is correct.** The prosecution's strongest argument is that the Federal Rules have adopted a broad interpretation of the *Hillmon* rule, which would allow a statement that implicates the conduct of a third person. The cases are split on this question.

   Answer (A) is incorrect because the statement is hearsay, and the only relevant purpose is to prove the truth of what it asserts. **Answer (B) is incorrect** because it was not made in furtherance of a conspiracy (X mumbled the words to himself). **Answer (C) is incorrect** because there is no indication X is unavailable. The prosecution knows where he is and can bring him in for the trial.

144. **Answer (B) is correct.** D's strongest argument against admissibility would state that the *Hillmon* rule does not reach this far. That is, the rule allows statements of the declarant's then existing intention to act in a certain way, but it does not allow such a statement to prove another person's intent to participate in that act. The attack should be made on the basis that the policies behind the hearsay rule would be violated by admission.

   Answer (A) is incorrect because the declarant's statement appears to be non-testimonial. X was mumbling to himself, which hardly suggests that X intended to have his statement used in a prosecution of D. **Answer (C) is incorrect** because the burden under FRE 403 is very heavily weighted against exclusion, and the prejudice here doesn't seem terribly great. **Answer (D) is incorrect** because the statement probably was a direct statement of X's state of mind. Additionally, it does not matter whether the statement is a direct statement of X's intention and thus potentially admissible under the hearsay exception for such statements (FRE 803(3)), or whether the statement constitutes circumstantial evidence of X's intention. The ruling on D's objection does not depend on this distinction.

145. **Answer (A) is correct.** A's statement asserts that D was planning to be in Chicago the next day, and would be hearsay if offered to prove D in fact planned to be in Chicago. But if D authorized A to speak for her about the matter, the statement would qualify as an authorized party admission under FRE 801(d)(2)(C). An agent is undoubtedly authorized to speak to the press for the client; that is one of the agent's primary jobs.

Answer (B) is incorrect because a party admission is non-hearsay under the FRE. It is not an exception to the hearsay rule.

Answer (C) is incorrect because there is no indication that D is unavailable. In addition, there is nothing to suggest that at the time A made the statement on D's behalf, a reasonable person in D's position would believe it was against her interest to make the statement.

Answer (D) is incorrect because the residual exception is a last-resort, and the argument for admission as an authorized party admission is much stronger. In addition, it is unlikely that A's statement meets all the requirements of FRE 807.

146. The court should overrule D1's objection but sustain D2's objection. D1's statement is a simple party admission under FRE 801(d)(2)(A). It is not a party admission of D2, however. There is no indication that D2 authorized D1 to speak for her, or that D1 was speaking as D2's agent/employee. It does not qualify as a coconspirator statement because any conspiracy had ended at that point and was therefore not made "during" the conspiracy.

147. Objection sustained in part, overruled in part. X, the driver, made a two-part statement while she was employed by D. The first part concerned a matter within the scope of her job as an employee-salesperson. It therefore qualifies as an agency admission under FRE 801(d)(2)(D). The second part is not within the scope of her employment. In addition, absent evidence to the contrary, the court will not assume that a salesperson has authority to tell a customer that the boss will pay the medical bills. Thus, the statement is not admissible as an authorized admission under FRE 801(d)(2)(C). Even if she did have such authority, the statement would be excluded under FRE 409 as an offer to pay medical expenses.

148. **Answer (A) is correct.** Under FRE 801(d)(1)(C), a statement of prior identification of a person after perceiving the person is admissible as non-hearsay if the declarant testifies at the trial and is subject to cross-examination concerning the statement. Here, X testified at the trial. Nothing suggests that X is unwilling to answer questions concerning the identification, which the Supreme Court has held is sufficient to make X subject to cross-examination. *See United States v. Owens*, 484 U.S. 554 (1988). It doesn't matter that another witness actually provided the testimony about the identification X made of D in the lineup.

Answer (B) is incorrect for the reasons given above.

Answer (C) is incorrect for the reasons given above. The rule does not require that the prosecution recall X to verify that she made the identification of D.

Answer (D) is incorrect because the best evidence rule does not apply here. PO did not testify about the contents of a "writing, recording, or photograph." PO testified from memory.

149. **Answer (B) is correct.** The statement is hearsay and relevant to show who did it. Because it is against X's penal interests, and X is now unavailable, it can be admitted as a declaration against interest. *See* FRE 804(b)(3). Although (B) is the best answer, there are two problems. The part of the statement referring to "some blond guy" could be challenged under *Williamson v. United States*, 512 U.S. 594 (1994), as not against the declarant's interest because it was made to a police officer. The statement may also be challenged as "testimonial" under the Confrontation Clause (as opposed to an offhand remark). However, the causal way the remark was made suggests it was not made to curry favor with the police or intended as a "testimonial" statement.

Answer (A) is incorrect because X is not a party. Answer (C) is incorrect because the statement did not concern the cause or circumstances of impending death, and there is no indication X believed he was about to die when he made the statement. Answer (D) is incorrect because the evidence is relevant.

150. **Answer (A) is correct.** V testified at the trial or hearing. Under *United States v. Owens*, 484 U.S. 554 (1988), he would be "subject to cross examination about a statement." (The facts here are very similar to those in *Owens*.) The statement was one of identification of a person as someone the declarant perceived earlier. *See* FRE 801(d)(1)(C). Under the rule, it doesn't matter that PO is the one who actually testifies about who V identified.

Answer (B) is incorrect under the rule in *Owens*. Answer (C) is incorrect because PO need not have personal knowledge of the correctness of the identification, only of who V identified. Answer (D) is incorrect because there was sufficient evidence to support a finding that V had personal knowledge. The standard under FRE 602 is easy to satisfy.

151. Objection sustained. V's statement, "I was so depressed that day" is relevant because it makes it more likely that V would have tried to take her own life. The statement is hearsay because it asserts that V was previously depressed and it is offered to prove that fact (and thus that V tried to commit suicide). The state of mind exception in FRE 803(3) does not apply, however, because this was not a statement of V's *then existing* state of mind, meaning it did not concern V's state of mind at the time V made the statement. It was a statement that V had been depressed at a previous time.

152. **Answer (A) is correct.** V's statement is relevant because, if true, it put V in a position to have been murdered by D. The statement is hearsay because it is an assertion of V's plans to do something that night (drop off something at D's apartment), and it is offered to prove that V in fact did that thing that night. The statement fits into the *Hillmon* rule, codified in FRE 803(3), because it is a statement of one's intention to do something in the future, offered to prove the intention, and thus, that the act occurred. It is therefore admissible.

Note that the statement of one person of an intention to do something in the future is not generally admissible to prove that another person acted in a certain way. Thus, the statement,

"D is planning to go to the bowling alley tonight" probably is not admissible to prove D's intention to go to the bowling alley, and thus that D did so. But the statement in the present question is relevant without implying anything about D's actions. There is thus no need to redact the statement in any way. (If D's name were removed, the statement wouldn't be relevant, or, if relevant, would have minimal probative value and would not give the prosecution evidence to which it is entitled. "I'm planning to drop something off somewhere tonight" has little if any value.)

Answer (B) is incorrect for the reason given above. There is legitimate value to the evidence as an indication of V's intentions, and that value would be lost without allowing the jury to hear where V intended to go.

Answer (C) is incorrect for the same reason.

Answer (D) is incorrect because, as explained above, there is substantial probative value to the evidence as an indication of V's intentions. True, the evidence also implies that D would be present to accept the package, but the statement itself says nothing about what D planned to do.

153. **Answer (C) is correct.** W's notes impliedly indicate that P said these things, and this is what the notes are offered to prove. (They are not offered to prove the truth of what he said about quantum theory.) Thus, the notes are hearsay. But because W states that the notes were taken during the class, that they accurately reflect what was said, that she no longer remembers what was said, the notes can be read to the jury under the recorded recollection exception. *See* FRE 803(5).

Answer (A) is incorrect because it misconstrues the purpose for which the notes are offered. **Answer (B) is incorrect** because there is no requirement that W had a "legal duty" to record accurately. **Answer (D) is incorrect** because the attorney is not using the notes merely to refresh W's recollection.

154. **Answer (D) is correct.** The statement is hearsay because it is offered to prove the truth of what it asserts (that P suffered certain injuries). Facts are given that would justify its admission under exceptions for excited utterances, present sense impressions, statements of then existing physical condition, and statements for purposes of medical diagnosis or treatment.

Answer (A) is incorrect because it is not an admission. P is offering her own statement. **Answers (B) and (C) are incorrect** because they are not as complete as answer (D).

155. **Answer (C) is correct.** The prosecution's best response would be to argue that the preliminary fact of whether D heard the accusation should be decided by the jury under FRE 104(b)—that this is a case of "conditional relevancy." That argument would be fairly strong here because W's statement to D is independently admissible as a non-hearsay prior identification under FRE 801(d)(1)(C). Thus, there is little danger in allowing the jury to decide the preliminary fact of whether D heard the accusation; even if he did not, the accusation is admissible independently.

Answer (A) is incorrect because the facts do not indicate that W was speaking under the stress of excitement caused by a startling event. Also, the prosecution would be better off with an argument that the jury should decide the preliminary fact. That way, the jury would be more likely to hear the evidence. **Answer (B) is incorrect** for the same reason. **Answer (D) is incorrect** because the preliminary facts for prior identifications are for the court under FRE 104(a).

156. Objection sustained. The note is hearsay if offered to prove the truth of the matter asserted (that CDs were delivered to P on that date). The facts do not support the use of the note as a business record because there is no showing that the note was made in the regular course of business or that it was the regular practice of the business to make such a note. On the evidence given, the making of the note simply does not appear to be a routine matter for D's business. *See* FRE 803(6). Finally, the note also might be self-serving and thus untrustworthy.

On the information given, the requirements of the recorded recollection exception are not met. D has not testified to a lack of memory concerning the fact covered in the note (delivery of the CDs to P on that date). *See* FRE 803(5).

157. **Answer (D) is correct.** This is a typical case of former testimony. D's motive to cross-examine W now would be the same as at the civil trial (to shake W's story). D had the opportunity to conduct that cross-examination at the civil trial (and in fact did so, though the rule does not seem to require that he did). W is now unavailable.

Answer (A) is incorrect because the courts do not generally view the different stakes in criminal cases and civil cases as sufficient to make the motive different under this rule if the issue is the same. **Answer (B) is incorrect** because it doesn't matter which trial took place first as long as the rule's other requirements are met. **Answer (C) is incorrect** because D did have an opportunity to confront W, and in fact had that chance when W was under oath and subject to penalty for perjury.

158. **Answer (B) is correct.** The former testimony exception does not apply because X, a criminal defendant, *never* had the opportunity to confront W, and the "predecessor in interest" language of the former testimony exception only applies in civil cases. **Answer (A) is incorrect** because the facts do not indicate that her motive would be different from the motive D had in the civil trial. **Answer (C) is incorrect** because the "predecessor in interest" language of the rule does not apply here. **Answer (D) is wrong.** Evidence admissible against one party is not necessarily admissible against another party.

159. **Answer (A) is correct.** This is hearsay within hearsay. The "inner" statement is that of W1 ("D was surfing carefully"). The "outer" statement is that of X ("W1 said …"). Both are hearsay because both are offered to prove the truth of what they assert. (Another way to see this is to say that both statements must be true in order for the evidence to be useful to prove that D was surfing carefully.) No exception applies to either statement.

Answer (B) is incorrect because both W1's statement and X's statement are hearsay. In addition, if the W1's statement had been admissible as a prior inconsistent statement, a later opportunity for W1 to explain or deny the statement is permissible.

Answer (C) is incorrect because neither W1's statement nor X's statement is a declaration against interest. *See* FRE 804(b)(3).

Answer (D) is incorrect for the reasons stated above.

160. **Answer (D) is correct.** W's statement as a grand jury witness qualifies as a prior inconsistent statement that may be admitted to prove the truth of the matter asserted under FRE 801(d)(1)(A). W has testified at the trial, W appears to be subject to cross-examination about the statement, the prior statement is inconsistent with W's trial testimony, and the prior statement was made under penalty of perjury, at a formal hearing (the grand jury). It therefore qualifies as non-hearsay and may be offered to prove the truth of what it asserts: that W committed the bank robbery.

Answers (A), (B), and (C) are incorrect for the reasons stated above.

161. **Answer (A) is correct.** X is unavailable even though she is on the stand. (*See* FRE 804(a)(2).) The statement is against X's interest in that it might subject her to civil liability.

Answer (B) is incorrect because X is not a party. **Answer (C) is incorrect** because the facts do not support the foundation for excited utterances. **Answer (D) is incorrect** because it wrongly assumes X is not unavailable.

162. **Answer (D) is correct.** The problem states that X's statement is offered to prove D knew the substance was cocaine. Because it is not offered to prove the truth of the matter asserted by X (that this was cocaine), the statement is not hearsay. **Answers (A), (B), and (C) are incorrect** for the reasons given.

163. **Answer (A) is correct.** Because X is not a party defendant, her statement cannot be an admission under FRE 801(d)(2)(A). The statement might be an admission of X's employer D under FRE 801(d)(2)(D). To qualify, three requirements must be met: (1) the statement must have been made by the party's agent; (2) it must concern a matter within the scope of the agent's employment; and (3) it must have been made while the agent was employed.

Requirements (1) and (3) are easily satisfied here. X worked for D as service manager. That almost certainly makes X an agent of D. The problem also makes clear that at the time X spoke to P, X was working as the service manager. Thus, the statement was made during the course of X's employment.

The real issue here is whether the statement concerned a matter within the scope of X's employment. To answer this, one would need to know something about the nature of X's job. As service manager, X probably was required to diagnose problems with vehicles brought to the dealership, but we can't really be sure of this without more information.

That raises the second big question in this problem: Whose responsibility is it to decide whether the statement concerned a matter within the scope of X's employment? Under FRE 104, most preliminary questions of fact are to be decided by the court (and the standard is preponderance of the evidence). However, if the relevance of the evidence depends on whether a condition of fact is satisfied (FRE 104(b)), the court's job is only to determine whether there is evidence sufficient to support a finding that the condition is satisfied. Here, the question would be as follows: Is X's statement relevant even if X's job did not include diagnosing problems with vehicles? The answer is yes. The statement, "the car's steering mechanism was not put together properly," is relevant even if X's job did not include diagnosis of the problems with cars brought to the dealership. The consequence is that this is *not* a problem that fits into FRE 104(b). That, in turn, means that the court must decide the preliminary fact question under FRE 104(a). **Answer (B) is incorrect** for this reason.

Note that under FRE 801(d)(2)(D), there is no requirement that the declarant be *authorized* to make the statement. This is a departure from the common law in many states, which did not recognize vicarious admissions unless the declarant was authorized to speak for the other person. The drafters of the Federal Rules decided that agency, scope of employment, and the making of the statement during the employment were sufficient in themselves to support admission of the evidence. The drafters created a second exemption, for authorized admissions. That exemption can be found in FRE 801(d)(2)(C).

Answer (C) is incorrect because courts tend not to apply the personal knowledge requirement to admissions. **Answer (D) is incorrect** because the statement is not hearsay if it is an admission under FRE 801(d).

164. **Answer (C) is correct.** X's statement essentially asserts that D did not commit the crimes. The statement is relevant because it increases the probability of D's innocence, so **answer (A) is incorrect.** X does not lack personal knowledge because she claims to know firsthand that D could not have committed the crimes, so **answer (B) is incorrect.** The statement is hearsay, however. Even if X was authorized to speak for D, the statement cannot qualify as an authorized admission under FRE 801(d)(2)(C) because the statement is being offered *by, not against*, D.

Because the statement is inadmissible hearsay, there is no need to consider the application of FRE 403. That rule applies only to exclude otherwise admissible evidence. This evidence is inadmissible. Thus, **answer (D) is incorrect.**

165. **Answer (B) is correct.** This problem raises the question of how FRE 801(d)(2)(E), the co-conspirator rule, should be applied. There are several preliminary facts that must be found before a statement qualifies as a coconspirator statement: (1) there must be a conspiracy; (2) the statement must have been made by a coconspirator of the party against whom the statement is offered; (3) the statement must have been made during the conspiracy; and (4) the statement must have been made "in furtherance" of the conspiracy. The third and fourth prerequisites are not really in issue here because the problem strongly suggests that the statement was made at a time when the conspiracy was still going on and that the statement helped further the conspiracy's goals.

The real questions here are whether there was in fact a conspiracy and whether the declarant, X, was a member of the conspiracy. Once again, we are faced with a problem involving the decision-making authority with respect to preliminary facts. Consider first the question whether there was a conspiracy. Is the statement (which asserts among other things that D was involved) relevant even if there was no conspiracy? Yes. Even if there was no conspiracy, the statement still increases the likelihood of D's guilt on the ground that D could have acted alone in importing the software. Thus, the existence of the conspiracy must be decided by the court under FRE 104(a).

Moving to the second question: Was the declarant (X) a coconspirator? Even if X was not a coconspirator, the statement is relevant because, once again, it increases the likelihood of D's guilt. So, again, the court must decide this question of preliminary fact under FRE 104(a).

Based on these considerations, answer (B) is correct because it recognizes that the court must decide the preliminary facts. **Answer (A) is incorrect** because it assumes FRE 104(b) applies, which it does not.

Answer (D) is incorrect because, even if X is a defendant (and the problem does not state whether that is true), X's statement would only be an admission of X, not of D, unless the statement qualifies under the coconspirator rule. One cannot use a personal admission of one party as an admission of another party unless the statement qualifies under FRE 801(d)(2)(C), (D), or (E).

Answer (C) is incorrect as well. The answer is attractive on its face because it is true that the jury must eventually decide whether there was a conspiracy. That's one of the charges against D. But there is a fundamental difference between the following two things: (1) deciding the existence of a fact for purposes of determining guilt; and (2) deciding the existence of a fact merely as a prerequisite to the admission of a piece of evidence. When the court decides the question for purposes of admitting the evidence (applying the preponderance of the evidence standard), all it is doing is admitting the evidence. And there is no reason for the court to inform the jury that it made that finding. By not saying anything about the facts the court had to decide in order to admit the evidence, the court avoids unduly swaying the jury.

166. **Answer (B) is correct.** FRE 602 tells us that a witness may testify to a fact "only if evidence is introduced sufficient to support a finding that the witness has personal knowledge of the matter." (Of course, this rule does not apply to experts in most situations.) Compare this standard to the one in FRE 104(b), and it should be clear that they are the same. Thus, FRE 602 treats issues concerning personal knowledge as problems of conditional relevance. Under that standard, the court does not decide whether the witness had personal knowledge; it merely decides whether there is evidence "sufficient to support a finding" of personal knowledge. This is the essence of answer (B), and it explains why **answer (A) is incorrect.**

Answer (C) is incorrect because FRE 602 makes clear that the witness's own testimony may be considered in determining whether there is evidence sufficient to support a finding of personal knowledge. ("Evidence to prove personal knowledge may consist of the witness's own testimony.") That the witness's testimony might be self-serving does not mean the court (and ultimately the jury) may not consider it.

Answer (D) is incorrect because the problem does not supply sufficient facts to determine whether the court should admit the evidence.

167. **Answer (D) is correct.** The preliminary facts necessary to the admission of a statement as a dying declaration under FRE 804(b)(2) are for the court under FRE 104(a). (That is because the statement will be relevant even if those facts are not true.) The last sentence of FRE 104(a) states that "[i]n so deciding, the court is not bound by evidence rules, except those on privilege." That means the court may consider all of the items listed in answers (A) and (B). (Even the statement itself may be used to support its own admissibility.)

As the language quoted above indicates, the only constraint on the court is the application of evidentiary privileges. In *United States v. Zolin*, 491 U.S. 554 (1989), the Supreme Court held that in making preliminary determinations concerning the application of the crime-fraud exception to the attorney-client privilege, the court was permitted to consider any evidence that had not already been found privileged. Thus, the type of evidence referred to in **answer (C)** may be considered as well as the types mentioned in **answers (A) and (B)**.

168. **Answer (C) is correct.** X's statement is hearsay because it asserts that X committed the crime, and it is offered to prove that fact, which decreases the likelihood that D committed it. However, the statement qualifies as a declaration against interest. FRE 804(b)(3) sets forth a number of prerequisites to the admission of hearsay under this exception. All of the prerequisites are for the court to decide under FRE 104(a).

    First, the declarant must be unavailable. Under FRE 804(a)(2), a person is unavailable if she "refuses to testify about the subject matter despite a court order to do so." That is what X has done here. Thus, for purposes of the rule she is unavailable, even though she is sitting on the witness stand.

    Next, under FRE 804(b)(3)(A), at the time of its making, the statement must have been "so contrary to" any of a number of interests that "a reasonable person in the declarant's position would have made [it] only if the person believed it to be true." Here, the statement is clearly against X's penal interest. There is every reason to believe that in these circumstances, a reasonable person would believe that admitting to the commission of a crime might subject her to prosecution. Even though the statement was made to a friend, most people would feel that it is risky to make such a statement.

    Next, under FRE 804(b)(3)(B), a statement tending to expose the declarant to criminal liability is not admissible unless it "is supported by corroborating circumstances that clearly indicate its trustworthiness." Here, the statement does expose X to criminal liability, and it is being offered to exculpate D, the accused. But the facts indicate that D called a friend of X to testify to X's involvement in the crime. That appears to be evidence linking X to the crime, satisfying the corroboration requirement.

    Answer (A) is incorrect because to be an admission, a statement must have been made by a party. **Answer (B) is incorrect** because, as explained above, the statement qualifies as a declaration against interest. **Answer (D) is incorrect** because, even if the friend to whom X made the statement testifies, the statement will still be hearsay. (Remember that the question whether a statement is hearsay does not depend on who the *witness* is. It depends on who the *declarant* is.)

169. **Answer (D) is correct.** The declarant is P. P stated that D was not planning to deliver the CDs on time. The statement is offered to prove that D was not planning to deliver the CDs on time. From that, it can be inferred that D did not in fact deliver the CDs on time. (Note the difference between the phrase "to prove" for relevance purposes, and the same statement for hearsay purposes. For relevance, one must consider the entire chain of reasoning. If the chain leads to a conclusion of fact that is of consequence to the action, the evidence is relevant. For hearsay purposes, however, "to prove" only requires looking at the first inference. The first

inference from the statement here is the same as the fact it asserts—that D was not planning to deliver the CDs on time. The statement is therefore hearsay.)

The question here is whether the statement satisfies any exception or fits into an exemption. **Answer (A) is incorrect** because, even though P's out-of-court statement implies something that D said, P did not tell her secretary, "D says...." Thus, D is not a declarant, and the statement is not admissible as an admission because P is offering her own statement, not that of D.

Still, we would want the law of evidence to be rational, and not to reach different conclusions based on tiny differences in wording. So, even if P had said, "D told me, 'I'm not going to deliver the CDs on time,'" there would still be a hearsay problem here. D's admission, in a sense, would be "trapped" within P's assertion that D made the statement. Because P's assertion is also hearsay (it must be true that D made the statement for the whole thing to be relevant), there must be a hearsay exception for P's statement or the whole thing will be excluded unless P's statement fits within an exception or exemption.

Answer (B) is incorrect because the state of mind exception (FRE 803(3)) does not apply. That is because what P *thinks* about what D plans to do is not relevant. What matters is what D *in fact* plans to do.

Answer (C) is incorrect because P's statement does not constitute words of independent legal significance. It is merely *evidence of* D's repudiation, just as D's own statement, "I'm not going to deliver the CDs" would be.

170. **Answer (C) is correct.** There are two layers of hearsay in this case. The inner layer is W's testimony, which was that X was not paying attention and was swerving from side to side as she drove. It is hearsay because it is offered to prove the truth of the matter asserted—that X was driving that way.

The outer layer is the transcript, which amounts to the court reporter's statement that this is what W testified at the trial. That statement is also hearsay because it is offered to prove that W in fact gave that testimony. (If W did not give that testimony, the transcript would be irrelevant.)

The transcript almost certainly qualifies as a business record of the court reporter under FRE 803(6). The transcript might also serve as the court reporter's recorded recollection under FRE 803(5).

Starting from the inside and working outward, the question is whether W's testimony qualifies under the former testimony exception in FRE 804(b)(1). To qualify, (1) the declarant must be unavailable; (2) the statement was given "at a trial, hearing, or lawful deposition, whether given during the current proceeding or a different one"; and (3) the statement "is now offered against a party who had—or, in a civil case, whose predecessor in interest had—an opportunity and similar motive to develop it by direct, cross-, or redirect examination."

W is dead, so W is unavailable to testify at the current trial. The statement was given by W as a witness in the criminal trial. The first two requirements are therefore satisfied. The real question concerns "opportunity and similar motive to develop ... [the testimony]." It is vital to consider separately each party against whom the evidence is offered. As to X, there is no problem. X was a party to the criminal prosecution (X was the defendant), and had an opportunity to cross-examine W at that time. X's motive at the criminal trial would have been to impeach W's testimony by showing that W was wrong when she said X was not paying attention and was swerving. That is exactly the same thing X would seek to do if W were present to testify at the civil trial. Thus, the transcript is admissible against X.

Is the transcript admissible against D Corp.? Because D Corp. was not a party to the criminal prosecution, it had no opportunity to cross-examine W at that trial. But because the present action is a civil case, the "predecessor in interest" language of FRE 804(b)(1)(B) might apply. The courts have generally interpreted the phrase broadly, and not limited "predecessor in interest" only to a party that would qualify under the law of property. Instead, courts tend to treat a party as a predecessor in interest under this rule if that party's interests are a good proxy for those of the current party. In other words, the courts tend to ask whether there was a party who had an opportunity to cross-examine the witness at the prior trial and whether that party would have used cross-examination for the same purposes as would the current party. That translates to the following question in the present case: Were X's interests in cross-examining W in the criminal trial the same as D Corp.'s interests in the current trial? The answer is yes because D Corp. claims that X was not driving recklessly. That was exactly X's defense in the first trial. Thus, the courts hold that X's cross-examination adequately protects D Corp.'s interests. (If X's lawyer did an egregiously bad job cross-examining W in the criminal trial, there is a chance that the current court will not apply the rule. Otherwise, D Corp. is pretty much stuck with the cross-examination X's lawyer conducted.)

The bottom line, therefore, is that the transcript is admissible against both D Corp. and X. **Answer (C) is correct.**

Answer (A) is incorrect because the transcript is offered to prove the truth of the matter asserted. In fact, both statements are offered to prove the truth of the matter asserted, as explained above. **Answer (B) is incorrect** because both statements were made out of court. **Answer (D) is incorrect** because, as explained, the transcript qualifies under the former testimony hearsay exception.

171. **Answer (B) is correct.** The statement X made to Y is hearsay if offered to prove that D was going to be the lookout unless the statement qualifies as non-hearsay under FRE 801(d)(2)(E), the coconspirator rule. That rule applies if the court finds by a preponderance of the evidence that there was a conspiracy, that X was a coconspirator, that the statement was made "during" the conspiracy, and that it was made "in furtherance" of the conspiracy.

Answer (A) is incorrect because the prosecution is not offering testimony about the contents of the audiotape; it is offering the witness's recollection of the conversation. Thus, the best evidence rule does not apply (even though the tape is probably a more accurate piece of evidence of what was said than the witness's memory).

Answer (C) is incorrect because it does not matter that the statement concerned another person's intentions. It is a coconspirator statement if it satisfies the foundational facts noted above.

Answer (D) is incorrect because the coconspirator rule applies even if conspiracy is not one of the charges involved in the case.

172. **Answer (C) is correct.** Under FRE 801(d)(2)(B), a party may adopt another's statement as her own, making it an admission. This will be the case if "the party manifested that it adopted or believed to be true." That fact, in turn, depends on whether the party heard and understood the statement and whether, under the circumstances, a reasonable person in the position of the party would deny the truth of the statement if it isn't true.

The problem here is that X is not a party. As a result, the adoptive admission rule does not apply. Therefore, **answer (A) is incorrect.**

Answer (B) is incorrect because the facts do not support the conclusion that D's statement is an excited utterance. D does not seem to have been under the influence of stress caused by a startling event, and some time had passed since D was placed under arrest. This was probably enough time to allow for reflection about the situation.

Answer (D) is incorrect because there has not been a showing that X is unavailable.

That leaves answer (C). D's statement is hearsay for which no exception applies, and if the jury does not hear D's statement, X's response is irrelevant.

173. D could object on two grounds: authentication and hearsay. To authenticate the bill, P needs to do more than merely state that it came from D. P will have to show something distinctive about the bill or something else showing that it came from D to meet the "sufficient to support a finding" standard of FRE 901(a). The document clearly will be hearsay because it will be offered to prove what it asserts: that P received certain medical services from the doctor for a certain amount of money. It might qualify as a business record under FRE 803(6), but P will have to establish that foundation.

174. The court should overrule Smith's objection but sustain Jones's objection. W's testimony is hearsay when offered to prove the truth of what W asserted (that she saw Smith and Jones kill V). The former testimony exception will apply easily to Smith, who was the defendant in the earlier trial. W is unavailable (*see* FRE 804(a)(2)), Smith had an opportunity to cross-examine W at the earlier trial (and did, though that is not required), and his motive was the same as it would be if W testified in the civil trial: to show that W was wrong or lying. Note that "motive" question is answered by looking to how the party might want to develop the witness's factual testimony, not to the ultimate consequence of an adverse judgment in the case. Thus, the evidence is admissible against Smith even though the consequences in the civil case (a money judgment, most likely) are different from those in a criminal case (most likely imprisonment). Thus, the transcript is admissible against Smith.

The transcript is not admissible against Jones, however. If W were present at the present trial, Jones would want to undercut W's identification of Jones as one of the perpetrators. This is something Smith would not have been motivated in any particularly strong way to do. Thus, Smith's cross-examination of W did not protect Jones's interests in the same way as Jones's cross-examination of W would support Jones if W were available in the present trial. The former testimony exception does not apply to Jones.

175. **Answer (A) is correct.** The document is hearsay because it asserts that the lumber was delivered on a certain date (two weeks later than it was supposed to arrive), and it is offered to prove that the lumber was delivered on that date. The question is whether any exception applies.

Answer (A) assumes the business records exception (FRE 803(6)) applies, which is correct. The preliminary facts are for the judge under FRE 104(a). The document, on its face, appears to be a "record of an ... event." The witness's testimony tends to show that records of this kind are made by the job foreperson (a person with knowledge) when building supplies arrive. The witness has testified that the document was kept in the place the company customarily keeps such records. That the document was written by a person who was unaware of any potential dispute between P and D means there are no meaningful indicia of lack of trustworthiness. The document qualifies as a business record.

Answer (B) is incorrect because the recorded recollection exception only applies when a writing made or adopted by a witness with knowledge of the facts, but who now lacks sufficient recollection to testify fully, is used as a substitute for the witness's testimony. *See* FRE 803(5). The custodian of records never had a personal knowledge of the lumber delivery date, so the record cannot be used as a substitute for her testimony.

Answer (C) is incorrect because the witness laying the foundation for business records is not required to have personal knowledge of the truth of the facts recited in the record.

Answer (D) is incorrect because the witness has no recollection of the delivery of the lumber that can be refreshed by the document.

176. **Answer (C) is correct.** Testimony concerning what P said at the earlier civil trial is hearsay. P is the declarant, and her statements about losing money to X in the scheme are offered in the present trial for the same purpose they were offered in the earlier trial: to prove that X in fact committed those acts.

The basic approach to the former testimony exception has already been discussed. From that discussion it should be clear that P's testimony, offered through the recollections of W, is admissible against X. X had an opportunity to cross-examine P in the earlier trial, and X's motive at that time was the same as it would be at the current trial if P were available: presumably to impeach P by showing she was wrong or being untruthful. There is no second layer of hearsay in this case because P's former testimony is being offered through a live witness who was present and can recount what P said.

The evidence is not admissible against D, however. D was not a party to the earlier action. Because the current case is a criminal prosecution, the "predecessor in interest" provision of FRE 804(b)(1)(B) does not apply. That means the evidence may not be offered against D.

Answers (A), (B), and (D) are incorrect for the reasons given.

177. **Answer (B) is correct.** There are two layers of hearsay in this problem. Because V's statement is offered to prove that another person committed the crime, it is hearsay unless it qualifies under the prior identification rule (FRE 801(d)(1)(C)). That statement is contained within a

police report, which is also hearsay because it is offered to prove the truth of the matters asserted (that V made the identification, and that the other facts recited in the report are true).

Is V's statement one that "identifies a person as someone the declarant perceived earlier"? It appears to be. An identification of a person's photo qualifies. Other requirements must be satisfied as well, however. The declarant (V) must testify at the trial or hearing and be subject to cross-examination about the statement. Here, V has not yet testified, but D has represented that she will call V. There is no requirement that the declarant testify before the statement is offered. (If V never testifies at the trial, the court, on the prosecution's motion, will strike the testimony about V's identification from the record and instruct the jury to ignore it.) In *United States v. Owens*, 484 U.S. 554 (1988), the Supreme Court read the phrase "subject to cross-examination about a prior statement" very loosely. Basically, as long as V takes the stand and willingly answers questions about the statement, the requirement will be satisfied. (Even if V proves forgetful about the incident or the photo identification, it appears that she will be deemed "subject to cross-examination about a prior statement.") Thus, V's statement qualifies as a non-hearsay statement of prior identification.

PO's report is hearsay, as noted above, but it appears to qualify as a public record or report under FRE 803(8)(A). It is a report of a public office that sets forth "a matter observed while under a legal duty to report" and "factual findings from a legally authorized investigation." On its face, "a matter observed" requirement, on its face, does not apply in criminal cases to matters observed by police and other law enforcement personnel. But courts have read this rule as applying only when the report is offered against the defendant, not the government. The "factual findings" part of the report is clearly admissible because the exclusion (the exception to the exceptions in part (iii)) does not apply when the record is offered against the government.

The hearsay rule therefore does not exclude the report, including the part that tells about V's identification. Answer (B) states the law correctly as applied to this problem.

Answers (A), (C), and (D) are incorrect for the reasons given.

178. **Answer (B) is correct.** X's written statement qualifies as "testimonial" because it was made at the request of the police, and X certainly would have thought the statement would be used in the investigation and prosecution of the person responsible for the murder. Under the Supreme Court's confrontation rules, testimonial statements are not admissible if the declarant is unavailable and the defendant did not have an opportunity to cross-examine the declarant about the statement. That is what happened here. X is dead and the facts do not reveal that D had any opportunity to cross-examine X.

Answer (A) is incorrect because it does not take account of the need for analysis under the Confrontation Clause. It is not enough that the evidence meets the requirements of a hearsay exception.

Answer (C) is incorrect because X's statement was testimonial.

Answer (D) is incorrect because it is based on the pre-*Crawford* confrontation analysis.

179. **Answer (D) is best.** The ticket is hearsay when offered to prove that D was present, which it certainly asserts. It appears that PO's testimony lays the foundation for the recorded recollection exception (FRE 803(5)). But the public records exception (FRE 803(8)(A)(ii)) specifically forbids the use of public records such as police reports against criminal defendants when those records concern the results of police investigations or "a matter observed" by law enforcement personnel. Thus, the rule is explicit regarding the type of document involved here: a ticket resulting from PO's observation of D's speeding violation. D's strongest argument is that, even if the ticket satisfies another hearsay exception such as the recorded recollection exception, the explicit rule excluding such records when offered against criminal defendants overrides, and the ticket is inadmissible. However, since PO can be cross-examined, some courts would admit the ticket.

   Answer (A) is incorrect because there is no multiple hearsay in this hypothetical.

   Answer (B) is incorrect because, as noted above, the record probably satisfies the recorded recollection exception.

   Answer (C) is incorrect because a FRE 403 argument rarely is successful; the rule is heavily weighted in favor of admissibility and is usually a last resort. Thus, this is not as strong as an argument of the type contained in **(D)**.

180. **Answer (D) is correct.** The first issue here is one of personal knowledge. That prerequisite applies to hearsay declarants, not just witnesses. (The courts do not apply the personal knowledge requirement to party admissions, but this is not a party admission.) Under FRE 602, personal knowledge is a FRE 104(b)-type fact, meaning that the court need only determine whether there is evidence sufficient to support a finding that the person had personal knowledge.

   If the court determines that there is evidence sufficient to support a finding that X had personal knowledge, it must next deal with the hearsay issue. X's statement is hearsay if offered to prove that the blue car ran the light and struck the red car. It might be an excited utterance, however, if there was a startling event, if declarant (X) was under the stress of excitement caused by the event, and if the statement relates to the event. These are facts for the court to decide under FRE 104(a).

   Answer (A) is incorrect because it is permissible — and usually wise practice — to lead a witness on cross-examination. **Answer (B) is incorrect** because the prior inconsistent statement rules apply when the same person has made inconsistent statements. That is not the case here. **Answer (C) is incorrect** because we do not have sufficient information to determine whether the excited utterance exception is satisfied. In addition, as noted above, the court will not reach the hearsay issue unless it determines that there is evidence sufficient to support a finding that the declarant had personal knowledge.

181. **Answer (B) is correct.** D's statement is hearsay because it was made out of court, it asserts that D is planning to fill P's order, and it is offered to prove that D did in fact fill P's order. The statement satisfies the state of mind exception (FRE 803(3)) because it was a statement of D's then-existing state of mind (here, the intention to do something in the future, an ap-

plication of the *Hillmon* doctrine). Note that this is a very self-serving statement, but that does not matter for purposes of the application of FRE 803(3). That rule contains no specific trustworthiness requirement.

Answer (A) is incorrect because a statement of a party is not an admission unless offered *against* the party who made it. This statement was offered *by* the party who made it.

Answer (C) is incorrect because as long as it is reasonable to conclude that D was referring to the order at issue, the statement is relevant. It will be up to the jury to decide, ultimately, whether this is what D meant, and the amount of probative value the statement has.

Answer (D) is incorrect because it is very difficult to discern any *unfair* prejudice to P from the evidence. True, the evidence hurts P's case, but it does not appear to do so improperly. Even if there is some potential for prejudice (perhaps the jury will overvalue the evidence as an indication of D's performance of the contract), it is extremely unlikely that the unfair prejudice will substantially outweigh the statement's legitimate probative value.

182. **Answer (A) is correct.** The father's statement is hearsay because it was made out of court, it asserts that P's arm hurt and that she cannot move it, and the statement is offered to prove those facts. The statement appears to qualify as a statement for purposes of medical diagnosis or treatment under FRE 803(4). That rule applies even if the declarant is seeking diagnosis or treatment for somebody other than herself. Here, as long as the father's purpose in making the statement to the admitting nurse was to obtain diagnosis or treatment for P, the statement will qualify. The preliminary facts are for the judge under FRE 104(a).

Answer (B) is incorrect because the facts do not suggest that the father was speaking while under the stress of excitement caused by a startling event or condition.

Answer (C) is incorrect because, as discussed above, the statement is hearsay.

Answer (D) is incorrect because, as discussed above, the statement almost certainly satisfies the exception in FRE 803(4).

183. **Answer (B) is correct.** There are two statements here. The "inner" statement is P's statement to the doctor, "My arm hurt a lot after I collided with another person." That statement is hearsay because it asserts that P suffered a collision with another person and that arm pain followed. The statement appears to satisfy the requirements of FRE 803(4), however, because P probably made the statement for purposes of obtaining treatment. This statement is "trapped," however, because it is contained within another statement: that of the doctor, who wrote that P made the statement just discussed. That statement, too, is hearsay because it asserts that P made the statement and is offered to prove that P made the statement.

FRE 805 provides that hearsay within hearsay is admissible if both levels of hearsay fit within an exception. In this case, the exception covering the doctor's statement is probably the business records exception. The requirements of FRE 803(6) have been discussed previously. The only real issue seems to be whether "the source of the information [or] other circumstances indicate a lack of trustworthiness." Whether that is the case here depends on whether the doctor has a business duty to listen and record accurately everything the patient said. Certainly, there is no problem with the part of P's statement that asserts that she had a lot of pain in her arm after the collision. The existence of pain in a particular part of the body would be something a doctor would want to know about. As a result, she is likely to listen carefully and to record accurately what the patient says about the pain. The same is probably true with the word "collision." A doctor would be interested not only in the existence of pain, but also about the general source of the pain. What about the patient's statement that the collision was with "another person"? Would that be "reasonably pertinent" to medical diagnosis or treatment (to borrow a phrase from FRE 803(4))? This might be the subject of argument, and perhaps testimony to the court, but it seems entirely likely that a doctor would consider it important to know whether a person's injury derived from a collision with another person or, for example, an automobile. That information might affect the diagnosis or treatment protocols the doctor follows. (If the patient had given the name of the person with whom she collided, it is unlikely the doctor would listen carefully to that information or take the trouble to record it accurately. The same would be true if the patient's injury derived from an automobile collision and the patient gave the make and color of the other car.)

Because it appears the business records exception would cover all parts of what the doctor recorded, and the "medical diagnosis or treatment" exception covers all parts of the patient's statement, it appears the document is admissible. All of the other answers are flawed. **Answer (A) is incorrect** because it asserts that no exception applies to the document. **Answer (C) is incorrect** because it identifies the doctor's statement about what the patient said as non-hearsay. **Answer (D) is incorrect** because, while it is true that the patient's statement might be self-serving, that is not a reason for the court to exclude it under FRE 803(4). (Moreover, in the circumstances, there was probably no reason for the patient to lie about the injury or exaggerate its effects.)

184. **Answer (B) is correct.** The statement in the chart is being offered to prove the truth of the matter asserted: that P suffered permanent injuries to his left leg. The testimony of W, the custodian of records, shows that the requirements of the business records exception (FRE 803(6)) have been met because the patient chart was prepared by a person with knowledge of the facts recorded (Dr. X), the chart was kept in the ordinary course of a business, it was the regular practice of the business to make the chart, and there is no reason to suspect that the chart is untrustworthy (the doctor did not work for P, but examined P for the state to determine P's eligibility for disability benefits).

Answer (A) is incorrect because, even though the chart states an expert opinion, FRE 803(6) allows the admission of records containing "an act, event, condition, opinion, or diagnosis".

Answer (C) is incorrect because the physician-patient privilege, if any, does not apply when the patient tenders his condition in issue, which is the case here. P has made his medical condition an issue in the case, at least insofar as it was affected by the accident.

Answer (D) is incorrect for the reasons stated above.

185. **Answer (A) is correct.** X's statement is hearsay because it asserts that D was the aggressor in the fight, which is what the prosecution is offering it to prove. It appears to satisfy the requirements of the excited utterance exception in FRE 803(2) because there was a startling event (D's alleged attack on V), and the circumstances suggest that the statement was made under the stress of excitement caused by the event, which had just occurred. The statement appears to be "non-testimonial" in nature because it was made during the event and a reasonable person in X's position would not have thought she was making a statement that would be used in the investigation or prosecution of the crime. In addition, that the statement was not made to law enforcement also tends to show that it was non-testimonial. The Supreme Court's decisions in *Crawford* and its progeny make clear that non-testimonial hearsay that satisfies a hearsay exception may be admitted without consideration of the Confrontation Clause. Thus, the evidence is admissible as long as the court finds that it satisfies the requirements of FRE 803(2).

    Answer (B) is incorrect because it assumes further inquiry into reliability is required.

    Answer (C) is incorrect because the statement is, in fact, hearsay. **Answer (D) is incorrect** for the reasons stated above concerning non-testimonial hearsay.

186. **Answer (D) is correct.** There are two statements. The "inner" statement is the Chairperson's statement, "What a piece of junk!" The "outer" statement is the secretary's assertion that this is what the Chairperson said. The Chairperson's statement is not hearsay because it is *not* offered to prove that the ad was in fact terrible (which is what the Chairperson probably meant to assert). Instead, it is offered as circumstantial evidence that the board later rejected the ad (and thus that the corporation was not required to pay for it). That is why the Chairperson's statement is relevant. The "outer" statement (the secretary's statement) is hearsay because it is an assertion that the Chairperson made the other statement, and is offered to prove that the Chairperson in fact did make that statement. The secretary's statement qualifies as a business record, however. It is the ordinary course of the business to take minutes of board meetings, and the secretary is required to keep and file those minutes in a certain way. Although it is true that the statement serves the interest of the party offering it, there is no real indication that at the time it was made, the company had reason to think there would be litigation over payment for the ad. Thus, this portion of the minutes is probably admissible.

    Answers (A), (B), and (C) are incorrect for the reasons given.

187. **Answer (B) is correct.** The report is relevant because it tends to show that P had in fact suffered liver damage as of a certain time. The doctor's statement is hearsay, however, because it asserts that P has suffered liver damage and it is offered to prove that fact. The doctor's testimony appears to satisfy all prerequisites for the business records exception. As to the trustworthiness issue, the report does not appear to lack trustworthiness when considered in context. The doctor prepared the report in connection with P's application to obtain health insurance. No litigation was anticipated at that time. In fact, if one wants to obtain medical insurance, any incentive to be dishonest would be to not disclose the patient's medical problems, or to minimize rather than exaggerate them. Thus, there are no indicia of lack of trustworthiness.

Answer (A) is incorrect because, even if the doctor was speaking for P, the statement is being offered by P rather than against her. **Answer (C) is incorrect** because courts tend to hold that statements made by the medical professional are not within the FRE 803(4) exception. (Thus, statements made to obtain medical diagnosis or treatment are admissible under the exception, not statements that constitute medical diagnosis.) **Answer (D) is incorrect** because the report is admissible hearsay.

188. **Answer (D) is correct.** There are actually three statements here: D's statement, Officer X's statement about what D said, and W's report stating what Officer X said. All three statements were made out of court. The innermost statement (that of D) is not hearsay because it is a party admission under FRE 801(d)(2)(A). That means Officer X, who heard D make the statement, could certainly testify that D made the statement.

Officer X's statement was made in her capacity as a police officer involved in the case, and thus appears to be the type of statement that qualifies for inclusion in a business or public record. And as the author of the police report, W is a person required to make such reports in the ordinary course of police work. This is probably the type of report envisioned by FRE 803(8)(A)(iii) ("factual findings from a legally authorized investigation").

So far so good. There is one big problem, however: FRE 803(8)(C) only applies in civil cases and against the government in criminal cases. The purpose of this limitation is to prevent trial by affidavit (trials at which the government presents reports rather than percipient witnesses who can be cross-examined). Thus, FRE 803(8) is not available here. But what about FRE 803(6), the business records exception? Most courts that have considered this issue have held that because FRE 803(8) establishes a clear prohibition of using certain types of police reports against criminal defendants, admitting the reports under the more general business records exception would improperly circumvent that rule. So the report is inadmissible hearsay.

Because D's statement is "trapped" within an inadmissible police report, it is inadmissible in the manner offered. But recall what was said above: The government may still call Officer X to testify to what D said. This makes Officer X subject to cross-examination to test whether she correctly reported D's statements, which is what the drafters of the rules wanted to happen.

Answer (A) is incorrect for the reasons just given. **Answer (B) is incorrect** because the witness, W, never had personal knowledge of what D said. This means that although the report *might* be admissible to prove what Officer X said (assuming the requirements of FRE 803(5) can be satisfied), W has no way to verify the accuracy of Officer X's report of what D said. If Officer X was the witness, and Officer X could not remember what D said, the police report *might* be admissible under the recorded recollection doctrine *if*, at a time when she still remembered well what D said, Officer X adopted the report as an accurate reflection of D's statement. Even then, there might be a problem, as some courts have held that because FRE 803(8) seeks to prevent most police reports from being used against criminal defendants, those reports cannot be admitted under *any* hearsay exception, including the exception for recorded recollection.

Answer (C) is incorrect because D's statement, while against her interest, does not qualify under FRE 804(b)(3). This is because D is not unavailable.

189. **Answer (D) is correct.** Suppose the note simply said, "I examined P's car and noticed a large dent on the right front door." In that situation, the note almost certainly would satisfy the recorded recollection doctrine because W will testify that she no longer remembers the facts recorded in the note, but that at the time she wrote the note, she remembered the condition of the car well, and that she recorded the facts accurately. The problem here is that the note records the statement of another person, who asserted that D ran the red light. W, the writer of the note, has no personal knowledge of the truth of this witness's statement. That statement is hearsay when offered to prove that D ran the red light, and on the facts given, no exception applies to it. Thus, the note is inadmissible.

   Answer (A) is incorrect for the reasons just given. **Answer (B) is incorrect** both for the reasons just given and because when the recorded recollection exception applies, the writing may not be admitted as an exhibit unless offered by the adverse party. **Answer (C) is incorrect** because W has not laid the foundation for business records. This was an informal note written by the witness and kept at home, not the type of record that is kept as part of the regular practice of W's business.

190. The statement constitutes hearsay if offered to prove that X and a person other than D committed the crime, but it might be admissible as a declaration against interest under FRE 804(b)(3). X is unavailable because he is dead. According to this rule, if a statement against interest is offered in a criminal case as one that tends to expose the declarant to criminal liability, it is not admissible unless it is "supported by corroborating circumstances that clearly indicate its trustworthiness." In *Williamson v. United States*, 512 U.S. 594 (1994), the Supreme Court held that each part of a statement offered under this provision must be against the interest of the declarant. Here, the part taking responsibility is against X's interest. Arguably, X's statement that he and another person committed the crime, and that the other person was not D, is against X's interest because it shows familiarity with certain details of the crime. The same is true for the statement about where the body was dumped, something that might only have been known to a few people at the time X told the police about it. This is a close case. Some courts are likely to hold that the entire statement comes in as against X's interest, while others are likely to hold that the part stating that D was not involved is not against X's interest because, for one thing, X and D were friends, giving X a motive to protect D.

   Finally, there must be "corroborating circumstances that clearly indicate [the statement's] trustworthiness." X's knowledge of the number of people involved and the location of the body is one such circumstance. More information is needed to determine if this requirement is met, though it probably is satisfied.

191. The court probably should sustain P's objection. The document is hearsay because it asserts that P was responsible for the accident and it is offered to prove that fact. The closest fit among the hearsay exceptions is FRE 803(6), the business records exception. Most of the requirements of that rule have been satisfied. From the custodian's testimony and the doc-

ument itself, this appears to be a report of a type regularly made, kept in the regular course of the business, containing information from a person with knowledge of the facts. But the document will be inadmissible if "the source of information or the method or circumstances of preparation indicate a lack of trustworthiness." The person who supplied the information in the report was the driver whose conduct was at issue, and who thus had a significant incentive to give a version that would suggest she was not responsible for the accident. In addition, a key purpose of such reports is probably to help prepare for litigation arising from accidents. In *Palmer v. Hoffman*, 318 U.S. 109 (1943), the Supreme Court held that a report analogous to the one in this problem was inadmissible for the same reason. Though *Palmer* has been criticized and its precedential value narrowed, it has never been overruled. If there is anything left of the *Palmer* rule, it would certainly cover the facts of this case. Note that the burden of persuasion to show the record is not trustworthy is on the opponent.

192. The court should overrule the objection. The "order log" is hearsay because it is an assertion of all orders placed between certain dates, offered to prove that these were the only orders placed. Because P's name does not appear in the log, the log tends to show that D received no order from P. The log is probably admissible as a business record under FRE 803(7) ("[a]bsence of a record of a regularly conducted activity"). The custodian's testimony shows that this was a record of a type regularly made, kept in the regular course of the business, containing information from a person with knowledge of the facts. In addition, even though the report is to some extent self-serving, it is routine and almost certainly not made in anticipation of litigation. Rather, it was made as an important part of the day-to-day conduct of D's business. The business probably relies on this record. Thus, the circumstances do not suggest lack of trustworthiness. The *Palmer v. Hoffman* rule will not exclude the record.

193. The court should overrule X's objection but sustain D's objection. The transcript of W's testimony from the earlier civil trial will be used to show that X ran a red light and struck V in a crosswalk. The transcript is hearsay within hearsay. The testimony of W will be offered to prove the facts W stated, and the transcript itself is an assertion of the court reporter that W in fact made those statements. The transcript is admissible hearsay because it is the court reporter's business record.

The real problem is with W's testimony. FRE 804(b)(1), the former testimony exception, may be used to admit the testimony against X because X had an opportunity to cross-examine W at the civil trial, and X's motive in that cross-examination was the same as it would be if W were available to testify at the criminal trial (to show that W was wrong about aspects of her testimony). D, however, was not a party to the civil trial, and the "predecessor in interest" language of the rule only applies in civil trials. Thus, the transcript may not be offered against D, who never had an opportunity to cross-examine W at the civil trial.

194. **Answer (D) is correct.** V's statement is hearsay because it is offered to prove that D was planning to kill V, which is what the statement asserted. No hearsay exception applies, as noted below.

Answer (A) is incorrect because the state of mind exception does not apply when the declarant (here, V) is referring to the state of mind of another person (here, D).

Answer (B) is incorrect. In *Giles v. California*, 554 U.S. 353 (2008), the Supreme Court specifically held that the forfeiture doctrine (both constitutional and as embodied in FRE 804(b)(6)) only applies when the actor's conduct that procured the unavailability of the declarant as a witness was committed for the primary purpose of preventing the declarant from testifying. In a typical murder case, that is not the perpetrator's primary purpose. To put it simply, the killer does not kill the victim to prevent the victim from testifying in the killer's murder trial.

Answer (C) is incorrect because V's statement does not appear to be "testimonial" in this context. That is, it does not appear that V made the statement to W expecting it to be used in the investigation or prosecution of D for a crime that had not yet taken place. Because the Supreme Court has held in *Crawford* and its progeny that non-testimonial statements are not subject to confrontation analysis, the Confrontation Clause is not applicable here.

195. **Answer (A) is correct.** X's statement is hearsay because it asserts that a blue Exterminator was weaving all over the road, and it is offered to prove that fact. (It is relevant because if D was weaving "in and out of lanes like it's a sports car" just before the accident, D might have been behaving in the same way at the time of the accident as well.) The evidence fits within FRE 803(1), the present sense impression exception, because the circumstances strongly suggest that X made the statement while observing an event, or immediately after observing it, and the statement described the event.

    Answer (B) is incorrect because there is no requirement that anybody be present to verify the accuracy of the declarant's statement. **Answer (C) is incorrect** because X's statement, while implicitly containing an opinion, is primarily descriptive of the facts. Also, it is "rationally based on the witness's perception'" (FRE 701(a)) and will help the jury understand the facts. **Answer (D) is incorrect** because there is no suggestion that this was a "startling event or condition" and that X was speaking while under the stress of excitement caused by such a condition.

196. **Answer.** Objection overruled. W1's prior statement qualifies as a prior consistent statement under FRE 801(d)(1)(B)(i): (1) W1 has testified at the trial, (2) W1 appears to be subject to cross-examination about the prior statement, (3) the prior statement is consistent with W1's trial testimony, (4) D has raised the issue of whether W1 might have had a motive to testify in P's favor (because of the job offer), and (5) W1's prior statement was made before such motive arose (before P made the job offer). Because all of these requirements are met, the prior statement is admissible as non-hearsay.

197. **Answer (A) is correct.** The document is hearsay if offered to prove what it asserts—that D was a patient during those dates. It qualifies as a record of regularly conducted activity (business record) under FRE 803(6) because W's testimony indicates that it is a memorandum concerning an act or condition, made by people with knowledge at or near the time of the act or condition, and that it was the regular practice of the hospital to make the record. Although it is self-serving in the sense that the business that made the record is the one offering it, there is nothing to suggest that at the time it was made, the person who recorded the information had any reason to be untruthful.

Answer (B) is incorrect for the reason given above.

Answer (C) is incorrect because, although it is true that computer logs can be tampered with, nothing here suggests that this happened. The possibility of tampering therefore should go to weight, not admissibility.

Answer (D) is incorrect because the court can take judicial notice of the accuracy of the log without resort to an expert witness.

198. **Answer (A) is correct.** X's statement is hearsay because it asserts that certain things had happened and it is offered to prove that those things happened. The statement is probably an excited utterance because the altercation was most likely a "startling event," the statement relates to the event, and it appears to have been made under the stress of excitement caused by the event. The statement is not likely a present sense impression because enough time has passed since the events to allow for reflection on X's part. Under the Supreme Court's confrontation jurisprudence, the statement is almost certainly not "testimonial" because it describes an ongoing emergency and is not part of a law enforcement effort to investigate a past event. The fact that D had gone into the house arguably did not end the emergency; it is reasonable to be concerned that D might have gone into the house to retrieve a weapon, or at least that D was still close enough to V to pose a continuing threat. Thus, the statement may be admitted over D's confrontation objection.

Answers (B), (C), and (D) are incorrect for the reasons stated above.

199. The court might conclude that X's statement does not violate the hearsay rule, but the court should sustain the confrontation objection. X's statement is hearsay if offered to prove D's involvement. It probably satisfies the declaration against interest exception (FRE 804(b)(3)) because it was against his interest in that it revealed X's involvement in the crime as well as X's knowledge of the details of the crime. (It is possible that a court would hold that the parts of the statement naming D were not against X's interest, and if so, those parts are inadmissible hearsay. But some courts would hold otherwise on the rationale that knowing details of the crime is self-incriminatory.) The court should exclude the statement on confrontation grounds, however, because the statement is clearly "testimonial" in nature. It was made to a police officer under circumstances in which a reasonable person would believe the statement would be used to help convict D of the crime. In addition, X is unavailable, and D did not have a prior opportunity to cross-examine X about the statement.

200. **Answer (A) is correct.** X's grand jury testimony is hearsay when offered in the present case because it was made other than while testifying at "the" trial or hearing (meaning the present case) and it is offered to prove the truth of the matter asserted: that X and D planned and carried out the murder. Parts of X's grand jury testimony will satisfy the declaration against interest exception (FRE 804(b)(3)), and it is possible that even those parts naming D qualify (though without more facts we can't determine whether those parts are really against X's interest). Even so, the grand jury testimony is clearly "testimonial" in nature; it *is* testimony. For that reason, admission in D's criminal trial would violate the 6th Amendment Confrontation Clause because D never had a chance to cross-examine X.

Answer (B) is incorrect because the evidence does not satisfy the former testimony exception. D did not have an opportunity to cross-examine X at the grand jury. Generally speaking, there is no "defendant" at that kind of proceeding, nor is there any "cross-examination."

Answer (C) is incorrect because it is not clear that X's grand jury testimony naming D qualifies as a declaration against interest, and trustworthiness does not satisfy the Confrontation Clause.

Answer (D) is incorrect because it fails to take into account the "testimonial" test for determining Confrontation Clause violations.

201. **Answer (D) is correct.** If it is relevant, X's act of pointing and the words, "Stop him! Stop him!" are an assertion that the person to whom X was pointing had committed the murder. Because the evidence would be offered to prove that fact, it is hearsay. However, it probably qualifies as an excited utterance. The murder appears to have been a startling event (judging from its nature and the nature of X's reaction), it concerns that event, and it was made under the stress of excitement caused by that event (the timing suggests as much).

The statement might also qualify as a present sense impression, but it would be more difficult to establish the foundation. The utterance must be made during or immediately after perceiving the event or condition. X's pointing and utterance might not qualify because they required at least a certain amount of reflection—of thinking back on the event. That suggests it might not meet the assumption behind the timing requirement, which is that statements made without reflection are more likely to be truthful.

Answer (A) is incorrect because, as explained above, this does appear to be an excited utterance. The declarant does not need to testify to lay the foundation.

Answer (B) is incorrect because X's availability is not required.

Answer (C) is incorrect because reliability is a question for the jury.

202. **Answer (C) is correct.** P's statement is hearsay because it was made other than while testifying at the trial and it is being offered to prove the truth of the matter asserted: that "that guy" ran over P's head and that P expected to die. This, in turn, might implicate D (if evidence suggests that D was "that guy") and might also suggest that P suffered a serious injury. The statement probably qualifies as an excited utterance under FRE 803(2) because the accident was a startling event, the statement relates to that event, and the statement appears to have been made under the stress of excitement caused by the event.

Answer (A) is incorrect because the statement is not a party admission when offered by the party who made it. It would qualify as a party admission only if offered by D.

Answer (B) is incorrect because the statement does not qualify as a dying declaration. P is not unavailable.

Answer (D) is incorrect because, as explained above, the statement appears to satisfy the requirements of the excited utterance exception.

Evidence of Character, "Other Crimes, Wrongs, or Acts," Habit, and Similar Events

203. **Answer (B) is correct.** "Character" is something internal to a person that tells us something about the person's morality. Having a disease does not speak to a person's morality.

Answer (A) is incorrect because carelessness as a driver tells us something bad about the driver's sense of morality.

Answer (C) is incorrect for much the same reason. Frugality is a moral trait.

Answer (D) is incorrect because, at least according to medical researchers, alcoholism is a disease, not a reflection of bad character. Many courts will exclude evidence of alcoholism because they fear that the jury will *treat* it as a character trait, but strictly speaking, it probably is not.

204. **Answer (B) is correct.** FRE 404(a)(1) forbids a party from offering evidence of another person's character or a trait of her character to prove "that on a particular occasion the person acted in accordance with the character or trait." There are several exceptions, none of which apply here. The government is seeking to infer guilt by showing that D's character would lead her to be the aggressor in the fight. This is exactly what the rule forbids.

Answer (A) is incorrect. Although the evidence is hearsay (reputation is what the community says about a person; when offered to prove what the community says, it is hearsay), FRE 803(21) provides an exception for "[a] reputation among a person's associates or in the community concerning the person's character." The character rule is what bars the evidence here.

Answer (C) is incorrect because character is not in issue. For character to be in issue ("an essential element of a charge, claim or defense," to use the language of FRE 405(b)), a person's character must be a required element. It is not an element of self-defense. True, a character for violent behavior might make self-defense less probable, but this is merely the use of character as circumstantial evidence of behavior. To determine whether character is in issue, ask yourself the following question: Does the law require proof of character in order to establish this charge, claim, or defense? If not, character is not in issue.

Answer (D) is incorrect because, when evidence is barred by a specific rule, the court does not have discretion to admit it if it has particularly high probative value. In other words, there is no "reverse-403" rule.

205. Objection sustained. In a criminal trial, defendant may offer evidence of a "pertinent trait" of her character to prove she did not commit the crime. Peacefulness is not pertinent to whether D committed a crime of fraud that involved no element of violence.

206. **Answer (B) is correct.** Until the Federal Rules were amended in the mid-1990s, there was no exception to the ban on character evidence that would allow the court to admit evidence of a defendant's character to prove action in accordance with that character in sexual assault or child molestation cases. The enactment of FRE 413–415 changed that situation by adding exceptions for these types of cases, both civil and criminal. In this hypothetical, the prosecution wishes to offer evidence that the defendant committed another act of child molestation. The purpose of the evidence is to prove, circumstantially, that the defendant committed the charged crime. FRE 414(a) specifically makes this evidence admissible "on any matter to which it is relevant." Thus, the prosecution may ask the jury to infer from D's prior act of child molestation that D is the kind of person who would commit such crimes, and that D therefore committed the charged crime. That is why **answer (A) is incorrect.**

The courts have held, however, that FRE 413–415 do not *require* admission of the evidence, and that trial courts may exclude the evidence if its probative value is substantially outweighed by the danger of unfair prejudice. That is why **answer (D) is incorrect.**

Answer (C) is incorrect because, even though the *modus operandi* theory is still available after the enactment of FRE 413–415, the facts here do not show such a distinctive method as to earmark the charged crime as having been committed by D. *See* FRE 404(b). Thus, *modus operandi* is not a legitimate theory on the facts given.

207. **Answer (D) is correct.** Character evidence is not admissible here because this is a civil action, and none of the exceptions in FRE 404(a) apply. (FRE 415 applies to civil cases, but only ones dealing with sexual assault and child molestation.) Thus, **answer (A) is incorrect.**

Answer (B) is incorrect because there is insufficient evidence to establish the existence of a habit. Habit is a specific reaction to a specific stimulus, and the person must have encountered the stimulus enough times to show that she acts in that specific way almost every time. It need not be an unconscious reaction, but there must be a sufficient number of instances to show that this is how the person reacts almost all the time.

Answer (C) is incorrect because character is not admissible to prove conduct in this situation. It is true that usually, when character may be offered as circumstantial evidence of a person's behavior, the party may use only reputation and opinion evidence on direct examination. But that question is never reached here because evidence of character is simply not admissible.

208. **Answer (D) is correct.** In this example, D is trying to show that P committed the burglaries mentioned in the newspaper article by showing that P committed other burglaries. The inference from the older burglaries is being used to show that P has the character of a burglar, and that P committed the burglaries mentioned in the article. That use is forbidden by FRE 404(a). Thus, the evidence is inadmissible. **Answer (C) is incorrect** because the question of

what form of character evidence may be used is never reached; character evidence in any form is forbidden here.

Answer (A) is incorrect because character is not in issue. In many defamation cases, reputation is in issue, and thus reputation may be proven. But D's defense does not put reputation in issue. D is simply asserting that the story was true. There are many ways D can prove that fact; character is not required. Thus, character is not "an essential element of a charge, claim, or defense."

Answer (B) is incorrect because good faith is not D's defense. D claims the article was true, not that she published an untrue article in good faith.

209. **Answer (C) is correct.** Evidence concerning D's tendency to drive through that particular intersection without yielding might constitute habit evidence, but the way in which it is being offered here is hearsay for which no exception applies. W is not testifying that D has a habit of driving through that intersection without yielding. W is testifying that people tell her D does this. If P wishes to prove D's habit, P should call as witnesses the people familiar with D's behavior. That would allow them to be subjected to cross-examination. For these reasons, **answer (D) is incorrect.**

Answer (A) is incorrect because the evidence probably does amount to habit rather than character. As explained above, it is not being offered in an appropriate way.

Answer (B) is incorrect because the habit rule is not so harsh as to require that a person *invariably* acts in a certain way. A court may conclude that it is sufficient that a person almost always reacts to the same stimulus in the same way.

210. **Answer (D) is correct.** FRE 404(a)(2)(A) allows a criminal defendant to offer evidence of a pertinent trait of her character to prove action in accordance with that trait. A person with a character trait of peacefulness is less likely to commit murder than is one with a violent character. Thus, the evidence is relevant. FRE 405(a) allows D to use evidence of reputation or opinion on direct examination of the character witness. This discussion shows why **answers (A) and (B) are incorrect.**

Answer (C) is incorrect because bias does not render a witness incompetent to offer her opinion. The jury may consider bias as it assesses W's credibility, but the court may not exclude the evidence simply because of the witness's bias.

211. **Answer (A) is correct.** FRE 405(a) allows a party cross-examining a character witness to refer to specific instances of conduct. The main purpose is to impeach the character witness by demonstrating that she lacks adequate information on which to base her testimony on direct examination. Here, if W was unaware of D's involvement in a barroom brawl, W's opinion about D's peacefulness would carry less value with the fact-finder.

Answer (B) is incorrect for the reasons just given. **Answer (C) is incorrect** because leading questions are permissible, and usually favored, on cross-examination. **Answer (D) is incorrect**

because for these purposes, the court may admit the evidence even if the two events are not very similar. If the incident in the bar is something a person would use to inform herself about D's character for peacefulness, W's possible ignorance of that event casts doubt on W's assessment of D's character.

212. **Answer (A) is correct.** In *Michelson v. United States*, 335 U.S. 469 (1948), the Supreme Court approved limits the common law had placed on a character evidence offered by a criminal defendant and on the rebuttal the prosecution is allowed to make. One rule provided that if the prosecutor seeks to cross-examine a character witness by inquiring about whether the witness has heard about an event inconsistent with the witness's character testimony, the prosecutor must show the court that it has a good faith belief that the event actually occurred. The Court noted that this is somewhat illogical because what should matter is that stories were circulating, even if untrue. (The witness's ignorance of those stories would show that her reputation testimony is questionable.) Nevertheless, to keep the inquiry within reasonable bounds and protect the defendant from unfair prejudice, the Court approved the requirement that the prosecutor show a good faith belief that the event occurred.

Answer (B) is incorrect because a reputation witness is more properly asked the "have you heard" form of question rather than the "did you know" form. This is because reputation is what one has heard, not what one knows about the individual personally. (In any event, today, as both reputation and opinion are admissible, the courts will not usually reverse on such a technicality.)

Answer (C) is incorrect because the last sentence of FRE 405(a) allows a cross-examiner to mention "relevant specific instances of the person's conduct."

Answer (D) is incorrect because, as noted above, the evidence is not admissible if the prosecutor does not have a good faith belief that the event occurred. Here, the prosecutor knows that D was not in fact involved. Thus, the evidence is inadmissible.

213. The court should overrule the objection as long as D shows that W has sufficient knowledge of V's community reputation. FRE 404(a)(2)(B) allows a criminal defendant to offer evidence of a pertinent trait of the character of a crime victim for the purpose of showing action in accordance with that trait on a specific occasion. Peacefulness or lack of peacefulness is a pertinent trait because P alleges that V was the aggressor in the fight. FRE 405(a) allows evidence of reputation or opinion on direct examination of a character witness. As long as W has sufficient knowledge of V's community reputation for peacefulness or lack of peacefulness, the testimony is proper.

214. The court should overrule D's objection as long as W2 has sufficient knowledge of V's character for peacefulness to be able to offer a valid opinion. FRE 404(a)(2)(C) applies here. In prosecutions for homicide where the defendant claims the victim was the first aggressor, the prosecution may rebut the defendant's evidence by offering evidence of the victim's character for peacefulness. It does not matter that D did not try to prove V's action using character evidence. The rule only requires that D try to prove that the victim was the first aggressor. FRE 405(a) limits the direct examination of character witnesses to reputation or opinion. Here, the prosecution is offering opinion evidence.

215. **Answer (D) is correct.** Although the evidence reveals another crime, it is relevant for a non-character purpose: to show that D had a motive to kill V (to be able to keep all the loot netted in the fraud). Motive, in turn, tends to show that the killing was not an accident. The probative value of the evidence is high for that purpose, and the risk of unfair prejudice caused by the jury's misuse of the evidence almost certainly does not substantially outweigh the probative value.

   Answer (A) is incorrect for the reasons just given. The evidence does not violate the character ban when used in this way.

   Answer (B) is incorrect because similarity of the charged and uncharged acts does not matter in this situation.

   Answer (C) is incorrect because the evidence, as explained, tends strongly to undermine D's defense.

216. **Answer (D) is correct.** The admissibility of this evidence is governed by FRE 404(b) because it concerns conduct of D other than that charged in the case. It will not be admissible to prove D's character and action in accordance with character, but it might be admissible if it is relevant on another basis. Here, that basis might be to show identity by means of *modus operandi*. It would be reasonable for a court to conclude that this was a very distinctive type of robbery, almost a "signature" of the person. Thus, the evidence is not being used to prove character, but just identity by means of "doctrine of chances" reasoning: the same person committed both crimes. There is no requirement that D have been found to have committed the other crime. All that is needed is evidence sufficient to support a finding that she did; FRE 104(b) applies.

   Answers (A), (B), and (C) are incorrect for the reasons given above.

217. **Answer (A) is correct.** FRE 404 only forbids the use of other crimes, wrongs, or acts when their relevance depends on an inference of the actor's character. Here, the evidence appears to be relevant to D's identity as the embezzler by means other than character. The theory is *plan*. A person who has a plan to act in a certain way is more likely to act in that way than is a person chosen randomly. In theory, this is not character-based propensity reasoning. Here, the existence of the plan may be inferred from D's subsequent embezzlement from the same trust. This explains why **answer (D) is incorrect**.

   Answer (B) is incorrect because evidence of D's subsequent embezzlement does not contradict her claim that somebody else committed the charged crime.

   Answer (C) is incorrect because the relevance of the plan theory as used here does not depend on the other crime having occurred before the charged crime.

218. The court should overrule D's objection because W3's testimony is proper to rebut D's claim that she does not have the character of an embezzler, and thus did not commit the crime. The trait of honesty is "pertinent" to the charge of embezzlement, which is a crime involving dishonesty. The prosecution has presented W3's testimony in the form of opinion, which is permissible under FRE 405(a). Because the prosecution has not offered W3's testimony to impeach D, it does not matter that D never testified.

219. **Answer (D) is correct.** FRE 404(a)(2)(B)(ii) permits the prosecution to meet D's evidence concerning the victim's character with evidence of the same trait of D's character. (This assumes D has not offered evidence of her own character.) **Answer (A) is incorrect** for the reasons just explained.

Answer (B) is incorrect because FRE 803(21) provides a hearsay exception for evidence of a person's reputation.

Answer (C) is incorrect because the prosecution may rebut both by cross-examining D's character witnesses and by calling its own witnesses.

220. **Answer (C) is correct.** The evidence in this case is potentially admissible under FRE 404(b), which would allow a *modus operandi* theory to show identity—that D is the person who committed the charged crime. The theory is that the method D used in the uncharged prior robbery was so distinctive as to mark the robbery as his, and that the later robbery, committed in the same distinctive way, bore that mark. The evidence does not offend the character ban of FRE 404(a) because the courts hold that the *modus operandi* theory does not depend on an inference of the person's character.

Though the *modus operandi* theory potentially applies, the Supreme Court held in *Huddleston v. United States*, 485 U.S. 681 (1988), that when there is a dispute about the person's commission of the uncharged act, the standard of FRE 104(b) applies. That means the court may admit the evidence if it finds that there is evidence sufficient to support a finding that the person committed the uncharged act.

Answer (C) tracks the law as just discussed. **Answer (A) is incorrect** because FRE 404(b)(1) admits "a crime, wrong, or other act" without regard to whether the person was charged criminally. **Answers (B) and (D) are incorrect** because they misconstrue the rules of law discussed above.

221. **Answer (B) is correct.** The theory here is that the evidence, though relevant on an impermissible character-propensity basis, is also relevant on a non-character basis supplied by the doctrine of chances. To state that theory in a common-sense way: What is the probability that four home care patients would die of poisoning while in D's care and without D's involvement? One would think the odds would be overwhelmingly against such an event happening four times. Though one patient might die of poisoning without D's involvement, four seems beyond the realm of coincidence. (The point is not that this *couldn't* happen. It is that such a chain of events is extremely unlikely to happen without wrongdoing on D's part.)

Note that this theory applies even without specific proof that D poisoned the other three patients. The jury is being asked to put all four incidents together and to determine the likelihood of guilt based on the informal probability reasoning discussed above. Thus, **answer (D) is incorrect** because admissibility does not depend on the prosecution proving D's guilt in each of the three prior incidents.

Answer (A) is incorrect because although the prosecution may rebut D's good character evidence by calling its own witnesses, those witnesses would be limited to testifying on direct examination in the form of reputation and opinion evidence, not specific instances of conduct.

Answer (C) is incorrect because FRE 608(b) only allows specific instances of a witness's conduct to impeach the witness's credibility if those instances are "probative of the character for truthfulness or untruthfulness." The courts do not consider murder to be probative of truthfulness or untruthfulness.

222. **Answer (D) is correct.** "Rape-shield" statutes such as those contained in FRE 412 are designed to exclude evidence concerning an alleged rape victim's prior sexual behavior or reputation. FRE 412 contains several exceptions, but none apply here on the facts given. (Defendant's best chance is to argue that exclusion violates his 6th Amendment right to present a defense, but the facts do not show why that is true here and not in many other rape prosecutions in which defendant claims consent.)

Answers (A), (B), and (C) are incorrect for the reasons given.

223. The best answer is objection sustained. The court must apply the standard of FRE 412(b)(2), which allows evidence of the sexual behavior of the alleged victim "if its probative value substantially outweighs the danger of harm to any victim and of unfair prejudice to any party." P's argument is very strong in this case given the standard set forth in FRE 412(b)(2), which is heavily weighted in favor of *exclusion* of the evidence. Note that the standard is the opposite of that contained in FRE 403. Here, the probative value of the evidence must substantially outweigh prejudice, not the other way around. Because P never made a rape claim against the other three men, the court is likely to hold that the probative value of the evidence is not particularly great. At the same time, the potential prejudice to P is quite high. Specifically, there is a good chance that the jury will use the three prior incidents to show that P has poor morals and will punish her by finding in favor of D.

224. The court should overrule D's objection for at least two reasons. First, evidence that D tried to spend the money the day before and that D was told the money was phony is arguably not another "crime, wrong, or other act." It is an act, of course, but it is not a culpable act, which is what the rule almost certainly regulates. Even if this qualifies as another "crime, wrong, or other act," however, the evidence is admissible to show D's knowledge that the bill was counterfeit when she tried to pass it on the charged occasion. The inference is not based on character. It derives from the simple generalization that a person will tend to retain knowledge the person obtained fairly recently. This applies regardless of the person's character. Thus, the evidence is likely admissible to prove knowledge under FRE 404(b).

225. **Answer (D) is correct.** This is not a situation in which character is in issue because neither P's claim nor D's defense requires proof of D's character for care. Thus, **answer (B) is incorrect.** Evidence of character is also not admissible here as circumstantial evidence of D's conduct because the case does not fit within any of the exceptions in FRE 404(a). Thus, **answer (C) is incorrect.**

If the evidence is to be admitted, it must be on the basis that the evidence is being used to show a habit, not character. That argument will fail, however. Habit under FRE 406 is a specific response to a specific stimulus. It is not a general tendency. That D tends to be "a careful driver who always pays attention" is not a specific response to a specific stimulus; it is far too general to be evidence of habit. Rather, it is evidence of D's character for care as a driver. Thus, **answer (A) is incorrect.**

226. **Answer (B) is correct.** This problem presents a simple example of motive evidence. FRE 404 is not implicated because the evidence is not about D1 and D2, but about the victims, and is not being offered to prove how anyone acted, but merely to show a basis for the existence of a motive to kill the victims, and motive is relevant to showing identity.

Answer (A) is incorrect because the evidence is not being offered to show a tendency toward violence. **Answer (C) is incorrect** because the evidence does not include any out-of-court statement. **Answer (D) is incorrect** because it is difficult to discern any unfair prejudice to the four victims, who are not parties to the action. There is a possibility the evidence would unfairly prejudice the prosecution in that the jury might acquit thinking that the victims deserved to die, but that seems highly unlikely.

227. **Answer (C) is correct.** D, a criminal defendant, is permitted to offer evidence of a pertinent trait of her character to prove that she did not commit the crime. Here, however, that evidence is being offered by way of an out-of-court statement asserting the declarant's opinion of D's character for peacefulness. No exception applies. Thus, **answer (A) is incorrect.**

Answer (B) is incorrect because the evidence reveals no pattern of behavior. It is simply a general opinion.

Answer (D) is incorrect because the reliability of the evidence is a question for the fact-finder, not for the court in deciding admissibility.

228. **Answer (D) is correct.** The issue here is identity—whether D is the person who shot V. Thus, **answer (B) is incorrect,** as the evidence will not be admissible to prove the perpetrator's intent. The evidence does not show conduct specific enough, nor are there enough incidents, to prove the existence of a habit. **Answer (A) is incorrect** for this reason.

Answer (C) is incorrect because it misconstrues the scope of "pattern" or "common scheme or plan." It is true that D has exhibited a sort of pattern, and that the two prior and one currently charged offenses have something in common. Two similar incidents in the past do show a tendency to act in that way. However, if FRE 404(b) is read to permit the admission of evidence of prior similar acts in a situation as this, without showing some connection among the acts other than their similarity, FRE 404(b) would pretty much swallow the rule excluding character whenever a person is charged with a crime of the same sort she has committed previously. If a person is charged with bank robbery, for example, evidence that she has robbed a bank before would be admissible. Though some courts have taken a very broad view of the ideas of "pattern" and "common scheme or plan," the better view is that some connection is required before the evidence should be admitted. Such a connection might be shown, for example, if the person has figured out a scheme that involves all of the charged and uncharged acts. (But the scheme must be more than a desire to rob banks. There must be a specific connection among the robberies.) For these reasons, the court should sustain the objection in the present case.

229. **Answer (A) is correct.** Unlike the facts of the previous problem, this case shows a real connection between the events. The evidence strongly suggests that the salesperson developed a scheme to defraud customers that involved a particular type of lie. The evidence carries significant probative value on that score.

Answer (B) is incorrect because in this situation, even five similar incidents of this kind probably do not constitute sufficient evidence to establish a habit. Though behavior does not need to be unconscious to be classified as habitual, neither should it be the type of behavior that a person needs to think about carefully each time she engages in it. Courts would be reluctant to call this behavior habitual.

Answer (C) is incorrect for the reasons given above. The evidence is not being offered on a character-based theory. The relevance of the evidence does not depend on an inference that D has a particular character trait.

Answer (D) is incorrect because FRE 404(b) applies in both civil and criminal cases.

230. Evidence of similar events is admissible to show a dangerous condition if the events occurred under substantially the same circumstances as those involved in the present case. FRE 403 applies; the more similar the conditions, the more probative value and the less risk of misleading the jury. Here, the court would want to know (1) whether the escalator was maintained in the same way when the other people fell, (2) whether the other people were riding the escalator in the same way as P, (3) whether the conditions on the escalator were the same (number of people, for example), and (4) perhaps other facts. If the court concludes that the circumstances are substantially similar, the court will admit the evidence. If D requests a limiting instruction, the court is obligated to give it. *See* FRE 105. The instruction would inform the jury that it may not use the evidence to infer negligence on the basis that the department store operators have a character for carelessness, but merely to show that the condition is dangerous.

231. The court would need to know (1) whether there were any changes to the condition of the stairs during the two-year period prior to P's accident, (2) whether the stadium manager was in a position to receive reports of injuries if any occurred, (3) whether the circumstances surrounding the accident differed meaningfully from the circumstances of the prior two-year period, and (4) anything else that might affect the probative value of the stadium manager's proposed testimony. If the circumstances of the prior two years were similar enough to those in which P fell, the evidence would be relevant. It might also possess significant probative value, making it unlikely the court would exclude the evidence because of the danger of jury confusion. FRE 403 applies; the more similar the conditions, the more probative value and the less risk of misleading the jury.

232. **Answer (C) is correct.** FRE 415 allows evidence of prior acts of sexual assault in a civil action alleging sexual assault and prior acts of child molestation in a civil action alleging child molestation. The rule is an exception to the general ban on character to prove conduct contained in FRE 404(a). (The court may exclude the evidence, however, if it finds that its probative value is substantially outweighed by the risk of unfair prejudice or other factors listed in FRE 403.)

Answer (A) is incorrect because no hearsay has been offered. There is no out-of-court statement.

Answer (B) is incorrect because the rule does not require the witness to provide the factual basis for her testimony beyond that already required by the firsthand knowledge rule (FRE 602). Naturally, D may explore this issue on cross-examination (though doing so might be a risky strategy).

Answer (D) is incorrect because there is nothing in the given facts to suggest a violation of D's due process rights. For example, the facts do not state that the court has denied D the opportunity to cross-examine W or otherwise to undermine W's testimony.

Topic 9: Answers

Evidence of Subsequent Remedial Measures, Compromise, Humanitarian Assistance, Criminal Pleas, and Liability Insurance

233. **Answer (C) is correct.** The act of patrolling for spills more often than before the accident qualifies as a subsequent remedial measure because it is a step that, if taken earlier, would have made the accident less likely to occur. Evidence of subsequent remedial measures is relevant because it is rational to infer that one who undertakes such a measure believes herself to be responsible for the accident. Thus, it is an implied recognition of responsibility. (Of course, there could be many explanations other than this in a given case. For example, the person might simply have acted to reduce what was already a very low risk. But that does not mean the evidence is irrelevant. As long as it is rational to conclude that the taking of the measure represents an implied recognition of responsibility, it is relevant evidence.) This means **answer (B) is incorrect.**

FRE 407, however, excludes the evidence when offered to prove fault in this way. In the present problem, the facts disclose no other possible purpose for the evidence. As a result, the court must exclude it. **Answer (D) is incorrect** because it fails to account for the subsequent remedial measures rule.

Answer (A) is incorrect because, under the modern definition of hearsay as recognized in the Federal Rules, conduct is not hearsay unless the actor *intended the conduct as an assertion of the matter the conduct is offered to prove.* Here, there is no reason to believe that by having her employees patrol for spills more often, D intended to assert that the condition at the time of the accident was unreasonably unsafe.

234. **Answer (D) is correct.** In this case, the evidence concerning D's subsequent remedial measure, while not admissible to prove D's negligence in patrolling only as often as was done before the accident, is admissible to impeach the testimony of D's manager. The method of impeachment is impeachment by contradiction. While that theory arguably has been applied too broadly by some courts, in this case it is appropriate to admit the evidence because it very directly contradicts the manager's testimony. The manager has left the clear impression that everything is fine with the store's operations, but the manager's own conduct contradicts her. This potentially calls into question the whole of the manager's testimony, and the jury should hear the evidence to help it evaluate the manager's credibility.

Answers (A) and (B) are incorrect for the reasons discussed in connection with the previous problem. **Answer (C) is incorrect** for the reasons just given.

235. **Answer (D) is correct.** In the previous problem, the evidence had a clear and strong tendency to impeach the witness by contradiction. That is not the situation here. The evidence, in fact, does not contradict W's testimony, nor is it inconsistent with it in any meaningful way. The only way in which the evidence is relevant is as an implied recognition of responsibility, and for that purpose it is inadmissible.

    Answers (A) and (B) are incorrect because they both involve the type of inference FRE 407 forbids. **Answer (C) is incorrect** for the reason just stated.

236. **Answer (C) is correct.** The evidence here is admissible for two reasons. First, it tends to impeach the expert witness by contradiction. The evidence suggests that the expert was wrong when she testified that this was the strongest, most wind-resistant available glass for this type of window. If she was wrong about that fact, she might have been wrong about other facts to which she testified. The evidence is also admissible to show the feasibility of precautionary measures. Evidence is only admissible for that purpose when the party whose conduct is at issue "disputes" feasibility (in other words, when the party argues that safer measures were not feasible). Here, the expert's testimony certainly contests feasibility. Hence, the evidence is admissible to prove feasibility.

    Answer (A) is incorrect because although FRE 407 initially was unclear about its application to product liability cases, an amendment to the rule makes clear that it does apply to such cases. **Answer (B) is incorrect** because it essentially states the forbidden use of the evidence. (A party who knows of a defect and who fails to fix it is more likely responsible than one who does not know of the defect.) **Answer (D) is incorrect** for the reasons given above.

237. D should argue that its claim concerning cost-effectiveness did not constitute contravention of feasibility. D should argue that feasibility is only disputed when a party claims something *could not have been done* for such reasons as lack of technology, and that feasibility is not disputed by cost-benefit arguments such as the one made here. D is not claiming the stronger glass could not have been used; D is only claiming it would have cost too much under the circumstances. D might conclude the argument by suggesting that if the court read the "feasibility" concept as broadly as P would like, it would practically subvert the policy of the exclusionary rule by making the evidence admissible in too many cases.

238. **Answer (D) is correct.** Evidence of subsequent remedial measures may be admitted if offered to prove the actor's ownership of or control over the instrumentality of the accident, where the actor denies ownership or control. Here, D has asserted that the road was private and that it had no authority to repair it. Evidence that a city road crew did in fact repair the pothole after the accident tends to show that the city did in fact have such authority.

    Answers (A) and (B) are incorrect for the reasons just discussed. **Answer (C) is incorrect** because the act is only evidence of ownership or control; it does not have "independent legal significance."

239. The court probably should sustain D's objection. Evidence of the subsequent design change qualifies as a subsequent remedial measure, which is inadmissible to show the prior design was defective. The testimony of D's expert does not state that a stronger design was not feasible, but only that other manufacturers used the same metal. In addition, the testimony is not impeached by evidence of the design change; that evidence does not contradict anything the expert said. There is no other purpose for which the evidence is relevant (other than the purpose for which it is inadmissible: to show that the design was defective). Therefore, the evidence is not admissible.

240. **Answer (D) is correct.** FRE 408 excludes compromise evidence. Included are offers to compromise disputed claims, completed compromises of such claims, and statements made during compromise negotiations. Here, a disputed claim exists. P's statement to D was both an offer to compromise (the offer to accept $5000) and a statement made during compromise negotiations (the assertion that D was negligent but that P was distracted). On the facts given, the statement appears relevant only to prove "the validity or amount of a disputed claim."

Answers **(A) and (B) are incorrect** because even though P's statement (the entire statement) is a party admission, it is excluded by FRE 408. That evidence is not excluded by one rule does not mean it is admissible. Other rules might exclude it. **Answer (C) is incorrect** because the statement is not a declaration against interest (P is not unavailable). Even if the statement were a declaration against interest, the compromise rule would still exclude it.

241. **Answer (A) is correct.** P's strongest argument in reply to D's claim that the letter is inadmissible under the compromise rule (FRE 408) is that there was no dispute as to liability or its amount. That is a strong argument here. The letter doesn't claim D was not liable; it merely claims that D can't afford to pay more.

Answer (B) is incorrect because it does not matter that the letter is a party admission. If it is inadmissible under the compromise rule, the fact that it is not barred by the hearsay rule does not matter.

Answer (C) is incorrect for the same reason.

Answer (D) is incorrect because an argument relying on FRE 403 is generally a last resort and usually fails. Nothing in the facts given suggests that there is any "unfair" prejudice that might outweigh the probative value of the evidence.

242. **Answer (A) is correct.** From the facts, it is clear that D was not disputing either the validity of the claim or its amount. (The statement, in fact, appears to concede liability.) Because FRE 408 only excludes offers and statements relating to disputed claims, the rule does not reach this statement. The hearsay rule also does not stand in the way of admission, because the statement is a party admission. **Answers (B), (C), and (D) are incorrect** for the reasons just given.

243. **Answer (C) is correct.** Evidence that D settled with W is relevant to D's fault because a person who settles a case with another who has made a claim is more likely to believe herself liable than one who does not settle. However, when offered for this purpose, the evidence is excluded by FRE 408. **Answers (B) and (D) are incorrect** for this reason. The rule permits the court to admit compromise evidence when it is offered to prove "a witness's bias or prejudice." That is the case here. A person who accepts money from one against whom she has made a claim is more likely to act favorably toward that person than is one who has not settled. To help the jury assess W's credibility when she testified that P crossed the center line and struck D, the jury should hear that W and D settled W's claim. **Answer (A) is incorrect** because, as explained above, the evidence is admissible to prove W's bias.

244. **Answer (B) is correct.** D's attorney's statement almost certainly was an authorized admission, and thus is not hearsay. FRE 801(d)(2)(C). Thus, **answer (A) is incorrect**. The compromise rule excludes statements made during negotiations to compromise "the validity or amount of a disputed claim." Here, even though D did not dispute the validity of the basic claim, D did dispute the damages element. Thus, the statement by D's attorney falls within the prohibition of FRE 408. This explains why **answer (C) is incorrect.**

Answer **(D) is incorrect** because there is no such thing as a "reverse-403" rule. That is, there is no rule that allows a court to admit otherwise inadmissible evidence if its probative value substantially outweighs unfair prejudice or other dangers the evidence might present. The court does not have the authority to admit this evidence if FRE 408 excludes it, which it does.

245. Objection sustained. Under FRE 410, if the court allows a criminal defendant to withdraw a guilty plea, the plea is inadmissible against the defendant. It does not matter that the evidence might not violate other rules such as the hearsay rule, and it does not matter if the plea is only used to impeach the defendant. There are very limited exceptions in FRE 410, but the facts given do not support the applicability of any of those exceptions.

246. **Answer (D) is correct.** The evidence is relevant because it constitutes D's acknowledgment of guilt in the very situation for which she is now being sued for battery. FRE 410 excludes withdrawn guilty pleas and pleas of *nolo contendere*. It does not exclude pleas of guilty that were never withdrawn. The hearsay rule does not bar this evidence because the guilty plea is a statement by D. When offered by P, it is a party admission. FRE 801(d)(2)(A).

Answer **(A) is incorrect** because, on the facts, it is not possible to state that the probative value is substantially outweighed by the danger of unfair prejudice. In fact, the evidence appears to have significant probative value, and it is unlikely that the jury will use the evidence *improperly*, making it unlikely that there is much potential for unfair prejudice.

Answer **(B) is incorrect** because the evidence is not offered for an impermissible character purpose. FRE 404(a) forbids character evidence when offered as circumstantial evidence of conduct on a particular occasion. The guilty plea here did not arise out of another incident from which the jury will be asked to infer conduct on the occasion in question. The evidence concerns the very conduct at issue, and D's guilty plea is an indication of guilt.

Answer **(C) is incorrect** because it misconstrues the nature of relevance analysis. The fact that an item of evidence might have several logical uses does not destroy its relevance if one of those uses is the one for which it is offered.

247. **Answer (D) is correct.** When P paid the jaywalking fine, P essentially pleaded guilty of the offense and accepted the penalty. An unwithdrawn guilty plea is admissible (FRE 410 does not apply to unwithdrawn guilty pleas). The evidence is relevant because it shows consciousness of guilt, as does the payment of the fine. Of course, D is free to argue that the evidence has low probative value because many people pay traffic and similar fines because it's too burdensome to contest the matter.

Answer (A) is incorrect because the evidence is relevant even if many or even most people pay rather than contest. A reasonable juror may still conclude that the evidence has some probative value.

Answer (B) is incorrect because the rule is clear: unwithdrawn guilty pleas are admissible. The court has no room in which to ignore the rule. (The court might apply FRE 403 in an unusual case, but there is little if any risk of unfair prejudice from admission of the evidence in this case.)

Answer (C) is incorrect because the evidence is relevant.

248. **Answer (A) is correct.** The prior guilty plea is relevant because it tends to show that at one time at least, D believed herself to be guilty of the crime charged. However, FRE 410 excludes guilty pleas that have been withdrawn. Evidence of the plea is not admissible to prove guilt or to impeach the pleader's credibility.

Answers (B), (C), and (D) are incorrect for the reasons given above.

249. **Answer (D) is correct.** W's statement ("D and I committed the crime") is hearsay when offered for that purpose in D's trial. No exception applies.

Answer (A) is incorrect because W is not unavailable. Thus, W's statement, though against W's interest, does not qualify as a declaration against interest under FRE 804(b)(3).

Answer (B) is incorrect for the reason noted above.

Answer (C) is incorrect because, although the statement is inadmissible hearsay, the plea bargaining rule (FRE 410) does not apply. That is because W's statement was not made to a prosecutor. There is no indication that the police officers to whom W made the statement were acting as agents of the prosecutor.

250. The court should sustain D's objection. D's statement is a party admission, and thus not hearsay. FRE 801(d)(2)(A). However, the statement is made inadmissible by FRE 410(a)(3), which excludes not only a withdrawn guilty plea, but any statements the person made during a hearing to enter the plea. The purposes for exclusion are primarily fairness and avoidance of unfair prejudice. If the court permits a person to withdraw a guilty plea, all consequences of the plea should also be removed. Allowing the prosecution to present evidence of the withdrawn plea would invite the jury to infer guilt from the very plea the court permitted the defendant to withdraw.

251. The court should overrule D's objection. D's statement is not hearsay because it constitutes a party admission. FRE 801(d)(2)(A). In addition, FRE 410(a)(4) only excludes "a statement made during plea discussions *with an attorney for the prosecuting authority* if the discussions did not result in a guilty plea or they resulted in a later-withdrawn guilty plea." (emphasis added). Statements made to police in an effort to plea bargain usually do not qualify because police officers are not prosecutors. If the police officers were acting as agents of the prosecuting authority, D's statements might be excluded, but the problem supplies no facts on which to base that conclusion.

252. The court should overrule D's objection. Although many people pay traffic fines rather than take the trouble to contest them, the evidence is still relevant because one reasonable inference from the payment is that the person paying the fine believed herself to be guilty. In addition, FRE 410 does not exclude guilty pleas that were never withdrawn. D's best bet in this case is to argue that the jury should give the evidence very little weight because payment of traffic citations often is not an indication of guilt, but D should also be aware that the jury might consider the evidence to have significant probative value in light of the fact that D might have known that P was injured, that P might sue, and that a guilty plea would be used against D.

253. **Answer (C) is correct.** D's offer to take P to the hospital constitutes the type of conduct made inadmissible by FRE 409 because it is an offer "to pay medical, hospital, or similar expenses resulting from an injury."

   Answer (A) is incorrect because even if the statement is a party admission, it is still excluded by FRE 409. **Answer (D) is incorrect** because the evidence is relevant. It is somewhat more likely that a person who offers to pay for another person's medical or related expenses is responsible for the other's injuries than is one who does not make an offer.

   Answer (B) is incorrect because there is no indication that this was an offer to settle a disputed claim.

254. **Answer (D) is correct.** The offer to pay P's medical bills is a party admission but is barred by FRE 409. The statement, "I didn't see you in the street," is not barred by that rule, however. Note that unlike the compromise rule (FRE 408), the medical payments rule does not exclude evidence of statements made in connection with the payment or offer to pay expenses. Thus, the statement accompanying the offer to pay is admissible. **Answer (A) is incorrect** because it assumes the entire statement is admissible as a party admission. **Answer (C) is incorrect** for the opposite reason; part of the statement is admissible.

   Answer (B) is incorrect because there was no disputed claim at the time D made the statement. Thus, the evidence does not fit within the compromise rule.

255. **Answer (D) is correct.** What D did for P was nice, and the law likes to encourage nice gestures, but no rule would exclude this evidence. It was not an offer to pay hospital, medical, or related expenses. It was not an offer to compromise a disputed claim. And of course, the evidence is relevant because a person who replaces the property of another that was destroyed

in an accident involving the two people is more likely responsible for the injury than is one who does not act in that way. **Answers (A), (B), and (C) are incorrect** for these reasons.

256. The court should sustain the objection. It is not likely that people who have liability insurance are more careless than people without liability insurance. In fact, the opposite might be true because having liability insurance shows a degree of responsibility. (Of course, many states require liability insurance, so having it might mean little or nothing.) Though relevant, FRE 411 makes the evidence inadmissible when offered to prove that the person "acted negligently or otherwise wrongfully." That is the only purpose for which the evidence might be relevant on the facts given. Thus, the evidence is inadmissible.

257. The court should sustain D's objection. FRE 411 only excludes evidence of liability insurance when it is offered to prove negligence or other wrongful conduct. Such evidence is admissible for other purposes, including proving a witness's bias. Here, P might argue that because D and D's expert witness both maintain malpractice insurance with the same company, D's expert might tend to favor D in order to keep her insurance company from having to pay P's claim. This, in turn, might keep premiums down. However, most courts would hold that having a common malpractice insurance carrier is not sufficient to establish bias, or even if it does show possible bias, the potential unfair prejudice from the evidence substantially exceeds any value to show bias.

258. The court should probably overrule D's objection. Technically, FRE 411 might not apply because this is jury selection, not a question of admissibility or inadmissibility of evidence offered formally at trial. Nevertheless, parties are entitled to an unbiased jury, and a person who works for a party's insurance company might favor the employer (and thus the party) in deliberations. The court should try to elicit this information as carefully as possible so as to avoid unduly emphasizing the existence of liability insurance, but P is probably entitled to determine if any jurors are employed by the insurer.

Impeachment and Cross-Examination of Witnesses

259. **Answer (C) is correct.** This is an attempt to impeach the credibility of W1 by showing that W1 has a disability that might have affected her ability to perceive accurately. There is no prohibition on the use of extrinsic evidence when this is the form of impeachment being used.

Answer (A) is incorrect because for this method of impeachment, there is no requirement that W1 be given the opportunity to explain or deny the accuracy of W2's testimony.

Answer (B) is incorrect because this is not an attack on W1's character for truthfulness, but only on her capacity to perceive accurately.

Answer (D) is incorrect for the reason given above.

260. **Answer (D) is correct.** The character trait of peacefulness is not "pertinent" to whether a person has committed perjury. Thus, under FRE 404(a)(1), it is not admissible to prove her innocence, meaning that **answer (A) is incorrect.** The evidence is also inadmissible to support D's credibility by showing that she did not lie when she denied committing the crime. Under FRE 608(a), opinions that are probative of a person's "character for truthfulness or untruthfulness" are admissible to attack or support the witness's character for truthfulness. Being a peaceful person is not probative of truthfulness or untruthfulness. In addition, even opinion testimony concerning the proper trait of character is not admissible unless the witness's character for truthfulness has been attacked by opinion, reputation, or otherwise. Thus, **answer (B) is incorrect. Answer (C) is incorrect** for the same reasons.

261. **Answer (A) is correct.** Under FRE 608(a), it is permissible to impeach a witness using opinion or reputation evidence to show that the witness has a bad character for truthfulness. That is what P has done here. The rule does not forbid the use of extrinsic evidence.

Answer (B) is incorrect because, as noted above, extrinsic evidence is permitted.

Answer (C) is incorrect because the rule allows the use of character to impeach a witness whether the case is civil or criminal.

Answer (D) is incorrect because specific instances of conduct may not be used for the present purpose except on cross-examination.

262. **Answer (D) is correct.** D is attempting to impeach W1 by showing lack of opportunity to observe accurately. There are no broad limits to that impeachment tool, but the evidence produced must be admissible under other rules. Here, the problem is that the evidence is in the form of hearsay (W1's statement to W2 that a bus partially blocked her line of sight). No exception applies.

Answer (A) is incorrect for the same reason and because the prior statement isn't really inconsistent with W1's testimony. Even a partially blocked view might be good enough to allow a person to see what happened.

Answer (B) is incorrect for the hearsay reason and because the prior statement doesn't particularly contradict W1.

Answer (C) is incorrect for the hearsay reason.

263. **Answer (C) is correct.** The evidence probably qualifies as another "crime, wrong, or other act" that might be admissible under FRE 404(b)(2) to show a motive to rob a liquor store to obtain money with which to purchase drugs.

Answer (A) is incorrect because being a drug addict with a $500 a day habit is not probative of a witness's character for truthfulness or untruthfulness, and thus under FRE 608(b), the evidence is not admissible to impeach D's credibility.

Answer (B) is incorrect because, without more, the evidence is not relevant to show D does not recollect accurately.

Answer (D) is incorrect because questions going to a person's motive to commit a crime are not beyond the scope of the direct examination when the person testified that she did not commit the crime.

264. **Answer (B) is correct.** W testified that D was on the driveway at the time of the collision. Previously, W implied that D was on the sidewalk at that time. The prior statement is therefore inconsistent with the trial testimony, and is admissible to impeach W's credibility.

Because the prior statement was not made under oath and subject to penalty of perjury, it is not admissible as non-hearsay under FRE 801(d)(1)(A). This means that **answers (A) and (C) are incorrect.** Because the evidence is admissible to impeach W, **answer (D) is incorrect.**

265. **Answer (A) is correct.** In this iteration of the skating problem, the prior inconsistent statement is being proved by extrinsic evidence. Under FRE 613(b), all that is required is that the witness be given the opportunity to explain or deny the statement. That was done here, because W was asked on cross-examination about the statement. (P was not required to do it this way. P could have avoided mentioning the prior inconsistent statement on cross-examination, elicited the statement from X, and then re-called W to confront her with the statement.) Because the prior statement was not made under oath subject to penalty of perjury, it is not admissible substantively (to prove the truth of the matter asserted). *See* FRE 801(d)(1)(A). It is only admissible to impeach W's credibility by showing inconsistency.

Answers (B), (C), and (D) are incorrect for the reasons just given and for those noted in the answer to the previous question.

266. **Answer (D) is correct.** Begin with the purpose of the evidence. P wishes to do one or both of two things. First, P might wish to impeach W's credibility by means of a prior inconsistent statement. W, who testified that D was on the driveway, previously said that D was on the sidewalk. This is a prior inconsistent statement. Under FRE 613(b), a party may offer extrinsic evidence of a prior inconsistent statement as long as the witness being impeached is given an opportunity to explain or deny making the statement. W had that opportunity here, because she was confronted with the statement on cross-examination. If Z had heard W's prior inconsistent statement, she could have testified about it.

The problem is that Z did not hear the prior inconsistent statement. X heard it. X made the out-of-court statement to Z that W had made the statement. This makes X a hearsay declarant. (X's statement asserted that W said, "D was just learning to skate and should not have been on the sidewalk." X's statement is offered to prove what it asserts—that W made that statement.) There is no exception covering X's statement. Thus, Z's testimony is inadmissible hearsay.

Answers (A), (B), and (C) are incorrect for the reasons just given.

267. **Answer (A) is correct.** As in the previous problems involving these facts, the evidence at issue is a prior inconsistent statement. Here, the statement was made under penalty of perjury in a deposition. That means it is admissible non-hearsay under FRE 801(d)(1)(A) if the declarant testifies at the trial or hearing and is subject to cross-examination concerning the statement. Those requirements are satisfied here. Thus, the prior statement is admissible to show that D was on the sidewalk (the truth of the matter asserted).

The prior inconsistent statement is also admissible to impeach. It is unlikely P will want to use it for that purpose, as P would like W to be believed when she made the prior statement. But technically, it is admissible to impeach.

Answers (B), (C), and (D) are incorrect for the reasons just given.

268. **Answer (B) is correct.** Under FRE 608(a), the character of a witness for truthfulness may be attacked by opinion or reputation evidence as to truthfulness. The evidence is not admissible to prove that D set the fire, however, because FRE 404(a) prohibits the prosecution from offering evidence of the defendant's character for that purpose unless one of the exceptions applies (example: D offers evidence of her good character to prove she did not start the fire). Even when character is admissible to prove action in accordance with that character, the trait must be a "pertinent" one, and truthfulness or untruthfulness is not "pertinent" to whether one would start a forest fire.

Answers (A), (C), and (D) are incorrect for the reasons given above.

269. **Answer (A) is correct.** Evidence that W testified incorrectly about what outfit she was wearing when she saw the crime take place is relevant because it suggests that she might be wrong about other things. Thus, this is impeachment by contradiction. There is no rule limiting the nature of contradictory matter raised *during the cross-examination of a witness*. Thus, it

does not matter that the color of W's outfit is "collateral." The question is proper. This means that **answer (C) is incorrect.**

Answer (B) is incorrect because the question does not deal with W's ability to perceive.

Answer (D) is incorrect because a possible error concerning what the witness was wearing when she saw the crime take place does not tend to show that the witness has a bad character for truthfulness or untruthfulness.

270. **Answer (D) is correct.** Using a false identification is an act that is "probative of the character for truthfulness or untruthfulness." Under FRE 608(b), such acts are admissible in the discretion of the court if not proven by extrinsic evidence. A question asked during cross-examination is not extrinsic to the witness. Thus, this is a proper attempt to impeach W by showing character for untruthfulness, meaning that **answer (A) is incorrect.**

Answer (B) is incorrect because the question does not suggest facts that contradict W's testimony.

Answer (C) is incorrect because questions going to the witness's credibility are not beyond the scope of the direct examination. It does not matter that the incident with the false identification was not mentioned during direct examination. *See* FRE 611(b).

271. **Answer (A) is correct.** Felony robbery is a crime punishable by imprisonment for more than a year. *See* FRE 609(a)(1)(A). It is not a crime that requires dishonesty or false statement. Thus, the conviction will be admissible as long as it is not excluded by FRE 403. That rule is strongly tilted toward admissibility.

Answer (B) is incorrect because the same type of conviction is harder to admit against a witness who is a criminal defendant. The standard in that case requires that the probative value of the conviction outweigh its prejudicial effect. *See* FRE 609(a)(1)(B). This means the prosecution will have to convince the court (albeit by just a little) it should admit the evidence.

Answer (C) is incorrect because any conviction older than 10 years (even a conviction for a crime the elements of which require dishonesty or false statement) is only admissible if the court decides, in the interests of justice, and supported by specific facts and circumstances, that the probative value substantially outweighs the prejudicial effect. *See* FRE 609(b). This is the reverse of FRE 403; the rule is heavily tilted toward exclusion.

Answer (D) is incorrect because a misdemeanor conviction of a crime that does not require dishonesty or false statement is never admissible to impeach the witness's credibility.

272. **Answer (C) is best.** Under FRE 609, a prior felony conviction of a testifying criminal defendant (for a crime that doesn't require an act of dishonesty or false statement) is admissible only if the court finds that its probative value exceeds the danger of unfair prejudice to the defendant. The age of the conviction affects its probative value; the older it is, the less it is likely to say about the defendant's truthfulness as a witness. In addition, if admission of the conviction would make it less likely that the defendant will testify, a court should take that fact into ac-

count because the defendant's testimony might increase the likelihood of an accurate verdict. Thus, the facts stated in both answers (A) and (B) would make it more likely that the court would grant D's motion to exclude the previous conviction for impeachment purposes.

Answers (A) and (B), while accurate, are not as good as (C).

Answer (D) is incorrect for the reasons stated above.

273. **Answer (A) is correct.** Under FRE 608(a), it is permissible to impeach a witness's truthful character using evidence of reputation for untruthfulness. That is what is happening in this problem. There is no "extrinsic evidence" rule; the party attacking the witness may call another witness to testify to the first witness's reputation for truthfulness.

Answer (B) is incorrect because FRE 608(a) contains no requirement that the witness's truthfulness has first been supported. In fact, the opposite is true: character for truthfulness may not be proven by reputation or opinion unless a witness's truthful character has been attacked.

Answer (C) is incorrect because it does not matter that this is a civil action.

Answer (D) is incorrect because the credibility of witnesses is relevant.

274. **Answer (C) is correct.** The purpose of the prosecutor's question is to impeach D with a prior conviction. This is governed by FRE 609. Under FRE 609(a)(1), because murder is not a crime involving "a dishonest act or false statement," evidence of the conviction is not admissible automatically. Thus, **answer (B) is incorrect.** Because murder is a crime "punishable by death or by imprisonment for more than one year," the crime *might* be admissible to impeach. Thus, **answer (A) is incorrect.** The standard depends on who the witness is. If the witness is the accused, the evidence is only admissible if the probative value exceeds the danger of unfair prejudice. (Note that this is *not* the FRE 403 standard.) Thus, answer (C) is correct, and **answer (D) is incorrect.**

275. D should argue that the testimony undercuts W1's capacity to observe, recollect, and narrate accurately, and that it is not an attack on W1's character for truthfulness. If it impeaches by capacity, there is no rule that specifically governs the evidence, and thus the court should simply decide whether the evidence is relevant and whether its potential for prejudice, consumption of time, or distraction of the jury substantially outweighs its probative value. (The court should also consider whether the evidence has too great a tendency to embarrass the witness, which would run afoul of FRE 611(a)(3), which provides that "[t]he court should exercise reasonable control over the mode and order of examining witnesses and presenting evidence so as to … protect witnesses from harassment or undue embarrassment.") It would have been much better for D to call the psychiatrist rather than a lay person who happens to know that W1 is under the psychiatrist's care, but this does not make the evidence inadmissible per se.

276. **Answer (D) is correct.** D's question violates the common law rule, that one may not impeach a witness by contradiction on a collateral matter using extrinsic evidence (what a mouthful!). Even though the Federal Rules do not mention this rule, it is sensible because it avoids wasting time on matters the only purpose of which is to impeach by contradiction, and even then,

involves matters so unimportant that the witness's error says virtually nothing about her credibility. Though the Federal Rules do not adopt the common law rule, many courts would exclude this evidence as a waste of time under FRE 403.

The problem here is not in asking whether W1 owns a blue raincoat, but in using extrinsic evidence to establish that she does not. If D wanted to show that W1 did not own a blue raincoat, D should have asked W1 that question. Unfortunately, however, if W1 had insisted that she did own a blue raincoat, D would have been stuck with that answer.

Answer (A) is incorrect for the reasons just given. **Answer (B) is incorrect** because whether W1 owns a blue raincoat or not does not affect her character for truthfulness. **Answer (C) is incorrect** because evidence that goes to the credibility of a witness is not irrelevant.

277. **Answer (D) is correct.** The prosecution is attempting to impeach W with a prior conviction. The conviction is not one for a crime involving dishonesty or false statement, so it is not automatically admissible. Thus, **answer (B) is incorrect.** Because murder is a crime "punishable by death or by imprisonment for more than one year," the court has discretion to admit the evidence. Thus, **answer (A) is incorrect.** Because the witness is a witness other than the accused, the evidence "must be admitted, subject to Rule 403." That means the evidence is admissible unless the probative value is substantially outweighed by the danger of unfair prejudice. This is the test stated in answer (D). **Answer (C) is incorrect** because it states the standard that would apply if the witness being impeached were the accused.

278. **Answer (A) is correct.** D's goal is to impeach W1 by showing a motive to testify against D. There is no specific rule in the FRE governing this type of impeachment, but the Supreme Court confirmed that this important form of impeachment is still available in *United States v. Abel*, 469 U.S. 45 (1984). The Court indicated that this method of impeachment is controlled by FRE 403. Because FRE 403 is heavily slanted toward admission (exclusion may only occur if the probative value of the evidence is substantially outweighed by the dangers mentioned in the rule), this form of impeachment is readily available. Here, the evidence will be admissible because the evidence carries substantial probative value and there is little danger of jury misuse of the evidence.

Answer (B) is incorrect because there is no prohibition of extrinsic evidence when the method of impeachment is bias or motive.

Answer (C) is incorrect because D's purpose is not to impeach W1's character for truthfulness. (If that was D's purpose, the evidence would not be admissible because FRE 608(b) does contain a prohibition on extrinsic evidence.)

Answer (D) is incorrect because FRE 408, the compromise rule, does not bar the evidence when used to impeach a witness by showing bias.

279. **Answer (C) is correct.** D's goal is to impeach W with a prior conviction. Medicare fraud is a crime involving dishonesty or false statement. Under FRE 609(a)(2), such a crime "must be admitted" regardless of the punishment associated with it. Courts have held that the trial court has no discretion to exclude the evidence. Thus, the court must overrule the objection.

Answers (A), (B), and (D) are incorrect for the reasons just given.

280. **Answer (B) is correct.** The prosecutor is seeking to elicit a prior inconsistent statement on cross-examination. Because the statement was not made under penalty of perjury in a trial, hearing, deposition, or other formal proceeding, it is hearsay and not admissible to prove the truth of the matter asserted. *See* FRE 801(d)(1)(A). The statement is admissible to impeach the witness's credibility, however. In addition, the question does not violate D's right to confrontation because D may conduct redirect examination of the witness concerning the inconsistent statement.

Answer (A) is incorrect for the reasons given above. The statement may not be offered to prove W's and D's whereabouts because it is inadmissible hearsay.

Answer (C) is incorrect for the reasons given above.

Answer (D) is incorrect for the reasons given above.

281. **Answer (A) is correct.** P is attempting to offer her own prior *consistent* statement. Under FRE 801(d)(1)(B)(i), a prior consistent statement is only admissible if the declarant testifies at the trial or hearing, is subject to cross-examination about the prior statement, and the statement is offered "to rebut an express or implied charge that the declarant recently fabricated it or acted from a recent improper influence or motive in so testifying." In *Tome v. United States*, 513 U.S. 150 (1995), the Supreme Court also held that the rule incorporates the additional common law requirement that the statement was made before the charge of fabrication was made or before the influence or motive came into being. Here, the problem is that P made the statement when she already had a motive to lie. In addition, the statement is not offered to rehabilitate credibility under FRE 801(d)(B)(ii) because there has been no impeachment. Thus, the statement is inadmissible hearsay.

Answer (B) is incorrect because it is an overly broad statement. The rules only regulate some methods of enhancing the credibility of a witness. There is nothing impermissible about supporting a witness's credibility by showing that she has very good vision, for example.

Answer (C) is incorrect because a prior inconsistent statement, if admissible, does not have to be proven by the declarant's testimony.

Answer (D) is incorrect because the evidence is inadmissible.

282. **Answer (A) is correct.** W's prior statement that he was at the movies for the entire night is inconsistent with his trial testimony that he was across the street from the car dealer at the crucial time that night. Because the statement was not made under penalty of perjury, the statement is not admissible to prove the truth of the matter asserted (FRE 801(d)(1)(A)). It is only admissible to impeach. The requirements of FRE 613(a) have been satisfied.

Answers (B), (C), and (D) are incorrect for the reasons just given.

283. **Answer (C) is correct.** As in the previous problem, the method of impeachment being used here is prior inconsistent statement. FRE 613(b) provides that if extrinsic evidence of a prior statement is offered, the declarant must be given the opportunity to explain or deny the statement. That occurred here, during W's cross-examination. Thus, the evidence is admissible to impeach W by prior inconsistent statement.

Answer (A) is incorrect because, as just shown, the rules governing the use of prior statements do not contain an extrinsic evidence prohibition.

Answer (B) is incorrect because the matter of W's whereabouts at the crucial time is not collateral.

Answer (D) is incorrect because D is not offering the evidence to prove that W has a bad character for truthfulness.

284. **Answer (C) is best.** The prosecution is using a prior *consistent* statement in this problem. The requirements of FRE 801(d)(1)(B) have been satisfied. W has testified at the trial, is subject to cross-examination concerning the prior consistent statement, the statement is being offered to rebut a charge of recent fabrication (as raised by the defense), and W made the statement before that charge had been leveled. This means **answer (A) is correct**: the question is a permissible attempt to establish W's credibility.

When a prior consistent statement satisfies the requirements of FRE 801(d)(1)(B), it can be used both to support the witness's credibility and to prove the truth of the matter asserted (here, that W was at Mel's Diner at the crucial time). Thus, **answer (B) is also correct**: the question is a permissible attempt to establish W's whereabouts on the evening of February 6.

Because the evidence is admissible for both credibility and substantive purposes, answer (C) is the correct answer. **Answer (D) is incorrect** for the reasons just given.

285. The court should sustain P's hearsay objection but overrule P's impeachment objection. The cross-examination question seeks to elicit a prior inconsistent statement of X. It does not matter that X was not a witness. Under FRE 806, when a hearsay statement is introduced, the declarant becomes a sort of witness who may be impeached in the same ways as would be permitted if she had in fact testified. Here, X's statement that another person clubbed P is inconsistent with the statement of X that D clubbed P, and that P introduced into evidence. (Presumably, that was admitted as an excited utterance under FRE 803(2).) Because that statement was not made subject to penalty of perjury in a trial, hearing, deposition, or other formal context, it is not admissible as non-hearsay to prove the truth of the matter asserted. *See* FRE 801(d)(1)(A). It is only admissible to impeach W's credibility.

286. **Answer (C) is correct.** If D hates poodles, it is not likely he would travel to another city to attend a poodle show. This is therefore an attempt to impeach D by showing the implausibility of his alibi. There is no specific provision in the Federal Rules governing this type of impeachment. Therefore, it is subject only to the general requirements of FRE 102 and 611(a) (which deal with such things as fairness, witness harassment, and needless consumption of time), and to FRE 403. There is no reason to think that the probative value of the evidence for its legitimate purpose of impeaching D's credibility is substantially outweighed by the danger of unfair prejudice or other dangers mentioned in FRE 403.

Answer (A) is incorrect because evidence going to the credibility of a witness is not irrelevant.

Answer (B) is incorrect because hating poodles does not affect a person's character for truthfulness.

Answer (D) is incorrect because a bias against poodles is not relevant to D's credibility in this instance. (Had D been on trial for attacking a poodle, and D denied doing so, the evidence might be admissible to impeach by showing a bias against poodles or a motive to hurt them.)

287. **Answer (C) is correct.** The applicable standard for admission of the evidence is in FRE 609(a)(1)(B). If the witness being impeached with a prior conviction is the criminal defendant, the evidence is admissible only if the probative value exceeds the risk of unfair prejudice. The fact that the conviction was for the same crime as the one for which D is now on trial increases the risk of unfair prejudice, but does not make the evidence per se inadmissible. Thus, **answer (A) is incorrect.**

Answer (B) is incorrect because it is based on the wrong standard.

Answer (D) is incorrect because battery is not a crime involving dishonesty or false statement, so the conviction is not automatically admissible to impeach D.

288. **Answer (C) is correct.** The evidence is relevant on two grounds. First, it supplies a motive for D to attack V. If D was having an affair with W, D might have had a motive to kill V to remove her from the picture. Thus, the evidence is admissible substantively. Second, the evidence tends to supply a motive for W to lie. W might want to protect D to preserve their relationship.

Answers (A), (B), and (D) are incorrect for the reasons just stated.

289. **Answer (A) is correct.** Evidence that W1 was watching "Beetleman" instead of "Bar Wars" impeaches W1 by contradiction. But which movie W1 was attending has no value to the case except to impeach in this way. Thus, the matter of what movie W1 was watching is considered "collateral." Although the Federal Rules do not adopt the common law rule, most federal courts would exclude evidence that impeaches a witness by contradiction on a collateral matter *using extrinsic evidence* under FRE 403 because it is a waste of time. Calling another witness (W2) is extrinsic evidence. Thus, this was an improper attempt to impeach by contradiction.

Note that the result would be the same if the evidence was that W1 *told W2* that she had seen "Beetleman." This would be a prior inconsistent statement. Because the matter about which W1 spoke inconsistently is collateral, most courts would forbid the use of extrinsic evidence to prove the prior inconsistent statement. This rule is not contained in the Federal Rules, but it follows naturally from the common law rule just discussed, and most federal courts today would exclude the evidence as a waste of time under FRE 403.

Answers (B), (C), and (D) are incorrect for the reasons just given.

290. **Answer (D) is correct.** The statement by X was admissible as an excited utterance. Thus, even though X has not testified at the trial, X's credibility is on the table. FRE 806 provides that "[w]hen a hearsay statement—or a statement described in Rule 801(d)(2)(C), (D), or (E)— has been admitted in evidence, the declarant's credibility may be attacked, and then sup-

ported, by any evidence that would be admissible for those purposes if the declarant had testified as a witness." That rule would make X's prior conviction admissible if it satisfies the requirements of FRE 609. Because forgery is a crime involving dishonesty or false statement, it is admissible per se pursuant to FRE 609(a)(2).

Answers (A), (B), and (C) are incorrect for the reasons just stated.

291. **Answer (B) is correct.** The evidence seeks to support D's credibility by showing a good character for truthfulness. FRE 608(a) provides that such evidence in the form of reputation or opinion is admissible "only after the witness's character for truthfulness has been attacked." The facts do not reveal that the prosecution attacked D's character for truthfulness. Thus, the evidence is inadmissible. **Answers (A) and (C) are incorrect** for the reasons just stated. **Answer (D) is incorrect** because W's opinion, stated on the witness stand, is not hearsay.

Note that in this situation, the evidence would not be admissible under FRE 404(a) because truthfulness is not a "pertinent" trait of character in this situation. D allegedly stole the cards while the child was playing with them; she is not alleged to have used any fraud or other dishonesty to cause the child to part with the cards.

292. **Answer (C) is correct.** FRE 609(b)(1) provides that if more than 10 years have elapsed from the date of conviction or release from confinement, whichever is later, evidence of a prior conviction is inadmissible unless "its probative value, supported by specific facts and circumstances, substantially outweighs its prejudicial effect." Note that this is the opposite of the FRE 403 standard. Here, the usual result will be exclusion, not admission. This rule applies even to crimes involving dishonesty or false statement, such as the perjury conviction in this case.

Answers (A) and (B) are incorrect for the reasons just stated. **Answer (D) is incorrect** because the facts given in the problem do not reveal whether the prosecution can meet its burden under FRE 609(b).

293. **Answer (D) is correct.** FRE 607 provides that "[a]ny party, including the party that called the witness, may attack the witness's credibility." The purpose of this rule was to do away with the common law rule that a party vouches for her own witnesses and may not impeach her own witness unless the witness turns hostile. At the same time, the courts have held that there are limits to a party's rights under FRE 607. Specifically, a party may not abuse the intent of the rule by calling a witness for the sole purpose of impeaching her through a method that reveals otherwise inadmissible evidence.

That is what the prosecution has done in this case. If W never testified, the prosecution would have no legitimate way to introduce W's statement to her friend that incriminated D. It would not be admissible substantively because of the hearsay rule, and if W neither testifies nor is a prior statement of W admitted pursuant to an exception to or exemption from the hearsay rule, there would be no basis for impeachment of W. Here, the prosecutor's probable objective is to place before the jury the statement incriminating D. That statement would purportedly be offered only as a prior inconsistent statement to impeach W, but the prosecutor un-doubtedly knows that the jury will have a hard time abiding by a limiting instruction, and will instead consider the evidence for what it asserts.

This answer assumes that the prosecution really does "know" that W will stick to the story she gave before the grand jury. The courts will not require absolute certainty, but a reasonably high standard of knowledge should be required in order to avoid losing potentially relevant information. Thus, if the prosecutor has a legitimate reason to believe that W will testify differently at trial than at the grand jury, the court should allow the prosecutor to call W.

Answers (A) and (C) are incorrect for the reasons given. **Answer B is incorrect** because the prosecutor had no reason to believe that W might change her testimony. The prosecutor is not entitled to place W before the jury, and introduce her prior inconsistent statement, on the sole ground that her demeanor will reveal that she is being untruthful. (In an extreme case this might be possible, but the facts here do not appear to support such a result.)

294. The court should overrule the objection. Even though Z never testified at the trial, Z's excited utterance was admitted to prove that D rammed X's car. Admission of that statement places Z's credibility in issue. FRE 806 provides that "[w]hen a hearsay statement — or a statement described in Rule 801(d)(2)(C), (D), or (E) — has been admitted in evidence, the declarant's credibility may be attacked, and then supported, by any evidence that would be admissible for those purposes if the declarant had testified as a witness." The rule further provides that an inconsistent statement may be introduced for that purpose without being subject to the requirement that the declarant be afforded an opportunity to explain or deny the statement (a requirement contained in FRE 613(b)). In this case, D is availing herself of the opportunity to impeach Z with a prior inconsistent statement.

295. The court should sustain the objection. FRE 610 provides that "[e]vidence of a witness's religious beliefs or opinions is not admissible to attack or support the witness's credibility." D's question was designed to impeach W by virtue of her religious beliefs — to show that a person who believes all people with blue eyes are evil should not be believed. This falls within the prohibition of FRE 610.

296. The court should overrule the objection. D is not attempting to impeach W by means of the nature of her religious beliefs, but trying to establish a possible bias or motive to testify in favor of the church to which W belongs. FRE 610 therefore does not apply. The court may still exclude the evidence under FRE 403, but that will be a difficult standard to satisfy, especially in light of the fact that the courts tend to treat bias or motive impeachment as strongly affecting the credibility of a witness. If the P church congregation is huge and W is not an active member, the probative value of the evidence to impeach by showing bias or motive is not as great as if the congregation was smaller and W was an active member. Even there, however, most courts would probably overrule the objection. Of course, if P requests a limiting instruction informing jurors of the limited purpose for which the court admitted the evidence, the court must grant the request. *See* FRE 105.

297. The court should overrule P's objection. Evidence that P is a "liar extraordinaire" is not relevant to whether D struck P or vice versa, but it does tend to impeach P's statement that D struck her. Normally, a person who does not testify at the trial is not subject to impeachment. However, FRE 806 provides that a hearsay declarant whose statement has been offered at trial may be impeached. That is the situation here. P's statement was admitted, probably as an excited utterance. This made P subject to impeachment. FRE 608(a) allows reputation or opinion evidence on the issue of a person's reputation for truthfulness. W2's proposed testimony fits into the reputation category, and is proper.

298. The court should sustain the prosecutor's objection and not permit W1 to testify concerning the weather. D is attempting to impeach W1 by contradiction. The common law rule is that one may not impeach a witness by contradiction on a collateral matter using extrinsic evidence. In this hypothetical, the weather is collateral because the events took place inside a bank, not outside. Thus, without more information, it does not appear that the fact that it was raining is relevant except insofar as it tends to impeach W1 by contradiction. (If D could show that most of the illumination in the bank was supplied by windows, and that it was dark in the bank because it was raining outside, the evidence concerning the weather might take on some value because it might have affected W1's ability to identify the robber. But those facts are not given.) Although the Federal Rules did not adopt the common law rule just described, federal courts will usually exclude evidence of this kind under FRE 403.

    Because the weather is a collateral fact, D is restricted to cross-examination, and is stuck with W1's response. D may not use W2 to show that it was raining.

299. **Answer (C) is correct.** D's statement is a party admission when offered by the prosecution. *See* FRE 801(d)(2)(A). It is therefore admissible to prove what it asserts: that D taught V a lesson. The statement is relevant because it suggests that D committed the assault and battery on V. The statement is also inconsistent with D's testimony at trial that she did not commit the crime. Thus, the statement is also admissible as a prior inconsistent statement, and may be used to impeach D's credibility as a witness.

    Answers (A), (B), and (D) are incorrect for the reasons given above.

300. The court should sustain the objection. This appears to be an effort to impeach W1's credibility by contradiction—by showing that W1 was wrong about something (the CD she was buying) and therefore might have been wrong about something else (the title of the CDs being unloaded). W2's testimony is "extrinsic" evidence when used for that purpose. The common law rule did not allow extrinsic evidence to impeach by contradiction on a "collateral" matter, meaning something unimportant to the case except insofar as it tends to impeach by contradiction. The name of the CD W1 was buying that day is certainly "collateral"; it means nothing to the facts of the case. The FRE do not codify the common law rule, but evidence meeting these requirements is a waste of time and usually will be excluded under FRE 403, which balances probative value against dangers including distracting the jury and wasting time.

Authentication

301. **Answer (A) is correct.** FRE 901(a) provides that a piece of evidence is authenticated if the court finds that there is sufficient evidence to support a finding that the evidence is what its proponent claims. FRE 901(b)(6)(B) provides an illustration of authentication involving telephone conversations: "evidence that a call was made to the number assigned at the time to … a particular business, if the call was made to a business and the call related to business reasonably transacted over the telephone." Here, P has testified that she placed the call to a number identified with D in the phone book, and that the answering party identified himself as a "heating service." This is sufficient evidence to support a finding that P actually placed the call to D.

   Answer (B) is incorrect because it assumes that the court must make the finding of whether the call was actually placed. This is not the standard of FRE 901(a).

   Answer (C) is incorrect because the answering party need not identify itself specifically as a particular business in order for there to be sufficient evidence to support a finding that the call was actually placed to the business.

   Answer (D) is incorrect because the very purpose of a motion to strike is to remove evidence from consideration that the jury has already heard. Normally, the court will also instruct the jury to ignore the evidence.

302. The prosecution will probably try to establish chain of custody. One or more witnesses will testify to the location of the bat from the time it was found (presumably in D's possession) until the time it was brought into court. Often, a police officer will testify that she marked the item at the scene and placed it in a secure location (such as an evidence locker). That witness or other witnesses will establish the movements (if any) of the item from the time it was discovered until the time of trial. Any breaks in the chain might be fatal, but need not be. The basic standard for authentication is the same for all other situations: whether there is evidence sufficient to support a finding that the item is what its proponent claims (FRE 901(a)).

303. **Answer (D) is correct.** P's testimony is sufficient to authenticate the photograph. P has personal knowledge of the positions of the cars immediately after the crash, and has testified that the photograph accurately depicts that scene. There is no requirement that the photographer testify.

   Answer (A) is incorrect for the reason just given. The photographer is not a necessary witness as long as someone with personal knowledge testifies.

   Answer (B) is incorrect because P's testimony is sufficient to support a finding that the cars were not moved between the accident and the time the photograph was taken.

Answer (C) is incorrect because the best evidence rule has not been violated in this situation. P is not testifying about the contents of the photograph without using the photograph. P has brought the photograph to court and will use it to prove its own contents.

304. **Answer (B) is correct.** Authentication is satisfied by showing that there is evidence sufficient to support a finding that the item is what the proponent claims. *See* FRE 901(a). It is not a very demanding standard. On the facts presented, the standard probably has been satisfied by V's testimony about the crushed corner. *See* FRE 901(b)(4) (distinctive characteristics).

Answer (A) is incorrect because it states the wrong standard for authentication.

Answer (C) is incorrect because it is simply not true. Some cartons of CDs will be identifiable for a variety of reasons including distinctive markings or other features.

Answer (D) is incorrect because V has testified that she recognizes the carton. That is one fact that would make her qualified to authenticate it.

305. One way would be to obtain an expert's opinion, as discussed in FRE 901(b)(3). P could obtain a handwriting exemplar from D, which the court would order D to provide if D is unwilling to do so voluntarily. That exemplar could be authenticated simply by testimony, from someone with knowledge, that D provided it. The expert would then testify that she compared the exemplar with the questioned letter and concluded that they were written by the same person.

A second way to authenticate the letter would be by the testimony of a lay witness familiar with D's handwriting (and whose familiarity was not acquired for purposes of the litigation). *See* FRE 901(b)(2).

In either case, the evidence would be admissible if the court concludes that there is evidence sufficient to support a finding that D wrote the questioned letter. That is an easy standard to satisfy.

306. **Answer (D) is correct.** According to FRE 902(6), "[p]rinted material purporting to be a newspaper or periodical" is self-authenticating, meaning that "they require no extrinsic evidence of authenticity in order to be admitted."

Answer (A) is incorrect because it fails to recognize the application of the self-authentication doctrine, and because even under normal authentication doctrine (FRE 901(a)), this issue is to be decided according to a different standard: whether there is sufficient evidence to support a finding that the item is what its proponent claims.

Answer (B) is incorrect because the objection was made on the basis of authentication, not the best evidence rule. Even if D had objected on best evidence rule grounds, the court should overrule the objection because that rule does not require a party to offer the "best evidence" to prove a point except when the issue is the contents of a writing and the party offers secondary evidence of the writing rather than the writing itself.

Answer (C) is incorrect because it fails to recognize the application of the self-authentication doctrine. If this were a normal authentication situation, the answer would be correct.

Note that if P had objected on hearsay grounds, the court probably would have sustained the objection. The article asserts that all the goods in D's warehouse were destroyed by flooding, and it is offered to prove that fact.

The Best Evidence Rule

307. Answer (D) is correct. The best evidence (or original writing) rule only applies when a party seeks to prove the contents of a writing, recording, or photograph. In that situation, unless an exception applies, the party must offer the writing, not secondary evidence (such as testimony about what the writing says). Here, P has not testified about the contents of her medical records. She has merely testified that she suffered complications that required amputation. Though her testimony might not be the "best evidence" of the condition that led to the need for amputation, the best evidence rule does not require P to produce the "best evidence" to prove anything except the contents of a writing.

Answer (A) is incorrect for the reasons just stated.

Answer (B) is incorrect because, if the best evidence rule does not apply, there is no requirement that the party produce the writing that would support her testimony.

Answer (C) is incorrect because it lays out an exception to the best evidence rule. Exceptions are not needed if the rule itself does not apply, which is the case here.

308. Answer (D) is correct for the same reasons as in the previous question. Even though the transcript is clearly the "best evidence" of X's testimony, the best evidence rule does not apply for one simple reason: W is not testifying about the contents of the transcript; she is testifying about the contents of her memory of what X said at the trial. Thus, if W testifies that X testified at the first trial, "Defendant shot the victim," W's testimony does not violate the best evidence rule. If W had testified that the transcript reports that X testified, "Defendant shot the victim," that testimony would violate the best evidence rule because W will have testified about the contents of a writing.

Answers (A), (B), and (C) are incorrect for the same reasons as in the previous question.

309. Answer (A) is correct. An X-ray is a "photograph" as defined in FRE 1001(c), and photographs are covered by the best evidence rule. Dr. W will testify about the contents of the X-ray, which presumably shows the condition of the bones of P's leg. The best evidence rule requires that unless certain exceptions apply (and none are applicable on the facts given here), the writing itself must be offered to prove its contents.

Note that as long as the writing is offered, there is no rule forbidding secondary evidence from being offered as well. Thus, Dr. W could explain what the X-ray shows. She could also testify about other facts that led her to conclude that P's leg was broken. And of course, P is not required to use the X-ray to prove her leg was broken. The best evidence rule simply provides that if a party wishes to prove the contents of a writing, recording, or photograph, the item itself must be offered.

Answer (B) is incorrect for the reason given above. An X-ray is covered by the rule.

Answer (C) is incorrect because, although it seems illogical, there is no exception to the rule for writings, recordings, or photographs that a fact-finder would be unable to understand or interpret.

Answer (D) is incorrect because the proposed testimony is about what the X-ray shows, even if it requires some interpretation. As long as Dr. W will testify that the X-ray shows a break in P's leg, the X-ray must be produced (barring application of an exception).

310. **Answer (A) is correct.** The issue concerns the terms of the agreement. The agreement is in writing. If D wants to prove the terms, she must therefore offer the writing. It does not matter that a contract is actually something that exists between two minds and that the writing is only a memorandum. In law, the writing takes on special significance; its terms *become* the terms of the agreement.

Answers (B) and (C) are incorrect for the reasons just given. D is required to offer the writing to prove the terms of the contract.

Answer (D) is incorrect because there is no exception to the best evidence rule for situations in which the writing is central to the case. In fact, just the opposite is true; FRE 1004(d) sets forth an exception for situations in which the writing goes to a collateral matter (where it "is not closely related to a controlling issue").

311. The best evidence rule only applies if the witness is testifying about the "contents" of a writing, and not simply the writing's existence. If the only issue were whether there was a piece of paper on the car's windshield, there would be no best evidence rule problem. If the issue were the exact nature of the citation (the precise violation it states, for example), the best evidence rule would apply. This case falls between. Though the parking ticket is a "writing," one argument is that the witness is simply identifying it as a parking ticket, not testifying to its contents. The opposite argument is that to testify that it was a parking ticket is to testify about its contents. The better argument is that this is not a best evidence rule violation, for the reason given above and one more—the importance of the ticket is its context in time: that it was on the car at that particular moment. The fact-finder would gain little by seeing the ticket in court.

An analogy: A witness will testify that the person who approached him was wearing a police badge. Probably, the testimony will not violate the best evidence rule.

312. A tombstone satisfies the definition of a "writing" in FRE 1001(a) because it consists of "letters, words, numbers … set down in any form." Thus, it appears the best evidence rule applies. But it is not likely possible to produce the tombstone in court. FRE 1004(b) provides an exception for situations in which "an original cannot be obtained by any available judicial process." This is such a situation. The best evidence rule will not bar the witness's testimony.

The hearsay rule also would not prevent the testimony. The words "Elvis Aaron Presley" are hearsay because they are an assertion of a person, made other than while testifying at the trial or hearing, and they are offered in evidence to prove the truth of what they assert (that Elvis is dead). FRE 803(13), however, provides an exception for "[a] statement of fact about personal or family history contained … on [a] … burial marker."

313. P's hearsay objection should be overruled because there is no out-of-court statement of a person; there was merely the reading on a mechanical instrument. FRE 801(b) defines "declarant" as a "*person* who made the statement." (emphasis added). Objection sustained on best evidence rule grounds, however. D proposes to testify about the reading on the face of the speedometer. That number constitutes a "writing" in this context. D's proposed testimony therefore violates the best evidence rule.

314. **Answer (C) is correct.** A photocopy qualifies as a "duplicate" under FRE 1001(e) because it is "a counterpart produced by a mechanical, photographic, chemical, electronic, or other equivalent process or technique that accurately reproduces the original." Photocopying qualifies under this definition. Normally, a duplicate is admissible to the same extent as the original (FRE 1003). However, the same rule provides that the court should exclude the duplicate if "a genuine question is raised about the original's authenticity or the circumstances make it unfair to admit the duplicate." This case seems to satisfy the second test. D has claimed P tampered with the photocopy. It would be unfair to permit P to use the photocopy in lieu of the original.

Answer (A) is incorrect because it fails to take account of the exception in FRE 1003.

Answer (B) is incorrect because a photocopy does qualify as a duplicate.

Answer (D) is incorrect because it ignores the application of the best evidence rule, which is supposed to encourage the use of originals as a means of advancing the likelihood of learning the truth. In this case, requiring P to produce the original will serve that purpose. P may also produce the photocopy in addition to the original, but not in lieu of it.

315. The court should overrule both objections. The elevator permit is a "writing." The best evidence rule states that if a party wishes to prove the content of a writing, recording, or photograph, the original must be produced. FRE 1002. Here, P wishes to testify about what the permit stated, which is testimony about its contents. Thus, the best evidence rule applies. However, FRE 1004(c) states that if the original is in the control of the opponent, and the party wishing to testify about it notifies the opponent in advance that it intends to prove the contents, secondary evidence is admissible if the opponent fails to produce the original. That is what happened here. Thus, P's testimony does not violate the best evidence rule. Also, the testimony probably is not hearsay. The expiration date arguably is not a statement about a fact; it is a fact that, in itself, has independent legal significance ("verbal act"). If the permit has expired, that fact in itself is some indication of D's negligence. Thus, the testimony is not hearsay.

Topic 13: Answers

Judicial Notice

316. **Answer (C) is correct.** FRE 201 governs the taking of judicial notice of adjudicative facts. FRE 201(b) provides that to be a proper subject of judicial notice, a fact must be one "not subject to reasonable dispute because it: (1) is generally known within the trial court's territorial jurisdiction; or (2) can be accurately and readily determined from sources whose accuracy cannot reasonably be questioned."

Answer (A) is incorrect because it presents a fact that is subject to judicial notice under subpart (b)(2) of FRE 201. This fact is one that is not subject to reasonable dispute because there are authoritative horticultural sources that will clearly state that palm trees grow better in warm climates than in cold climates.

Answer (B) is incorrect because it falls into the same category as answer (A). Sources whose accuracy is not subject to dispute will verify the molecular structure of deuterium.

Answer (D) is incorrect because it presents a fact that is subject to judicial notice under subpart (b)(1) of FRE 201. If a certain state forbids the sale of packaged liquor on Sundays, this fact is very likely to be known generally within that state.

Barring additional facts not given in the problem, answer (C) does not state a fact of which judicial notice may be taken. It is quite unlikely that people within the court's territorial jurisdiction will generally be aware that a particular road was not plowed for twenty-four hours after a particular snow storm. It is possible that many people know this to be true, but it is very unlikely that the fact is "generally known." Also, this is not a fact that is likely to be found in "sources whose accuracy cannot reasonably be questioned." Even a contemporaneous newspaper account that stated the fact might be disputed because newspapers often contain inaccuracies.

317. **Answer (D) is correct.** FRE 201(f) provides that "[i]n a civil case, the court *must* instruct the jury to accept the noticed fact as conclusive." (emphasis added) The language makes clear that this is mandatory.

Answer (A) is incorrect because, once the court has taken notice of the fact, no contrary evidence may be offered.

Answer (B) is incorrect because such an argument would run directly contrary to the provision of FRE 201(f) that the court's taking of notice is conclusive as to the fact. It is therefore improper to argue to the jury that it should make a contrary factual finding.

Answer (C) is incorrect because, as noted above, the court is *required* to give the instruction.

318. **Answer (A) is correct.** Certainly, the danger posed by AIDS is generally known within the territorial jurisdiction of the trial court. If for some reason it is not, D can certainly provide the court with authoritative sources establishing that fact.

Answer (B) is incorrect because the importance of facts to the claim or defense does not affect the propriety of taking judicial notice.

Answer (C) is incorrect because FRE 201(d) provides that "[t]he court may take judicial notice at any stage of the proceeding." Thus, notice may be taken even after the trial begins. (In fact, notice is sometimes taken at the appellate stage.)

Answer (D) is incorrect because FRE 104(a) provides that the court may rely on any non-privileged evidence in making evidentiary rulings. Thus, even if D supports her judicial notice request with hearsay (the reliable source is likely hearsay, for example), the court may consider the hearsay in making its ruling.

319. **Answer (C) is correct.** FRE 201 does not forbid the taking of judicial notice in criminal cases, even against the defendant and even if the fact noticed constitutes an essential element of the crime. Thus, **answers (A) and (B) are incorrect.**

If the court takes notice in a criminal case, however, FRE 201(f) states that "the court must instruct the jury that it may or may not accept the noticed fact as conclusive." The purpose of this rule is to preserve a criminal defendant's right to trial by jury. **Answer (D) is incorrect** because it is phrased in permissive terms (the court "may" instruct the jury). The instruction that the jury need not consider the fact conclusively established is a mandatory instruction.

320. The court may take notice of the fact, but not on the basis of FRE 201. This is not an "adjudicative fact," but a "legislative fact." In the words of the Advisory Committee note to FRE 201, legislative facts "are those which have relevance to legal reasoning and the lawmaking process, whether in the formulation of a legal principle or ruling by a judge or court or in the enactment of a legislative body." In other words, legislative facts are the kinds of "facts" that rule-makers take into consideration when deciding on the appropriate rule. Those facts often are disputable; indeed, they are often hotly contested. If legislatures and courts were not permitted to take such facts into account, lawmaking would be virtually impossible to undertake.

Burdens of Proof and Presumptions

321. **Answer (A) is correct.** The party who has the burden of persuasion as to an issue generally must also bear the burden of producing evidence. Here, P has the burden of persuading the jury that D was negligent, and must also produce evidence of D's negligence. The testimony of P's witness is certainly sufficient to meet a burden of production. This does not mean, however, that P has met a burden of *persuasion*. It only means that P has produced sufficient evidence to *allow* the jury to render a verdict for P on the negligence issue. The burden of persuasion remains with P.

What happens if D fails to produce any contrary evidence on the negligence question? Barring very unusual circumstances in which the evidence presented by the party with the burden of persuasion (here P) is so overwhelming as to make a decision for the other party irrational, there is still a jury question. Thus, by failing to offer evidence of non-negligence, D has taken a risk that the jury will find in P's favor on that question, but no more. The burden of persuasion is still with P, and the court should not direct a verdict for P on the issue.

(A) is therefore the correct answer. The case goes to the jury on the negligence issue, and the jury should be instructed that P bears the burden of persuasion.

Answer (B) is incorrect because, as stated above, the effect of D's failure to offer evidence is not to order the issue decided for P, but to let the case go to the jury.

Answer (C) is incorrect because it assumes that the burden of persuasion has shifted to D. As explained above, it has not.

Answer (D) is incorrect because the evidence discussed only goes to the issue of negligence, not to the entire *prima facie* case.

322. **Answer (D) is correct.** P has the burden of persuasion on the negligence issue, and also has the burden of producing evidence on that issue. P has failed to produce any affirmative evidence of D's negligence. Thus, P has not met a burden of producing evidence on this essential element of the *prima facie* case. There is no reason to force D to present any evidence at all. The court should direct a verdict for D. Note that the directed verdict will be on the entire negligence claim; the failure of any essential element of the *prima facie* case means the entire claim fails.

Answer (A) is incorrect because, by failing to meet a burden of production, P has not earned the right to have the jury decide in her favor.

Answer (B) is incorrect because D has no obligation to present evidence if P has not met a burden of production on an essential element of her claim.

Answer (C) is incorrect because the court has sufficient information before it to rule on D's motion. Of course, the court may choose to give P another opportunity to present evidence as to D's negligence, but it should not force D to present a case unless, and until, P presents such evidence.

323. The court should still grant D's motion. P is arguing that even though she has no affirmative evidence of negligence, she should be given the opportunity to produce it from D's witnesses, or, even if not, show the jury by the witnesses' demeanor that they are lying. If the court were to allow the case to go forward based on this argument, directed verdicts would practically disappear. It is possible that granting such motions will work injustice occasionally, but that will not likely happen often. Remember that in civil cases, there is ample opportunity for discovery. P should use that opportunity to take the depositions of D's witnesses. If P really believes that she can show that D's witnesses are lying, or get them to change their stories, she can thus establish a record to place before the court in opposition to D's motion for directed verdict.

324. **Answer (C) is correct.** According to the "bursting bubble" theory of presumptions, a presumption only shifts the burden of production to the opponent, and when the opponent offers sufficient evidence of the non-existence of the *presumed fact* to meet a burden of production, the presumption disappears from the case. Here, P has produced sufficient evidence to meet her burden of production. This causes the presumption to come into being, and shifts the burden of production to D. However, D's blood test evidence is clearly sufficient to meet a burden of production. That causes the presumption to disappear, leaving only logical inferences. (Note that D's evidence destroys only the presumption, not the logical inference. In other words, D's evidence is not so overwhelming as to require a directed verdict for D.)

As a result of the evidence produced by P and D, the situation is as follows: P's cohabitation evidence gives rise to a logical inference that D is the father of the child, and D's blood test evidence gives rise to a logical inference that he was not the father of the child. The jury will simply decide whether D is the father taking into account all the evidence, as it normally would do.

Answer (A) is incorrect because, even though P has produced sufficient evidence to meet a burden of production as to the foundational facts, D's evidence destroys the presumption, making an instruction on the presumption inappropriate under the bursting bubble theory. The burden of persuasion remains with P.

Answer (B) is incorrect because it assumes that P's evidence is so strong as to require a decision that D was the father. This is not true. P's evidence is only sufficient to meet a burden of production. And as explained above, under the bursting bubble theory of presumptions, D's evidence has destroyed the presumption, making an instruction about the presumption inappropriate.

Answer (D) is incorrect because, even though D's blood test evidence is rather strong, it is probably not strong enough to *require* a verdict in D's favor on the paternity issue. This is still a jury question.

325. **Answer (A) is correct.** In this case, P's evidence is sufficient to meet a burden of production on all of the foundational facts (deed purports to create an interest in property, it is at least 30 years old, it is in such condition as to create no suspicion as to its authenticity, it was kept in a place where such a writing is likely to be found, and it has been acted on as authentic by persons having an interest in the matter). This meets a burden of production. D's evidence, in turn, only challenges one of the foundational facts (keeping the deed in a place where such a writing is likely to be found), and does not challenge the presumed fact (that the deed is authentic). That means P has caused the presumption to come into force. That means an instruction concerning the presumption is appropriate.

Note that it does not matter whether the jurisdiction follows the majority theory of presumptions (bursting bubble) theory or the minority theory (Morgan-McCormick). The theories operate the same way when the opponent does not produce evidence to challenge the presumed facts. That is the case here.

Answer (B) is incorrect because all P has done is to produce enough evidence to meet a burden of production as to the existence of the foundational facts. P has not produced such overwhelming evidence that a finding in P's favor is required. This is true even as to those foundational facts that D has not challenged. The jury can still choose to disbelieve P's evidence on one or more of the foundational facts.

Answer (C) is incorrect because, even though D may have produced sufficient evidence to meet a burden of production as to one of the foundational facts, this does not destroy the presumption. The court should still give the instruction.

Answer (D) is incorrect because D's evidence concerning where P kept the deed was not so strong as to compel a finding that it was kept in the car glove box rather than in a safe deposit box. All D has done is produce sufficient evidence to support such a conclusion.

326. **Answer (B) is correct.** The Supreme Court has held that generally, true presumptions (what it called "mandatory presumptions") may not operate against a criminal defendant. At the same time, the Court has held that if the statutory device was presented to the jury in a *permissive* fashion, it does not violate the defendant's right to a trial by jury or due process. The instruction in (B) mentions the statutory device but does not tell the jury that it *must* conclude that D was in possession if it finds that D was an occupant of the vehicle at the relevant time. The phrase "may, but need not" connotes a permissive inference.

Answer (A) is incorrect because it instructs the jury that the device is mandatory.

Answer (C) is incorrect because it suggests that D has a burden of proof with regard to an element of the crime. The Constitution forbids this.

Answer (D) is incorrect because the Supreme Court has not forbidden any mention of an inference that might arise from a statutory device, even if that device is written in "presumption" form. As long as the jury instruction does not suggest that the jury must make a finding from the existence of certain facts, it is not improper to issue the instruction. (Of course, one might argue that under some circumstances, it is unfair to mention one inference a jury might draw and not mention others, but that argument should be made in the context of a particular case in which the instruction might amount to an inappropriate comment on the evidence by the court.)

327. **Answer (D) is correct.** A "conclusive presumption" is really a rule of law that makes the foundational facts the important facts and renders the actual truth of the presumed fact irrelevant. So-called conclusive presumptions are enacted to serve an important social purpose. In this case, the presumption is probably designed to protect children born to married, cohabiting couples from having their legitimacy dragged before the courts. In effect, the presumption provides that if the conditions are met, it is no longer legally important whether the man is actually the biological father. That essentially renders evidence contesting whether D was the biological father irrelevant. In this case, D's evidence would attack the now-irrelevant factual issue of whether he was the biological father. The evidence should not be admitted.

There is still a question for the jury, however: whether the foundational facts are true. That D has not challenged P's evidence on the foundational facts does not mean they are established; the jury must still decide whether to accept P's evidence as accurate. The court should instruct the jury that if it finds that those foundational facts are true, it must find that D is the father.

Answer (A) is incorrect because it assumes D's blood test evidence is admissible, which it is not. Also, the answer assumes there is some means of weighing the presumption against D's evidence, which makes no sense.

Answer (B) is incorrect because it assumes D's blood test evidence is admissible, which it is not. Also, the answer assumes that the presumption shifts the burden of persuasion on the paternity issue to D. It does not do that.

Answer (C) is incorrect because it does not take into account that there is still a question for the jury considering the truth of the foundational facts. The presumption will only operate against D if the jury finds those facts to be true.

328. **Answer (B) is correct.** Under the "bursting bubble" theory of presumptions, evidence that challenges only the foundational facts does not destroy the presumption. The jury should be told to determine whether the foundational facts exist, and that if they do, that it must find that the presumed fact (lack of payment) is true.

Answer (A) is incorrect because this is a civil case, where the applicable standard for the jury is preponderance of the evidence.

Answer (C) is incorrect because it misstates how the "bursting bubble" theory of presumptions applies in this situation.

Answer (D) is incorrect because, as explained above, the presumption has not been destroyed and the instruction should be given.

Topic 15: Answers

Evidentiary Privileges

329. **Answer (D) is correct.** A client has a privilege for confidential attorney-client communications. Of course, the communications must deal with the legal matter on which the client has sought assistance. Without more information, there is no basis to conclude that this conversation was anything but confidential. It also dealt with the attorney's representation of D on the murder charge. The privilege covers a person's admission to wrongdoing. Unless there is some unknown code between D and this attorney, asking for help to "beat this charge" is not seeking the attorney's assistance to cover up the crime. The privilege applies.

   Answer (A) is incorrect because the mere fact that the prosecutor has learned of the conversation is not sufficient to prove waiver by D. The prosecutor has produced no evidence to show that D has manifested a desire to waive the privilege. Even if the jurisdiction still maintains the old "eavesdropper rule," by which overheard conversations are not privileged, we do not know that this is how the prosecutor learned of the statement.

   Answer (B) is incorrect because a guilty client—even one who admits guilt—is just as entitled to the attorney-client privilege as an innocent one, and asking for help to "beat this charge" is not tantamount to seeking the attorney's help to cover up the crime.

   Answer (C) is incorrect because, as discussed above, the entire communication is privileged.

330. **Answer (D) is correct.** The communication is still privileged despite the presence of D's spouse and the attorney's secretary. Explanations follow.

   Answer (A) is incorrect because, even if the husband is not the client, there is a privilege for confidential communications between spouses. The court would treat the communication between D and the attorney in the spouse's presence as within the scope of both privileges.

   Answer (B) is incorrect because the secretary is probably a party whose presence is part of the provision of legal services to D, the client. Thus, the secretary is within the scope of the privilege.

   Answer (C) is incorrect because, as explained above, it is the privilege for confidential spousal communications that draws the husband within the scope of privilege here.

331. Application of the crime-fraud exception is a question for the court under FRE 104(a). In *United States v. Zolin*, 491 U.S. 554 (1989), the Supreme Court held that even though FRE 104(a) provides that the court is bound by rules of privilege in deciding preliminary facts, the court may still conduct an *in camera* inspection of allegedly privileged materials if it finds that there is a factual basis adequate to support a good faith belief that the crime-fraud ex-

ception applies. Here, the court may use the secretary's notes as well as any other material that has not already been found privileged to decide whether that standard has been met. If the judge decides that an adequate basis exists to conduct the *in camera* inspection, she will listen to the tape and decide whether the crime-fraud exception applies.

332. **Answer (C) is correct.** FRE 501 states that in civil cases in which state law provides the rule of decision, the court is to apply the state privilege law. Here, the state has adopted a general physician-patient privilege, so the court must apply it. Commonly, that privilege does not apply if the patient has placed her medical condition in issue, which is the case when the person seeks damages for personal injuries, as here.

Answer (A) is incorrect because state privilege law applies.

Answer (B) is incorrect because there is no rule that provides that testimonial privileges do not apply when there is a strong need for the evidence.

Answer (D) is incorrect because there is no rule excluding unprivileged statements under circumstances such as these.

333. **Answer (A) is correct.** The prosecution here is claiming that D met with A (the attorney) for the purpose of obtaining A's assistance in avoiding detection of D's crime. If true, the crime-fraud exception to the attorney-client privilege applies. To prove that the preliminary facts necessary to the crime-fraud exception are present, the prosecution has asked the court to inspect the tape recording. FRE 104(a), however, states that in making rulings of admissibility, the court is not bound by evidence rules "except those on privilege." This means that normally, the court may consider possibly inadmissible evidence when making its rulings, but that this does not apply to privilege rules. In *United States v. Zolin*, 491 U.S. 554 (1989), the Supreme Court held that this provision does not categorically prevent the trial court from conducting *in camera* inspection of allegedly privileged materials. Instead, the Court set out a test for when the trial court may look at such materials. Answer (A) sets forth that test.

Answer (B) is incorrect because it fails to take account of the final phrase of FRE 104(a).

Answer (C) is incorrect because it fails to consider the Supreme Court's decision in *Zolin*.

Answer (D) is incorrect because X's presence at the meeting did not waive the privilege. X, the secretary, was needed to take notes in order to help the attorney render legal assistance to the client.

334. **Answer (A) is correct.** Dr. X is serving as a conduit for the transmission of confidential information between P and P's attorney. In a sense, X is like an interpreter. Her participation is necessary in order for P to communicate fully with her attorney. As long as the examination was conducted in private and the report sent to the attorney in confidence, the attorney-client privilege will apply.

Answer (B) is incorrect because Dr. X's examination and report are not subject to the physician-patient privilege. The primary reason is that by bringing an action for personal injuries, P has waived any physician-patient privilege covering communications relevant to the condition for which she seeks compensation. This is often known as the "patient-litigant" exception.

Answer (C) is incorrect because it assumes a physician-patient privilege applies, which is incorrect.

Answer (D) is incorrect because it does not take account of the attorney-client privilege.

335. **Answer (D) is correct.** Under federal law, a spouse has a privilege not to testify against her spouse in a criminal action. The testifying spouse is the only holder, meaning that even if the party spouse objects to her testimony, he cannot prevent her from testifying. This privilege is not based on confidential communications. It is simply a privilege not to testify against the spouse. Thus, it doesn't matter that W's friend also saw D's wet clothes and muddy shoes. Because W is willing to testify, D cannot prevent her from doing so.

Answer (A) is incorrect because the privilege for confidential spousal communications does not apply to this situation. There are two reasons. First, there is no indication of any communication in these facts; D's conduct was not communicative. Second, even if there was a communication, the fact that it was made in the presence of a third party (W's friend) means it was not confidential.

Answer (B) is incorrect because, as noted above, the adverse testimony privilege is held by the testifying spouse. If, as in this case, she is willing to testify, her spouse may not prevent her from doing so.

Answer (C) is incorrect because the privilege for confidential spousal communications does not apply here.

336. **Answer (A) is correct.** In this situation, the privilege for confidential communications will apply. That privilege continues even after the marriage ends. It covers confidential communications, which in this case would be the statement D made to W. The adverse spousal testimony privilege will not apply, however. That privilege ends when the marriage ends. Because D and W are not married at the time of the trial, D cannot prevent W from testifying against him.

Answers (B), (C), and (D) are incorrect for the reasons noted above.

337. **Answer (A) is correct.** The attorney-client privilege protects statements made in confidence to one's attorney. Here, D's statement qualifies. If the privilege did not apply, the statement would not be hearsay when offered by P because it is a party admission.

Answer (B) is incorrect because the statement is not hearsay when offered by P.

Answer (C) is incorrect because the attorney-client privilege applies even when it deprives the opponent of crucial evidence.

Answer (D) is incorrect because of the attorney-client privilege.

338. There is a privilege at common law protecting confidential communications between spouses. There is no privilege, however, when the trial concerns an alleged crime committed by one spouse against the other. Anything D said would qualify as a party admission when offered by the prosecution, so the hearsay rule is not a bar to the admission of D's statements. *See* FRE 801(d)(2)(A).

339. **Answer (C) is correct.** FRE 501 provides that when state law supplies the rule of decision, state privilege law applies. The current case is in federal court under diversity jurisdiction, so state law applies to the substantive claim. State law recognizes a privilege for confidential communications between parent and child, so the court should apply that privilege and refuse to order W to testify.

   Answer (A) is incorrect because it fails to recognize that state privilege law applies.

   Answer (B) is incorrect for the same reason.

   Answer (D) is incorrect because no such exception exists. Some states have an exception to privileges when the matter concerns spousal or child abuse and the statement was that of a spouse or child, but there is no exception to any privilege of the kind described in this answer. Any such exception would pretty much nullify the privilege.

340. **Answer (D) is correct.** In *Jaffee v. Redmond*, 518 U.S. 1 (1996), the Supreme Court recognized a psychotherapist-patient privilege under federal law, and applied that privilege to a licensed clinical social worker. There is little doubt that the privilege would extend to a psychiatric social worker as well. The privilege belongs to the patient, who has manifested her intention to maintain the privilege (by instructing PSW not to answer the questions).

   Answer (A) is incorrect because privileges operate at all stages of a case, not only at trial.

   Answer (B) is incorrect because privileges may be asserted by non-parties as well as parties.

   Answer (C) is incorrect because, as noted above, there is a psychotherapist-patient privilege in federal court, and it would apply to the W-PSW relationship.

341. Privileges represent a compromise. On one side of the scale is the need for evidence in order to learn the truth. On the other side of the scale are several values, among them the encouragement of full and frank discussion between parties to certain relationships and the protection of privacy. Courts believe that parents and minor children are likely to communicate fully and frankly even without a privilege, and that the need for evidence to learn the truth outweighs both this value and the value in protecting the privacy of parents and minor children.

342. **Answer (B) is correct.** In *Upjohn Co. v. United States*, 449 U.S. 383 (1981), the Supreme Court declined to state a specific test for attorney-client privilege in the corporate context, but it did reject the "control group" test that some courts had used. Instead of adopting that test, the Court named a number of factors that made the communications at issue in the case privileged. Among those factors were (1) that the communications were made by corporate employees to corporate counsel at the direction of corporate superiors; (2) that the purpose of the communications was to secure legal advice for the corporation; (3) that upper-echelon

management did not possess all the information necessary to obtain the advice; (4) that the communications concerned matters within the scope of the employees' duties; (5) that the employees knew the purpose of the communications was to obtain legal advice; and (6) that the employees were instructed that the communications were to be kept confidential. Most, if not all, of those factors are present in Answer (B).

Answer (A) is incorrect because it essentially states the control group test, which the Supreme Court rejected in *Upjohn*.

Answer (C) is incorrect because there is an attorney-client privilege for corporations.

Answer (D) is incorrect because it states too broad a test for covered communications. Not all communications between a corporate employee and the corporation's counsel are protected by the privilege.

343. **Answer (C) is correct.** When the attorney brings an action against the client for breach of duty (such as failure to pay the attorney's fees), or the client sues the attorney for breach of duty (such as legal malpractice), there is no privilege between the attorney and the client as to communications that relate to the matter being litigated between them. Without such an exception, it would be virtually impossible to establish the facts necessary to prove any alleged breach of duty.

Answer (A) is incorrect because if an exception applies, the holder has no privilege to claim.

Answer (B) is incorrect because if an exception applies, there is no privilege even if the client still exists.

Answer (D) is incorrect because the attorney-client privilege does not apply here. Also, where the privilege does apply, it covers both confidential communications to the attorney and the attorney's confidential communications to the client.

Lay and Expert Opinion; Scientific Evidence

344. **Answer (C) is correct.** Under FRE 701, lay opinion testimony is admissible if it is "(a) rationally based on the witness's perception," "(b) helpful to clearly understanding the witness's testimony or to determining a fact in issue," and (c) not based on scientific, technical, or other specialized knowledge within the scope of Rule 702. The opinion in answer (C) depends on more than the witness's "rational perception." It probably requires expertise to determine whether the water seepage really caused the damage. Thus, a lay witness's testimony is not likely to be "helpful" to the trier of fact.

Answer (A) is incorrect because a lay witness can describe the impressions of her senses, such as appearance, sound, or smell. There is, in fact, hardly any way to describe the smell without giving an opinion.

Answer (B) is incorrect because lay witnesses are probably capable of rendering opinions as to the speed of automobiles from their everyday experience. The jury would be helped by this testimony much more than from hearing a vague factual description about the car's movement.

Answer (D) is incorrect for the same reasons as in answer (A). From our real-world experience, we tend to be able to recognize the outward effects of intoxication. In addition, we tend to develop a holistic sense of a person's state of sobriety; it isn't any one thing as much as a combination of factors that lead us to conclude that another person might be intoxicated. The jury would be helped by this testimony.

345. **Answer (B) is correct.** Though the court is unlikely to sustain the objection, W arguably lacks personal knowledge of her relationship to D. That knowledge is second-hand, raising a possible violation of FRE 602 ("A witness may testify to a matter only if evidence is introduced sufficient to support a finding that the witness has personal knowledge of the matter.").

Answer (A) is incorrect. At least on the surface, W is stating a fact, not an opinion. Naturally, all statements of fact are actually statements of one's opinion about the fact (when a person says, "the light was green," she is really saying that in her opinion, the light was green), but the opinion rule is designed to exclude only statements that would be considered opinions in a more narrow sense. Even so, this answer does have some merit.

Answer (C) is incorrect because W is not *testifying* about an out-of-court statement. True, W is basing her testimony on what she's been told, but she does not testify directly to the out-of-court statement. Some courts have found that the hearsay rule is violated in situations such as this, but that conclusion does not seem to be supported by the language of FRE

801(c), which strongly suggests that hearsay is *testimony about* an out-of-court statement, offered to prove the truth of the matter asserted, and not merely *testimony based upon* an out-of-court statement offered to prove the truth of the matter asserted. (Note that if W had testified, "my mom told me D is my father," that testimony would be hearsay.)

It is also possible, though unlikely, that W's testimony, even if hearsay, fits within the exception established in FRE 803(19), which concerns testimony in the form of reputation evidence concerning personal or family history. That evidence can be community reputation, but can also be reputation among family members. Here, W has not testified in terms of reputation, so the exception might not apply.

Answer (D) is incorrect because FRE 601 provides that "[e]very person is competent to be a witness" except as specifically provided. There is no specific provision making children incompetent. In some jurisdictions, children under a certain age are presumed incompetent, but an eight-year-old is not covered by that presumption.

346. **Answer (C) is correct.** Though "erratically" is an opinion, it is closer to a statement of fact than the other answers. "Erratic" behavior can be defined as wandering behavior, that which lacks a fixed course, consistency, or regularity. These are descriptive terms, and though they embody opinions, they are less removed from the witness's actual observations than are the other answers.

Answer (A) is incorrect because "carelessly" is more clearly an opinion. In addition, the jury will not be helped meaningfully by hearing a witness testify that D drove "carelessly." The jury would want to know what led W to reach this conclusion. (A court might still allow this opinion, however, if it believes the jury would benefit from hearing it.)

Answer (B) is incorrect because "negligently" is a legal conclusion. Even though FRE 704(a) permits a witness to testify to an opinion that "embraces" an ultimate fact, courts generally have not interpreted that rule to allow such a bald statement of opinion on an ultimate issue, especially when the term used carries specialized meaning in the law. Under FRE 701, the opinion is not helpful. In addition, W's use of the term "negligence" might not accord with the legal definition. It is the court's job to instruct the jury as to the meaning of legal terms. Finally, the jury is helped by evidence of what D did, not of the witness's opinion about whether D's actions amounted to negligence.

Answer (D) is incorrect for the same reasons as answer (B). "Recklessly" is also a technical term in the law, and W's statement that D was driving "recklessly" is not particularly useful to the jury; the jury should hear facts instead.

347. **Answer (C) is correct.** P's witness is an orthopedic surgeon. Her expertise does not extend to engineering questions involving the strength of the structures surrounding automobile passengers.

Answers (A), (B), and (D) are incorrect because each states an opinion that an orthopedic surgeon probably would be permitted to give. Under answer (A), an orthopedic surgeon is most likely qualified to assess the cause of a bone fracture as well as know how to treat it.

The opinion in answer (B) would be permitted because it relies on the witness's expertise about the force necessary to fracture limbs, something an orthopedic surgeon probably understands.

The opinion in answer (D) would be permitted because an orthopedic surgeon is probably qualified to render an opinion about any permanent impairment that might result from a leg fracture.

348. **Answer (D) is correct.** Neither objection is well-taken.

Answer (A) is incorrect because W is very likely qualified as an expert. FRE 702 provides that a person may qualify as an expert if she has obtained "knowledge, skill, experience, training, or education." There is no general requirement that a person have become an expert through formal education. (Obviously, some fields require formal training. One may not be an expert physician without having completed the necessary formal education, for example.)

Answer (B) is incorrect because FRE 703 provides that an expert witness may base an opinion on otherwise inadmissible evidence (including hearsay) *as long as experts in the field reasonably rely on such facts or data.* Here, W based her opinion, in part, on hearsay—the out-of-court statements of eyewitnesses. The facts state that in doing so, W was using techniques learned through experience. This strongly suggests that expert arson investigators reasonably rely on bystander statements in drawing conclusions about the origins of fires.

Answer (C) is incorrect because, as discussed above, the court should overrule both objections.

349. **Answer (B) is correct.** W's testimony is admissible to demonstrate the underlying basis for W's conclusion that the fire was arson-caused. This is necessary to assist the jury in deciding how much credit to give W's testimony. If, for example, other admissible evidence persuades the jury that the bystander statements were accurate (suppose the bystanders testify to what they saw), the jury is likely to give greater credit to W's conclusion. But if the prosecution's admissible evidence does not persuade the jurors that the facts relied on by W actually occurred, the jury is likely to ignore W's conclusion that the fire was arson-caused. Answer (B) is correct because the proposed instruction would inform the jury that it may only consider the bystander statements to explain the basis of W's testimony. As will be shown next, the statements are not admissible to prove the truth of the matters asserted.

Answer (A) is incorrect because FRE 703 does not establish a hearsay exception. This means that the bystander statements are not admissible to prove the truth of the matters asserted—that the fire proceeded as the statements describe. Answer (A) violates that rule.

(Note that the distinction between admissible only to show the basis of the expert's opinion and admissible to prove the truth of the matters asserted in the statements is very likely to be lost on the jury. Even so, the law draws the distinction.)

Answer (C) is incorrect because the bystanders' beliefs about how the fire proceeded are not relevant. This is not a valid argument to avoid the hearsay rule. What matters is what happened, not what the bystanders believed happened.

Answer (D) is incorrect because, pursuant to FRE 105, when evidence is admissible for one purpose but not another purpose, the court "on timely request, *must* restrict the evidence to its proper scope and instruct the jury accordingly" (emphasis added).

350. **Answer (D) is correct.** All of these factors are relevant under the *Daubert* standard.

351. **Answer (B) is correct.** FRE 704(b) provides that "[i]n a criminal case, an expert witness must not state an opinion about whether the defendant did or did not have a mental state or condition that constitutes an element of the crime charged or of a defense." This rule was intended to prohibit an opinion as to whether the relevant test is met or not. In the case of the insanity defense (the matter the drafters chiefly had in mind), the rule was designed to forbid an opinion as to whether the test for insanity was met. Answer (B) states the federal test for insanity and gives the opinion that D satisfied that test. The opinion is therefore inadmissible.

Answer (A) is incorrect because the disease of paranoid schizophrenia is not a mental state that forms an element of a crime or defense. **Answer (D) is incorrect** for the same reason.

Answer (C) is incorrect for much the same reason: it does not specify a particular mental state that is an element of the defense, and thus does not violate the rule stated in FRE 704(b).

352. **Answer (C) is correct.** Dr. W's testimony is offered to show that V lacks credibility because of a mental condition that causes V to fantasize. Such testimony is a proper subject of expertise. The court has the responsibility under FRE 104(a) to determine whether Dr. W is qualified as an expert in the field in which she will testify (psychiatry, and perhaps more specifically the type of psychiatric condition allegedly exhibited by V). The court must also decide, under FRE 703, whether observations of V for several hours under various circumstances is a means of gathering information that experts in the field reasonably rely upon. If the court answers both questions in the affirmative (using a preponderance standard), the court should allow Dr. W to testify in the manner indicated.

Answer (A) is incorrect because FRE 704(b) only forbids an expert witness to testify that a criminal defendant has a certain mental state or condition that constitutes an element of the crime or of a defense. Here, the testimony concerns the alleged victim, not the criminal defendant, and the mental condition about which Dr. W will testify is not an element of the crime or any defense.

Answer (B) is incorrect because the competency of an expert witness is a matter for the court to decide under FRE 104(a).

Answer (D) is incorrect because a court may admit expert testimony that goes to a witness's credibility. It is not the sort of opinion that a lay witness would be qualified to give. (In some instances, the court might exclude such testimony as a waste of time, but no rule forbids the court from allowing the testimony.)

353. **Answer (D) is correct.** According to FRE 703, an expert may base her opinion on any source that is reasonably relied upon by experts in the field. A psychiatrist often bases her conclusions on tests and observations she conducts personally. At times, a psychiatrist uses tests performed by other mental health professionals. And a hypothetical question is a common way to convey facts to the expert. FRE 705 makes clear that the hypothetical need not be asked of the witness while she is on the witness stand. Therefore, **answers (A), (B), and (C) are incorrect** because each states a proper source of the facts or data upon which the expert may rely in forming an opinion.

354. **Answer (A) is correct.** In *Frye v. United States*, 293 F. 1013 (D.C. Cir. 1923), the court held that an expert opinion based on a scientific technique is not admissible unless it is "generally accepted" in the relevant scientific community: "Just when a scientific principle or discovery crosses the line between the experimental and demonstrable stages is difficult to define. Somewhere in this twilight zone the evidential force of the principle must be recognized, and while courts will go a long way in admitting expert testimony deduced from a well-recognized scientific principle or discovery, the thing from which the deduction is made must be sufficiently established to have gained general acceptance in the particular field in which it belongs." This standard, which placed a great deal of faith in the scientific community to determine the validity of a novel scientific theory or technique, was the prevailing standard for many decades, and some courts continue to adhere to that standard today.

Answer (A) is correct because it embodies the *Frye* test. **Answers (C) and (D) are incorrect** because they do not state the *Frye* standard. **Answer (B) is incorrect** because, although it states a correct basic standard, it incorrectly assumes that the question involved is one of conditional relevancy under FRE 104(b). The question must be decided by the judge under FRE 104(a).

355. **Answer (C) is correct.** In *Daubert v. Merrell Dow Pharmaceuticals, Inc.*, 509 U.S. 579 (1993), the Supreme Court held that the Federal Rules had abolished the *Frye* general acceptance test and replaced that test with one requiring the court to assess the reliability and relevance of scientific testimony. Reliability is to be shown according to a flexible standard that looks at several factors including peer review and publication, error rates, and general acceptance, with no single factor serving as a *per se* test. In addition, the court must find a fit between the expert's testimony and the facts of the case — that the testimony is relevant to an issue in the case (here, causation). FRE 702 was later amended to essentially codify the basic principles of *Daubert*. Answer (C) states the general test.

Answer (A) is incorrect because it states the *Frye* test. Although some states still apply that test (or a version of it), the federal courts no longer do so, as explained above.

Answer (B) is incorrect because it allocates the fact-finding authority largely to the jury. *Daubert* and FRE 702 do not do this. The judge is to be the "gate-keeper," and the jury will only hear purported scientific testimony if the judge finds (by a preponderance of the evidence) that it is reliable and relevant.

Answer (D) is incorrect because publication and peer review is only one factor in the test for determining admissibility. It is not a *per se* factor. As explained above, the test is flexible.

356. P's chances on appeal are not good. In *General Electric Co. v. Joiner*, 522 U.S. 156 (1997), the Supreme Court held that the "abuse of discretion" standard applies to trial court *Daubert* rulings. That standard gives the trial court broad discretion, and appellate courts usually show substantial deference to such decisions. The court will typically affirm the trial court's decision even if it would have reached a different conclusion, as long as the trial court's conclusion is within the broad range of its discretion.

Even if the court finds that the trial court has erred in excluding the evidence, the court will not reverse unless exclusion affected "a substantial right of the party" (FRE 103(a)). In this situation, exclusion of P's expert was probably fatal to P's case, making causation difficult or impossible to prove. Thus, if there was error, reversal probably would be required.

Answers

Practice Final Exam

Part I:
Multiple Choice Questions Answers

357. **Answer (C) is correct.** The document asserts that the interview took place at a certain date and time, and it is being offered to prove the truth of that statement. Thus, it is hearsay. However, the document appears to satisfy the requirements of FRE 803(8), the public records exception. Because the document is being offered by, rather than against, the criminal defendant, the exclusions from the exception in parts (A)(ii) and (iii) of the rule do not apply.

   Answer (A) is incorrect because the witness did not profess to a loss of memory that the document refreshed. **Answer (B) is incorrect** for a similar reason. FRE 803(5) (recorded recollection) only applies when the witness does not remember a fact to which she has been asked to testify. **Answer (D) is incorrect** because the document is admissible as a public record.

358. **Answer (A) is correct.** The statements in the article are the act over which the suit has been brought, so they are not hearsay. (They fall into the category of words of independent legal significance ("verbal act"); they are the libel itself.) However, when a party wishes to prove the contents of a writing, the best evidence rule (FRE 1002) requires that the writing itself be produced. It was not, and no reason was given, nor does any exception apply.

   Answer (B) is incorrect because the evidence is not hearsay. **Answer (C) is incorrect** because the testimony does violate the best evidence rule. **Answer (D) is incorrect** because the testimony is inadmissible.

359. **Answer (B) is correct.** When "a crime, wrong, or other act" is offered to prove a relevant fact, those acts might be admissible under FRE 404(b) if their relevance does not depend on an inference of the actor's character. Here, the prosecution is using another very similar bank robbery to show that D committed the current robbery, and the theory is *modus operandi* to prove identity. That theory only applies when the events are both very unusual and very similar. That requirement is probably satisfied here because of the dance the robbers forced the tellers to perform. **Answer (D) is incorrect** for this reason.

   This does not mean the evidence will be admissible, however. The court first must determine whether there is evidence sufficient to support a finding that the actor did engage in the uncharged act. This is a FRE 104(b) test. **Answer (C) is incorrect** because it assumes the applicable test is that set forth in FRE 104(a), under which the court decides the existence of the preliminary fact. Even if the court decides that the FRE 104(b) test is met, the court must

281

still determine whether the evidence is relevant (which it is here, because D denies involvement in the bank robbery).

For the evidence to be admissible, the court must also examine its relevance to the crime for which D is charged and determine whether it should be excluded by FRE 403. **Answer (A) is incorrect** because it assumes that the evidence is automatically admissible without consideration of these issues.

360. **Answer (D) is correct.** W's statement is hearsay because it asserted that D robbed the bank, and it is offered to prove that fact. D's laughing response might, however, amount to an adoption of W's statement, and if so the statement and D's response will constitute non-hearsay under FRE 801(d)(2)(B). **Answer (A) is incorrect** because the facts do not support a conclusion that W was speaking while under the stress of excitement caused by a startling event. *See* FRE 803(2). **Answer (B) is incorrect** because W's statement reflected on an event that had occurred an hour earlier, which is too long to qualify the statement as a present sense impression under the circumstances. *See* FRE 803(1). **Answer (C) is incorrect** because FRE 804(b)(3), the declaration against interest exception, only applies if the declarant is unavailable, and D is available.

361. **Answer (A) is correct.** D1 and D2 admit possession of V's wallet, but claim lack of intent to steal. Evidence that D1 and D2 had possessed two other wallets for a period of several weeks is intuitively strong on the issue of intent because one would think it extremely unlikely that D1 and D2 would innocently find three wallets on the street in a matter of a few weeks. Thus, the evidence is admissible to prove intent on doctrine of chances reasoning.

Answer (B) is incorrect because identity is not an issue here. D1 and D2 admit possession but deny intent to steal. Even if identity were an issue, the facts state that the method allegedly used is common among pickpockets. This makes the *modus operandi* theory inapplicable.

Answer (C) is incorrect because a few similar incidents do not rise to the level of habit. Moreover, the level of conscious deliberation needed to steal wallets in this way argues against characterizing the behavior as habitual. Though a conscious act may be classified as a habit, the more conscious it is, the less likely it will qualify.

Answer (D) is incorrect because, as discussed above, the evidence is admissible to prove intent.

362. **Answer (A) is correct.** P's statement to her doctor is not hearsay because it is a party admission under FRE 801(d)(2)(A). It is also not subject to the physician-patient privilege because of the patient-litigant exception. By bringing the personal injury action against D, P waived her physician-patient privilege with respect to relevant aspects of her medical condition.

Answers (B), (C), and (D) are incorrect for the reasons just discussed.

363. **Answer (D) is correct.** D's own statement is not a party admission if D offers it. Thus, it is inadmissible hearsay when offered to prove that V attacked D with a moose head. The statement is not admissible as a prior consistent statement under FRE 801(d)(1)(B)(i) because D made the statement at a time when he had a motive to lie (he was about to go to trial for as-

sault with a deadly weapon). In addition, the statement is not admissible under FRE 801(D)(1)(B)(ii) to rehabilitate credibility because there has been no impeachment.

Answer (A) is incorrect because D's statement does not qualify for admission as a prior consistent statement, and thus may not be used to prove D's self-defense claim. **Answer (B) is incorrect** because a prior consistent statement may not be offered for any purpose unless it satisfies the requirements of FRE 801(d)(1)(B). **Answer (C) is incorrect** for the same reasons that answers (A) and (B) are incorrect.

364. **Answer (D) is correct.** This is a direct application of the Supreme Court's holding in *United States v. Zolin*, 491 U.S. 554 (1989). **Answers (A), (B), and (C) are incorrect** because they do not correctly state the holding of that case.

365. **Answer (B) is correct.** Under the Federal Rules definition of hearsay, an utterance is not classified as hearsay unless it makes an assertion of fact and is offered to prove that fact. X's statement does not assert a fact; it is a request to do something. The request is relevant because it is circumstantial evidence that X was planning to set a fire. Because it is offered for that purpose, but does not assert that fact, it is not hearsay.

Under a declarant-based definition of hearsay, an utterance can be classified as hearsay if its value depends on the credibility of the declarant. Here, there might be significant credibility issues. Most importantly, we might not understand what X meant by the request; X might not have been trying to convey anything about a possible fire (thus raising issues of ambiguity). Also, X might have misperceived some fact that led X to make the statement (raising issues of perception), or X might have been insincere, or have had a faulty memory. Because of these concerns, a declarant-based definition of hearsay probably would characterize the utterance as hearsay. **Answers (C) and (D) are incorrect** for this reason.

Answer (A) is incorrect because X is not a party. Thus, her statements cannot constitute party admissions.

366. **Answer (A) is correct.** This question raises the privilege for confidential communications between spouses. Generally, both spouses are holders. This means that if D does not want W to testify about what D told W in confidence, D may prevent W from testifying. **Answer (C) is incorrect** because it fails to recognize that D is also a holder of the privilege for confidential communications between spouses. **Answer (B) is incorrect** because D's statement, offered by the prosecution, is a non-hearsay party admission. **Answer (D) is incorrect** because a privilege does apply in this case.

367. **Answer (B) is correct.** The evidence of V's violent character is relevant because it makes it more likely that V did in fact attack D first, causing D to respond in self-defense. The idea is that a person with a reputation for violence is more likely to have an actual character for violence than is one without such reputation. From that, one may infer that the person is more likely to start a fight than is one who is not violent. On the facts of this case, this evidence is relevant even though D was unaware of V's reputation for violence, because the evidence is

being offered to show V's behavior, not D's. (Note that if D's theory of self-defense was that she feared V, the reputation evidence in question would not be relevant unless D had heard about it.)

The next question is whether the evidence is *admissible* to prove that V attacked D. Under the FRE 404(a)(2)(B) exception to the general ban on character to prove conduct, a criminal defendant may offer evidence of a pertinent trait of the character of the alleged victim. FRE 405(a) permits the use of reputation and opinion evidence. Thus, this evidence is admissible to prove that V attacked D. **Answer (A) is incorrect** for this reason.

Answer (C) is incorrect because the evidence is not being offered to impeach V. V was not a witness, nor were any statements by V offered into evidence.

Answer (D) is incorrect because, as explained above, the evidence fits into an exception to the general ban on character evidence to prove conduct.

368. **Answer (A) is correct.** If this statement is to be admissible, it will be as an authorized admission under FRE 801(d)(2)(C). For that to be the case, X must have been authorized to speak for D Corp. about this matter. Under the Federal Rules, authorization is a question to be decided by the court under FRE 104(a) because the statement will be relevant even if the declarant was not authorized to speak. (In other words, this is not a case of conditional relevancy.)

Answer (B) is incorrect because the statement can be non-hearsay even if X is not a party. As noted above, the statement might be admissible as an authorized admission, which is not hearsay under the Federal Rules.

Answer (C) is incorrect because in making its ruling, the trial court is permitted to take into account any non-privileged information, even inadmissible evidence, and even the very evidence at issue. Here, that evidence (X's statement) contains an assertion of authority to speak for C Corp. The trial court may use that assertion as part of its basis for finding that X was authorized to speak for D Corp.

Answer (D) is incorrect because it assumes authority is a question of conditional relevancy to be treated under the standard of FRE 104(b). As explained above, it is not.

369. **Answer (C) is correct.** The Supreme Court has strongly suggested that the dying declaration exception is *sui generis*—that statements qualifying under that exception are admissible even if they would seem otherwise to violate the Confrontation Clause. (In part, the Court reached this conclusion on the basis that the exception pre-dated the Confrontation Clause and was well known to the drafters, suggesting that they did not intend such statements to be affected by the Clause.) Thus, if the court in this case determines that the dying declaration exception applies, and it appears that it does, it appears that the court should admit V's statement.

Answers (A), (B), and (D) are incorrect because, if the statement meets the requirements of the dying declaration exception, no further inquiry is needed, nor need the defendant have had a prior opportunity to cross-examine the declarant.

370. **Answer (D) is correct.** X's statement about the accident is relevant, of course, to prove what happened. It is also hearsay, but might fit within the excited utterance exception. The foundational facts necessary to establishing applicability of the excited utterance exception are to be decided by the court pursuant to FRE 104(a). That is because the statement will be relevant even if the foundational (preliminary) facts are not true. (In other words, this is not an example of conditional relevancy.) Thus, the court must decide whether X's statement about the accident was made under the stress of excitement caused by the accident. **Answer (A) is incorrect** because it is not clear that X's statement fails to satisfy the requirements of the excited utterance exception. **Answer (B) is incorrect** because it assumes that the standard of FRE 104(b) applies. As discussed above, FRE 104(a) applies.

X's earlier statement, about the weather, is not offered to prove the truth of the matter asserted (what the weather was like), but as circumstantial evidence that X was not experiencing the stress of the accident. Thus, it is not hearsay. That statement is relevant not because of what X said about the weather, but because it suggests that the so-called excited utterance should not be given as much weight as otherwise. The theory here is that if excited utterances tend to be trustworthy because they are made under stress and before the declarant has an opportunity to reflect, evidence that the person was not suffering from the stress of the accident, and that some time had passed after the event, would tend to undercut its probative value. The jury is therefore entitled to learn that X might not have been under quite as much stress as it seems from hearing only the second statement. (The assumptions about the reliability of excited utterances are questionable, but the rule persists.)

Answer (C) is incorrect because the fact that X spoke about the weather is still relevant even if the other statement qualifies as an excited utterance.

371. **Answer (B) is correct.** The declarant-based definition of hearsay will classify utterances as hearsay when their value depends on the credibility of the declarant. There are meaningful issues concerning the credibility of the declarants in this hypothetical. For example, they might not have understood the nature of D's establishment, or they might have been trying to frame D. Thus, there is a good chance that these utterances would be classified as hearsay under a declarant-based definition of hearsay.

The assertion-based definition will not classify an utterance as hearsay unless it is a statement, which is defined as an assertion, and unless the statement is being offered to prove the truth of the matter asserted. These utterances are relevant because they suggest that the callers believed D was running a house of prostitution, but the utterances did not assert that fact. Thus, most courts applying the assertion-based definition of hearsay (the definition in the Federal Rules) would not characterize these utterances as hearsay.

Answers (A), (C), and (D) are incorrect because they do not apply the principles stated above correctly.

372. **Answer (A) is correct.** This is a leading question because it suggests the answer P wants the witness to give. Thus, **answer (C) is incorrect.** However, it is proper to lead an adverse witness on direct examination. FRE 611(c). D is obviously adverse to P. Thus, P may lead D. **Answer**

(B) **is incorrect** for this reason. **Answer (D) is incorrect** because the question does not assume a fact not in evidence; it asks about a fact, though in a leading way.

373. **Answer (D) is correct.** FRE 404(a)(2)(B) permits a criminal defendant to offer evidence of a pertinent trait of the character of an alleged crime victim. V is the alleged victim. Thus, **answer (C) is incorrect**. D has offered evidence of V's violent reputation, which is pertinent to whether V would have attacked another person. FRE 405(a) provides that on direct examination, character may be proven by reputation or opinion. This was reputation evidence. The evidence is admissible.

    Answer (A) is incorrect because, as explained above, the evidence does relate to whether V might have attacked D. A person with a violent character is more likely to act violently than is one without such a character. **Answer (B) is incorrect** because the evidence, although hearsay, satisfies FRE 803(21), which creates an exception for evidence of reputation about a person's character.

374. **Answer (C) is correct.** In *Luce v. United States*, 469 U.S. 38 (1984), the Supreme Court held that in order to preserve for appeal the question of whether the court committed error in allowing the prosecution to offer evidence of defendant's prior conviction to impeach, D must subject herself to that impeachment by testifying at trial. Because D did not take the stand, he did not preserve the issue for appeal. Note, as well, that **answer (A) is incorrect** for another reason: a prior conviction for burglary is not automatically admissible because it is not a crime involving dishonesty or false statement. *See* FRE 609(a)(2).

    Answer (B) is incorrect because it is not true that appellate courts may not review trial court decisions admitting or excluding prior conviction evidence. The problem here is that D did not properly preserve the issue for appeal, not that an appellate court may not review this type of ruling.

    Answer (D) is incorrect because the prosecution has no due process right to offer prior convictions to impeach.

375. **Answer (A) is correct.** Except where defendant offers evidence of her character to prove her innocence, and in sexual assault and child molestation cases, and where defendant offers evidence of the victim's character, the prosecution is not permitted to offer evidence of defendant's character to prove action in accordance therewith on a particular occasion. Thus, the evidence is not admissible to prove that D had a character that would lead her to embezzle. Thus, **answer (B) is incorrect**.

    A conviction for misdemeanor perjury is admissible, however, to impeach D's credibility under FRE 609(a)(2). Because perjury is a crime involving a false statement, the conviction is admissible regardless of the balance of probative value and prejudice. In fact, the trial court *must* admit the evidence; it has no discretion to exclude it under FRE 403. This is why **answer (C) is incorrect. Answer (D) is incorrect** because, as noted above, the evidence is admissible to impeach D's credibility.

376. **Answer (B) is correct.** This is a prior inconsistent statement, and it is relevant both to impeach W's credibility as a witness and to show that W's employer sometimes set back odometers.

The evidence is admissible to impeach simply because it is inconsistent with W's trial testimony. W has been given an opportunity to explain or deny making the statement, as required by FRE 613(b).

The statement is also admissible to prove the truth of the matter asserted at the deposition because W testified at the trial, was subject to cross-examination about the statement, the statement is inconsistent with the trial testimony, and the statement was made under oath, subject to penalty of perjury (at the deposition). Thus, the requirements of FRE 801(d)(1)(A) have been satisfied.

Answer (A) is incorrect because the evidence is admissible both to impeach and to prove that odometers sometimes were set back (and that by implication, the odometer on the car P bought might have been tampered with). **Answer (C) is incorrect** because unavailability is not a precondition for admission of prior inconsistent statements. **Answer (D) is incorrect** because a prior inconsistent statement made under penalty for perjury may be admitted substantively even if the declarant was not cross-examined when she made the statement.

377. **Answer (D) is correct.** The evidence concerning D's theft of office supplies from D's employer is relevant to impeach D if D testifies or if out-of-court statements of D are offered into evidence. Thus, **answer (B) is incorrect.** Here, there is no indication that either has occurred. Thus, D is not subject to impeachment.

Even if D has testified or is otherwise subject to impeachment, the method used here is impeachment by bad character for truthfulness. Under FRE 608(b), only acts probative of truthfulness or untruthfulness may be used. That requirement has been satisfied because an act of theft is probably minimally probative of untruthfulness. However, the rule forbids the use of extrinsic evidence, and D's personnel record is extrinsic evidence. The prosecution would have been allowed to ask D about the theft on cross-examination if D testified, but that is not what happened.

Note that the requirements of the business records exception are probably satisfied here (meaning that **answer (C) is incorrect**), but that does not matter because the evidence is inadmissible, as explained above. Thus, **answer (A) is incorrect.**

378. **Answer (D) is correct.** The prosecutor has simply used the document to refresh V's recollection. *See* FRE 612. A party may use anything to refresh a witness's recollection. All that is required before the witness testifies about the facts after the memory device has been used is that the witness testifies that she now remembers the facts. The device used to refresh recollection is not evidence, and is not read to the fact-finder.

Here, because V has stated that she now remembers the other items she found missing after the break-in, V may state what those items were.

Answer (A) is incorrect because the prosecution was not using the recorded recollection doctrine (FRE 803(5)) here.

Answer (B) is incorrect because the document was not being used; the witness's memory was being used. (Even if the document were being used, no rule prohibits the use of all documents against a criminal defendant.)

Answer (C) is incorrect because the prosecutor was not attempting to lay the foundation for the business records exception. The document need not be a business record or any specific kind of record. Because it is not evidence, no evidence rules restrict what can be used to refresh recollection.

379. **Answer (B) is correct.** W's testimony at the first trial is hearsay when offered at the second trial. The court reporter's transcript is also hearsay in that it is the statement of the reporter that W gave certain testimony, offered to prove that W gave that testimony. The transcript itself satisfies FRE 803(6), the business records exception to the hearsay rule. The former testimony exception (FRE 804(b)(1)) will cover W's testimony: (1) D was a party to the earlier civil action, (2) D had an opportunity to cross-examine W at that trial, (3) D's motive in cross-examining W at the second trial would be the same as at the first (to show that W was wrong when she stated that D ran a red light and struck V in a crosswalk), and, (4) W is unavailable under FRE 804(a)(2) because she refuses to drop her unsupported privacy claim even when ordered to do so by the court.

Answer (A) is incorrect because the importance of particular evidence is not a reason to admit it if it violates a rule of evidence. Thus, this is not a reason to admit the evidence.

Answer (C) is incorrect because W is unavailable, as explained above.

Answer (D) is incorrect because under the reasoning of the Supreme Court in *Crawford*, "testimonial" hearsay that fits within an exception satisfies the demands of the Confrontation Clause if the defendant had an opportunity to cross-examine the declarant and if the declarant is unavailable. Both conditions are satisfied here.

380. **Answer (D) is correct.** Messon's public relations officer is undoubtedly authorized to speak for the company. That is, in fact, the primary job of a public relations officer. Thus, authorization, the key requirement of FRE 801(d)(2)(C), is satisfied. Of course, the statement is also being offered against Messon, the party.

Answer (A) is incorrect because unavailability is a requirement of the declaration against interest exception (FRE 804(b)(3)), and Messon is not unavailable.

Answer (B) is incorrect because there is no indication this was an excited utterance. Even if the officer sounded excited, there is nothing in the facts to suggest that she was speaking while under the stress of excitement caused by a startling event or condition. Almost certainly, she was just doing her job of selling her company's point of view.

Answer (C) is incorrect for a rather technical reason: The statement is a direct statement of Messon's "state of mind." That is, it directly states Messon's beliefs about the state of the bay. (From that, of course, it may be inferred that it saw no reason to engage in more cleanup, which is why the statement is relevant.) Because the officer's utterance is a direct statement of her employer's beliefs, it is hearsay when offered to prove those beliefs.

381. **Answer (B) is correct.** Evidence that D and W1 are lovers tends to impeach W1 by showing a motive to testify in D's favor. This form of impeachment is not explicitly regulated by the Federal Rules. Therefore, it is not limited by any specific rule such as one forbidding the use of extrinsic evidence.

Answer (A) is incorrect because merely being D's lover does not show that W1 has a bad character for truthfulness.

Answer (C) is incorrect because the evidence does not contradict anything about which W1 testified. W1 never denied being D's lover.

Answer (D) is incorrect because, as explained above, the evidence is admissible to impeach W1 by showing a motive to testify favorably toward D.

382. **Answer (A) is correct.** The tape recording is relevant only if it actually was a recording of D's voice. Thus, whether it was D's voice would be a case of conditional relevancy even without a specific rule making it so. But such a rule exists: FRE 901(a) sets forth the FRE 104(b) standard for authentication issues. Thus, the court's task is to determine whether there is evidence sufficient to support a finding that the voice on the tape was D's. **Answer (B) is incorrect** because it sets forth a FRE 104(a) standard under which the judge makes the determination of preliminary fact.

Answer (C) is incorrect because the evidence is not hearsay. Rather, it constitutes words of independent legal significance ("verbal act"). If the recording contains D's voice, it is not evidence of the slander. It is the slander itself. (The machine recording does not add a level of hearsay; the machine's workings are questions of relevance and probative value, not hearsay.)

Answer (D) is incorrect because voice identification does not require an expert witness. The jury may hear the voice on the tape, compare it to D's voice, and make its own determination whether the voices are the same.

383. **Answer (D) is correct.** The right to jury trial includes the right not to be retried because the judge believes the jury reached the wrong decision. Put another way, a jury's acquittal is final. Also, retrial would violate the double jeopardy clause. Thus, **answer (A) is incorrect**; the court may not order a new trial.

Answers (B) and (C) are incorrect for a second reason. The jury's failure to consider crucial evidence and its disregard of the judge's instructions are not the type of juror behavior that can be the subject of testimony to impeach the verdict. FRE 606(b)(2)(A) and (B) forbid juror testimony or affidavits to impeach the verdict unless the testimony or affidavit would show that "extraneous prejudicial information was improperly brought to the jury's attention" or "an outside influence was improperly brought to bear upon any juror," respectively. What happened in this case does not fall into either category.

384. **Answer (B) is correct.** Whether this constitutes a habit under FRE 406 is a close question, but the fact that D rode with "no hands" for part of each of the 20 rides W observed creates at least a decent argument for habit.

   Answer (B) is incorrect because being a careless bicycle rider is probably character evidence, and character may not be offered in this situation to prove D acted in accordance with her character on a specific occasion. (None of the exceptions in FRE 404(a) apply.)

   Answer (C) is incorrect because W's testimony does not contradict D. D did not claim she never rode with "no hands"; she only testified that she did not do so on this occasion.

   Answer (D) is incorrect because D's intent to ride with "no hands" is not relevant. What is relevant is whether D in fact did so. Even if one might argue that intent to do so makes it more likely D did in fact do so, the character rule still would bar the testimony. That is because the conclusion that D would intend to ride with "no hands" is made possible by inferring from D's past conduct that she is a careless rider who would ride carelessly on this occasion. As explained above, character evidence is not admissible in this situation to prove D acted in accordance with her character on a specific occasion.

385. **Answer (A) is correct.** This is a leading question because it suggests the answer the prosecutor wants the witness to give. FRE 611(c) provides that generally, leading questions may not be asked on direct. However, the rule specifically allows leading questions "as necessary to develop the witness's testimony." That is the situation here. The prosecutor is using a leading question to help the witness provide her testimony.

   Answers (B) and (C) are incorrect for the reasons just given. **Answer (D) is incorrect** because the question is not argumentative nor is it compound. It is simply leading.

386. **Answer (D) is correct.** The evidence is relevant because it has a tendency to narrow the universe of possible perpetrators to that small group of people (of which D is a member) who know how to use this technique to crack safes. Thus **answer (A) is incorrect. Answer (B) is incorrect** because considerations of unfair prejudice do not make evidence irrelevant. Those considerations only lead to the exclusion of relevant evidence.

   FRE 404(b) permits the use of other crimes, wrongs, or acts to prove a relevant fact other than through an inference as to the person's character. That evidence is relevant on such a basis does not mean it is admissible, however. The Supreme Court in *Huddleston v. United States*, 485 U.S. 681 (1988), made clear that the court should still determine whether the probative value of the evidence is substantially outweighed by the danger of unfair prejudice. That is why **answer (C) is incorrect** and **answer (D) correct.**

387. **Answer (D) is correct.** Though it is unusual to call a witness to testify about another person's trial testimony, nothing in the rules prohibits a party from proving the testimony this way. The best evidence rule does not apply because P is not using X to prove the contents of a

writing (the transcript). *See* FRE 1002. Rather, P is trying to prove what W said, something X knows from personal knowledge. Thus, **answer (A) is incorrect.**

Though W's testimony at the first trial is hearsay when offered to prove its truth (that W caused the collision by running a red light), FRE 804(b)(1), the former testimony exception, applies here. The evidence was offered at the first trial against D. (It does not matter that W was an adverse witness; W's testimony was still being offered by P against D. Thus, **answer (B) is incorrect.**) At the first trial, D would have had a motive to cross-examine W in the hope of showing that W did not in fact run the light. That is the same motive D would have in the second trial. Thus, X's testimony is admissible.

Note that **answer (C) is incorrect** because it gets the matter exactly backward. One way to test the application of the rules of evidence is to take a step back and think about the fairness of applying them in certain ways. Here, *not* permitting P to prove W's testimony at the first trial would be unfair to P because it would make it more difficult to prove P's case for reasons beyond P's control, and under circumstances where the adverse party had an opportunity and a good reason to try to repair the damage caused by W's testimony. This fairness test will not work in all cases, of course; some evidence rules exist to promote values other than fairness and require rulings that seem unfair. But it cannot hurt to consider such matters as fairness in testing the application of the rules.

388. **Answer (A) is correct.** Under the "Morgan/McCormick" theory of presumptions, a presumption shifts *both* the burden of production *and* the burden of persuasion to the opponent. If the proponent produces sufficient evidence to meet a burden of production on the foundational facts, the presumption comes into existence and is not dispelled (rebutted) merely by offering evidence sufficient to meet a burden of production on the non-existence of the presumed facts. Instead, the presumption persists.

Here, if P has offered sufficient evidence to meet a burden of production on the existence of the foundational facts (the child was born within ten months of the last date on which a male and female were cohabiting), the presumption came into existence. This shifted to D the burden of persuading the jury that he was not the child's father (the presumed fact). This means the court should issue the instruction noted in answer (A).

Answer (B) is incorrect because it places the fact-finding role in the court's hands rather than the jury's. This is improper. The court's only role is to determine whether there is evidence sufficient to support a finding that the foundational facts are true.

Answer (C) is incorrect because, as explained above, under the Morgan/McCormick view of presumptions, evidence contradicting the presumed fact does not destroy the presumption.

Answer (D) is incorrect because, as in answer (B), it places the fact-finding role in the court's hands rather than the jury's. It is not up to the court to decide whether D's blood test evidence proves he was not the father. The court should decide only whether there is sufficient evidence to permit such a finding.

389. Answer (D) is correct. FRE 703 provides that "[a]n expert may base an opinion on facts or data in the case that the expert has been made aware of or personally observed." The only limitation is set forth in the second sentence of the rule: "If experts in the particular field would reasonably rely on those kinds of facts or data in forming an opinion on the subject, they need not be admissible...."

Looking at the choices in light of this rule, all meet the test of FRE 703: A psychiatrist may base her testimony on things she learned while treating the defendant. These facts were made known to the psychiatrist before the hearing. Thus, **answer (A)** sets forth a permissible source of knowledge. **Answer (B)** also sets forth a permissible source of information. This is information another expert gathered. It seems reasonable to assume that psychiatrists frequently rely on psychological tests performed by other experts. (If there is an objection on this ground, the party calling the expert will have to show that psychiatrists do indeed rely on this source of data.)

Hypothetical questions are still permitted, as well, as long as they are based on facts supported by testimony in the record. Thus, **answer (C)** also sets forth a permissible source of the expert's knowledge.

390. Answer (D) is correct. FRE 602 states that every person is competent to be a witness except as provided in the rules. There is no rule making children below a certain age incompetent. Thus, **answer (C) is incorrect.**

At the same time, there is no rule prohibiting the judge from asking questions of a prospective witness as the judge did here. It is possible that a person's mental condition would make her testimony so useless that it is a waste of time to allow the person to testify. Though this situation would be very rare, the judge could exclude the witness on the ground that the probative value of the witness's testimony is substantially outweighed by the waste of time involved. *See* FRE 403. Thus, **answer (A) is incorrect.**

The court's determination of all preliminary facts under FRE 104(a) is made on a "preponderance of the evidence" standard. In deciding whether to allow W to testify, the judge should not apply a stricter standard. Thus, **answer (B) is incorrect.**

391. Answer (A) is correct. The evidence is relevant because it shows that the ride acted in the same way alleged by P on another occasion close in time to P's injury, and that the person involved on that similar occasion was nearly thrown out of the car even though he was seated properly. Thus, the evidence tends to show that inadequate maintenance could have been the cause of the accident.

Answer (B) is incorrect because this is not a situation in which character evidence may be offered to prove action in accordance therewith on a particular occasion. None of the exceptions to the character ban in FRE 404(a) apply.

Answer (C) is incorrect because two incidents are not sufficient to establish a "habit" to maintain the ride poorly.

Answer (D) is incorrect because, as shown above, the evidence is relevant and admissible "similar accidents" evidence.

392. **Answer (A) is correct.** Under FRE 104(a), the court has the authority to determine "whether a witness is qualified." **Answer (C) is incorrect** because it assumes the jury has the ultimate authority to decide this question.

The trial court has made its ruling after arguments on the issue. At this point, only that much is on the record for possible appeal. P must also give the appellate court a basis for determining the effect of the error, if indeed the trial court's ruling was erroneous. This requires P to place on the record what the witness would have testified if permitted to do so. *See* FRE 103(a)(2). With that information, the appellate court can determine whether the error affected "a substantial right of the party." **Answer (B) is incorrect** because, as just shown, P has not preserved the point for appeal.

Answer (D) is incorrect because there is no crying in trial advocacy.

393. **Answer (C) is correct.** The issue here is one of authentication of the signature on the letter as that of D. Under FRE 901(a), authentication is an issue ultimately for the jury, as long as the court determines that there is "evidence sufficient to support a finding that the item is what the proponent claims it is."

A party wishing to authenticate a signature is not required to call an expert witness. In fact, FRE 901(b)(2) envisions non-expert testimony on handwriting from a person familiar with the individual's handwriting (as long as the familiarity was not acquired for purposes of litigation). FRE 901(b)(3) permits the jury to compare D's admitted handwriting sample with the writing on the allegedly libelous letter. The court need only look at the two items to decide whether there is evidence sufficient to support a finding that they were made by the same person. Thus, **answer (A) is incorrect.**

Answer (B) is incorrect for the same reason as well—because it assumes the court must decide that the letter was written by D rather than simply determine whether there is sufficient evidence for the jury to find that the letter is authentic. **Answer (D) is incorrect** for the same reason: it also appears to assume that the court must determine whether D wrote the letter.

394. **Answer (C) is correct.** Because P is basing her claim against D on D's own negligence in retaining the guard, an issue in the case is whether the guard was, in fact, unreliable. That places the guard's character for reliability "in issue." (In the words of FRE 405(b), this is a situation in which character is "an essential element of a ... claim.") Because the guard's character is in issue, FRE 405(b) allows evidence of character in the form of specific instances of conduct in addition to reputation and opinion as allowed under FRE 405(a). Thus, answer (C) is correct because the prior incidents are offered to show that the guard was in fact unreliable.

The evidence is also relevant on another basis: It shows possible notice to D of the guard's unreliability. In this negligence case, is it not enough to show that the guard was unreliable; P must also show that reasonable school officials would have discovered his unreliability. Evidence that the guard had been absent twice in the past month would tend to show notice. **Answer (D) is incorrect.** It starts out correctly, but goes wrong when it suggests that the incidents have low probative value which is substantially outweighed by the danger of unfair prejudice the evidence carries. That conclusion is incorrect on the facts because the jury will certainly use the evidence of the guard's absences for its proper purpose. Though there is some danger the jury will use the evidence to prove that the guard was absent on this occasion (see discussion of answer (A) below), that danger is unlikely to substantially outweigh the legitimate probative value of the evidence.

Answer (B) is incorrect because a jury is entitled to determine that two absences in the month prior to the accident should have put D on notice of the guard's unreliability. There is no need to prove a "pattern" per se; it is enough to raise suspicion of unreliability in reasonable school officials.

Answer (A) is incorrect because the evidence may *not* be used to prove the guard was absent on the day of P's accident. That would be an improper use of character evidence to prove action in accordance with that character on a particular occasion. Though character evidence is admissible in this case as explained above, it is not admissible to prove action in accordance.

395. **Answer (D) is correct.** If W has sued D's spouse, W might be biased against D, which might lead W to shade her testimony improperly in P's favor. No specific FRE governs bias impeachment, but the Supreme Court in *United States v. Abel*, 469 U.S. 45 (1984), made clear that this form of impeachment is still permitted.

Answer (A) is incorrect because, as shown above, the evidence is relevant to the witness's possible bias. **Answer (B) is incorrect** because there is no prohibition on the use of extrinsic evidence to impeach by showing bias. **Answer (C) is incorrect** because there is no prohibition on the use of a witness's specific instances of conduct to show bias.

396. **Answer (C) is correct.** V's utterance is hearsay because it asserts, among other things, that V was on the sidewalk, and it is offered to prove that fact. The statement would qualify as a dying declaration under FRE 804(b)(2) if the following requirements are satisfied: (1) this is a civil action or homicide prosecution (it is a civil action); (2) the declarant is unavailable (V is unavailable because he is dead); (3) the declarant believed death was imminent when he made the statement (*see* below); and (4) the statement concerned the cause or circumstances of what the declarant believed to be his impending death (that is clear here).

The issue here is whether V believed he was about to die when he made the statement. This preliminary fact (along with the others) must be decided by the court under FRE 104(a) because this is *not* a case of conditional relevancy. (The statement is relevant even if V did not believe she was about to die.) The court will apply the "preponderance of the evidence" standard to deciding this question.

Answer (A) is incorrect because the evidence is hearsay. **Answer (B) is incorrect** because the statement does concern the cause or circumstances of what V believed to be his impending death (where he was located when the crane hit him is part of the circumstances of the accident that killed V). **Answer (D) is incorrect** because it assumes that the disputed preliminary fact is to be decided according to the conditional relevancy standard of FRE 104(b), rather than the standard of FRE 104(a).

397. **Answer (D) is correct.** The possible objection here is under FRE 403, but the photographs have significant probative value. To the extent they show entry wounds in the back of V's head, they undercut D's self-defense claim because they suggest that V was retreating. True, the jury might be inflamed by the gruesome nature of the photographs, but any unfair prejudice that results is unlikely to "substantially outweigh[]" their probative value.

Answer (A) is incorrect because D's admission to killing V does not make the photographs irrelevant. If they suggest that V was retreating, they undercut D's self-defense claim. Thus, they meet the definition of relevant evidence in FRE 401 because they affect the likelihood of the existence of a fact of consequence to the action.

Answer (B) is incorrect because, as explained above, the photos have significant probative value that is likely to be "substantially outweighed" by their prejudicial effect.

Answer (C) is incorrect because there is a legitimate use for the photographs; the court will not assume an illegitimate use absent a showing that D has not made here.

398. **Answer (C) is correct.** D's prior attempt to pass the counterfeit bill supplied D with knowledge that the bill was counterfeit. The incident therefore undermines D's defense that he lacked such knowledge. Used in this way (*see* FRE 404(b)), the evidence does not violate the character rule in FRE 404(a). If the court does not find that the evidence should be excluded under FRE 403, it will admit the evidence. Almost certainly, the court will hold the evidence admissible.

Answer (A) is incorrect because the logic described above shows the relevance of the prior event to *provide* D with knowledge.

Answer (B) is incorrect because there is sufficient similarity between the two events. As long as the bill used was the same one, the "knowledge" theory works well.

Answer (D) is incorrect because W's testimony about what he told D is not being used to prove that the bill was counterfeit, but only to show that D *knew* the bill was counterfeit. (Presumably, the prosecution will present expert testimony that the bill was fake.)

399. **Answer (D) is correct.** The question concerns authentication. To authenticate something (here, a phone call), there must be evidence sufficient to support a finding that this is what its proponent claims it to be. Here, D claims the call was to P, and that it was a person working for P who answered and stated that the order would be canceled. The fact that D called P's published number, that the person answered consistently with P's business ("Videos"), and that the person acted as one would expect a P employee to act, all supply sufficient evidence to support a finding that the call actually was to P. *See* FRE 901(b)(6).

Answer (A) is incorrect because the person's statements are not hearsay; they are words of independent legal significance ("verbal act"): the act of canceling the order.

Answer (B) is incorrect because the proponent need not personally recognize the voice. Authentication can be accomplished in other ways.

Answer (C) is incorrect because even though there might be "better" evidence, the best evidence rule does not apply to a situation such as this. D is not testifying about the contents of any "writing, recording, or photograph"; D is merely testifying to her recollection of a phone conversation.

400. **Answer (D) is correct.** The speedometer reading is not hearsay. The instrument is a mechanical device and not a person. Thus, under FRE 801(b), it cannot be a "declarant." Even though D has testified about the reading on the instrument, and even though the reading was a "writing," the reading cannot have been preserved in any fashion. Thus, even if the speedometer survived the crash, it would not show the 50 mph measurement about which D has testified. The best evidence rule is not implicated. (Consider an analogy to a watch used to tell the time. D could testify that she knows a certain event took place at a certain time because she looked at her watch. Such testimony would not violate the best evidence rule.)

Answers (A) and (C) are incorrect for the reasons stated above.

401. **Answer (C) is correct.** Under FRE 404(a)(2)(B), a criminal defendant may offer evidence of a "pertinent" trait of the alleged victim's character. On direct examination, the character evidence may take the form of opinion or reputation. *See* FRE 405(a). If reputation evidence is offered to prove the victim's character and thus action in accordance (such as starting the fight, as here), it is hearsay. However, FRE 803(21) creates an exception for evidence of a person's community reputation for character.

Answers (A) and (B) are incorrect for the reasons stated above.

Answer (D) is incorrect because the prosecution need not place the alleged victim's character in issue in order for the defendant to offer evidence of that person's character.

402. **Answer (D) is correct.** Under FRE 106, when a party offers one part of a writing or recorded statement, the adverse party may offer another part of the writing or recorded statement that, in fairness, should be considered along with it. Here, P introduced a letter from D expressing regret for the injury. That letter was admissible as a party admission of D. Normally, D would not be permitted to introduce the letter because it is hearsay (not a party admission) and no exception appears to apply. But the parts of the letter introduced by P leave the impression that D was at fault. The court should allow D to introduce the part of the letter that corrects or otherwise contradicts that impression.

Answer (A) is incorrect because it fails to take into account the completeness doctrine of FRE 106.

Answer (B) is incorrect because there is no such rule; this is a sort of reverse-403, which does not exist.

Answer (C) is incorrect because, as noted above, a party may not introduce her own statement as a party admission.

403. **The correct answer is (B).** The compromise rule (FRE 408) excludes evidence of any statements made in the course of an effort to compromise a claim as long as the claim was disputed as to either liability or the proper amount owed. D's letter shows that D disputes the amount of damage P's car sustained. The letter is therefore inadmissible.

Answer (A) is incorrect because D's letter is a party admission.

Answer (C) is incorrect because, if the statement was made in the course of compromise, the entire statement, including the admission of responsibility, is inadmissible.

Answer (D) is incorrect because there is no requirement that D's statement have been made "*arguendo*" or "without prejudice." The compromise rule is intended to encourage frankness, including admission of responsibility. (Of course, the claim must be disputed, as noted above.)

404. **Answer (C) is correct.** An expert witness generally may give an opinion that "embraces" an ultimate fact (FRE 704), but the courts do not permit an expert to give an opinion using terminology that has special, technical meaning in the law about which the judge will instruct the jury. The phrase "crossing state lines with intent to distribute contraband" is undoubtedly a phrase in the applicable criminal statute. The expert may not use that terminology.

Answer (A) is incorrect because this is a typical sort of permissible expert opinion. It is not an opinion that a person is guilty or that this particular case actually involved gang behavior. In testifying that the killing was "consistent with" gang behavior, the witness is using her expertise to inform the jury that this is a method used by gangs, not that it actually was committed by a gang in this case.

Answer (B) is incorrect for basically the same reason. It is testimony that defendant possessed an amount of drugs common to those who sell drugs, not that this was what defendant was doing.

Answer (D) is incorrect because, as discussed above, the opinion in answer (C) is not permissible.

405. **Answer (C) is correct.** Under the common law *Frye* rule, "scientific" evidence is admissible only if the underlying technique or theory has been "generally accepted" in the relevant scientific community. That test disfavors new theories even if they are likely to become accepted. Because W's technique has not yet achieved general acceptance, W would not be permitted to testify based upon it.

Under the modern *Daubert* rule as modified and incorporated in FRE 702, scientific reliability is shown by looking to many factors including whether the theory has been generally accepted, whether it has been subjected to peer review and publication, whether it has a measurable error rate, and whether such rate is low. Here, the evidence probably satisfies the rule because most factors favor its reliability. Thus, the evidence most likely would be admissible in federal court.

Answers (A), (B), and (D) are incorrect for the reasons stated above.

406. Answer (D) is correct. Under the Supreme Court's confrontation decisions, "non-testimonial" hearsay may be offered against a criminal defendant; it does not implicate the defendant's confrontation right. Of course, the evidence must not violate applicable evidence rules, and the question indicates that the evidence satisfies the requirements of the residual exception.

Answers (A), (B), and (C) are incorrect for the reasons stated above. They do not apply the correct test.

407. Answer (D) is correct. X's statement is hearsay but seems to qualify as an excited utterance under FRE 803(2) because the event was a startling one, the statement relates to it, and the statement seems to have been made under the stress of excitement caused by the event. Under the Supreme Court's confrontation cases, the statement is not "testimonial." Chiefly, this is because it was not made under circumstances in which the declarant (X) would have expected it to be used to assist in the prosecution of D or anyone else for the crime. When hearsay is non-testimonial, the Court has held that the Confrontation Clause is not a bar to its admission.

Answer (A) is incorrect because it does not matter that D did not have an opportunity to cross-examine X at any time.

Answer (B) is incorrect because the prosecution has no obligation to demonstrate that X is unavailable.

Answer (C) is incorrect because the prosecution is not required to show that the statement is reliable; as long as it satisfies a hearsay exception, the Confrontation Clause is no bar to its admission. (There might be some circumstances in which admission of a hearsay statement would violate another constitutional right of a criminal defendant even if the statement satisfies the requirements of an exception, but the Court has not left much room for such cases, and nothing in this set of facts argues strongly for that result.)

408. Answer (D) is correct. W's testimony from the prior trial is hearsay when offered in the current trial because it is a statement about what happened, offered to prove what happened. The transcript of W's testimony is hearsay because it is a statement of what W said, offered to prove what W said. Under the former testimony exception, FRE 804(b)(1), the testimony will be admissible against D1 because (1) W is unavailable, (2) D1 was a party to the civil trial, (3) D1 had an opportunity to cross-examine W, and (4) D1 had a motive to try to show that W was wrong. The transcript is not admissible against D2, however. When the current trial is a criminal trial, and the party against whom the former testimony is offered was not a party to the earlier trial, the former testimony exception does not apply. The "predecessor in interest" rule applies only in civil cases.

Answers (A), (B), and (C) are incorrect for the reasons given above.

409. Answer (D) is correct. The transcript contains the deposition testimony of W, who testified at the current trial. The deposition testimony is hearsay if offered to prove the facts asserted, which are similar to those to which W testified at the trial. No exception applies.

Answer (A) is incorrect because the facts do not reveal that the deposition testimony is being offered to rebut a charge of recent fabrication or improper influence or motive, or to rehabilitate credibility. FRE 801(d)(1)(B).

Answer (B) is incorrect because the former testimony exception (FRE 804(b)(1)) does not apply. For one thing, W is not unavailable.

Answer (C) is incorrect because it presents a false argument against the deposition testimony being hearsay. All statements of fact are implicitly statements about the witness's opinion about the facts. If this argument were to be accepted, the hearsay rule would disappear.

410. **Answer (B) is correct.** Under FRE 801(d)(2)(A), the statement of a party is not hearsay when offered against the party. It is a party admission.

Answer (A) is incorrect because, as noted above, the statement qualifies as non-hearsay.

Answer (C) is incorrect because a statement of a party is admissible as a non-hearsay party admission regardless of the nature of the statement at the time it was made. A party admission need not have been against the party's interest when made (or ever, for that matter), as long as it is offered by a party opponent and not the declarant-party.

Answer (D) is incorrect because the statement is not hearsay, and even if it was, the declaration against interest exception (FRE 801(b)(3)) does not apply unless the declarant is unavailable, and D is not unavailable.

411. **Answer (A) is correct.** There are two reasons. First, the assistant manager's statement is hearsay because it asserted that the store would pay the medical bills and provide pain and suffering compensation, and it is offered to prove that the store would do so. The statement probably is not a party admission because the declarant's job did not include determining whether the store would compensate an injured customer (*see* FRE 801(d)(2)(D)), nor was the declarant authorized to speak for the owner about such matters (*see* FRE 801(d)(2)(C)). The second reason the statement is inadmissible is that an offer to pay medical and similar expenses is inadmissible under FRE 409.

Answer (B) is incorrect for the reasons stated above.

Answer (C) is incorrect because it states the wrong standard for authorization. This is not a situation in which the evidence is only "conditionally relevant." The assistant manager's statement is relevant even if the assistant manager did not have authority to speak. Thus, the applicable rule is FRE 104(a), and the courts have held that the standard for finding preliminary facts under that rule (here, authority) is preponderance of the evidence, not evidence "sufficient to support a finding").

Answer (D) is incorrect because, if the statement qualified as a party admission, there is no requirement of personal knowledge. Party admissions do not require that the declarant have personal knowledge of the facts stated.

412. **Answer (C) is correct.** Under FRE 201(b), a court may take judicial notice of an adjudicative fact if it is not subject to reasonable dispute, in that it is (1) generally known in the court's territorial jurisdiction; or (2) capable of accurate determination by looking to reliable sources. The names of a person's direct descendants would not qualify as the first kind of fact because the information would not be known generally. It is also unlikely that the court will hold that there are sources of this information that are so reliable that they can't reasonably be questioned.

   Answer (A) is incorrect because this information can be obtained from reliable sources such as the manufacturer's specifications.

   Answer (B) is incorrect because this information will be published in reliable sources such as the local government directory.

   Answer (D) is incorrect because the existence of a stop sign at a certain place is likely to be recorded in police department or other governmental records.

413. **Answer (A) is correct.** A lay witness may not give an opinion unless it is rationally based on the perception of the witness, is helpful to the jury in developing a clear understanding of the facts, and does not involve expertise. *See* FRE 701. The opinion that a person acted maliciously is not helpful to the jury and in fact usurps the jury's role. The witness should state the facts, not why she believes D acted with a state of mind that has a legal meaning that the judge will explain to the jury.

   Answer (B) is incorrect. Intoxication can be based rationally on the witness's perception, and often can't be conveyed simply by stating "facts." To help the jury, it is sometimes necessary to give a sort of holistic judgment. Intoxication is such a judgment, and it is one that does not require expertise.

   Answer (C) is incorrect because this seems more a recitation of what was going on (facts) than of an opinion. It involves some opinion beyond basic facts (I saw D put her hands around V's neck ...), but it helps the jury to hear what the witness believes was the effect of those facts.

   Answer (D) is incorrect because it is simply the recitation of facts.

414. **Answer (A) is correct.** Under FRE 103(a)(2), when a court sustains an objection to certain evidence, the party offering the evidence preserves the matter for appeal by placing into the record the substance of the evidence. Here, that would be done by stating on the record what W's testimony would have been.

   Answer (B) is incorrect because asking the question again violates the trial court's ruling.

   Answer (C) is incorrect because, even if the judge doesn't like it, the attorney must protect the client's interest by placing into the record the substance of the testimony the witness would have given.

   Answer (D) is incorrect because the ruling doesn't affect all other testimony W would have given. P's attorney should continue the examination of W.

415. **Answer (D) is correct.** W2's testimony is not relevant to any issue in the case. V's generosity and general good character do not in any way rebut D's alibi. In addition, V's character is not admissible in this situation because D has not offered any evidence suggesting that V had a bad character. Normally, an appellate court will not review alleged error in the admission of evidence unless the opponent stated a proper ground for excluding it. *See* FRE 103(a)(1). But an exception applies to situations of "plain error," which are those in which it is clear from the record what the objection should have been. *See* FRE 103(e). Here, the error in denying D's motion to strike W2's testimony is plain because the record clearly shows the testimony was inadmissible. Thus, the court may review the alleged error. It will not reverse, however, unless a "substantial right" of D has been affected. FRE 103(a).

Answer (A) is incorrect because the plain error rule applies.

Answer (B) is incorrect because a motion to strike testimony, while not as effective as an objection that stops the witness from answering the question, can be sufficient.

Answer (C) is incorrect because it fails to recognize that the trial court's commission of an error does not guarantee reversal. Reversal requires that the error affected a substantial right of a party.

416. **Answer (D) is correct.** Under the "bursting bubble" theory of presumptions, evidence attacking the presumed fact destroys the presumption and the judge should not mention the presumption to the jury. Here, the presumed fact is payment, and D has testified that she paid. This is sufficient to destroy the presumption.

Answers (A), (B), and (C) are incorrect because they misunderstand the "bursting bubble" theory.

417. **Answer (B) is correct.** The privilege for confidential communications between spouses does not apply because the statement was made to a group, and not confidentially. However, the privilege not to testify adversely to a spouse does apply because the testimony the prosecution seeks is against D's interest. In the federal courts, the holder of that privilege is the testifying spouse (here, W). If W does not wish to testify about D's statement, she cannot be compelled to do so.

Answer (A) is incorrect because it fails to account for the adverse testimony privilege.

Answer (C) is incorrect because it assumes D is the holder of the adverse testimony privilege. As noted, under federal law the holder is W.

Answer (D) is incorrect because D's statement is not hearsay; it is a party admission. *See* FRE 801(d)(2)(A) (statement of opposing party).

418. **Answer (B) is correct.** If true, the DNA evidence means that only one in a million people could have left a blood sample with these characteristics; because there are ten million people in the urban area, ten of them could have left the blood.

Answer (A) is an example of the "prosecutor's fallacy." Other evidence might suggest that there is a much greater or lesser chance that D committed the crime. If, for example, D was an inhabitant of the International Space Station when the crime was committed, there is a zero percent chance that D was the perpetrator. The DNA evidence is only one piece of evidence in the case, and it is purely statistical. It does not provide any information about what *actually* happened.

Answer (C) is an example of the "defense attorney's fallacy." It is the flip side of the "prosecutor's fallacy." Other evidence about what actually happened might show that the probability of guilt is much higher or much lower.

Answer (D) is incorrect for the same reason. The DNA evidence doesn't tell us that D "probably" committed the crime; it is only statistical in nature and doesn't indicate what actually happened.

419. **Answer (B) is best.** If D is in fact a cocaine user, D would have a reason to possess cocaine and to know that cocaine is present in the apartment. When used in this way, the evidence does not violate the character evidence ban in FRE 404(a) but is admissible on "motive" reasoning under FRE 404(b).

Answer (A) is incorrect because being a cocaine user is not conduct relevant to D's character for truthfulness. *See* FRE 608(b). It is therefore inadmissible for that purpose.

Answer (C) is incorrect for the reasons stated above.

Answer (D) is incorrect because no rule requires that D prove that W has a reason to lie before the prosecution may offer evidence of D's cocaine use.

420. **Answer (A) is correct.** This is an attempt to support D's character for truthfulness with opinion evidence that D is honest. FRE 608(a) does not allow this unless D's character for truthfulness has been attacked. Nothing in the facts suggests that this has occurred.

Answer (B) is incorrect because D's truthfulness is irrelevant to the question whether D started a forest fire.

Answer (C) is incorrect because, as explained above, the evidence is not admissible to show character for truthfulness unless such character has been attacked.

Answer (D) is incorrect for the reasons given above.

421. **Answer (D) is correct.** Under FRE 608(a), the character of a witness for truthfulness may be impeached using opinion and reputation evidence concerning that trait. W2's testimony is opinion evidence of V's untruthful character. The problem here is that V never testified. However, the court has admitted a statement of V, presumably under the dying declaration exception in FRE 804(b)(2). That means that V has been used, in some sense, as a witness, and it seems appropriate to permit D to impeach V as though V had testified. This is exactly what FRE 806 permits.

Answer (A) is incorrect because W2's testimony is relevant to the truthfulness of V, whose statement was admitted to prove that D set off the bomb.

Answer (B) is incorrect for the reasons stated above.

Answer (C) is incorrect because, even though W2's testimony is "extrinsic" to V, FRE 608(a) allows extrinsic impeachment of a witness's character for truthfulness using opinion (and reputation) evidence.

422. **Answer (A) is correct.** A judgment of conviction is a statement by the court that asserts that a person committed a crime. It is hearsay when offered to prove that the person committed the crime, but there is an exception in FRE 803(22) covering it. However, a conviction for a misdemeanor that does not require an act of dishonesty or false statement is never admissible to impeach a witness. *See* FRE 609(a)(2).

Answer (B) is incorrect for the reasons just given.

Answer (C) is incorrect because there is no rule requiring that a witness be given an opportunity to explain or deny a conviction if it is admitted to impeach the witness.

Answer (D) is incorrect because, as explained above, a conviction for a misdemeanor that does not require an act of dishonesty or false statement is never admissible to impeach.

Part II:
Short Answer Questions Answers

423. The court should grant D's motion and instruct the jury to disregard W's testimony. Unless W's testimony satisfies the requirements of FRE 801(d)(1)(C), the "prior identification" rule, it is inadmissible hearsay. In this case, the rule's requirements are not satisfied.

First, X's statement, "He's the one who robbed V" is offered to prove that D is the one who robbed V. So, too, is X's act of pointing, which qualifies as a "statement" under FRE 801(a) because it was "intended [by X] as an assertion." It is therefore hearsay unless it fits into an exemption or an exception. No exceptions apply here. (It is not a present sense impression because it describes an event that took place sometime earlier, not one taking place at the moment or immediately before.) The statement satisfies most of the requirements of the prior identification rule, but not all: The prosecution has failed to call X to testify as a witness at the trial. Thus, X was not "subject to cross-examination about a prior statement." In addition, there is a confrontation issue if X's statement is considered "testimonial," which depends on whether an ongoing emergency still existed. More facts are needed.

424. In *Daubert v. Merrill Dow Pharmaceuticals, Inc.*, 509 U.S. 579 (1993), the Supreme Court held that when the issue concerns the admissibility of purported scientific testimony, the court must determine whether the opinion represents scientific knowledge that will assist the trier of fact. FRE 702 was later amended to incorporate this basic idea. This test means that the court must decide both whether the evidence is reliable and whether it is relevant to the facts of the case. Reliability is not to be decided according to a categorical test of "general acceptance," as was the case under the *Frye* test. Rather, the court should look at such matters as whether W's theory has been subject to testing, whether it has been subjected to peer review and publication, whether it has an error rate and whether the error rate is known,

whether standards are maintained, and indeed whether the theory is generally accepted. Relevance is not a difficult issue in this case. It is clear that the evidence concerns the disputed issue of causation.

If the court decides that the theory underlying W's proposed testimony is reliable and that it is relevant to the facts of the case, the court should admit the evidence. Otherwise, the court should exercise its "gate-keeping" function by excluding the evidence.

425. At common law, witnesses were generally not allowed to give an opinion on an ultimate issue in the case. FRE 704(a) changes that rule by providing that "[a]n opinion is not objectionable just because it embraces an ultimate issue." That does not mean that all opinions are now admissible. The testimony must still be helpful (FRE 702), and it remains subject to exclusion under FRE 403. If a witness's proposed opinion testimony is given in the form of technical terms of a legal rule, the testimony invades the province of the court to instruct the jury about the meaning of legal terms. Moreover, the witness's interpretation of the legal rule may be erroneous. Here, the terms "aided and abetted" and perhaps other terms of the statute have special legal meaning, and it is the court's job to instruct the jury about the meanings of those terms, not the job of a witness. W can probably testify in another form that does not invade this judicial function. The court should sustain D's objection.

426. The court should overrule P's objection and allow D to ask the question. D's question is an attempt to impeach W by contradiction. The fact on which D is to be contradicted is collateral because its only value to the case is in contradicting W. Though the Federal Rules do not explicitly codify the common law rule that it is impermissible to impeach a witness by contradiction on a collateral matter with extrinsic evidence, most federal courts would exclude evidence that fits within the rule under FRE 403 because it is a waste of time. The rule was not violated because extrinsic evidence was not offered, and the court should overrule P's objection.

427. The court should sustain D's objection because the testimony violates the hearsay rule. The testimony is not simply that D twice committed similar crimes. It is that someone (the police chief) *told* W that D had done so. The police chief's statement is hearsay because it asserts that D committed these crimes, and it is offered to prove that fact. No exception applies in this situation.

If the prosecution offered the evidence in a way that did not violate the hearsay rule (such as by offering testimony of one who has personal knowledge of D's two prior crimes), it probably would be admissible to prove identity through *modus operandi*. *See* FRE 404(b). All three of the burglaries were committed in the same rather unusual way. It is likely that the same person committed all three. If D committed the two uncharged acts, D is more likely to have committee the charged crime.

428. The court should sustain the objection on both grounds. First, the bystander's statement in the police report is hearsay within hearsay. The "inner" layer is the bystander's statement that D ran the red light. This is offered to prove the truth of the matter asserted: that D ran the light. The "outer" layer is the report itself, which is the officer's statement that the bystander

made this statement. It, too, is hearsay. FRE 803(8)(A)(iii), part of the public records exception, covers the officer's statement (the shell of the report, in essence), but there is no exception covering the bystander's statement. FRE 805 states that hearsay within hearsay is admissible if each part fits within an exception. Because the "inner" part does not fit within an exception, the part of the report containing the bystander's statement is inadmissible hearsay.

P's proposed testimony also violates the best evidence rule, FRE 1002. P is testifying about what the report contains. This is testimony about the contents of a writing. The best evidence rule provides that to prove the contents of a writing, recording, or photograph, the writing, recording, or photograph must be produced. P has not produced it, and has not shown that an exception applies.

429. The court must overrule D's objection and allow the prosecution to ask W about the conviction. Under FRE 609(a)(2), a witness's conviction for a crime involving dishonesty or false statement is admissible to impeach the witness. Courts have held that admission is always permitted; FRE 403 may not be used to exclude it. The crime of filing a false federal income tax return is a crime involving dishonesty or false statement. It is therefore admissible automatically. The passage of seven years since conviction or the end of confinement (whichever is later) is not long enough to change the answer. The relevant period under FRE 609(b) is ten years.

430. The court should sustain D's objection to W's testimony about what D said to W, but should overrule the objection to W's testimony about the cat hair.

Both spousal privileges are implicated here. The privilege for confidential communications between spouses generally belongs to both spouses. Thus, D may prevent W from testifying about D's statement, which appears to have been made in confidence.

In federal court and many state courts, the privilege not to testify adversely to a spouse belongs to the testifying spouse. Thus, D may not prevent W from testifying about D's appearance if W wishes to do so.

431. The court should overrule D's objection. X's statement is hearsay because it was made other than while testifying at the trial, and is offered to prove the truth of the matter asserted (that D robbed the bank). FRE 804(b)(6) provides an exception for statements offered against a party when the party caused or acquiesced in the procurement of the declarant's unavailability. That is the case here. X's absence from the country qualifies as unavailability under FRE 804(a)(5). If the court concludes that D's threat caused X's unavailability, X's statement will be admissible under FRE 804(b)(6). (The result under the Confrontation Clause is the same.)

432. The court should overrule D's objection. FRE 404(a)(2)(B) allows a criminal defendant to offer evidence of a pertinent character trait of an alleged crime victim. Dishonesty in business dealings is a pertinent trait because it makes commission of fraud more likely. FRE 404(a)(2)(B)(ii) allows the prosecution, in this situation, to offer evidence concerning the same trait of the defendant's character. That was the purpose of W2's testimony. The evidence thus fits within FRE 404(a)(2)(B)(ii), and because it took the form of reputation testimony, it complies with FRE 405(a).

433. Objection overruled. Evidence that D stole the getaway car the day before the charged robbery is relevant to show "preparation," and thus to identify D as a person who might have been involved in the crime. *See* FRE 404(b). When used in this way, the evidence does not violate the character rule. In addition, the lack of similarity between the charged crime and the vehicle theft does not matter. The court should admit the evidence (1) if there is evidence sufficient to support a finding that D stole the getaway vehicle (*see Huddleston v. United* States, 485 U.S. 681 (1988)), and (2) unless its probative value is substantially outweighed by the danger of unfair prejudice (FRE 403), which is extremely unlikely to be the case.

Note that some courts might treat the evidence as an inseparable part of the charged crime, or "intrinsic" to it, and thus admissible. This is probably too broad a reading of the facts and of that theory. The vehicle theft was a separate act. In addition, even if the court views the theft as intrinsic, it should conduct the same analysis as it would under the "other crimes, wrongs, or acts" rule.

434. The court should overrule the objection unless it finds that the probative value of the evidence is substantially outweighed by the danger of unfair prejudice or other factors listed in FRE 403. Under FRE 413, evidence of a criminal defendant's prior act of sexual assault is admissible for any purpose for which it is relevant. That would include showing that defendant has a bad character and would commit another sexual assault. The rule overrides the general provision of FRE 404(a).

435. Objection overruled. A person may authenticate a letter even if she does not recognize the signature. For example, the letter might have distinctive characteristics taken in consideration with other circumstances (*see* FRE 901(b)(4)). Here, the letter refers to prior events at the concert, and in context seems to have come from D. The standard for authentication is "evidence sufficient to support a finding" (FRE 901(a)), which is not a very high bar.

436. Objection sustained. D has not offered testimony about V's character for peacefulness or violence. Therefore, the prosecution is not permitted to offer evidence concerning V's character. *See* FRE 404(a)(2)(B). If the crime was homicide, the prosecutor would be permitted to introduce this testimony. FRE 404(a)(2)(C).

437. Objection overruled. The log is hearsay because it contains assertions of when the floor was swept and it is offered to prove that those assertions were true. If they were true, the floor was not swept for an hour before and an hour after P fell. The log probably qualifies as a business record under FRE 803(6) because: (1) it was made by persons with knowledge (the people who did the sweeping); (2) it was made at about the time they did the job; (3) it was part of the regular practice of the business to make the log; (4) it was kept by the business in the ordinary course of business; and (5) there is no specific reason to think it was not accurate enough to be admitted in this situation.

438. The court should overrule both objections. The statement qualifies as a coconspirator statement because the court should find that (1) a conspiracy existed, (2) X (the declarant) was a member of the conspiracy, (3) the statement was made during the conspiracy, and (4) that the statement was made in furtherance of the conspiracy (because it was made to seek Y's participation). It is thus non-hearsay under FRE 801(d)(2)(E). The court should overrule the Confrontation Clause objection because it does not violate the standards set forth in *Crawford v. Washington* and its progeny. The statement was not "testimonial" in nature because it was not made under circumstances in which a reasonable person would expect it to be used in investigation or prosecution of a crime.

439. The court should overrule both objections. The transcript itself is hearsay but undoubtedly admissible as the business record of the court reporter. It contains the testimony of W, given during Smith's criminal trial. Because Smith had an opportunity to cross-examine W at that trial, and had a motive to show that W was wrong when she testified that she saw Smith and Jones in River City, and because that would be the same thing Smith would try to do if W were a witness in the present civil trial, the transcript is admissible against Smith. FRE 804(b)(1). It is also admissible against Jones because, even though Jones was not a party to the criminal trial, Smith was a "predecessor in interest"; Smith had the opportunity to cross-examine W and had the same motive Jones would have today: to show that W was wrong about seeing Smith and Jones in River City on that day. (It is true that Smith would have had a stronger motive to show that W was wrong about seeing Smith than about seeing Jones, but Smith would have wanted to undermine W's testimony as much as possible.) The transcript is therefore likely admissible against both Smith and Jones.

440. Objection overruled. P's statement is hearsay because offered to prove the fact asserted: that P's leg hurt. However, it appears to satisfy several exceptions: (1) present sense impression (FRE 803(1)), because it is a statement about a condition P was experiencing and made while she was experiencing it; (2) excited utterance (FRE 803(2)), because the accident was a "startling event," the statement relates to the event (actually, its effect on P), and the statement was made while under the stress of excitement caused by the event (as demonstrated by P's tone of voice); (3) statement of present physical condition (FRE 803(3)); and (4) statement for purposes of medical diagnosis or treatment (FRE 803(4)), because it appears that P was telling W about the leg and asking W to call 911 for the purpose of getting medical aid.

441. Objection sustained. FRE 407 forbids the use of subsequent remedial measures to prove the defectiveness of a product. Here, the redesign occurred after P's accident. Had it been done before P obtained the product, the accident wouldn't have occurred. Thus, the redesign was a subsequent remedial measure.

No exception applies. Note that the evidence is not admissible to impeach W. W has not testified in any way that is inconsistent with the product's redesign. Most courts would hold that merely testifying that the product was "sound" is not contradicted by or inconsistent with the later change in the product's design. (If W had testified that the product was "as safe as possible," such testimony would open the door to admission of the subsequent remedial evidence because the impression left by that testimony is directly contradicted by the product redesign.)

442. Objection overruled. This question implicates the subsequent remedial measures rule (FRE 407). Evidence that D Corp. redesigned the bicycle after the accident in a way that would have prevented the accident from occurring would not be admissible to prove the defectiveness of the prior design. Here, however, the testimony of D's expert stated that no stronger metal was available. That testimony constituted a statement that the stronger design was not feasible. Under those circumstances, the rule allows the use of the subsequent remedial measure to show feasibility. In addition, D's expert witness's testimony is contradicted by W's testimony that a stronger metal was available. Thus, W's testimony is also admissible to impeach the expert by contradiction. (Often, when evidence is admissible to prove feasibility, it is also admissible to impeach.)

443. The court should sustain D's objection as to the substantive use of the evidence but overrule D's improper impeachment objection. The theft that was the subject of the conviction is not admissible to prove that D is a person who has a character that would make it more likely that D would possess illegal drugs. FRE 404(a). In addition, theft is not a crime the elements of which require an act of dishonesty or false statement. Federal courts limit FRE 609(a)(2) to crimes that require deceit ("crimen falsi"). Because the conviction was for a misdemeanor, the evidence is per se inadmissible to impeach D's credibility as a witness. However, leaving the conviction off of a job application is an act of dishonesty that is admissible under FRE 608(b) as long as it is raised on cross-examination (which it was) and as long as the court does not hold it inadmissible under FRE 403. That is unlikely to happen here because the potential prejudicial effect of a mere misdemeanor theft conviction is small. Thus, the evidence is admissible to impeach D's credibility but for no other purpose.

444. The court should overrule the objection. This is an attempt to impeach W by a criminal conviction showing bad character for truthfulness. Under FRE 609(a)(2), a conviction for a crime that has dishonesty or false statement as an element is automatically admissible; the court may not exclude it under any other rule including FRE 403 (unless some other part of FRE 609 applies). Thus, here, the court must admit the evidence.

445. Objection sustained. This is an attempt to impeach D by showing a false statement: lying on her job application by saying she had never been convicted of a crime, when in fact she had been convicted of petty theft. FRE 608(b) permits this type of impeachment, but not using extrinsic evidence. Calling W to establish the lie is using extrinsic evidence, so it violates the rule.

Note that the petty theft conviction is not admissible under FRE 609 because it is not a crime an element of which requires an act of dishonesty or false statement and it is not a crime punishable by death or imprisonment in excess of a year.

446. The court should overrule both objections. First, leading questions are allowed on cross-examination (FRE 611(c)). Second, this is an example of impeachment of a witness's credibility by inquiring about a specific instance of conduct that bears on the witness's character for truthfulness. It is governed by FRE 608(b). That rule permits the use of specific instances relevant to character for truthfulness only on cross-examination of the witness, and without the use of extrinsic evidence. The question asked concerns an instance of deceit (untruthfulness).

447. The court should rule that the evidence is admissible to impeach W1 by showing a prior inconsistent statement but is inadmissible to prove that P ran into D. Under FRE 613(b), extrinsic evidence of a prior inconsistent statement may be offered as long as the declarant is given an opportunity to explain or deny the statement. That opportunity was provided to W1 during cross-examination. Thus, the testimony of W2 is admissible to impeach W1.

The testimony is not admissible to prove the truth of what W1 said (that P ran into D) because it is hearsay for that purpose. It does not qualify as a non-hearsay prior inconsistent statement under FRE 801(d)(1)(A) because W1's statement was not made under penalty of perjury, in a trial, hearing, deposition, or other proceeding. It was just an informal statement to X. Thus, it is not admissible to prove P ran into D.

448. The court should overrule the objection. In a negligent entrustment action involving an automobile accident, an element of the claim P must prove is that the person to whom the item was entrusted was in fact a reckless driver. The evidence P wishes to present in this case tends to prove that fact. It is character evidence in the form of specific instances of conduct, and FRE 405(b) explicitly allows such evidence.

449. W's testimony concerning what the teller told her is hearsay if offered to prove the truth of the matters asserted (what the teller had seen in the bank). There appears to be no exception to cover the statement unless it qualifies under the "statement offered against a party that wrongfully caused … the declarant's unavailability" exception embodied in FRE 804(b)(6). The problem here is that D is not the one who caused the absence of the declarant by making the threat. Thus, the court will have to determine if D "acquiesced" in the conduct that was designed to procure the teller's absence. The courts are split on this issue. Some would hold that because all conspirators are legally responsible for each others' acts, D's participation in the conspiracy constituted acquiescence to what X did. Other courts follow a more limited rule. For example, in *United States v. Cherry*, 217 F.3d 811 (10th Cir. 2000), the court held that the exception would apply to the non-actor if the other conspirator's acts are "in furtherance, within the scope, and reasonably foreseeable as a necessary or natural consequence of an ongoing conspiracy." Applying that rule, either result might be justified depending on the circumstances. Was there an explicit or implicit understanding among the conspirators that any people who saw their faces were to be killed or intimidated into leaving the jurisdiction? Even in the absence of such an understanding, it is "reasonably foreseeable as a necessary or natural consequence of the conspiracy" that one of the conspirators would make this kind of threat? The law still needs to develop, but it is likely that many courts would hold the evidence admissible here.

450. Objection sustained in part and overruled in part. The offer to pay the hospital bill is inadmissible under FRE 409 as an offer "to pay medical, hospital, or similar expenses resulting from an injury" if offered to prove liability for the injury. Because the question states that this was P's purpose in offering the testimony, it is inadmissible. The court should overrule the objection as to D's statement, "I don't know what came over me." This statement is a party admission (FRE 801(d)(2)(A)), and FRE 409 does not exclude other statements made in the

course of offering or paying medical, hospital, or similar expenses. So, the court should admit that statement.

451. The court should overrule the objection. FRE 606(b)(1) forbids juror testimony about "any statement made or incident that occurred during the jury's deliberations; the effect of anything on that juror's or another juror's vote; or any juror's mental processes concerning the verdict or indictment." The disparaging comment does not appear to be admissible under FRE 606(b)(1). Moreover, none of the exceptions in FRE 606(b)(2) apply. However, in *Pena-Rodriguez v. Colorado*, 137 S. Ct. 855, 869 (2017), the Supreme Court carved out an exception to Rule 606 based on constitutional grounds: "[W]here a juror makes a clear statement that indicates he or she relied on racial stereotypes or animus to convict a criminal defendant, the Sixth Amendment requires that the no-impeachment rule give way in order to permit the trial court to consider the evidence of the juror's statement and any resulting denial of the jury trial guarantee."

452. The court should overrule the objection. Originally, FRE 801(d)(1)(B) limited the substantive use of prior consistent statements to those offered to rebut a charge of recent fabrication or improper influence. A 2014 amendment also permits admission of prior consistent statements "to rehabilitate the declarant's credibility as a witness when attacked on another ground." The Advisory Committee note explains that "[t]he intent of the amendment is to extend substantive effect to consistent statements that rebut other attacks on a witness — such as the charges of inconsistency or *faulty memory*." (emphasis added) Thus, the statement is substantively admissible to rehabilitate W after impeachment showing a possible defect in memory.

453. The court should sustain the objection. Although V's statement that she feared D is hearsay, it satisfies the requirements of FRE 803(3) as a statement of V's then-existing state of mind. However, such testimony must still be relevant to the issues in the case. This is a problem. The victim's state of mind is not an element of murder. The prosecutor most likely offered the statement to suggest that D had done something bad to V in the past to make V fearful — e.g., threatened or assaulted her. However, FRE 803(3) cannot be used to establish past events. Had V stated, "I am scared because D threatened me," the last part of the statement would be inadmissible.

Note that there are some crimes in which fear is an element — e.g., extortion requires the victim to be put in fear. Domestic violence statutes are another example.

454. The court should overrule the objection. Like the prior question, the statement satisfies the requirements of FRE 803(3) (then-existing state of mind). However, unlike the prior question, the prosecutor has a viable relevance argument. Evidence that V expressed fear of D before the sexual conduct occurred is relevant to prove absence of consent — a person who is afraid of another would most likely not consent to sex. Defense may argue that the evidence should be inadmissible under FRE 403 as unfairly prejudicial, but this objection will likely fail.

455. The court should overrule the objection. In *Ohio v. Clark*, 135 S. Ct. 2173 (2015), the Supreme Court addressed this issue in a case in which a three-and-a-half-year-old child made statements about his injuries in response to questions by his preschool teachers. The Court

ruled that the primary purpose of the questioning was not "testimonial" and thus admitting the statements was not unconstitutional. In the Court's view, a number of factors supported this conclusion. First, the statements were made during "an ongoing emergency" involving possible child abuse: the teachers needed to know whether it was safe to release V to his father. "Thus, the immediate concern was to protect a vulnerable child who needed help." The intent was not to gather evidence for prosecution. Second, the conversation "was informal and spontaneous" in a preschool lunchroom and classroom. Third, "[s]tatements by very young children will rarely, if ever, implicate the Confrontation Clause. Few preschool students understand the details of our criminal justice system." Fourth, "[s]tatements made to someone who is not principally charged with uncovering and prosecuting criminal behavior are significantly less likely to be testimonial than statements given to law enforcement officers."

Index